INTERMEDIATE

ILLUSTRATED SERIES™

MICROSOFT® OFFICE 365™ ACCESS® 2016

FRIEDRICHSEN

For Microsoft® Office updates, go to sam.cengage.com

CENGAGE
Learning®

Australia • Brazil • Mexico • Singapore • United Kingdom • United States

CENGAGE
Learning·

Illustrated Microsoft® Office 365™ &
Access® 2016—Intermediate
Lisa Friedrichsen

SVP, GM Skills & Global Product Management:
 Dawn Gerrain

Product Director: Kathleen McMahon

Senior Product Team Manager: Lauren Murphy

Product Team Manager: Andrea Topping

Associate Product Manager: Melissa Stehler

Senior Director, Development: Marah Bellegarde

Product Development Manager: Leigh Hefferon

Senior Content Developer: Christina Kling-Garrett

Developmental Editor: Lisa Ruffolo

Product Assistant: Erica Chapman

Marketing Director: Michele McTighe

Marketing Manager: Stephanie Albracht

Marketing Coordinator: Cassie Cloutier

Senior Production Director: Wendy Troeger

Production Director: Patty Stephan

Senior Content Project Manager: Stacey Lamodi

Art Director: Diana Graham

Text Designer: Joseph Lee, Black Fish Design

Cover Template Designer: Lisa Kuhn, Curio Press, LLC
 www.curiopress.com

Composition: GEX Publishing Services

For product information and technology assistance, contact us at
Cengage Learning Customer & Sales Support, 1-800-354-9706

For permission to use material from this text or product, submit all requests online at **www.cengage.com/permissions**
Further permissions questions can be emailed to
permissionrequest@cengage.com

Mac users: If you're working through this product using a Mac, some of the steps may vary. Additional information for Mac users is included with the Data Files for this product.

Some of the product names and company names used in this book have been used for identification purposes only and may be trademarks or registered trademarks of their respective manufacturers and sellers.

Windows® is a registered trademark of Microsoft Corporation. © 2012 Microsoft. Microsoft and the Office logo are either registered trademarks or trademarks of Microsoft Corporation in the United States and/or other countries. Cengage Learning is an independent entity from Microsoft Corporation and not affiliated with Microsoft in any manner. Microsoft product screenshots used with permission from Microsoft Corporation. Unless otherwise noted, all clip art is courtesy of openclipart.org.

Disclaimer: Any fictional data related to persons or companies or URLs used throughout this text is intended for instructional purposes only. At the time this text was published, any such data was fictional and not belonging to any real persons or companies.

Disclaimer: The material in this text was written using Microsoft Windows 10 Professional and Office 365 Professional Plus and was Quality Assurance tested before the publication date. As Microsoft continually updates the Windows 10 operating system and Office 365, your software experience may vary slightly from what is presented in the printed text.

Library of Congress Control Number: 2016932629
Soft-cover Edition ISBN: 978-1-305-87799-3
Loose-leaf Edition ISBN: 978-1-337-25101-3

Cengage Learning
20 Channel Center Street
Boston, MA 02210
USA

Cengage Learning is a leading provider of customized learning solutions with employees residing in nearly 40 different countries and sales in more than 125 countries around the world. Find your local representative at **www.cengage.com**

Cengage Learning products are represented in Canada by Nelson Education, Ltd.

For your course and learning solutions, visit **www.cengage.com**

Purchase any of our products at your local college store or at our preferred online store **www.cengagebrain.com**

Printed in the United States of America
Print Number: 02   Print Year: 2017

Brief Contents

Contents

Productivity Apps for School and Work

Corinne Hoisington

Lochlan keeps track of his class notes, football plays, and internship meetings with OneNote.

Zoe is using the annotation features of Microsoft Edge to take and save web notes for her research paper.

Nori is creating a Sway site to highlight this year's activities for the Student Government Association.

Hunter is adding interactive videos and screen recordings to his PowerPoint resume.

© Rawpixel/Shutterstock.com

Being computer literate no longer means mastery of only Word, Excel, PowerPoint, Outlook, and Access. To become technology power users, Hunter, Nori, Zoe, and Lochlan are exploring Microsoft OneNote, Sway, Mix, and Edge in Office 2016 and Windows 10.

Learn to use productivity apps!
Links to companion **Sways**, featuring **videos** with hands-on instructions, are located on www.cengagebrain.com.

Introduction to OneNote 2016

notebook | section tab | To Do tag | screen clipping | note | template | Microsoft OneNote Mobile app | sync | drawing canvas | inked handwriting | Ink to Text

As you glance around any classroom, you invariably see paper notebooks and notepads on each desk. Because deciphering and sharing handwritten notes can be a challenge, Microsoft OneNote 2016 replaces physical notebooks, binders, and paper notes with a searchable, digital notebook. OneNote captures your ideas and schoolwork on any device so you can stay organized, share notes, and work with others on projects. Whether you are a student taking class notes as shown in **Figure 1** or an employee taking notes in company meetings, OneNote is the one place to keep notes for all of your projects.

Figure 1: OneNote 2016 notebook

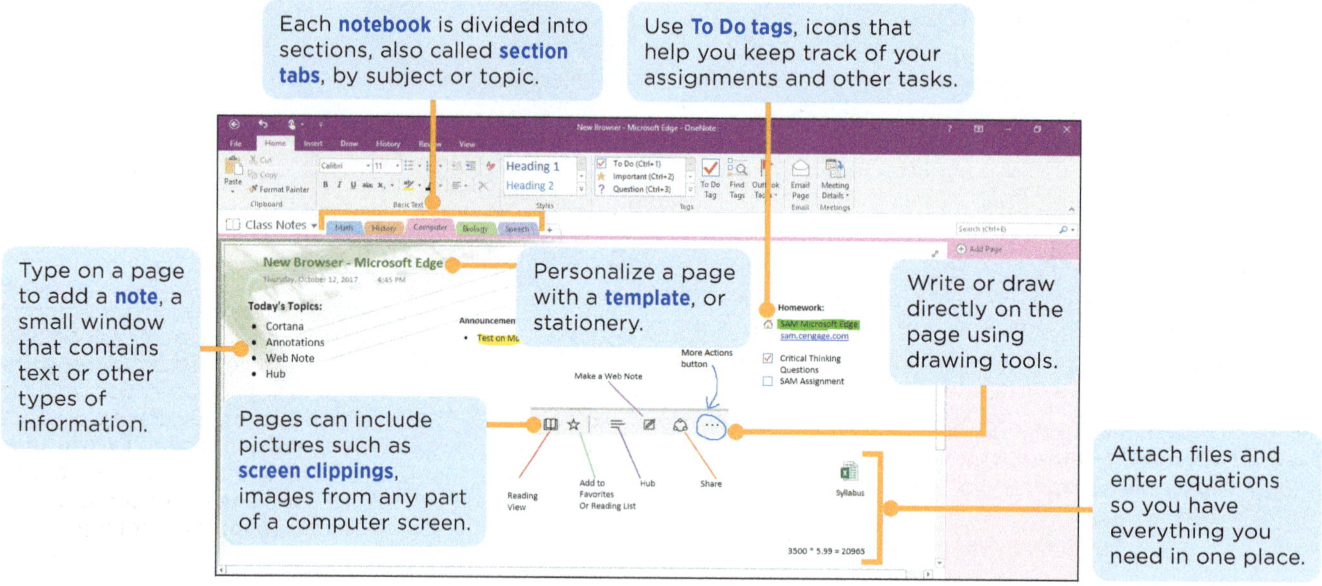

Each **notebook** is divided into sections, also called **section tabs**, by subject or topic.

Use **To Do tags**, icons that help you keep track of your assignments and other tasks.

Type on a page to add a **note**, a small window that contains text or other types of information.

Personalize a page with a **template**, or stationery.

Write or draw directly on the page using drawing tools.

Pages can include pictures such as **screen clippings**, images from any part of a computer screen.

Attach files and enter equations so you have everything you need in one place.

Creating a OneNote Notebook

OneNote is divided into sections similar to those in a spiral-bound notebook. Each OneNote notebook contains sections, pages, and other notebooks. You can use OneNote for school, business, and personal projects. Store information for each type of project in different notebooks to keep your tasks separate, or use any other organization that suits you. OneNote is flexible enough to adapt to the way you want to work.

When you create a notebook, it contains a blank page with a plain white background by default, though you can use templates, or stationery, to apply designs in categories such as Academic, Business, Decorative, and Planners. Start typing or use the buttons on the Insert tab to insert notes, which are small resizable windows that can contain text, equations, tables, on-screen writing, images, audio and video recordings, to-do lists, file attachments, and file printouts. Add as many notes as you need to each page.

Syncing a Notebook to the Cloud

OneNote saves your notes every time you make a change in a notebook. To make sure you can access your notebooks with a laptop, tablet, or smartphone wherever you are, OneNote uses cloud-based storage, such as OneDrive or SharePoint. **Microsoft OneNote Mobile app**, a lightweight version of OneNote 2016 shown in **Figure 2**, is available for free in the Windows Store, Google Play for Android devices, and the AppStore for iOS devices.

If you have a Microsoft account, OneNote saves your notes on OneDrive automatically for all your mobile devices and computers, which is called **syncing**. For example, you can use OneNote to take notes on your laptop during class, and then open OneNote on your phone to study later. To use a notebook stored on your computer with your OneNote Mobile app, move the notebook to OneDrive. You can quickly share notebook content with other people using OneDrive.

Figure 2: Microsoft OneNote Mobile app

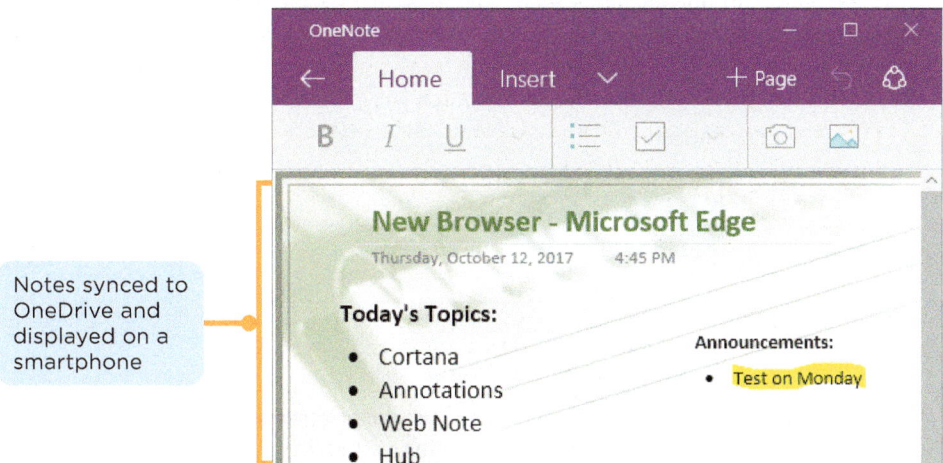

Notes synced to OneDrive and displayed on a smartphone

Taking Notes

Use OneNote pages to organize your notes by class and topic or lecture. Beyond simple typed notes, OneNote stores drawings, converts handwriting to searchable text and mathematical sketches to equations, and records audio and video.

OneNote includes drawing tools that let you sketch freehand drawings such as biological cell diagrams and financial supply-and-demand charts. As shown in **Figure 3**, the Draw tab on the ribbon provides these drawing tools along with shapes so you can insert diagrams and other illustrations to represent your ideas. When you draw on a page, OneNote creates a **drawing canvas**, which is a container for shapes and lines.

On the Job Now

OneNote is ideal for taking notes during meetings, whether you are recording minutes, documenting a discussion, sketching product diagrams, or listing follow-up items. Use a meeting template to add pages with content appropriate for meetings.

Figure 3: Tools on the Draw tab

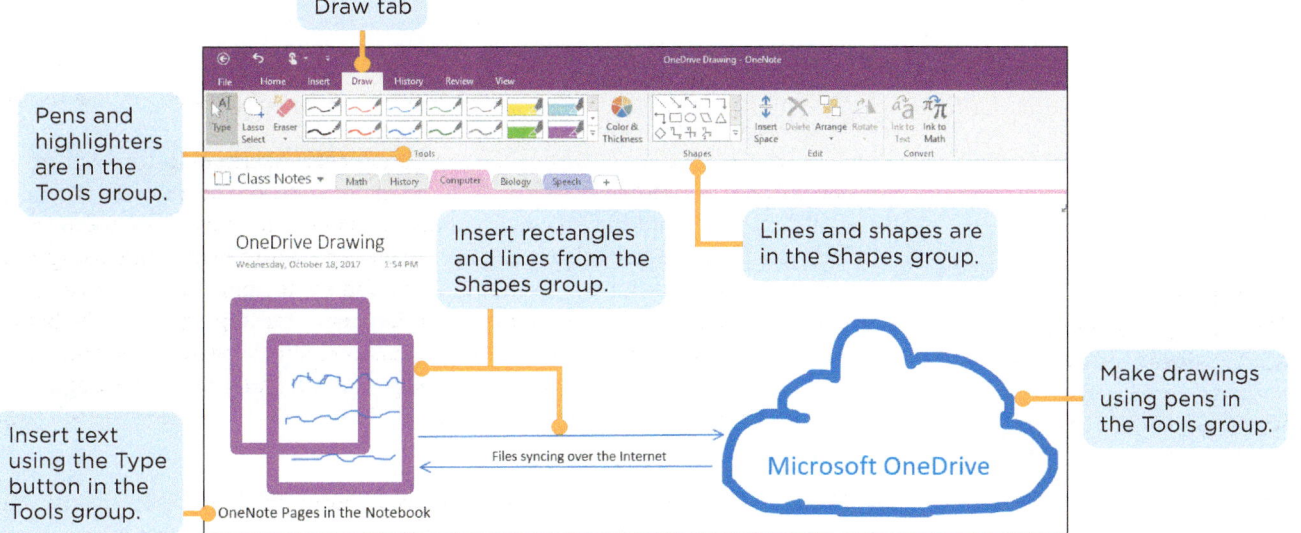

Draw tab

Pens and highlighters are in the Tools group.

Insert rectangles and lines from the Shapes group.

Lines and shapes are in the Shapes group.

Make drawings using pens in the Tools group.

Insert text using the Type button in the Tools group.

OneDrive Drawing
Wednesday, October 18, 2017   1:54 PM

Files syncing over the Internet

Microsoft OneDrive

OneNote Pages in the Notebook

Converting Handwriting to Text

When you use a pen tool to write on a notebook page, the text you enter is called **inked handwriting**. OneNote can convert inked handwriting to typed text when you use the **Ink to Text** button in the Convert group on the Draw tab, as shown in **Figure 4**. After OneNote converts the handwriting to text, you can use the Search box to find terms in the converted text or any other note in your notebooks.

Figure 4: Converting handwriting to text

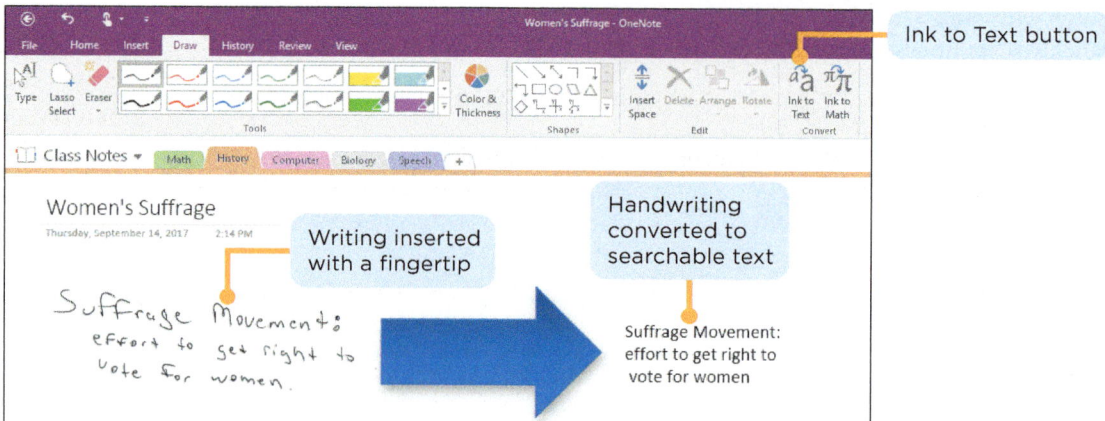

Ink to Text button

Women's Suffrage

Writing inserted with a fingertip

Handwriting converted to searchable text

Suffrage Movement: effort to get right to vote for women

On the Job Now

Use OneNote as a place to brainstorm ongoing work projects. If a notebook contains sensitive material, you can password-protect some or all of the notebook so that only certain people can open it.

Recording a Lecture

If your computer or mobile device has a microphone or camera, OneNote can record the audio or video from a lecture or business meeting as shown in **Figure 5**. When you record a lecture (with your instructor's permission), you can follow along, take regular notes at your own pace, and review the video recording later. You can control the start, pause, and stop motions of the recording when you play back the recording of your notes.

Figure 5: Video inserted in a notebook

Record Video button

Audio & Video Recording tab

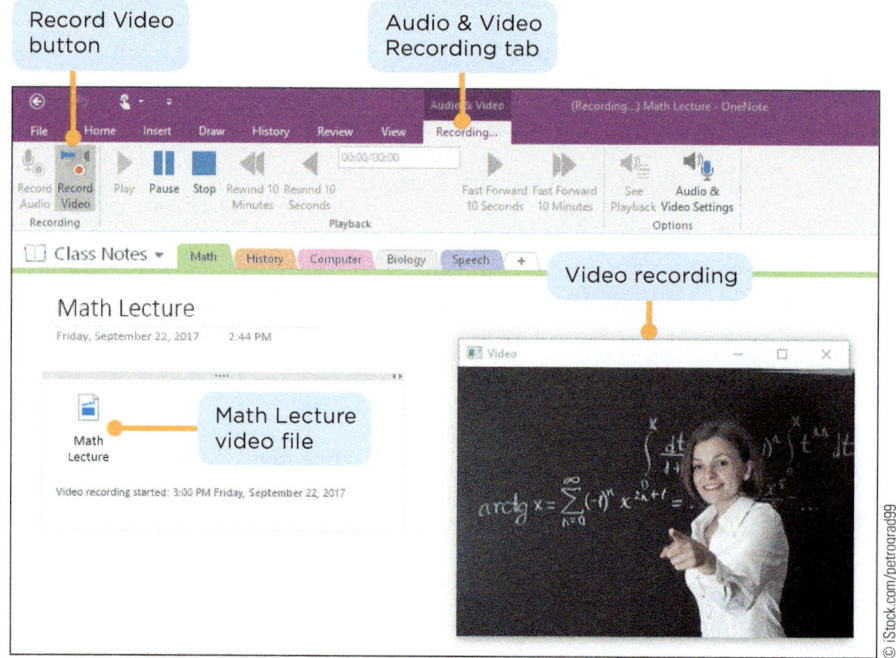

Video recording

Math Lecture

Math Lecture video file

© iStock.com/petrograd99

Try This Now

Learn to use OneNote!

Links to companion **Sways**, featuring **videos** with hands-on instructions, are located on www.cengagebrain.com.

1: Taking Notes for a Week

As a student, you can get organized by using OneNote to take detailed notes in your classes. Perform the following tasks:

a. Create a new OneNote notebook on your Microsoft OneDrive account (the default location for new notebooks). Name the notebook with your first name followed by "Notes," as in **Caleb Notes**.

b. Create four section tabs, each with a different class name.

c. Take detailed notes in those classes for one week. Be sure to include notes, drawings, and other types of content.

d. Sync your notes with your OneDrive. Submit your assignment in the format specified by your instructor.

2: Using OneNote to Organize a Research Paper

You have a research paper due on the topic of three habits of successful students. Use OneNote to organize your research. Perform the following tasks:

a. Create a new OneNote notebook on your Microsoft OneDrive account. Name the notebook **Success Research**.

b. Create three section tabs with the following names:

- **Take Detailed Notes**
- **Be Respectful in Class**
- **Come to Class Prepared**

c. On the web, research the topics and find three sources for each section. Copy a sentence from each source and paste the sentence into the appropriate section. When you paste the sentence, OneNote inserts it in a note with a link to the source.

d. Sync your notes with your OneDrive. Submit your assignment in the format specified by your instructor.

3: Planning Your Career

Note: This activity requires a webcam or built-in video camera on any type of device.

Consider an occupation that interests you. Using OneNote, examine the responsibilities, education requirements, potential salary, and employment outlook of a specific career. Perform the following tasks:

a. Create a new OneNote notebook on your Microsoft OneDrive account. Name the notebook with your first name followed by a career title, such as **Kara - App Developer**.

b. Create four section tabs with the names **Responsibilities, Education Requirements, Median Salary**, and **Employment Outlook**.

c. Research the responsibilities of your career path. Using OneNote, record a short video (approximately 30 seconds) of yourself explaining the responsibilities of your career path. Place the video in the Responsibilities section.

d. On the web, research the educational requirements for your career path and find two appropriate sources. Copy a paragraph from each source and paste them into the appropriate section. When you paste a paragraph, OneNote inserts it in a note with a link to the source.

e. Research the median salary for a single year for this career. Create a mathematical equation in the Median Salary section that multiplies the amount of the median salary times 20 years to calculate how much you will possibly earn.

f. For the Employment Outlook section, research the outlook for your career path. Take at least four notes about what you find when researching the topic.

g. Sync your notes with your OneDrive. Submit your assignment in the format specified by your instructor.

Introduction to Sway

Sway site | responsive design | Storyline | card | Creative Commons license | animation emphasis effects | Docs.com

Expressing your ideas in a presentation typically means creating PowerPoint slides or a Word document. Microsoft Sway gives you another way to engage an audience. Sway is a free Microsoft tool available at Sway.com or as an app in Office 365. Using Sway, you can combine text, images, videos, and social media in a website called a **Sway site** that you can share and display on any device. To get started, you create a digital story on a web-based canvas without borders, slides, cells, or page breaks. A Sway site organizes the text, images, and video into a **responsive design**, which means your content adapts perfectly to any screen size as shown in **Figure 6**. You store a Sway site in the cloud on OneDrive using a free Microsoft account.

Bottom Line

- Drag photos, videos, and files from your computer and content from Facebook and Twitter directly to your Sway presentation.
- Run Sway in a web browser or as an app on your smartphone, and save presentations as webpages.

Figure 6: Sway site with responsive design

You can display a Sway presentation in a web browser.

Sway uses responsive design to make sure pages fit perfectly on any device.

© iStock.com/marinello, © iStock.com/marekuliasz

Learn to use Sway!
Links to companion **Sways**, featuring **videos** with hands-on instructions, are located on www.cengagebrain.com.

Creating a Sway Presentation

You can use Sway to build a digital flyer, a club newsletter, a vacation blog, an informational site, a digital art portfolio, or a new product rollout. After you select your topic and sign into Sway with your Microsoft account, a **Storyline** opens, providing tools and a work area for composing your digital story. See **Figure 7**. Each story can include text, images, and videos. You create a Sway by adding text and media content into a Storyline section, or **card**. To add pictures, videos, or documents, select a card in the left pane and then select the Insert Content button. The first card in a Sway presentation contains a title and background image.

Figure 7: Creating a Sway site

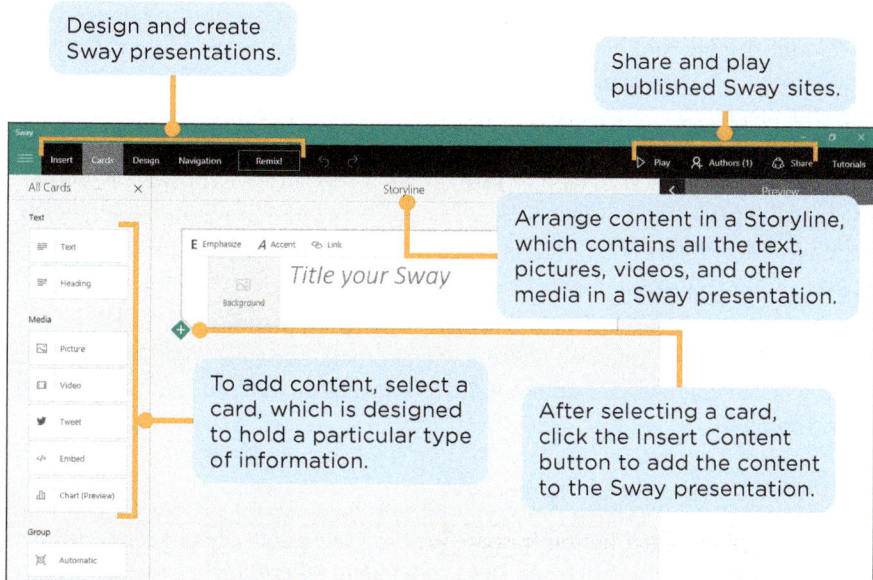

Design and create Sway presentations.

Share and play published Sway sites.

Arrange content in a Storyline, which contains all the text, pictures, videos, and other media in a Sway presentation.

To add content, select a card, which is designed to hold a particular type of information.

After selecting a card, click the Insert Content button to add the content to the Sway presentation.

Adding Content to Build a Story

As you work, Sway searches the Internet to help you find relevant images, videos, tweets, and other content from online sources such as Bing, YouTube, Twitter, and Facebook. You can drag content from the search results right into the Storyline. In addition, you can upload your own images and videos directly in the presentation. For example, if you are creating a Sway presentation about the market for commercial drones, Sway suggests content to incorporate into the presentation by displaying it in the left pane as search results. The search results include drone images tagged with **Creative Commons license** at online sources as shown in **Figure 8**. A Creative Commons license is a public copyright license that allows the free distribution of an otherwise copyrighted work. In addition, you can specify the source of the media. For example, you can add your own Facebook or OneNote pictures and videos in Sway without leaving the app.

On the Job Now

If you have a Microsoft Word document containing an outline of your business content, drag the outline into Sway to create a card for each topic.

Figure 8: Images in Sway search results

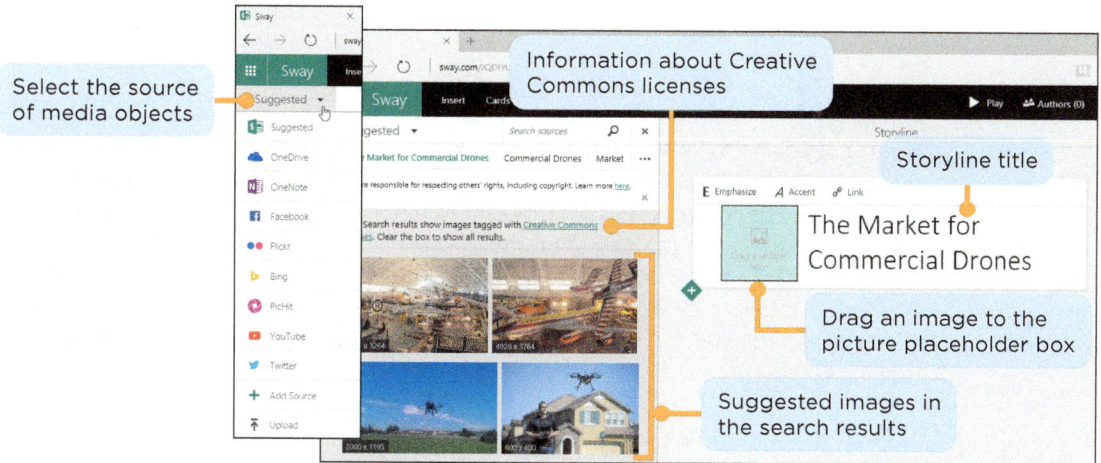

Select the source of media objects

Information about Creative Commons licenses

Storyline title

The Market for Commercial Drones

Drag an image to the picture placeholder box

Suggested images in the search results

On the Job Now

If your project team wants to collaborate on a Sway presentation, click the Authors button on the navigation bar to invite others to edit the presentation.

Designing a Sway

Sway professionally designs your Storyline content by resizing background images and fonts to fit your display, and by floating text, animating media, embedding video, and removing images as a page scrolls out of view. Sway also evaluates the images in your Storyline and suggests a color palette based on colors that appear in your photos. Use the Design button to display tools including color palettes, font choices, **animation emphasis effects**, and style templates to provide a personality for a Sway presentation. Instead of creating your own design, you can click the Remix button, which randomly selects unique designs for your Sway site.

Publishing a Sway

Use the Play button to display your finished Sway presentation as a website. The Address bar includes a unique web address where others can view your Sway site. As the author, you can edit a published Sway site by clicking the Edit button (pencil icon) on the Sway toolbar.

Sharing a Sway

When you are ready to share your Sway website, you have several options as shown in **Figure 9**. Use the Share slider button to share the Sway site publically or keep it private. If you add the Sway site to the Microsoft **Docs.com** public gallery, anyone worldwide can use Bing, Google, or other search engines to find, view, and share your Sway site. You can also share your Sway site using Facebook, Twitter, Google+, Yammer, and other social media sites. Link your presentation to any webpage or email the link to your audience. Sway can also generate a code for embedding the link within another webpage.

Figure 9: Sharing a Sway site

Share button

> Play   Authors (1)   Share

Share ●   Just me

Drag the slider button to Just me to keep the Sway site private

Share with the world

Post the Sway site on Docs.com

Docs.com - Your public gallery

Share with friends

Options differ depending on your Microsoft account

Send friends a link to the Sway site

https://sway.com/JQDFrUaxmg4lEbbk

More options

☑ Viewers can duplicate this Sway

Stop sharing

Try This Now

Learn to use Sway!
Links to companion **Sways**, featuring **videos** with hands-on instructions, are located on www.cengagebrain.com.

1: Creating a Sway Resume

Sway is a digital storytelling app. Create a Sway resume to share the skills, job experiences, and achievements you have that match the requirements of a future job interest. Perform the following tasks:

    a. Create a new presentation in Sway to use as a digital resume. Title the Sway Storyline with your full name and then select a background image.

    b. Create three separate sections titled **Academic Background, Work Experience**, and **Skills**, and insert text, a picture, and a paragraph or bulleted points in each section. Be sure to include your own picture.

    c. Add a fourth section that includes a video about your school that you find online.

    d. Customize the design of your presentation.

    e. Submit your assignment link in the format specified by your instructor.

2: Creating an Online Sway Newsletter

Newsletters are designed to capture the attention of their target audience. Using Sway, create a newsletter for a club, organization, or your favorite music group. Perform the following tasks:

    a. Create a new presentation in Sway to use as a digital newsletter for a club, organization, or your favorite music group. Provide a title for the Sway Storyline and select an appropriate background image.

    b. Select three separate sections with appropriate titles, such as Upcoming Events. In each section, insert text, a picture, and a paragraph or bulleted points.

    c. Add a fourth section that includes a video about your selected topic.

    d. Customize the design of your presentation.

    e. Submit your assignment link in the format specified by your instructor.

3: Creating and Sharing a Technology Presentation

To place a Sway presentation in the hands of your entire audience, you can share a link to the Sway presentation. Create a Sway presentation on a new technology and share it with your class. Perform the following tasks:

    a. Create a new presentation in Sway about a cutting-edge technology topic. Provide a title for the Sway Storyline and select a background image.

    b. Create four separate sections about your topic, and include text, a picture, and a paragraph in each section.

    c. Add a fifth section that includes a video about your topic.

    d. Customize the design of your presentation.

    e. Share the link to your Sway with your classmates and submit your assignment link in the format specified by your instructor.

Introduction to Office Mix

add-in | clip | slide recording | Slide Notes | screen recording | free-response quiz

Bottom Line

- Office Mix is a free PowerPoint add-in from Microsoft that adds features to PowerPoint.
- The Mix tab on the PowerPoint ribbon provides tools for creating screen recordings, videos, interactive quizzes, and live webpages.

To enliven business meetings and lectures, Microsoft adds a new dimension to presentations with a powerful toolset called Office Mix, a free add-in for PowerPoint. (An **add-in** is software that works with an installed app to extend its features.) Using Office Mix, you can record yourself on video, capture still and moving images on your desktop, and insert interactive elements such as quizzes and live webpages directly into PowerPoint slides. When you post the finished presentation to OneDrive, Office Mix provides a link you can share with friends and colleagues. Anyone with an Internet connection and a web browser can watch a published Office Mix presentation, such as the one in **Figure 10**, on a computer or mobile device.

Figure 10: Office Mix presentation

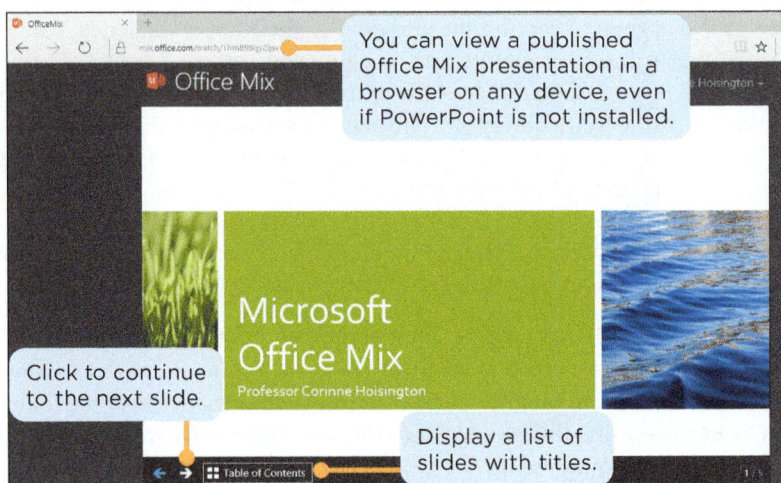

Adding Office Mix to PowerPoint

To get started, you create an Office Mix account at the website mix.office.com using an email address or a Facebook or Google account. Next, you download and install the Office Mix add-in (see **Figure 11**). Office Mix appears as a new tab named Mix on the PowerPoint ribbon in versions of Office 2013 and Office 2016 running on personal computers (PCs).

Learn to use Office Mix!

Links to companion **Sways**, featuring **videos** with hands-on instructions, are located on www.cengagebrain.com.

Figure 11: Getting started with Office Mix

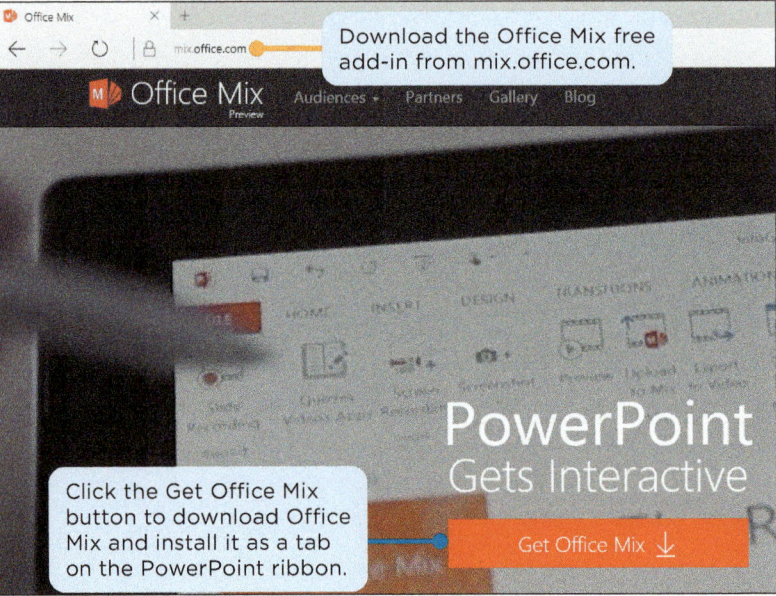

Capturing Video Clips

A **clip** is a short segment of audio, such as music, or video. After finishing the content on a PowerPoint slide, you can use Office Mix to add a video clip to animate or illustrate the content. Office Mix creates video clips in two ways: by recording live action on a webcam and by capturing screen images and movements. If your computer has a webcam, you can record yourself and annotate the slide to create a **slide recording** as shown in **Figure 12**.

Figure 12: Making a slide recording

When you are making a slide recording, you can record your spoken narration at the same time. The **Slide Notes** feature works like a teleprompter to help you focus on your presentation content instead of memorizing your narration. Use the Inking tools to make annotations or add highlighting using different pen types and colors. After finishing a recording, edit the video in PowerPoint to trim the length or set playback options.

The second way to create a video is to capture on-screen images and actions with or without a voiceover. This method is ideal if you want to show how to use your favorite website or demonstrate an app such as OneNote. To share your screen with an audience, select the part of the screen you want to show in the video. Office Mix captures everything that happens in that area to create a **screen recording**, as shown in **Figure 13**. Office Mix inserts the screen recording as a video in the slide.

Figure 13: Making a screen recording

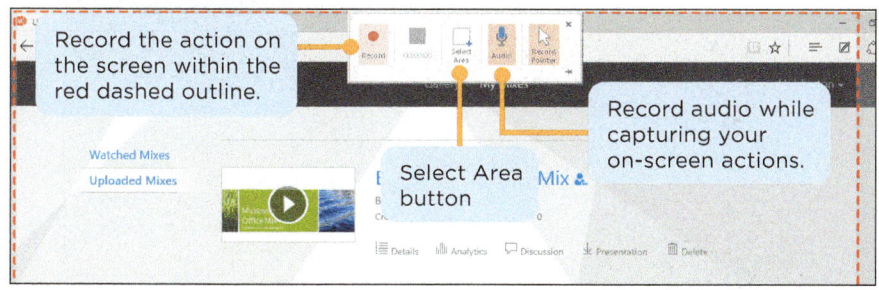

Inserting Quizzes, Live Webpages, and Apps

To enhance and assess audience understanding, make your slides interactive by adding quizzes, live webpages, and apps. Quizzes give immediate feedback to the user as shown in **Figure 14**. Office Mix supports several quiz formats, including a **free-response quiz** similar to a short answer quiz, and true/false, multiple-choice, and multiple-response formats.

Figure 14: Creating an interactive quiz

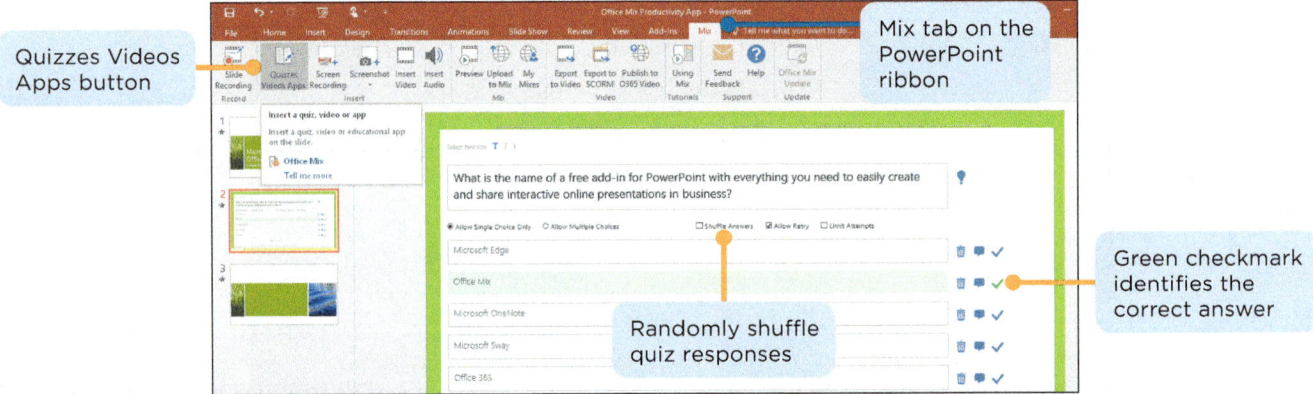

Sharing an Office Mix Presentation

When you complete your work with Office Mix, upload the presentation to your personal Office Mix dashboard as shown in **Figure 15**. Users of PCs, Macs, iOS devices, and Android devices can access and play Office Mix presentations. The Office Mix dashboard displays built-in analytics that include the quiz results and how much time viewers spent on each slide. You can play completed Office Mix presentations online or download them as movies.

Figure 15: Sharing an Office Mix presentation

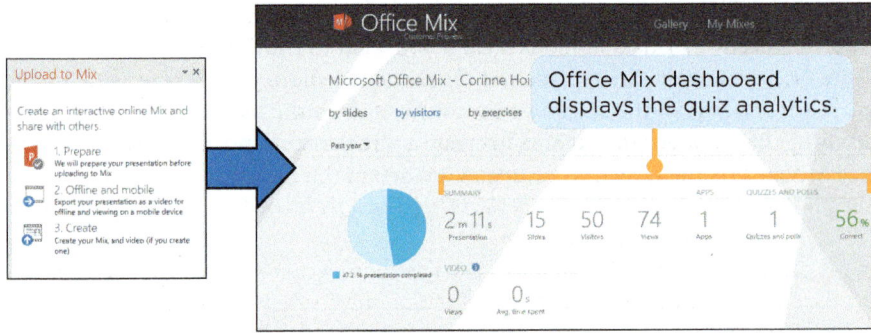

Try This Now

1: Creating an Office Mix Tutorial for OneNote

Learn to use Office Mix!
Links to companion **Sways**, featuring **videos** with hands-on instructions, are located on www.cengagebrain.com.

Note: This activity requires a microphone on your computer.

Office Mix makes it easy to record screens and their contents. Create PowerPoint slides with an Office Mix screen recording to show OneNote 2016 features. Perform the following tasks:

a. Create a PowerPoint presentation with the Ion Boardroom template. Create an opening slide with the title **My Favorite OneNote Features** and enter your name in the subtitle.
b. Create three additional slides, each titled with a new feature of OneNote. Open OneNote and use the Mix tab in PowerPoint to capture three separate screen recordings that teach your favorite features.
c. Add a fifth slide that quizzes the user with a multiple-choice question about OneNote and includes four responses. Be sure to insert a checkmark indicating the correct response.
d. Upload the completed presentation to your Office Mix dashboard and share the link with your instructor.
e. Submit your assignment link in the format specified by your instructor.

2: Teaching Augmented Reality with Office Mix

Note: This activity requires a webcam or built-in video camera on your computer.

A local elementary school has asked you to teach augmented reality to its students using Office Mix. Perform the following tasks:

a. Research augmented reality using your favorite online search tools.
b. Create a PowerPoint presentation with the Frame template. Create an opening slide with the title **Augmented Reality** and enter your name in the subtitle.
c. Create a slide with four bullets summarizing your research of augmented reality. Create a 20-second slide recording of yourself providing a quick overview of augmented reality.
d. Create another slide with a 30-second screen recording of a video about augmented reality from a site such as YouTube or another video-sharing site.
e. Add a final slide that quizzes the user with a true/false question about augmented reality. Be sure to insert a checkmark indicating the correct response.
f. Upload the completed presentation to your Office Mix dashboard and share the link with your instructor.
g. Submit your assignment link in the format specified by your instructor.

3: Marketing a Travel Destination with Office Mix

Note: This activity requires a webcam or built-in video camera on your computer.

To convince your audience to travel to a particular city, create a slide presentation marketing any city in the world using a slide recording, screen recording, and a quiz. Perform the following tasks:

a. Create a PowerPoint presentation with any template. Create an opening slide with the title of the city you are marketing as a travel destination and your name in the subtitle.
b. Create a slide with four bullets about the featured city. Create a 30-second slide recording of yourself explaining why this city is the perfect vacation destination.
c. Create another slide with a 20-second screen recording of a travel video about the city from a site such as YouTube or another video-sharing site.
d. Add a final slide that quizzes the user with a multiple-choice question about the featured city with five responses. Be sure to include a checkmark indicating the correct response.
e. Upload the completed presentation to your Office Mix dashboard and share your link with your instructor.
f. Submit your assignment link in the format specified by your instructor.

Introduction to Microsoft Edge

Reading view | Hub | Cortana | Web Note | Inking | sandbox

Microsoft Edge is the default web browser developed for the Windows 10 operating system as a replacement for Internet Explorer. Unlike its predecessor, Edge lets you write on webpages, read webpages without advertisements and other distractions, and search for information using a virtual personal assistant. The Edge interface is clean and basic, as shown in **Figure 16**, meaning you can pay more attention to the webpage content.

Figure 16: Microsoft Edge tools

Forward button
New tab button
Web address in the Address bar
Add to favorites or reading list button
Back button
Reading view button
More button
Share Web Note button
Refresh (F5) button
Hub (Favorites, reading list, history, and downloads) button
Make a Web Note button

Browsing the Web with Microsoft Edge

One of the fastest browsers available, Edge allows you to type search text directly in the Address bar. As you view the resulting webpage, you can switch to **Reading view**, which is available for most news and research sites, to eliminate distracting advertisements. For example, if you are catching up on technology news online, the webpage might be difficult to read due to a busy layout cluttered with ads. Switch to Reading view to refresh the page and remove the original page formatting, ads, and menu sidebars to read the article distraction-free.

Consider the **Hub** in Microsoft Edge as providing one-stop access to all the things you collect on the web, such as your favorite websites, reading list, surfing history, and downloaded files.

Locating Information with Cortana

Cortana, the Windows 10 virtual assistant, plays an important role in Microsoft Edge. After you turn on Cortana, it appears as an animated circle in the Address bar when you might need assistance, as shown in the restaurant website in **Figure 17**. When you click the Cortana icon, a pane slides in from the right of the browser window to display detailed information about the restaurant, including maps and reviews. Cortana can also assist you in defining words, finding the weather, suggesting coupons for shopping, updating stock market information, and calculating math.

Figure 17: Cortana providing restaurant information

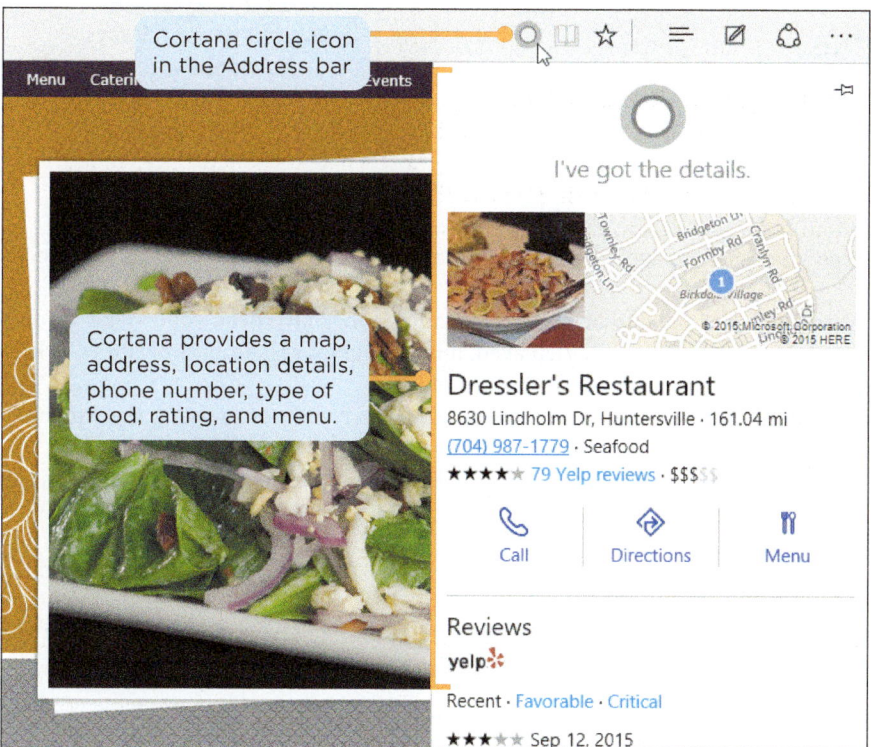

Figure 17: Cortana providing restaurant information

Annotating Webpages

One of the most impressive Microsoft Edge features are the **Web Note** tools, which you use to write on a webpage or to highlight text. When you click the Make a Web Note button, an **Inking** toolbar appears, as shown in **Figure 18**, that provides writing and drawing tools. These tools include an eraser, a pen, and a highlighter with different colors. You can also insert a typed note and copy a screen image (called a screen clipping). You can draw with a pointing device, fingertip, or stylus using different pen colors. Whether you add notes to a recipe, annotate sources for a research paper, or select a product while shopping online, the Web Note tools can enhance your productivity. After you complete your notes, click the Save button to save the annotations to OneNote, your Favorites list, or your Reading list. You can share the inked page with others using the Share Web Note button.

On the Job Now

To enhance security, Microsoft Edge runs in a partial sandbox, an arrangement that prevents attackers from gaining control of your computer. Browsing within the **sandbox** protects computer resources and information from hackers.

Figure 18: Web Note tools in Microsoft Edge

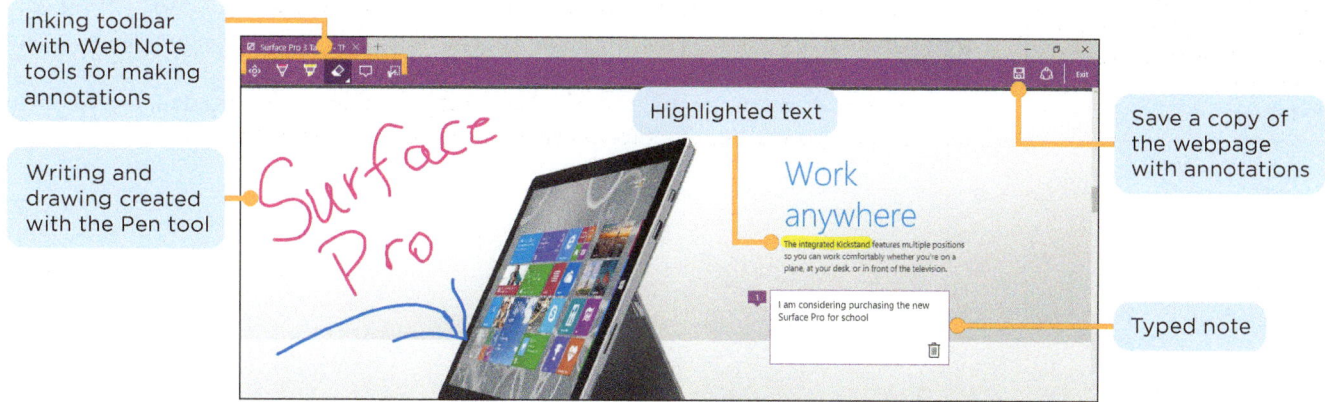

Try This Now

Learn to use Edge!
Links to companion **Sways**, featuring **videos** with hands-on instructions, are located on www.cengagebrain.com.

1: Using Cortana in Microsoft Edge

Note: This activity requires using Microsoft Edge on a Windows 10 computer.

Cortana can assist you in finding information on a webpage in Microsoft Edge. Perform the following tasks:

a. Create a Word document using the Word Screen Clipping tool to capture the following screenshots.

- Screenshot A—Using Microsoft Edge, open a webpage with a technology news article. Right-click a term in the article and ask Cortana to define it.
- Screenshot B—Using Microsoft Edge, open the website of a fancy restaurant in a city near you. Make sure the Cortana circle icon is displayed in the Address bar. (If it's not displayed, find a different restaurant website.) Click the Cortana circle icon to display a pane with information about the restaurant.
- Screenshot C—Using Microsoft Edge, type **10 USD to Euros** in the Address bar without pressing the Enter key. Cortana converts the U.S. dollars to Euros.
- Screenshot D—Using Microsoft Edge, type **Apple stock** in the Address bar without pressing the Enter key. Cortana displays the current stock quote.

b. Submit your assignment in the format specified by your instructor.

2: Viewing Online News with Reading View

Note: This activity requires using Microsoft Edge on a Windows 10 computer.

Reading view in Microsoft Edge can make a webpage less cluttered with ads and other distractions. Perform the following tasks:

a. Create a Word document using the Word Screen Clipping tool to capture the following screenshots.

- Screenshot A—Using Microsoft Edge, open the website **mashable.com**. Open a technology article. Click the Reading view button to display an ad-free page that uses only basic text formatting.
- Screenshot B—Using Microsoft Edge, open the website **bbc.com**. Open any news article. Click the Reading view button to display an ad-free page that uses only basic text formatting.
- Screenshot C—Make three types of annotations (Pen, Highlighter, and Add a typed note) on the BBC article page displayed in Reading view.

b. Submit your assignment in the format specified by your instructor.

3: Inking with Microsoft Edge

Note: This activity requires using Microsoft Edge on a Windows 10 computer.

Microsoft Edge provides many annotation options to record your ideas. Perform the following tasks:

a. Open the website **wolframalpha.com** in the Microsoft Edge browser. Wolfram Alpha is a well-respected academic search engine. Type **US$100 1965 dollars in 2015** in the Wolfram Alpha search text box and press the Enter key.

b. Click the Make a Web Note button to display the Web Note tools. Using the Pen tool, draw a circle around the result on the webpage. Save the page to OneNote.

c. In the Wolfram Alpha search text box, type the name of the city closest to where you live and press the Enter key. Using the Highlighter tool, highlight at least three interesting results. Add a note and then type a sentence about what you learned about this city. Save the page to OneNote. Share your OneNote notebook with your instructor.

d. Submit your assignment link in the format specified by your instructor.

Getting Started with Microsoft Office 2016

CASE ▶ This module introduces you to the most frequently used programs in Office, as well as common features they all share.

Module Objectives

After completing this module, you will be able to:

- Understand the Office 2016 suite
- Start an Office app
- Identify Office 2016 screen elements
- Create and save a file
- Open a file and save it with a new name
- View and print your work
- Get Help, close a file, and exit an app

Files You Will Need

OF 1-1.xlsx

Learning
Outcomes
- Identify Office suite components
- Describe the features of each app

Understand the Office 2016 Suite

Microsoft Office 2016 is a group of programs—which are also called applications or apps—designed to help you create documents, collaborate with coworkers, and track and analyze information. You use different Office programs to accomplish specific tasks, such as writing a letter or producing a presentation, yet all the programs have a similar look and feel. Microsoft Office 2016 apps feature a common, context-sensitive user interface, so you can get up to speed faster and use advanced features with greater ease. The Office apps are bundled together in a group called a **suite**. The Office suite is available in several configurations, but all include Word, Excel, PowerPoint, and OneNote. Some configurations include Access, Outlook, Publisher, Skype, and OneDrive. **CASE** *As part of your job, you need to understand how each Office app is best used to complete specific tasks.*

DETAILS

The Office apps covered in this book include:

- #### Microsoft Word 2016

  When you need to create any kind of text-based document, such as a memo, newsletter, or multipage report, Word is the program to use. You can easily make your documents look great by using formatting tools and inserting eye-catching graphics. The Word document shown in **FIGURE 1-1** contains a company logo and simple formatting.

- #### Microsoft Excel 2016

  Excel is the perfect solution when you need to work with numeric values and make calculations. It puts the power of formulas, functions, charts, and other analytical tools into the hands of every user, so you can analyze sales projections, calculate loan payments, and present your findings in a professional manner. The Excel worksheet shown in **FIGURE 1-1** tracks checkbook transactions. Because Excel automatically recalculates results whenever a value changes, the information is always up to date. A chart illustrates how the monthly expenses are broken down.

- #### Microsoft PowerPoint 2016

  Using PowerPoint, it's easy to create powerful presentations complete with graphics, transitions, and even a soundtrack. Using professionally designed themes and clip art, you can quickly and easily create dynamic slide shows such as the one shown in **FIGURE 1-1**.

- #### Microsoft Access 2016

  Access is a relational database program that helps you keep track of large amounts of quantitative data, such as product inventories or employee records. The form shown in **FIGURE 1-1** can be used to generate reports on customer invoices and tours.

Microsoft Office has benefits beyond the power of each program, including:

- #### Note-taking made simple; available on all devices

  Use OneNote to take notes (organized in tabbed pages) on information that can be accessed on your computer, tablet, or phone. Share the editable results with others. Contents can include text, web page clips (using OneNote Clipper), email contents (directly inserted into a default section), photos (using Office Lens), and web pages.

- #### Common user interface: Improving business processes

  Because the Office suite apps have a similar **interface**, your experience using one app's tools makes it easy to learn those in the other apps. Office documents are **compatible** with one another, so you can easily **integrate**, or combine, elements—for example, you can add an Excel chart to a PowerPoint slide, or an Access table to a Word document.

  Most Office programs include the capability to incorporate feedback—called **online collaboration**—across the Internet or a company network.

FIGURE 1-1: Microsoft Office 2016 documents

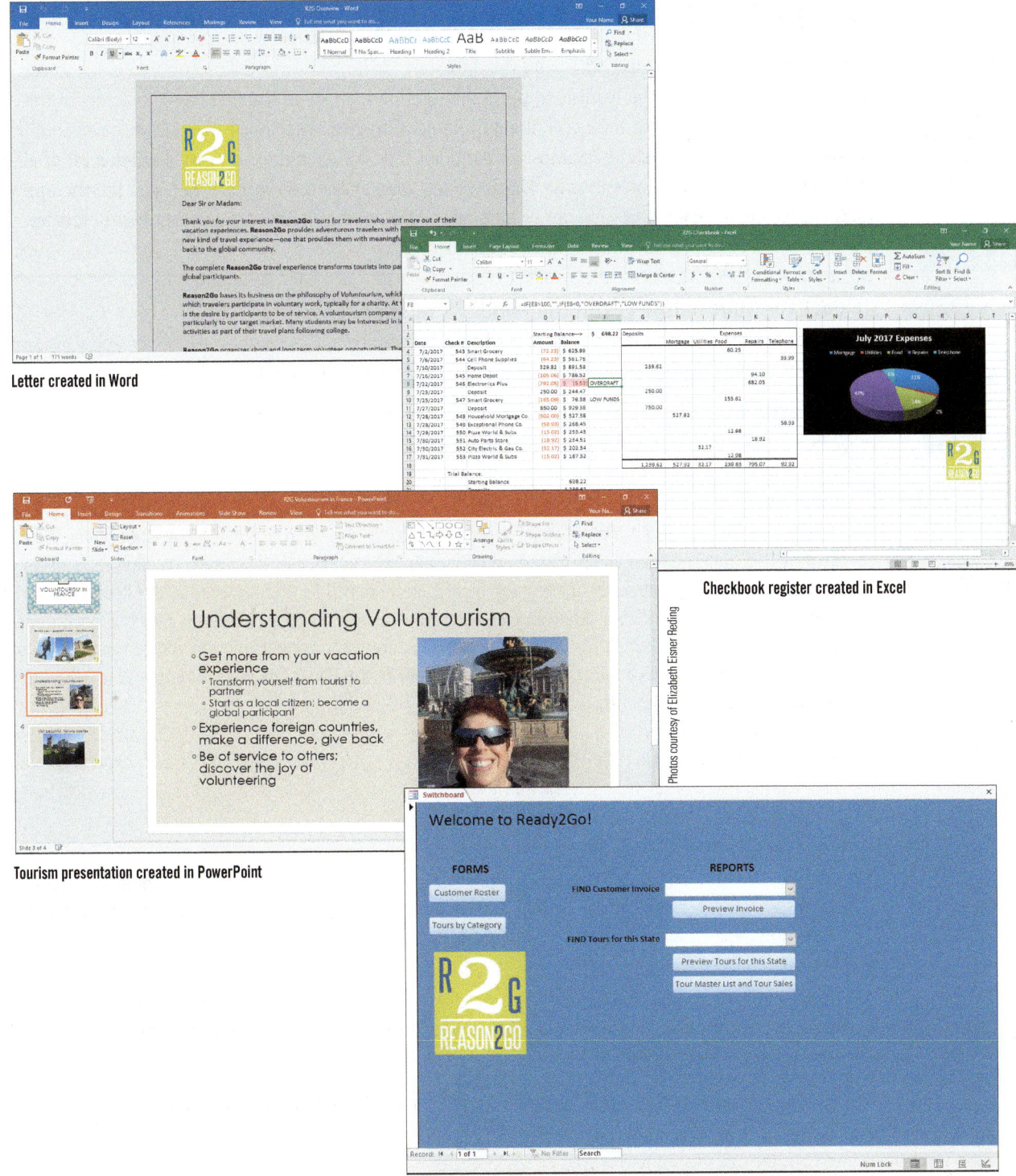

Letter created in Word

Checkbook register created in Excel

Tourism presentation created in PowerPoint

Form created in Access

Photos courtesy of Elizabeth Eisner Reding

What is Office 365?

Until recently, most consumers purchased Microsoft Office in a traditional way: by buying a retail package from a store or downloading it from Microsoft.com. You can still purchase Microsoft Office 2016 in this traditional way—but you can also now purchase it as a subscription service called Microsoft Office 365, which is available in a wide variety of configurations.

Depending on which configuration you purchase, you will always have access to the most up-to-date versions of the apps in your package and, in many cases, can install these apps on multiple computers, tablets, and phones. And if you change computers or devices, you can easily uninstall the apps from an old device and install them on a new one.

Start an Office App

Learning Outcomes
• Start an Office app
• Explain the purpose of a template
• Start a new blank document

To get started using Microsoft Office, you need to start, or **launch**, the Office app you want to use. An easy way to start the app you want is to press the Windows key, type the first few characters of the app name you want to search for, then click the app name In the Best match list. You will discover that there are many ways to accomplish just about any Windows task; for example, you can also see a list of all the apps on your computer by pressing the Windows key, then clicking All Apps. When you see the app you want, click its name. **CASE** ▶ *You decide to familiarize yourself with Office by starting Microsoft Word.*

STEPS

1. **Click the Start button ⊞ on the Windows taskbar**

   The Start menu opens, listing the most used apps on your computer. You can locate the app you want to open by clicking the app name if you see it, or you can type the app name to search for it.

2. **Type word**

   Your screen now displays "Word 2016" under "Best match", along with any other app that has "word" as part of its name (such as WordPad). See **FIGURE 1-2**.

3. **Click Word 2016**

   Word 2016 launches, and the Word **start screen** appears, as shown in **FIGURE 1-3**. The start screen is a landing page that appears when you first start an Office app. The left side of this screen displays recent files you have opened. (If you have never opened any files, then there will be no files listed under Recent.) The right side displays images depicting different templates you can use to create different types of documents. A **template** is a file containing professionally designed content and formatting that you can easily customize for your own needs. You can also start from scratch using the Blank Document template, which contains only minimal formatting settings.

Enabling touch mode

If you are using a touch screen with any of the Office 2016 apps, you can enable the touch mode to give the user interface a more spacious look, making it easier to navigate with your fingertips. Enable touch mode by clicking the Quick Access toolbar list arrow, then clicking Touch/Mouse Mode to select it. Then you'll see the Touch Mode button 👆 in the Quick Access toolbar. Click 👆, and you'll see the interface spread out.

Using shortcut keys to move between Office programs

You can switch between open apps using a keyboard shortcut. The [Alt][Tab] keyboard combination lets you either switch quickly to the next open program or file or choose one from a gallery. To switch immediately to the next open program or file, press [Alt][Tab]. To choose from all open programs and files, press and hold [Alt], then press and release [Tab] without releasing [Alt]. A gallery opens on screen, displaying the filename and a thumbnail image of each open program and file, as well as of the desktop. Each time you press [Tab] while holding [Alt], the selection cycles to the next open file or location. Release [Alt] when the program, file, or location you want to activate is selected.

FIGURE 1-2: Searching for the Word app

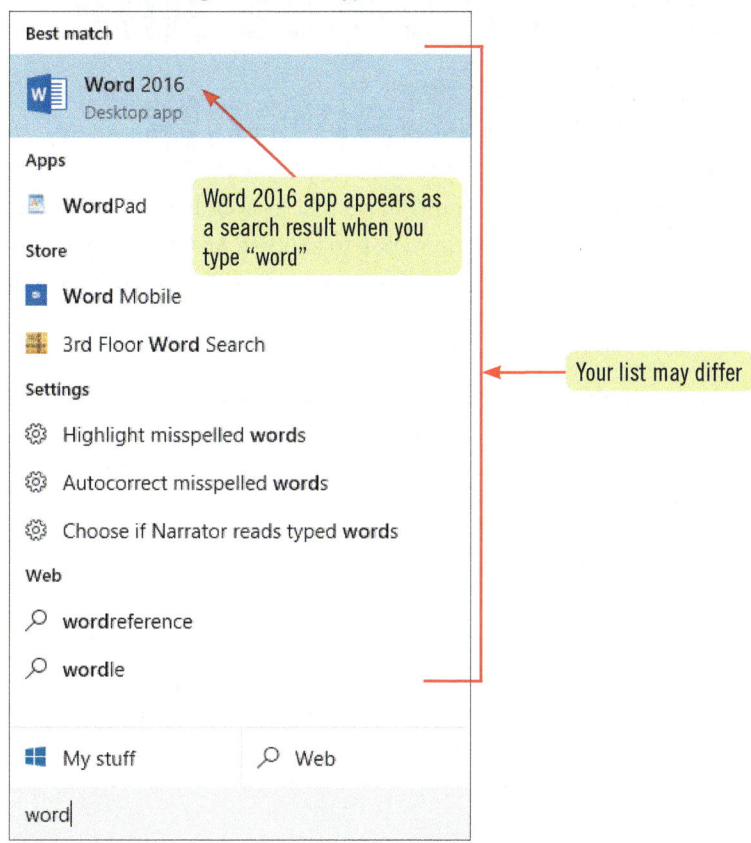

Word 2016 app appears as a search result when you type "word"

Your list may differ

FIGURE 1-3: Word start screen

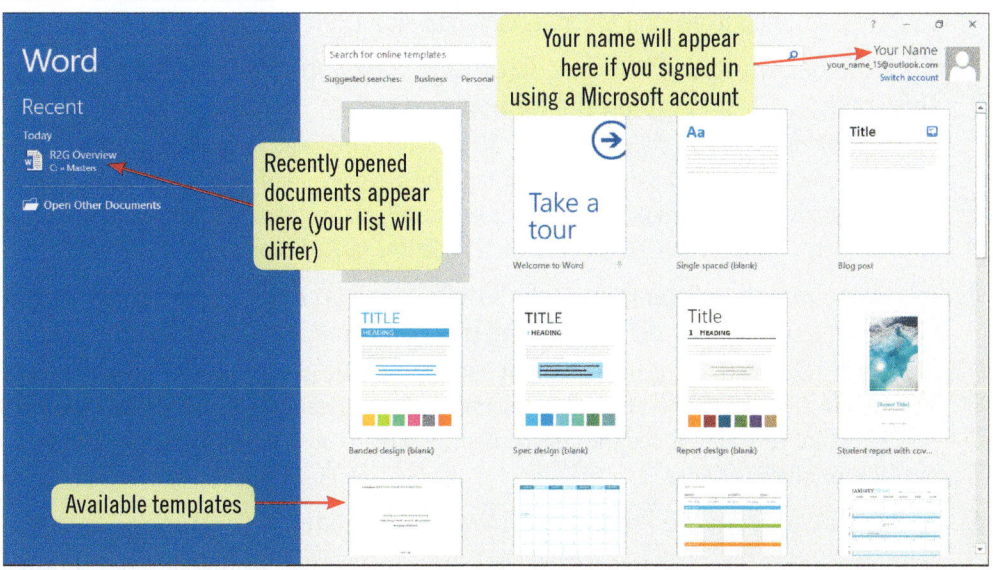

Your name will appear here if you signed in using a Microsoft account

Recently opened documents appear here (your list will differ)

Available templates

Using the Office Clipboard

You can use the Office Clipboard to cut and copy items from one Office program and paste them into others. The Office Clipboard can store a maximum of 24 items. To access it, open the Office Clipboard task pane by clicking the dialog box launcher in the Clipboard group on the Home tab. Each time you copy a selection, it is saved in the Office Clipboard. Each entry in the Office Clipboard includes an icon that tells you the program it was created in. To paste an entry, click in the document where you want it to appear, then click the item in the Office Clipboard. To delete an item from the Office Clipboard, right-click the item, then click Delete.

Office 2016

Identify Office 2016 Screen Elements

Learning Outcomes
- Identify basic components of the user interface
- Display and use Backstage view
- Adjust the zoom level

One of the benefits of using Office is that its apps have much in common, making them easy to learn and making it simple to move from one to another. All Office 2016 apps share a similar user interface, so you can use your knowledge of one to get up to speed in another. A **user interface** is a collective term for all the ways you interact with a software program. The user interface in Office 2016 provides intuitive ways to choose commands, work with files, and navigate in the program window. **CASE** *Familiarize yourself with some of the common interface elements in Office by examining the PowerPoint program window.*

STEPS

1. **Click the Start button ⊞ on the Windows taskbar, type pow, click PowerPoint 2016, then click Blank Presentation**

   PowerPoint starts and opens a new file, which contains a blank slide. Refer to **FIGURE 1-4** to identify common elements of the Office user interface. The **document window** occupies most of the screen. At the top of every Office program window is a **title bar** that displays the document name and program name. Below the title bar is the **Ribbon**, which displays commands you're likely to need for the current task. Commands are organized onto **tabs**. The tab names appear at the top of the Ribbon, and the active tab appears in front. The **Share button** in the upper-right corner lets you invite other users to view your cloud-stored Word, Excel, or Powerpoint file.

2. **Click the File tab**

   The File tab opens, displaying **Backstage view**. It is called Backstage view because the commands available here are for working with the files "behind the scenes." The navigation bar on the left side of Backstage view contains commands to perform actions common to most Office programs.

▶ 3. **Click the Back button ⊙ to close Backstage view and return to the document window, then click the Design tab on the Ribbon**

   To display a different tab, click its name. Each tab contains related commands arranged into **groups** to make features easy to find. On the Design tab, the Themes group displays available design themes in a **gallery**, or visual collection of choices you can browse. Many groups contain a **launcher**, which you can click to open a dialog box or pane from which to choose related commands.

4. **Move the mouse pointer ▷ over the Ion Boardroom theme in the Themes group as shown in FIGURE 1-5, but *do not click* the mouse button**

   The Ion Boardroom theme is temporarily applied to the slide in the document window. However, because you did not click the theme, you did not permanently change the slide. With the **Live Preview** feature, you can point to a choice, see the results, then decide if you want to make the change. Live Preview is available throughout Office.

▶ 5. **Move ▷ away from the Ribbon and towards the slide**

   If you had clicked the Ion theme, it would be applied to this slide. Instead, the slide remains unchanged.

▶ 6. **Point to the Zoom slider ▭—————▯——— + 100% on the status bar, then drag to the right until the Zoom level reads 166%**

   The slide display is enlarged. Zoom tools are located on the status bar. You can drag the slider or click the Zoom In or Zoom Out buttons to zoom in or out on an area of interest. **Zooming in** (a higher percentage), makes a document appear bigger on screen but less of it fits on the screen at once; **zooming out** (a lower percentage) lets you see more of the document at a reduced size.

7. **Click the Zoom Out button ▭ on the status bar to the left of the Zoom slider until the Zoom level reads 120%**

FIGURE 1-4: PowerPoint program window

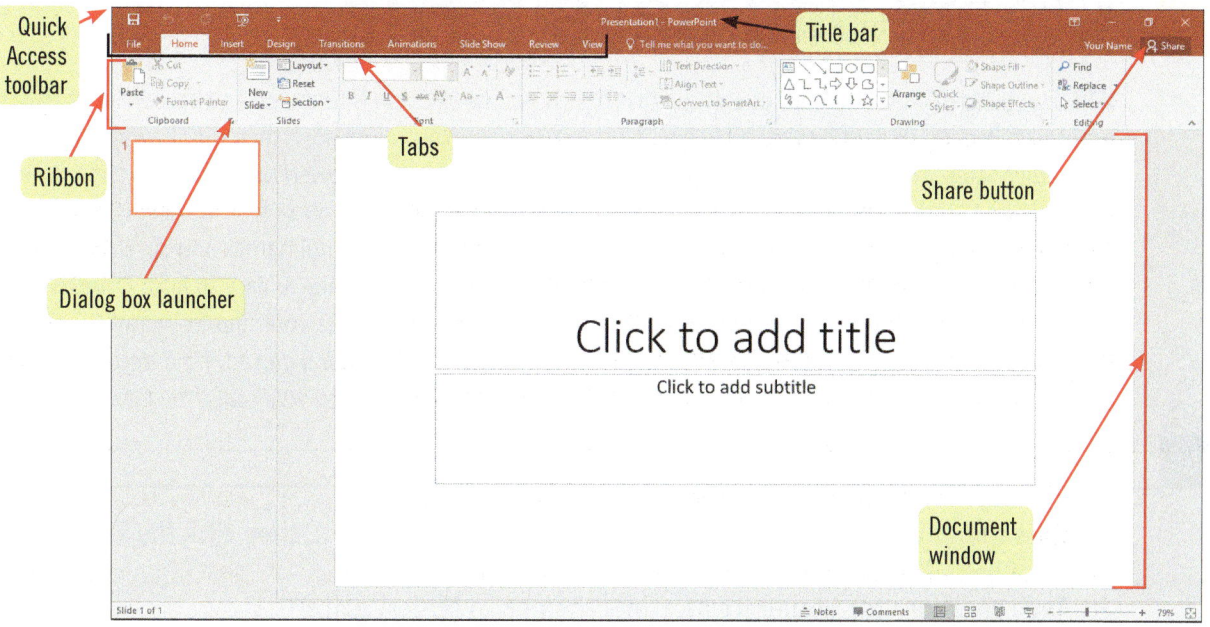

FIGURE 1-5: Viewing a theme with Live Preview

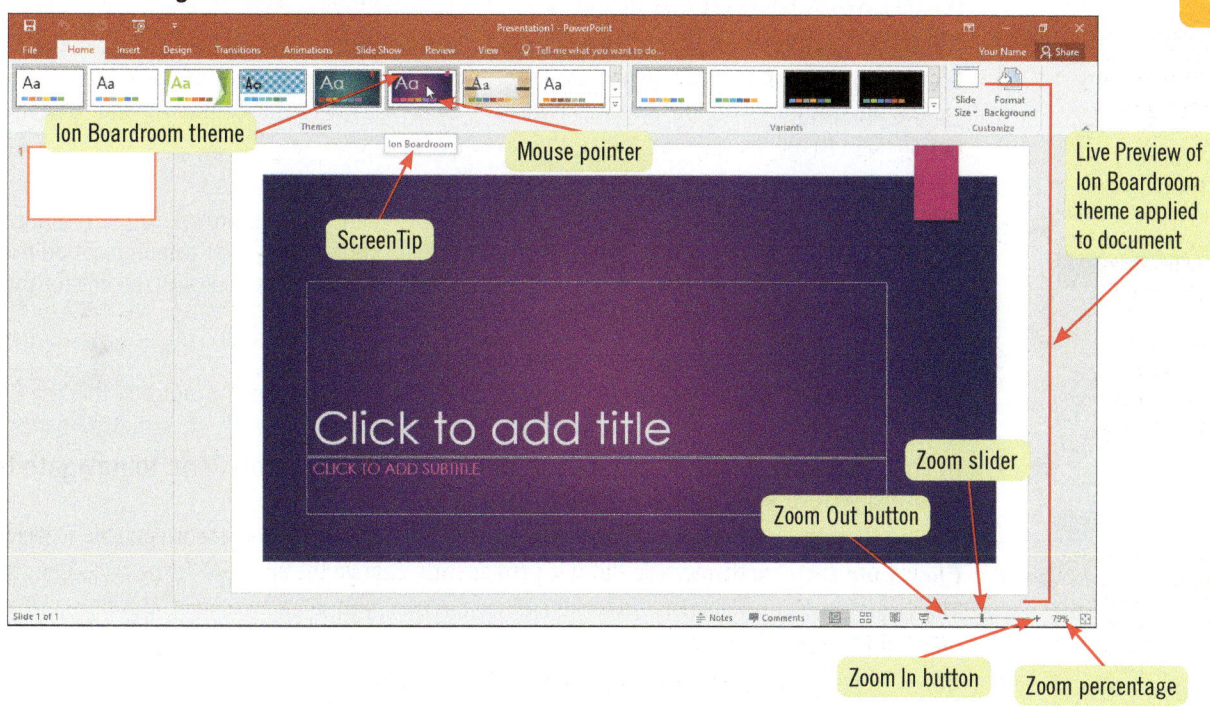

Office 2016

Create and Save a File

When working in an Office app, one of the first things you need to do is to create and save a file. A **file** is a stored collection of data. Saving a file enables you to work on a project now, then put it away and work on it again later. In some Office programs, including Word, Excel, and PowerPoint, you can open a new file when you start the app, then all you have to do is enter some data and save it. In Access, you must create a file before you enter any data. You should give your files meaningful names and save them in an appropriate location, such as a folder on your hard drive or OneDrive so they're easy to find. **OneDrive** is a Microsoft cloud storage system that lets you easily save, share, and access your files from anywhere you have Internet access. **CASE** ▶ *Use Word to familiarize yourself with creating and saving a document. First you'll type some notes about a possible location for a corporate meeting, then you'll save the information for later use.*

STEPS

1. **Click the Word button** ⬛ **on the taskbar, click Blank document, then click the Zoom In button** ➕ **until the level is 120%, if necessary**

2. **Type Locations for Corporate Meeting, then press [Enter] twice**

   The text appears in the document window, and the **insertion point** blinks on a new blank line. The insertion point indicates where the next typed text will appear.

3. **Type Las Vegas, NV, press [Enter], type Chicago, IL, press [Enter], type Seattle, WA, press [Enter] twice, then type your name**

4. ▶ **Click the Save button** 🖫 **on the Quick Access toolbar**

   Because this is the first time you are saving this new file, the Save place in Backstage view opens, showing various options for saving the file. See **FIGURE 1-6**. Once you save a file for the first time, clicking 🖫 saves any changes to the file *without* opening the Save As dialog box.

5. **Click Browse**

   The Save As dialog box opens, as shown in **FIGURE 1-7**, where you can browse to the location where you want to save the file. The Address bar in the Save As dialog box displays the default location for saving the file, but you can change it to any location. The File name field contains a suggested name for the document based on text in the file, but you can enter a different name.

6. **Type OF 1-Possible Corporate Meeting Locations**

   The text you type replaces the highlighted text. (The "OF 1-" in the filename indicates that the file is created in Office Module 1. You will see similar designations throughout this book when files are named.)

7. ▶ **In the Save As dialog box, use the Address bar or Navigation Pane to navigate to the location where you store your Data Files**

   You can store files on your computer, a network drive, your OneDrive, or any acceptable storage device.

8. ▶ **Click Save**

   The Save As dialog box closes, the new file is saved to the location you specified, and the name of the document appears in the title bar, as shown in **FIGURE 1-8**. (You may or may not see the file extension ".docx" after the filename.) See **TABLE 1-1** for a description of the different types of files you create in Office, and the file extensions associated with each.

TABLE 1-1: Common filenames and default file extensions

file created in	is called a	and has the default extension
Word	document	.docx
Excel	workbook	.xlsx
PowerPoint	presentation	.pptx
Access	database	.accdb

FIGURE 1-6: Save place in Backstage view

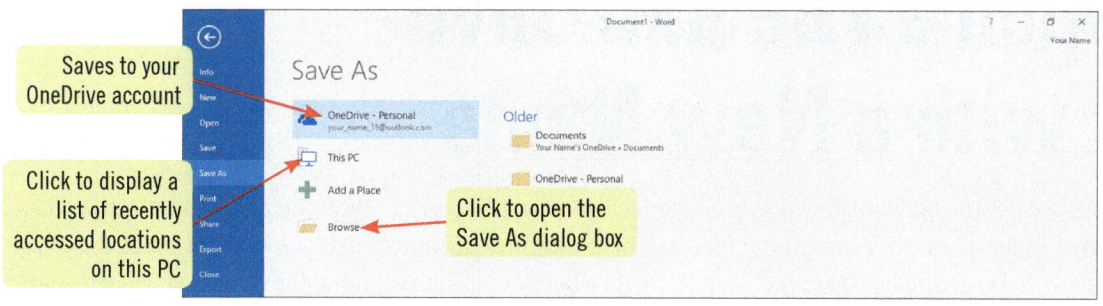

Saves to your OneDrive account

Click to display a list of recently accessed locations on this PC

Click to open the Save As dialog box

FIGURE 1-7: Save As dialog box

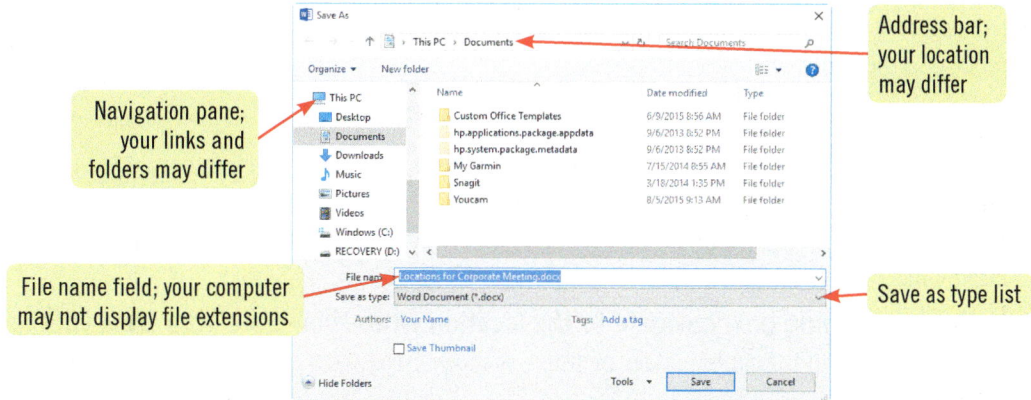

Navigation pane; your links and folders may differ

File name field; your computer may not display file extensions

Address bar; your location may differ

Save as type list

FIGURE 1-8: Saved and named Word document

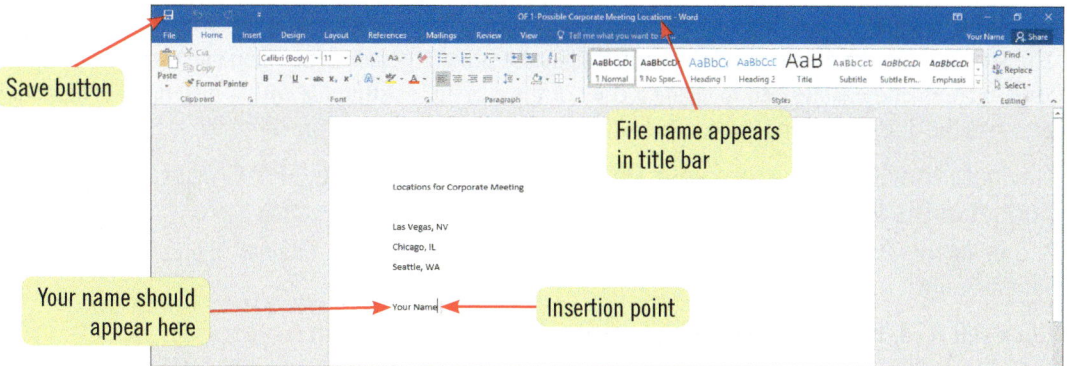

Save button

File name appears in title bar

Your name should appear here

Insertion point

Saving files to OneDrive

All Office programs include the capability to incorporate feedback—called **online collaboration**—across the Internet or a company network. Using **cloud computing** (work done in a virtual environment), you can store your work in the cloud. Using OneDrive, a file storage service from Microsoft, you and your colleagues can create and store documents in the cloud and make the documents available anywhere there is Internet access to whomever you choose. To use OneDrive, you need a Microsoft Account, which you obtain at onedrive.live.com. Pricing and storage plans vary based on the type of Microsoft account you have. When you are logged into your Microsoft account and you

save a file in any of the Office apps, the first option in the Save As screen is your OneDrive. Double-click your OneDrive option, and the Save As dialog box opens displaying a location in the address bar unique to your OneDrive account. Type a name in the File name text box, then click Save and your file is saved to your OneDrive. To sync your files with OneDrive, you'll need to download and install the OneDrive for Windows app. Then, when you open Explorer, you'll notice a new folder called OneDrive has been added to your folder. In this folder is a sub-folder called Documents. This means if your Internet connection fails, you can work on your files offline.

Learning
Outcomes
• Open an existing
  file
• Save a file with a
  new name

Open a File and Save It with a New Name

In many cases as you work in Office, you need to use an existing file. It might be a file you or a coworker created earlier as a work in progress, or it could be a complete document that you want to use as the basis for another. For example, you might want to create a budget for this year using the budget you created last year; instead of typing in all the categories and information from scratch, you could open last year's budget, save it with a new name, and just make changes to update it for the current year. By opening the existing file and saving it with the Save As command, you create a duplicate that you can modify to suit your needs, while the original file remains intact. **CASE** *Use Excel to open an existing workbook file, and save it with a new name so the original remains unchanged.*

STEPS

1. **Click the Start button ⊞ on the Windows taskbar, type exc, click Excel 2016, click Open Other Workbooks, This PC, then click Browse**

   The Open dialog box opens, where you can navigate to any drive or folder accessible to your computer to locate a file.

2. **In the Open dialog box, navigate to the location where you store your Data Files**

   The files available in the current folder are listed, as shown in FIGURE 1-9. This folder displays one file.

3. **Click OF 1-1.xlsx, then click Open**

   The dialog box closes, and the file opens in Excel. An Excel file is an electronic spreadsheet, so the new file displays a grid of rows and columns you can use to enter and organize data.

4. **Click the File tab, click Save As on the navigation bar, then click Browse**

   The Save As dialog box opens, and the current filename is highlighted in the File name text box. Using the Save As command enables you to create a copy of the current, existing file with a new name. This action preserves the original file and creates a new file that you can modify.

5. **Navigate to where you store your Data Files if necessary, type OF 1-Corporate Meeting Budget in the File name text box, as shown in FIGURE 1-10, then click Save**

   A copy of the existing workbook is created with the new name. The original file, OF 1-1.xlsx, closes automatically.

6. **Click cell A18, type your name, then press [Enter], as shown in FIGURE 1-11**

   In Excel, you enter data in cells, which are formed by the intersection of a row and a column. Cell A18 is at the intersection of column A and row 18. When you press [Enter], the cell pointer moves to cell A19.

7. **Click the Save button 🖫 on the Quick Access toolbar**

   Your name appears in the workbook, and your changes to the file are saved.

Exploring File Open options

You might have noticed that the Open button in the Open dialog box includes a list arrow to the right of the button. In a dialog box, if a button includes a list arrow you can click the button to invoke the command, or you can click the list arrow to see a list of related commands that you can apply to the currently selected file. The Open list arrow includes several related commands, including Open Read-Only and Open as Copy.

Clicking Open Read-Only opens a file that you can only save with a new name; you cannot make changes to the original file. Clicking Open as Copy creates and opens a copy of the selected file and inserts the word "Copy" in the file's title. Like the Save As command, these commands provide additional ways to use copies of existing files while ensuring that original files do not get changed by mistake.

FIGURE 1-9: Open dialog box

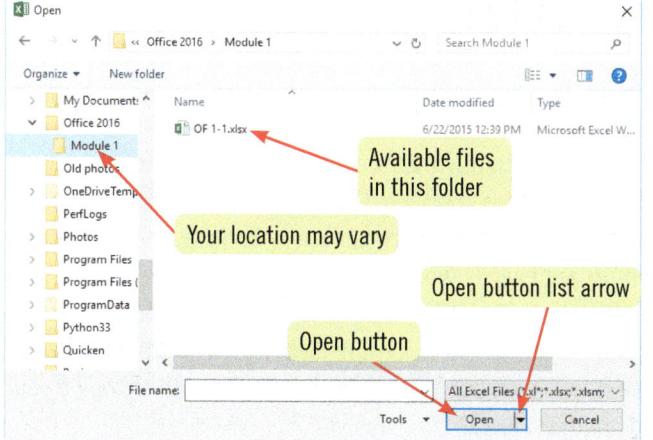

Available files in this folder

Your location may vary

Open button list arrow

Open button

FIGURE 1-10: Save As dialog box

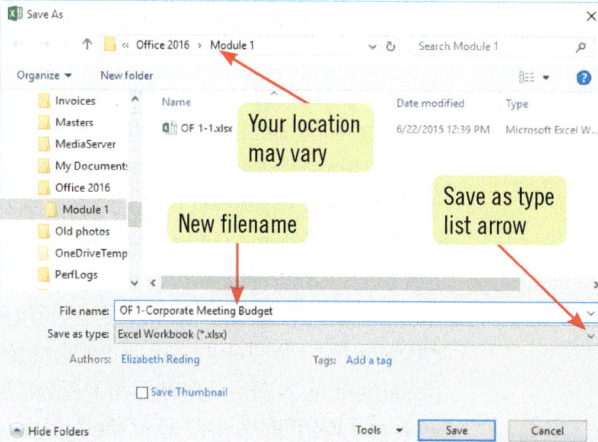

Your location may vary

Save as type list arrow

New filename

FIGURE 1-11: Your name added to the workbook

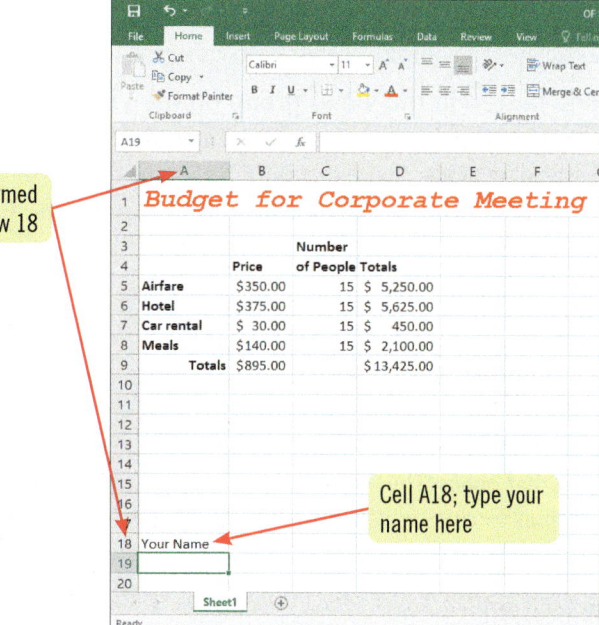

Address for cell A18 formed by column A and row 18

Cell A18; type your name here

Working in Compatibility Mode

Not everyone upgrades to the newest version of Office. As a general rule, new software versions are **backward compatible**, meaning that documents saved by an older version can be read by newer software. To open documents created in older Office versions, Office 2016 includes a feature called Compatibility Mode. When you use Office 2016 to open a file created in an earlier version of Office, "Compatibility Mode" appears in the title bar, letting you know the file was created in an earlier but usable version of the program. If you are working with someone who may not be using the newest version of the software, you can avoid possible incompatibility problems by saving your file in another, earlier format. To do this in an Office program, click the File tab, click Save As on the navigation bar, then click Browse. In the Save As dialog box, click the Save as type list arrow in the Save As dialog box, then click an option in the list. For example, if you're working in Excel, click Excel 97-2003 Workbook format in the Save as type list to save an Excel file so it can be opened in Excel 97 or Excel 2003.

View and Print Your Work

Learning Outcomes
• Describe and change views in an app
• Print a document

Each Microsoft Office program lets you switch among various **views** of the document window to show more or fewer details or a different combination of elements that make it easier to complete certain tasks, such as formatting or reading text. Changing your view of a document does not affect the file in any way, it affects only the way it looks on screen. If your computer is connected to a printer or a print server, you can easily print any Office document using the Print button in the Print place in Backstage view. Printing can be as simple as **previewing** the document to see exactly what the printed version will look like and then clicking the Print button. Or, you can customize the print job by printing only selected pages. You can also use the Share place in Backstage view or the Share button on the Ribbon (if available) to share a document, export to a different format, or save it to the cloud. **CASE** *Experiment with changing your view of a Word document, and then preview and print your work.*

STEPS

1. **Click the Word program button [W] on the taskbar**

   Word becomes active, and the program window fills the screen.

2. **Click the View tab on the Ribbon**

   In most Office programs, the View tab on the Ribbon includes groups and commands for changing your view of the current document. You can also change views using the View buttons on the status bar.

3. **Click the Read Mode button in the Views group on the View tab**

   The view changes to Read Mode view, as shown in **FIGURE 1-12**. This view shows the document in an easy-to-read, distraction-free reading mode. Notice that the Ribbon is no longer visible on screen.

4. **Click the Print Layout button [▦] on the Status bar**

   You return to Print Layout view, the default view in Word.

5. **Click the File tab, then click Print on the navigation bar**

   The Print place opens. The preview pane on the right displays a preview of how your document will look when printed. Compare your screen to **FIGURE 1-13**. Options in the Settings section enable you to change margins, orientation, and related options before printing. To change a setting, click it, and then click a new setting. For instance, to change from Letter paper size to Legal, click Letter in the Settings section, then click Legal on the menu that opens. The document preview updates as you change the settings. You also can use the Settings section to change which pages to print. If your computer is connected to multiple printers, you can click the current printer in the Printer section, then click the one you want to use. The Print section contains the Print button and also enables you to select the number of copies of the document to print.

6. **If your school allows printing, click the Print button in the Print place (otherwise, click the Back button [←])**

   If you chose to print, a copy of the document prints, and Backstage view closes.

Customizing the Quick Access toolbar

You can customize the Quick Access toolbar to display your favorite commands. To do so, click the Customize Quick Access Toolbar button [▾] in the title bar, then click the command you want to add. If you don't see the command in the list, click More Commands to open the Quick Access Toolbar tab of the current program's Options dialog box. In the Options dialog box, use the Choose commands from list to choose a category, click the desired command in the list on the left, click Add to add it to the Quick Access toolbar, then click OK. To remove a button from the toolbar, click the name in the list on the right in the Options dialog box, then click Remove. To add a command to the Quick Access toolbar as you work, simply right-click the button on the Ribbon, then click Add to Quick Access Toolbar on the shortcut menu. To move the Quick Access toolbar below the Ribbon, click the Customize Quick Access Toolbar button, and then click Show Below the Ribbon.

FIGURE 1-12: Read Mode view

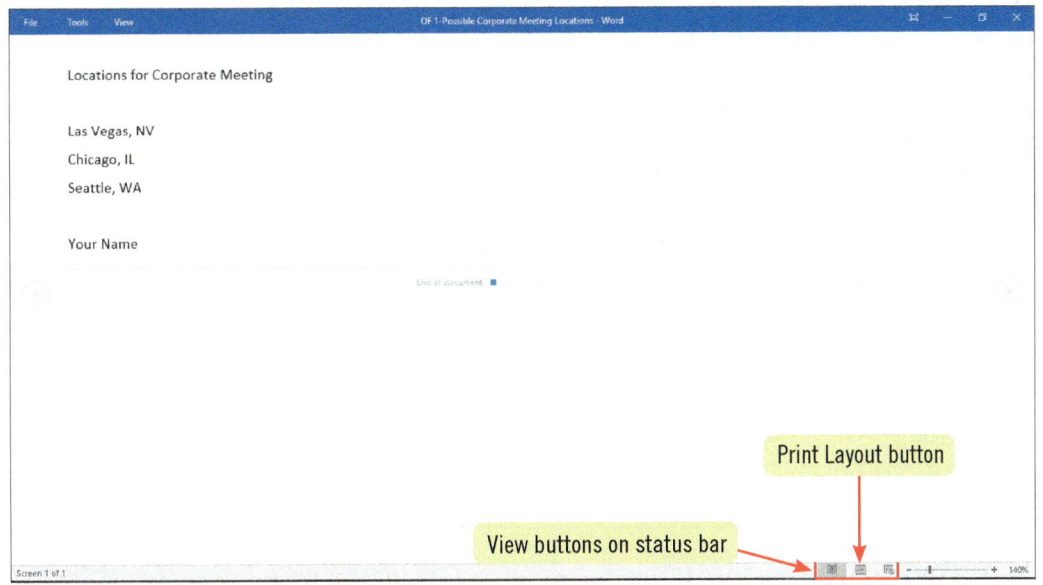

FIGURE 1-13: Print settings on the File tab

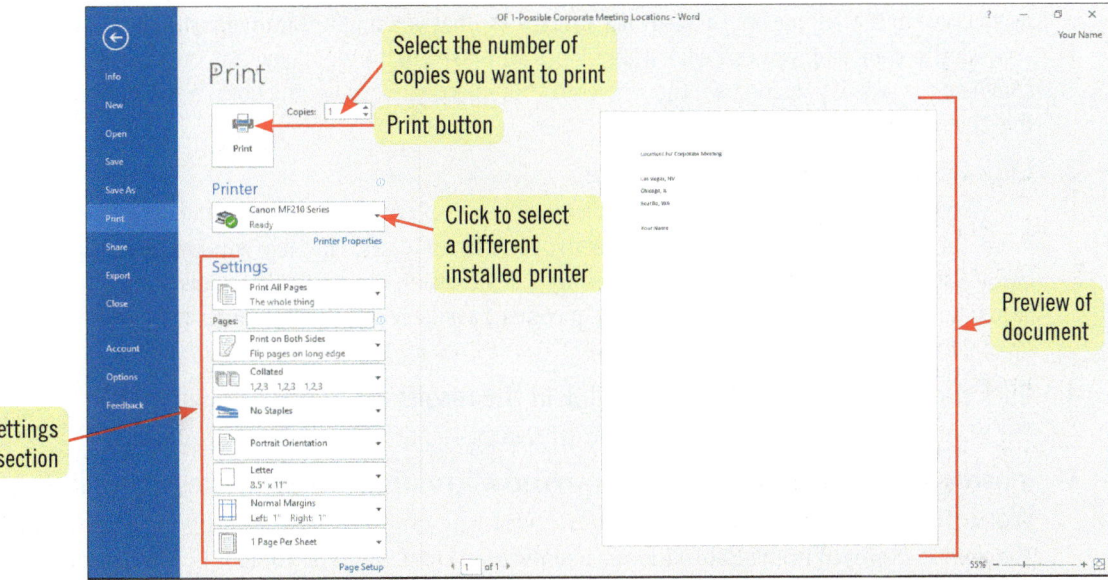

Creating a screen capture

A **screen capture** is a digital image of your screen, as if you took a picture of it with a camera. For instance, you might want to take a screen capture if an error message occurs and you want a Technical Support person to see exactly what's on the screen. You can create a screen capture using the Snipping Tool, an accessory designed to capture whole screens or portions of screens. To open the Snipping Tool, click the Start button on the Windows taskbar, type "sni", then click the Snipping Tool when it appears in the left panel. On the Snipping Tool toolbar, click New, then drag the pointer on the screen to select the area of the screen you want to capture. When you release the mouse button, the screen capture opens in the Snipping Tool window, and you can save, copy, or send it in an email. In Word, Excel, and PowerPoint 2016, you can capture screens or portions of screens and insert them in the current document using the Screenshot button in the Illustrations group on the Insert tab. Alternatively, you can create a screen capture by pressing [PrtScn]. (Keyboards differ, but you may find the [PrtScn] button in or near your keyboard's function keys.) Pressing this key places a digital image of your screen in the Windows temporary storage area known as the **Clipboard**. Open the document where you want the screen capture to appear, click the Home tab on the Ribbon (if necessary), then click the Paste button in the Clipboard group on the Home tab. The screen capture is pasted into the document.

Get Help, Close a File, and Exit an App

Learning Outcomes
• Display a ScreenTip
• Use Help
• Close a file
• Exit an app

You can get comprehensive help at any time by pressing [F1] in an Office app or clicking the Help button on the title bar. You can also get help in the form of a ScreenTip by pointing to almost any icon in the program window. When you're finished working in an Office document, you have a few choices for ending your work session. You close a file by clicking the File tab, then clicking Close; you exit a program by clicking the Close button on the title bar. Closing a file leaves a program running, while exiting a program closes all the open files in that program as well as the program itself. In all cases, Office reminds you if you try to close a file or exit a program and your document contains unsaved changes. **CASE** ▶ *Explore the Help system in Microsoft Office, and then close your documents and exit any open programs.*

STEPS

1. **Point to the Zoom button in the Zoom group on the View tab of the Ribbon**
   A ScreenTip appears that describes how the Zoom button works and explains where to find other zoom controls.

2. **Click the Tell me box above the Ribbon, then type Choose a template**
   As you type in the Tell me box, a Smart list anticipates what you might want help with. If you see the task you want to complete, you can click it and Word will take you to the dialog box or options you need to complete the task. If you don't see the answer to your query, you can use the bottom two options to search the database.

3. **Click Get Help on "choose a template"**
   The Word Help window opens, as shown in **FIGURE 1-14**, displaying help results for choosing a template in Word. Each entry is a hyperlink you can click to open a list of topics. The Help window also includes a toolbar of useful Help commands such as printing and increasing the font size for easier readability, and a Search field. Office.com supplements the help content available on your computer with a wide variety of up-to-date topics, templates, and training.

4. **Click the Where do I find templates link in the results list Word Help window**
   The Word Help window changes, and a more detailed explanation appears below the topic.

5. **If necessary, scroll down until the Download Microsoft Office templates topic fills the Word Help window**
   The topic is displayed in the Help window, as shown in **FIGURE 1-15**. The content in the window explains that you can create a wide variety of documents using a template (a pre-formatted document) and that you can get many templates free of charge.

6. **Click the Keep Help on Top button ⊣ in the lower-right corner of the window**
   The Pin Help button rotates so the pin point is pointed towards the bottom of the screen: this allows you to read the Help window while you work on your document.

7. **Click the Word document window, notice the Help window remains visible**

8. **Click a blank area of the Help window, click ⊥ to Unpin Help, click the Close button ✕ in the Help window, then click the Close button ✕ in the Word program window**
   Word closes, and the Excel program window is active.

9. **Click the Close button ✕ in the Excel program window, click the PowerPoint app button 🄿 on the taskbar if necessary, then click the Close button ✕ to exit PowerPoint**
   Excel and PowerPoint both close.

FIGURE 1-14: Word Help window

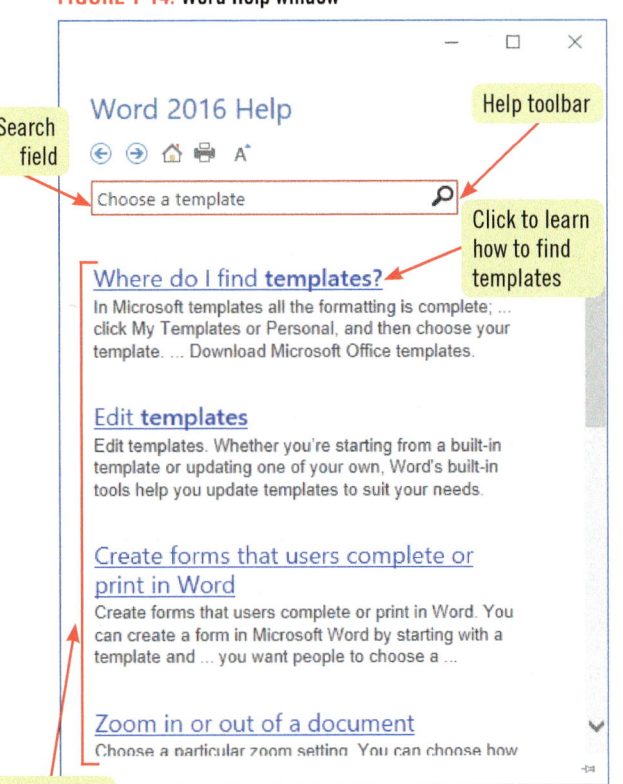

Search field

Help toolbar

Word 2016 Help

Choose a template

Click to learn how to find templates

Where do I find **templates?**
In Microsoft templates all the formatting is complete; ... click My Templates or Personal, and then choose your template. ... Download Microsoft Office templates.

Edit **templates**
Edit templates. Whether you're starting from a built-in template or updating one of your own, Word's built-in tools help you update templates to suit your needs.

Create forms that users complete or print in Word
Create forms that users complete or print in Word. You can create a form in Microsoft Word by starting with a template and ... you want people to choose a ...

Zoom in or out of a document
Choose a particular zoom setting. You can choose how

Help topics are updated frequently; your list may differ

FIGURE 1-15: Create a document Help topic

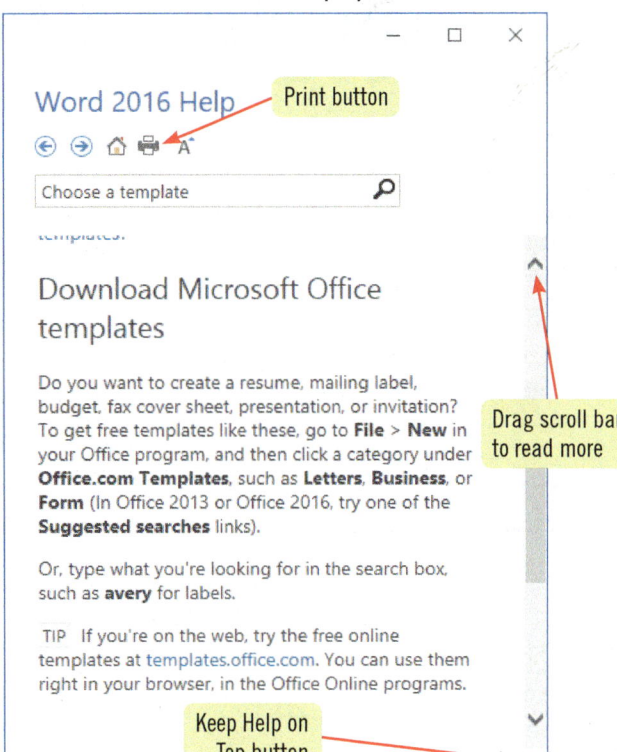

Word 2016 Help

Print button

Choose a template

templates.

Download Microsoft Office templates

Do you want to create a resume, mailing label, budget, fax cover sheet, presentation, or invitation? To get free templates like these, go to **File** > **New** in your Office program, and then click a category under **Office.com Templates**, such as **Letters**, **Business**, or **Form** (In Office 2013 or Office 2016, try one of the **Suggested searches** links).

Or, type what you're looking for in the search box, such as **avery** for labels.

 TIP   If you're on the web, try the free online templates at templates.office.com. You can use them right in your browser, in the Office Online programs.

Drag scroll bar to read more

Keep Help on Top button

Office 2016

Using sharing features and co-authoring capabilities

If you are using Word, Excel, or PowerPoint, you can take advantage of the Share feature, which makes it easy to share your files that have been saved to OneDrive. When you click the Share button, you will be asked to invite others to share the file. To do this, type in the name or email addresses in the Invite people text box. When you invite others, you have the opportunity to give them different levels of permission. You might want some people to have read-only privileges; you might want others to be able to make edits. Also available in Word, Excel, and PowerPoint is real-time co-authoring capabilities for files stored on OneDrive. Once a file on OneDrive is opened and all the users have been given editing privileges, all the users can make edits simultaneously. On first use, each user will be prompted to automatically share their changes.

Recovering a document

Each Office program has a built-in recovery feature that allows you to open and save files that were open at the time of an interruption such as a power failure. When you restart the program(s) after an interruption, the Document Recovery task pane opens on the left side of your screen displaying both original and recovered versions of the files that were open. If you're not sure which file to open (original or recovered), it's usually better to open the recovered file because it will contain the latest information. You can, however, open and review all versions of the file that were recovered and save the best one. Each file listed in the Document Recovery task pane displays a list arrow with options that allow you to open the file, save it as is, delete it, or show repairs made to it during recovery.

Practice

Concepts Review

Label the elements of the program window shown in FIGURE 1-16**.**

FIGURE 1-16

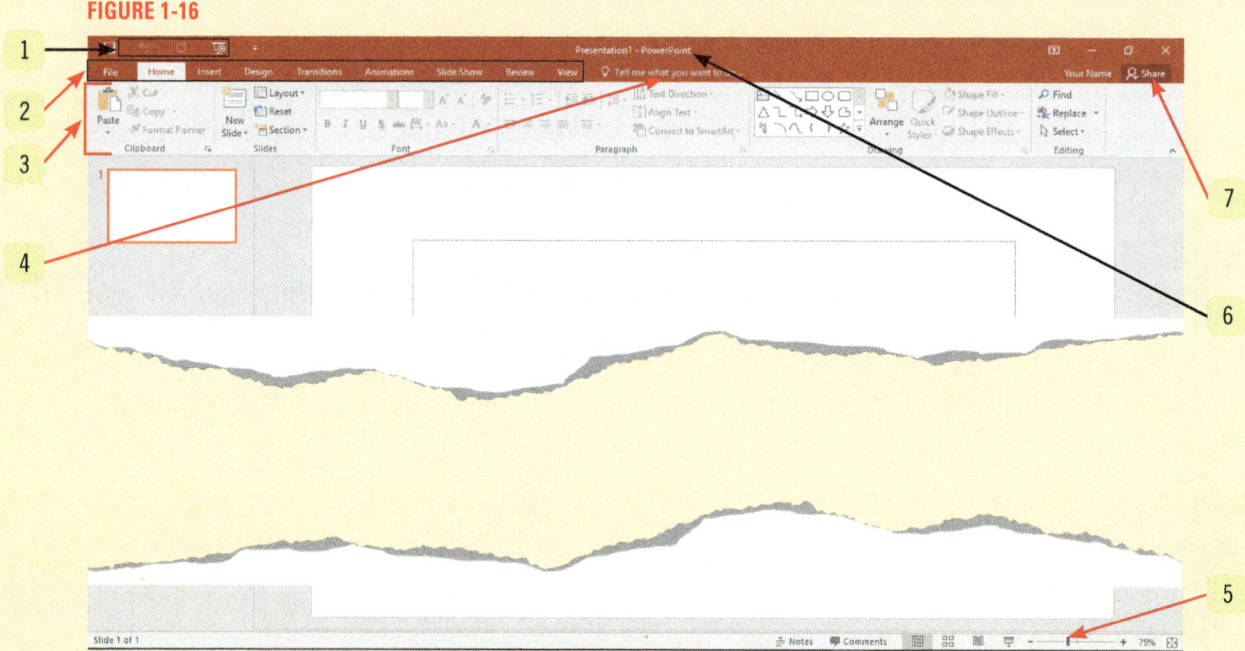

Match each project with the program for which it is best suited.

8. Microsoft PowerPoint   a. Corporate convention budget with expense projections

9. Microsoft Word   b. Presentation for city council meeting

10. Microsoft Excel   c. Business cover letter for a job application

11. Microsoft Access   d. Department store inventory

Independent Challenge 1

You just accepted an administrative position with a local independently owned insurance agent who has recently invested in computers and is now considering purchasing a subscription to Office 365. You have been asked to think of uses for the apps and you put your ideas in a Word document.

a. Start Word, create a new Blank document, then save the document as **OF 1-Microsoft Office Apps Uses** in the location where you store your Data Files.

b. Change the zoom factor to 120%, type **Microsoft Access**, press [Enter] twice, type **Microsoft Excel**, press [Enter] twice, type **Microsoft PowerPoint**, press [Enter] twice, type **Microsoft Word**, press [Enter] twice, then type your name.

c. Click the line beneath each program name, type at least two tasks you can perform using that program (each separated by a comma), then press [Enter].

d. Save the document, then submit your work to your instructor as directed.

e. Exit Word.

Getting Started with Access 2016

CASE — Julia Rice is the developer for a new initiative at Reason 2 Go (R2G), a specialized type of travel company that combines volunteer opportunities and tourism into meaningful experiences for its customers. Julia has been asked to create products to meet a market demand for shorter experiences in the United States. Julia uses Microsoft Access 2016 to store, maintain, and analyze customer and trip information.

Module Objectives

After completing this module, you will be able to:

- Understand relational databases
- Explore a database
- Create a database
- Create a table

- Create primary keys
- Relate two tables
- Enter data
- Edit data

Files You Will Need

R2G-1.accdb
LakeHomes-1.accdb
Salvage-1.accdb

Contacts-1.accdb
Basketball-1.accdb

Understand Relational Databases

Learning Outcomes
- Describe relational database concepts
- Explain when to use a database
- Compare a relational database to a spreadsheet

Microsoft Access 2016 is relational database software that runs on the Windows operating system. You use **relational database software** to manage data that is organized into lists, such as information about customers, products, vendors, employees, projects, or sales. Many small companies track customer, inventory, and sales information in a spreadsheet program such as Microsoft Excel. Although Excel offers some list management features, Access provides many more tools and advantages for managing data. Some advantages are due to Access using a relational database model whereas Excel manages data as a single list. TABLE 1-1 compares the two programs. **CASE** *You and Julia review the advantages of database software over spreadsheets for managing lists of information.*

DETAILS

The advantages of using Access for database management include the following:

- **Duplicate data is minimized**

  FIGURES 1-1 and 1-2 compare how you might store sales data in a single Excel spreadsheet list versus three related Access tables. With Access, you do not have to reenter information such as a customer's name and address or trip name every time a sale is made, because lists can be linked, or "related," in relational database software.

- **Information is more accurate, reliable, and consistent because duplicate data is minimized**

  The relational nature of data stored in an Access database allows you to minimize duplicate data entry, which creates more accurate, reliable, and consistent information. For example, customer data in a Customers table is entered only once, not every time a customer makes a purchase.

- **Data entry is faster and easier using Access forms**

  Data entry forms (screen layouts) make data entry faster, easier, and more accurate than entering data in a spreadsheet.

- **Information can be viewed and sorted in many ways using Access queries, forms, and reports**

  In Access, you can save multiple queries (questions about the data), data entry forms, and reports, allowing you to use them over and over without performing extra work to re-create a particular view of the data.

- **Information is more secure using Access passwords and security features**

  Access databases can be encrypted and password protected.

- **Several users can share and edit information at the same time**

  Unlike spreadsheets or word-processing documents, more than one person can enter, update, and analyze data in an Access database at the same time.

FIGURE 1-1: Using a spreadsheet to organize sales data

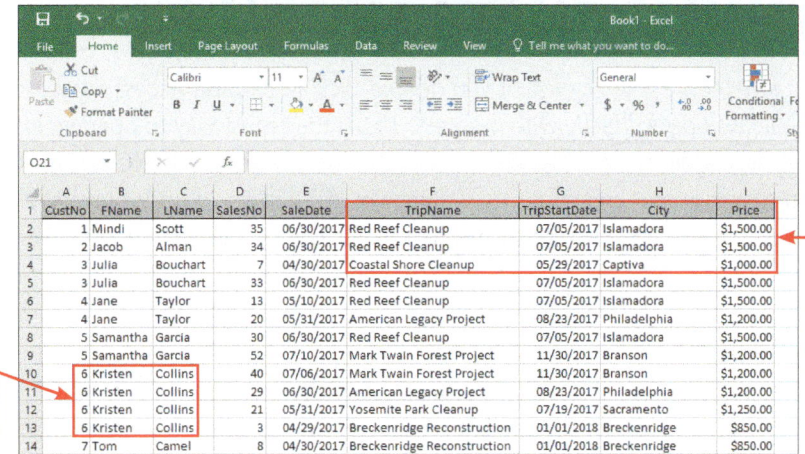

Customer information is duplicated when the same customer purchases multiple trips

Trip information is duplicated when the same trip is purchased by multiple customers

FIGURE 1-2: Using a relational database to organize sales data

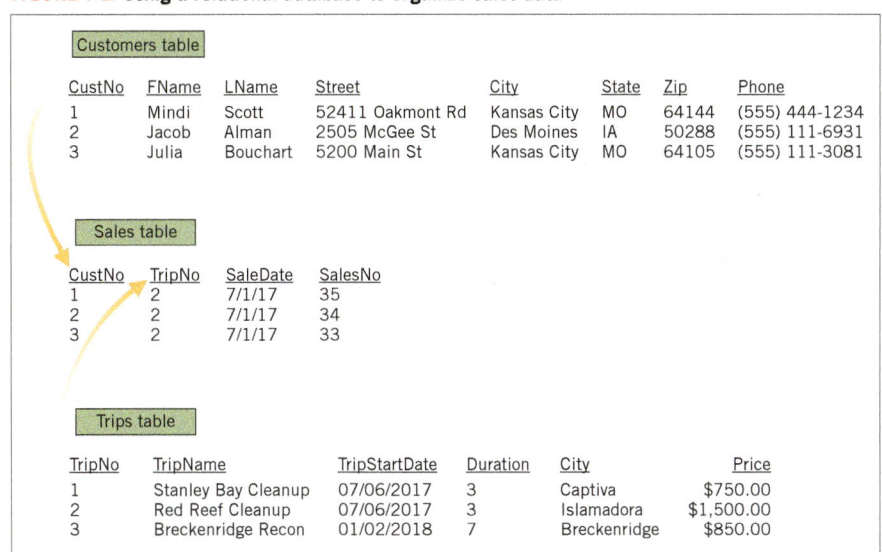

TABLE 1-1: Comparing Excel with Access

feature	Excel	Access
Layout	Provides only a tabular spreadsheet layout	Provides tabular layouts as well as the ability to create customized data entry screens called forms
Storage	Restricted to a file's limitations	Virtually unlimited when coupled with the ability to use Microsoft SQL Server to store data
Linked tables	Manages single lists of information—no relational database capabilities	Relates lists of information to reduce data redundancy and create a powerful relational database
Reporting	Limited	Provides the ability to create an unlimited number of reports
Security	Limited to file security options such as marking the file "read-only" or protecting a range of cells	When used with SQL Server, provides extensive security down to the user and data level
Multiuser capabilities	Not allowed	Allows multiple users to simultaneously enter and update data
Data entry	Provides only one spreadsheet layout	Provides the ability to create an unlimited number of data entry forms

Explore a Database

Learning
Outcomes
• Start Access and
open a database
• Open and define
Access objects

You can start Access in many ways. If you double-click an existing Access database icon or shortcut, that specific database opens directly within Access. This is the fastest way to open an existing Access database. If you start Access on its own, however, you see a window that requires you to make a choice between opening a database and creating a new database. **CASE** *Julia Rice has developed a database called R2G-1, which contains trip information. She asks you to start Access 2016 and review this database.*

STEPS

1. **Start Access**

   Access starts, as shown in **FIGURE 1-3**. This window allows you to open an existing database, create a new database from a template, or create a new blank database.

   TROUBLE
   If a yellow Security Warning bar appears below the Ribbon, click Enable Content.

2. **Click the Open Other Files link, navigate to the location where you store your Data Files, click the R2G-1.accdb database, click Open, then click the Maximize button ▣ if the Access window is not already maximized**

   The R2G-1.accdb Access database application contains five tables of data named Categories, Customers, Sales, States, and Trips. It also includes five queries, six forms, and four reports. Each of these items (table, query, form, and report) is a different type of **object** in an Access database application and is displayed in the **Navigation Pane**. The purpose of each object is defined in **TABLE 1-2**. To learn about an Access database application, you explore its objects.

   TROUBLE
   If the Navigation Pane is not open, click the Shutter Bar Open/Close Button ≫ to open it and view the database objects.

3. **In the Navigation Pane, double-click the Trips table to open it, then double-click the Customers table to open it**

   The Trips and Customers tables open in Datasheet View to display the data they store. A **table** is the fundamental building block of a relational database because it stores all of the data.

4. **In the Navigation Pane, double-click the TripSales query to open it, double-click any occurrence of Heritage in "American Heritage Tour," type Legacy, then click any other row**

   A **query** selects a subset of data from one or more tables. In this case, the TripSales query selects data from the Trips, Sales, and Customers tables. Entering or editing data in one object changes that information in every other object of the database, because all objects build on the same data stored only in the tables.

5. **Double-click the CustomerRoster form to open it, double-click Tour in "American Legacy Tour," type Project, then click any name in the middle part of the window**

   An Access **form** is a data entry screen. Users prefer forms for data entry (rather than editing and entering data in tables and queries) because forms can present information in any layout and include command buttons to make common tasks easy to perform.

6. **Double-click the TripSales report to open it**

   An Access **report** is a professional printout that can be distributed electronically or on paper. As shown in **FIGURE 1-4**, the edits made to the American Legacy Project name have carried through to the report, demonstrating the power and productivity of a relational database.

7. **Click the Close button ✕ in the upper-right corner of the window**

   Clicking the Close button in the upper-right corner of the window closes Access as well as the database on which you are working. Changes to data, such as the edits you made to the American Legacy Project record, are automatically saved as you work. Access will prompt you to save design changes to objects before it closes.

FIGURE 1-3: Opening the Microsoft Access 2016 window

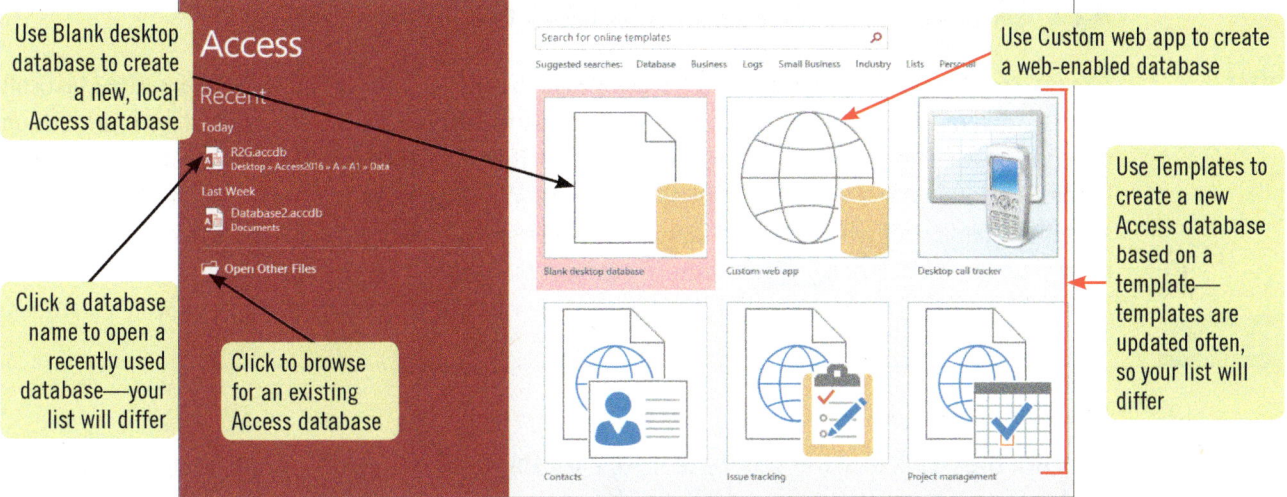

Use Blank desktop database to create a new, local Access database

Use Custom web app to create a web-enabled database

Use Templates to create a new Access database based on a template—templates are updated often, so your list will differ

Click a database name to open a recently used database—your list will differ

Click to browse for an existing Access database

FIGURE 1-4: Objects in the R2G-1 database

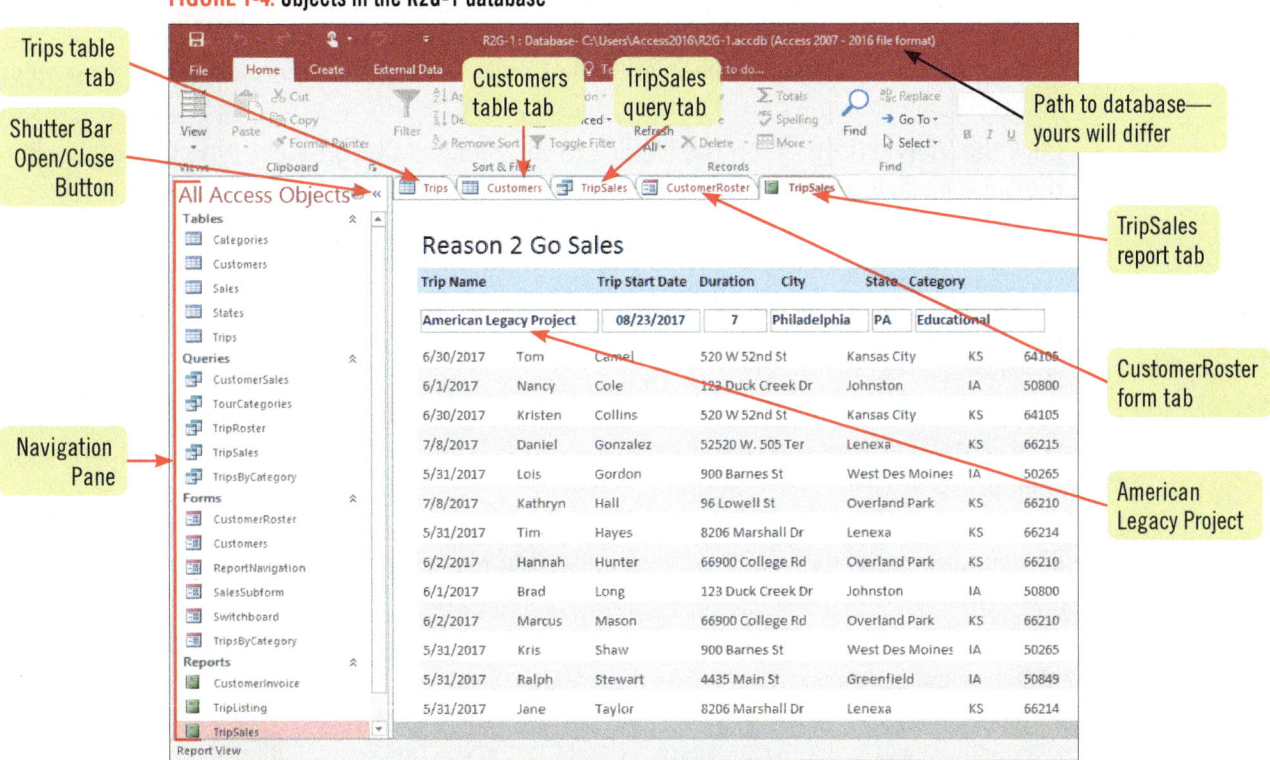

Trips table tab

Shutter Bar Open/Close Button

Customers table tab

TripSales query tab

Path to database—yours will differ

Navigation Pane

TripSales report tab

CustomerRoster form tab

American Legacy Project

TABLE 1-2: Access objects and their purpose

object	icon	purpose
Table		Contains all of the data within the database in a spreadsheet-like view called Datasheet View; tables are linked with a common field to create a relational database, which minimizes redundant data
Query		Allows you to select a subset of fields or records from one or more tables; create a query when you have a question about the data
Form		Provides an easy-to-use data entry screen
Report		Provides a professional presentation of data with headers, footers, graphics, and calculations on groups of records

Create a Database

You can create a database using an Access **template**, a sample database provided within the Microsoft Access program, or you can start with a blank database to create a database from scratch. Your decision depends on whether Access has a template that closely resembles the type of data you plan to manage. If it does, building your own database from a template might be faster than creating the database from scratch. Regardless of which method you use, you can always modify the database later, tailoring it to meet your specific needs. **CASE** *Julia Rice reasons that the best way for you to learn Access is to start a new database from scratch, so she asks you to create a new database that will track customer communication.*

STEPS

1. **Start Access**

2. **Click the Blank desktop database icon, click the Browse button 📂, navigate to the location where you store your Data Files, type R2G in the File name box, click OK, then click the Create button**

   A new database file with a single table named Table1 is created, as shown in **FIGURE 1-5**. Although you might be tempted to start entering data into the table, a better way to build a table is to first define the columns, or **fields**, of data that the table will store. **Table Design View** provides the most options for defining fields.

3. **Click the View button 📐 on the Fields tab to switch to Design View, type Customers in the Save As dialog box as the new table name, then click OK**

   The table name changes from Table1 to Customers, and you are positioned in Table Design View, a window you use to name and define the fields of a table. Access automatically created a field named ID with an AutoNumber data type. The **data type** is a significant characteristic of a field because it determines what type of data the field can store such as text, dates, or numbers. See **TABLE 1-3** for more information about data types.

4. **Type CustID to rename ID to CustID, press [▼] to move to the first blank Field Name cell, type FirstName, press [▼], type LastName, press [▼], type Phone, press [▼], type Birthday, then press [▼]**

   Be sure to always separate a person's first and last names into two fields so that you can easily sort, find, and filter on either part of the name later. The Birthday field will only contain dates, so you should change its data type from Short Text (the default data type) to Date/Time.

5. **Click Short Text in the Birthday row, click the list arrow, then click Date/Time**

   With these five fields properly defined for the new Customers table, as shown in **FIGURE 1-6**, you're ready to enter data. You switch back to Datasheet View to enter or edit data. **Datasheet View** is a spreadsheet-like view of the data in a table. A **datasheet** is a grid that displays fields as columns and records as rows. The new **field names** you just defined are listed at the top of each column.

6. **Click the View button ⊞ to switch to Datasheet View, click Yes when prompted to save the table, press [Tab] to move to the FirstName field, type *your* first name, press [Tab] to move to the LastName field, type *your* last name, press [Tab] to move to the Phone field, type 555-666-7777, press [Tab], type 1/32/1990, then press [Tab]**

   Because 1/32/1990 is not a valid date, Access does not allow you to make that entry and displays an error message, as shown in **FIGURE 1-7**. This shows that selecting the best data type for each field in Table Design View before entering data in Datasheet View helps prevent data entry errors.

7. **Press [Esc], edit the Birthday entry for the first record to 1/31/1990, press [Tab], enter two more sample records using realistic data, right-click the Customers table tab, then click Close to close the Customers table**

FIGURE 1-5: Creating a database with a new table

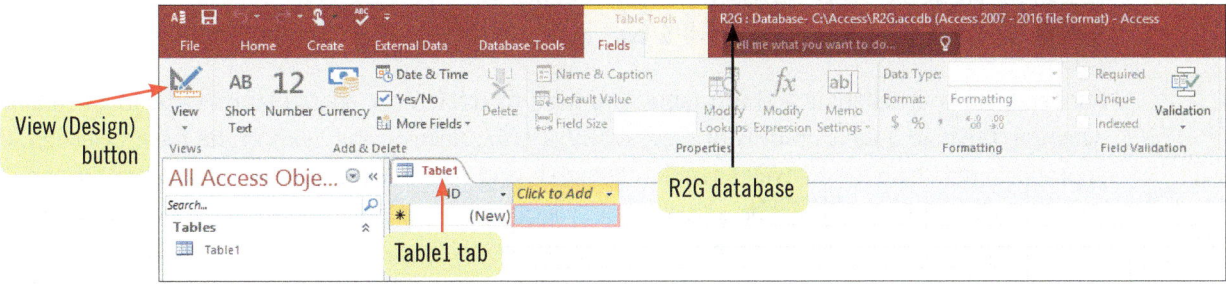

FIGURE 1-6: Defining field names and data types for the Customers table in Table Design View

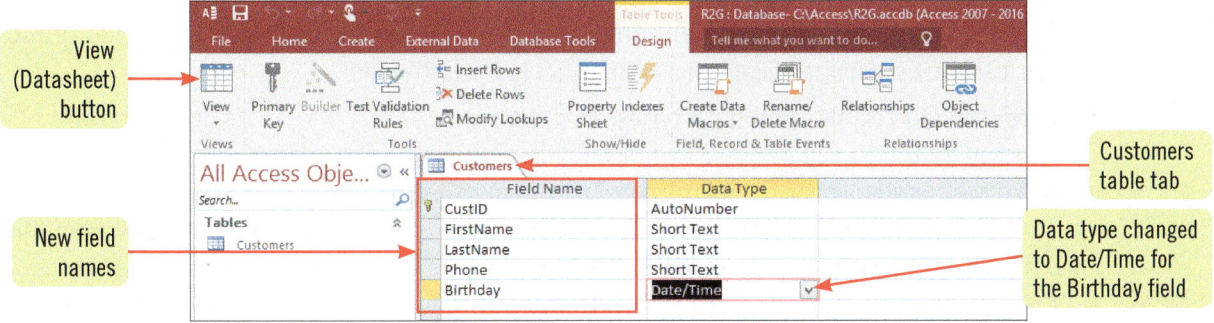

FIGURE 1-7: Entering your first record in the Customers table

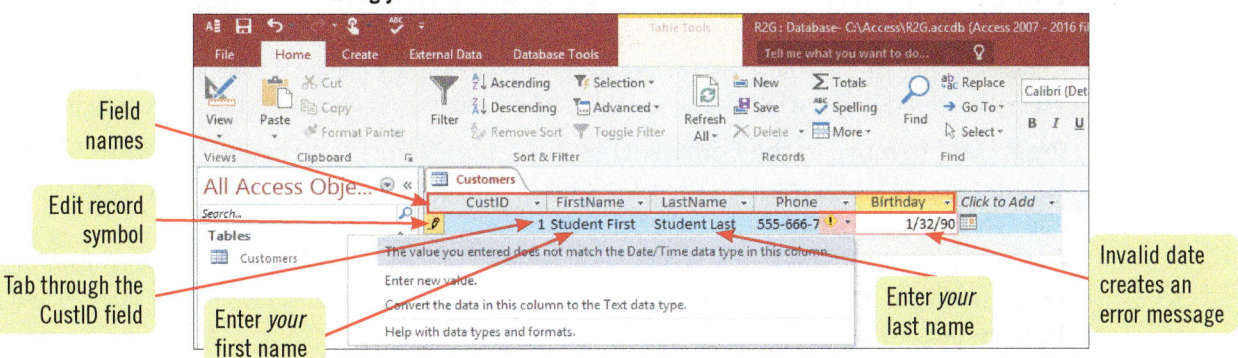

TABLE 1-3: Data types

data type	description of data
Short Text	Text or numbers not used in calculations such as a name, zip code, or phone number less than 255 characters
Long Text	Lengthy text greater than 255 characters, such as comments or notes
Number	Numeric data that can be used in calculations, such as quantities
Date/Time	Dates and times
Currency	Monetary values
AutoNumber	Sequential integers controlled by Access
Yes/No	Only two values: Yes or No
OLE Object	OLE (Object Linking and Embedding) objects such as an Excel spreadsheet or Word document
Hyperlink	Web and email addresses or links to local files
Attachment	Files such as .jpg images, spreadsheets, and documents
Calculated	Result of a calculation based on other fields in the table
Lookup Wizard	The Lookup Wizard helps you set Lookup properties, which display a drop-down list of values for the field; after using the Lookup Wizard, the final data type for the field is either Short Text or Number depending on the values in the drop-down list

Create a Table

Learning Outcomes
- Create a table in Table Design View
- Set appropriate data types for fields

After creating your database and first table, you need to create new, related tables to build a relational database. Creating a table consists of these essential tasks: defining the fields in the table, selecting an appropriate data type for each field, naming the table, and determining how the table will participate in the relational database. **CASE** *Julia Rice asks you to create another table to store customer comments. The new table will eventually be connected to the Customers table so each customer record in the Customers table may be related to many records in the Comments table.*

STEPS

1. **Click the Create tab on the Ribbon, then click the Table Design button in the Tables group**

   You create and manipulate the structure of an object in **Design View**.

2. **Enter the field names and data types, as shown in FIGURE 1-8**

   The Comments table will contain four fields. CommentID is set with an AutoNumber data type so each record is automatically numbered by Access. The CommentText field has a Long Text data type so a long comment can be recorded. CommentDate is a Date/Time field to identify the date of the comment. CustID has a Number data type and will be used to link the Comments table to the Customers table later.

   TROUBLE
   To rename an object, close it, right-click it in the Navigation Pane, and then click Rename.

3. **Click the View button 🔲 to switch to Datasheet View, click Yes when prompted to save the table, type Comments as the table name, click OK, then click No when prompted to create a primary key**

   A **primary key field** contains unique data for each record. You'll identify a primary key field for the Comments table later. For now, you'll enter the first record in the Comments table in Datasheet View. A **record** is a row of data in a table. Refer to **TABLE 1-4** for a summary of important database terminology.

4. **Press [Tab] to move to the CommentText field, type Wants to help with the Rose Bowl Parade, press [Tab], type 1/7/17 in the CommentDate field, press [Tab], then type 1 in the CustID field**

   You entered 1 in the CustID field to connect this comment with the customer in the Customers table that has a CustID value of 1. Knowing which CustID value to enter for each comment is difficult. After you relate the tables properly (a task you have not yet performed), Access can make it easier to link each comment to the correct customer.

   TROUBLE
   The CommentID field is an AutoNumber field, which will automatically increment to provide a unique value. If the number has already incremented beyond 1 for the first record, AutoNumber still works as intended.

5. **Point to the divider line between the CommentText and CommentDate field names, and then double-click the ↔ pointer to widen the CommentText field to read the entire comment, as shown in FIGURE 1-9**

6. **Right-click the Comments table tab, click Close, then click Yes if prompted to save the table**

Creating a table in Datasheet View

You can also create a new table in Datasheet View using the commands on the Fields tab of the Ribbon. However, if you use Design View to design your table before entering data, you will probably avoid some common data entry errors. Design View helps you focus on the appropriate data type for each field.

Selecting the best data type for each field before entering any data into that field helps prevent incorrect data and unintended typos. For example, if a field has a Number, Currency, or Date/Time data type, you will not be able to enter text into that field by mistake.

FIGURE 1-8: Creating the Comments table

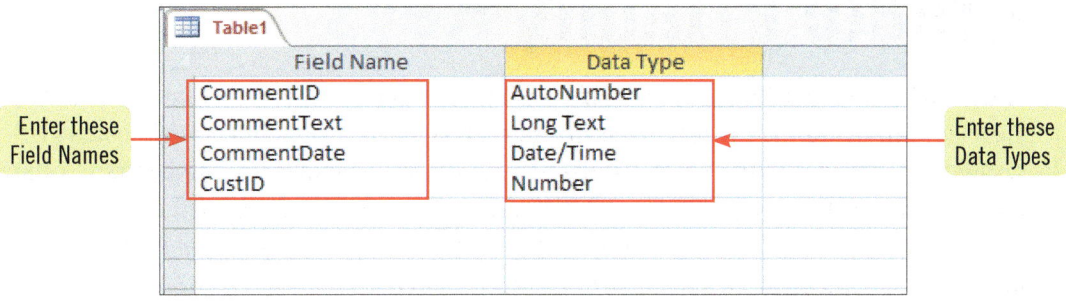

Enter these Field Names

Enter these Data Types

FIGURE 1-9: Entering a record in the Comments table

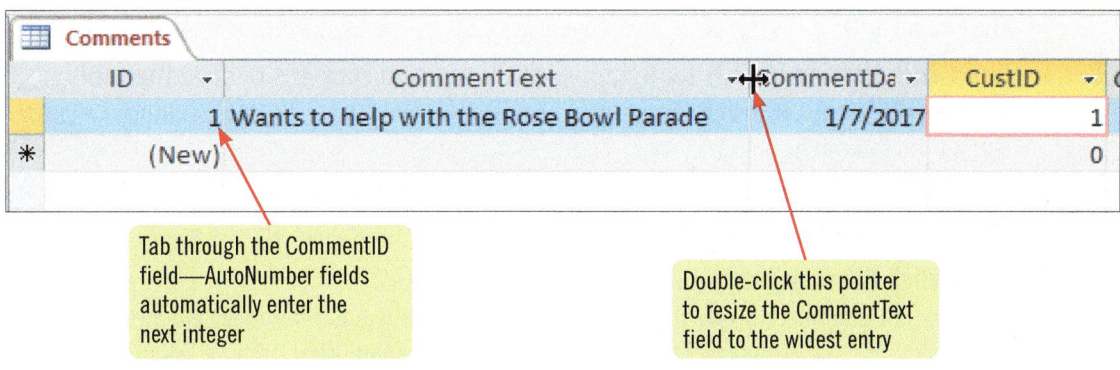

Tab through the CommentID field—AutoNumber fields automatically enter the next integer

Double-click this pointer to resize the CommentText field to the widest entry

TABLE 1-4: Important database terminology

term	description
Field	A specific piece or category of data such as a first name, last name, city, state, or phone number
Record	A group of related fields that describes a person, place, thing, or transaction such as a customer, location, product, or sale
Key field	A field that contains unique information for each record, such as a customer number for a customer
Table	A collection of records for a single subject such as Customers, Products, or Sales
Relational database	Multiple tables that are linked together to address a business process such as managing trips, sales, and customers at Reason 2 Go
Objects	The parts of an Access database that help you view, edit, manage, and analyze the data: tables, queries, forms, reports, macros, and modules

Create Primary Keys

Learning Outcomes
• Set the primary key field
• Define one-to-many relationships

The **primary key field** of a table serves two important purposes. First, it contains data that uniquely identifies each record. No two records can have the exact same entry in the field designated as the primary key field. Second, the primary key field helps relate one table to another in a **one-to-many relationship**, where one record from one table may be related to many records in the second table. For example, one record in the Customers table may be related to many records in the Comments table. (One customer may have many comments.) The primary key field is always on the "one" side of a one-to-many relationship between two tables. **CASE** ▶ *Julia Rice asks you to check that a primary key field has been appropriately identified for each table in the new R2G database.*

STEPS

1. **Right-click the Comments table in the Navigation Pane, then click Design View**

   Table Design View for the Comments table opens. The field with the AutoNumber data type is generally the best candidate for the primary key field in a table because it automatically contains a unique number for each record.

2. **Click the CommentID field if it is not already selected, then click the Primary Key button in the Tools group on the Design tab**

   The CommentID field is now set as the primary key field for the Comments table, as shown in **FIGURE 1-10**.

3. **Right-click the Comments table tab, click Close, then click Yes to save the table**

   Any time you must save design changes to an Access object such as a table, Access displays a dialog box to remind you to save the object.

4. **Right-click the Customers table in the Navigation Pane, then click Design View**

   Access has already set CustID as the primary key field for the Customers table, as shown in **FIGURE 1-11**.

5. **Right-click the Customers table tab, then click Close**

   You were not prompted to save the Customers table because you did not make any design changes. Now that you're sure that each table in the R2G database has an appropriate primary key field, you're ready to link the tables. The primary key field plays a critical role in this relationship.

Object views

Each object has a number of **views** that allow you to complete different tasks. For example, to enter and edit data into the database, use **Datasheet View** for tables and queries and **Form View** for forms. To change the structure of an object, you most often work in **Design View**. Use **Print Preview** to see how a report will appear on a physical piece of paper. Click the arrow at the bottom of the View button on the Design tab of the Ribbon to see all of the available views for an object.

Learning about field properties

Properties are the characteristics that define the field. Two properties are required for every field: Field Name and Data Type. Many other properties, such as Field Size, Format, Caption, and Default Value, are defined in the Field Properties pane in the lower half of a table's Design View. As you add more property entries, you are generally restricting the amount or type of data that can be entered in the field, which increases data entry accuracy. For example, you might change the Field Size property for a State field to 2 to eliminate an incorrect entry such as FLL. Field properties change depending on the data type of the selected field. For example, date fields do not have a Field Size property because Access controls the size of fields with a Date/Time data type.

FIGURE 1-10: Creating a primary key field for the Comments table

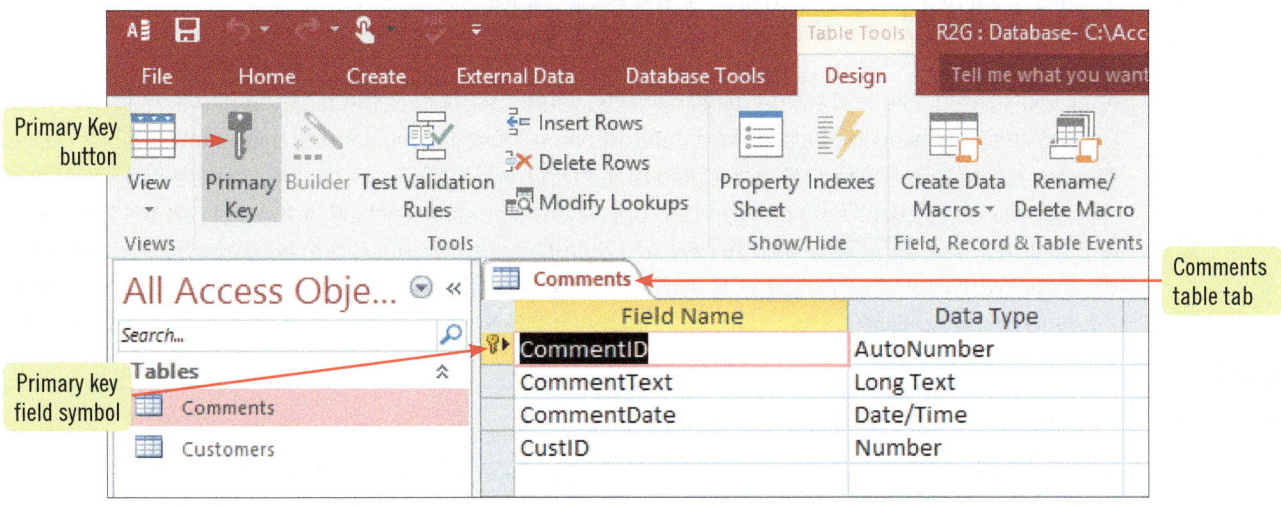

FIGURE 1-11: Confirming the primary key field for the Customers table

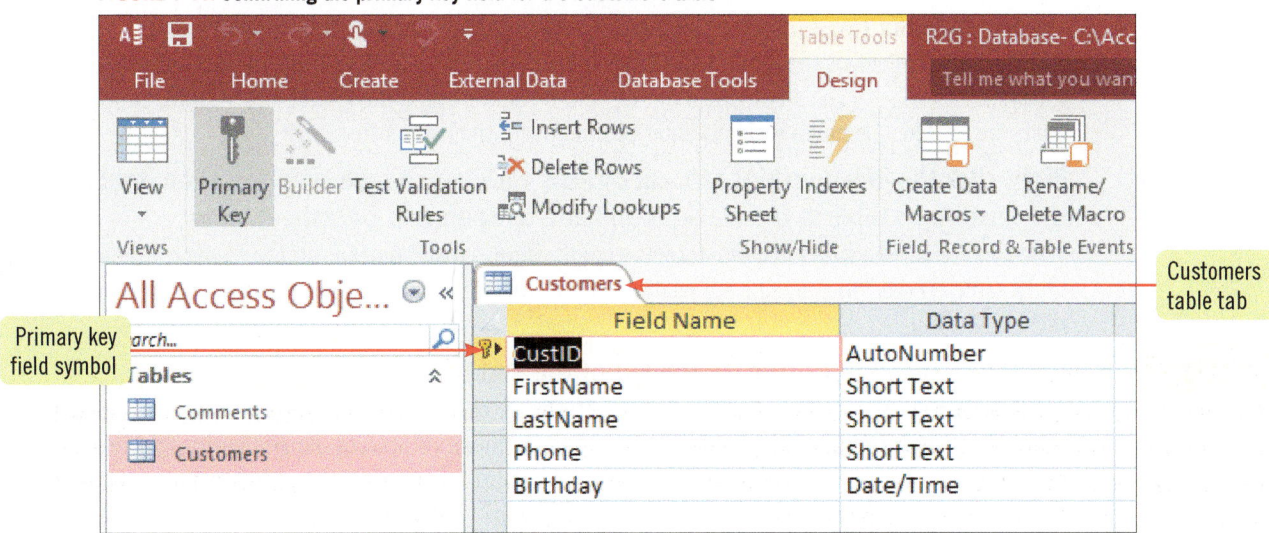

Relate Two Tables

Learning Outcomes
- Define foreign key field
- Create one-to-many relationships
- Set referential integrity

After you create tables and set primary key fields, you must connect the tables in one-to-many relationships to enjoy the benefits of a relational database. A one-to-many relationship between two tables means that one record from the first table is related to many records in the second table. You use a common field to make this connection. The common field is always the primary key field in the table on the "one" side of the relationship. **CASE** *Julia Rice explains that she has new comments to enter into the R2G database. To identify which customer is related to each comment, you define a one-to-many relationship between the Customers and Comments tables.*

STEPS

1. **Click the Database Tools tab on the Ribbon, then click the Relationships button**

TROUBLE
If the Show Table dialog box doesn't appear, click the Show Table button on the Design tab.

2. **In the Show Table dialog box, double-click Customers, double-click Comments, then click Close**

   Each table is represented by a small **field list** window that displays the table's field names. A **key symbol** identifies the primary key field in each table. To relate the two tables in a one-to-many relationship, you connect them using a common field, which is always the primary key field on the "one" side of the relationship.

QUICK TIP
Drag a table's title bar to move the field list.

3. **Drag CustID in the Customers field list to the CustID field in the Comments field list**

   The Edit Relationships dialog box opens, as shown in **FIGURE 1-12**. **Referential integrity**, a set of Access rules that governs data entry, helps ensure data accuracy.

TROUBLE
If you need to delete an incorrect relationship, right-click a relationship line, then click Delete.

4. **Click the Enforce Referential Integrity check box in the Edit Relationships dialog box, then click Create**

   The **one-to-many line** shows the link between the CustID field of the Customers table (the "one" side) and the CustID field of the Comments table (the "many" side, indicated by the **infinity symbol**), as shown in **FIGURE 1-13**. The linking field on the "many" side is called the **foreign key field**. Now that these tables are related, it is much easier to enter comments for the correct customer.

QUICK TIP
To print the Relationships window, click the Relationship Report button on the Design tab, then click Print.

5. **Right-click the Relationships tab, click Close, click Yes to save changes, then double-click the Customers table in the Navigation Pane to open it in Datasheet View**

   When you relate two tables in a one-to-many relationship, expand buttons appear to the left of each record in the table on the "one" side of the relationship. In this case, the Customers table is on the "one" side of the relationship.

6. **Click the expand button ⊞ to the left of the first record**

   A **subdatasheet** shows the related comment records for each customer. In other words, the subdatasheet shows the records on the "many" side of a one-to-many relationship. The expand button ⊞ also changed to the collapse button ⊟ for the first customer. Widening the CommentText field allows you to see the entire entry in the Comments subdatasheet. Now the task of entering comments for the correct customer is much more straightforward.

TROUBLE
Be careful to enter complete comments for the correct customer, as shown in **FIGURE 1-14**.

7. **Enter two more comments, as shown in FIGURE 1-14**

   Interestingly, the CustID field in the Comments table (the foreign key field) is not displayed in the subdatasheet. Behind the scenes, Access is entering the correct CustID value in the Comments table, which is the glue that ties each comment to the correct customer.

8. **Close the Customers table, then click Yes if prompted to save changes**

FIGURE 1-12: Edit Relationships dialog box

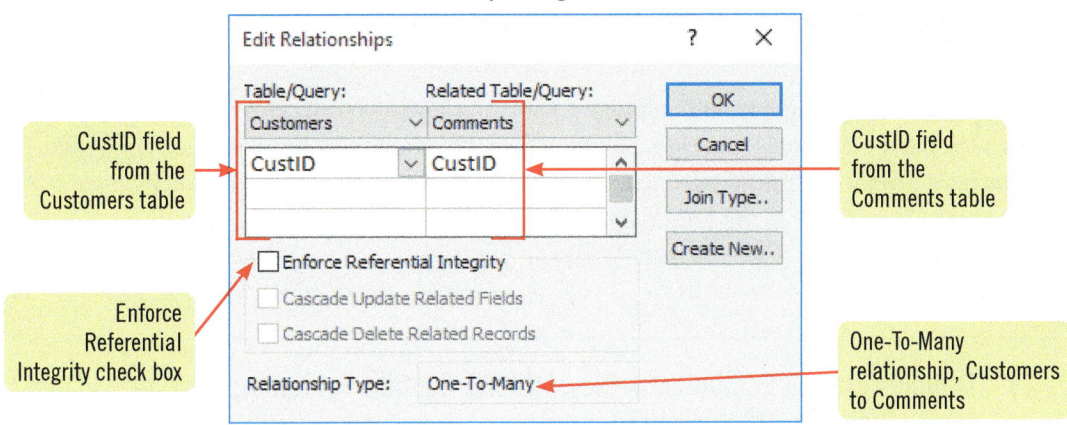

- CustID field from the Customers table
- CustID field from the Comments table
- Enforce Referential Integrity check box
- One-To-Many relationship, Customers to Comments

FIGURE 1-13: Linking the Customers and Comments tables

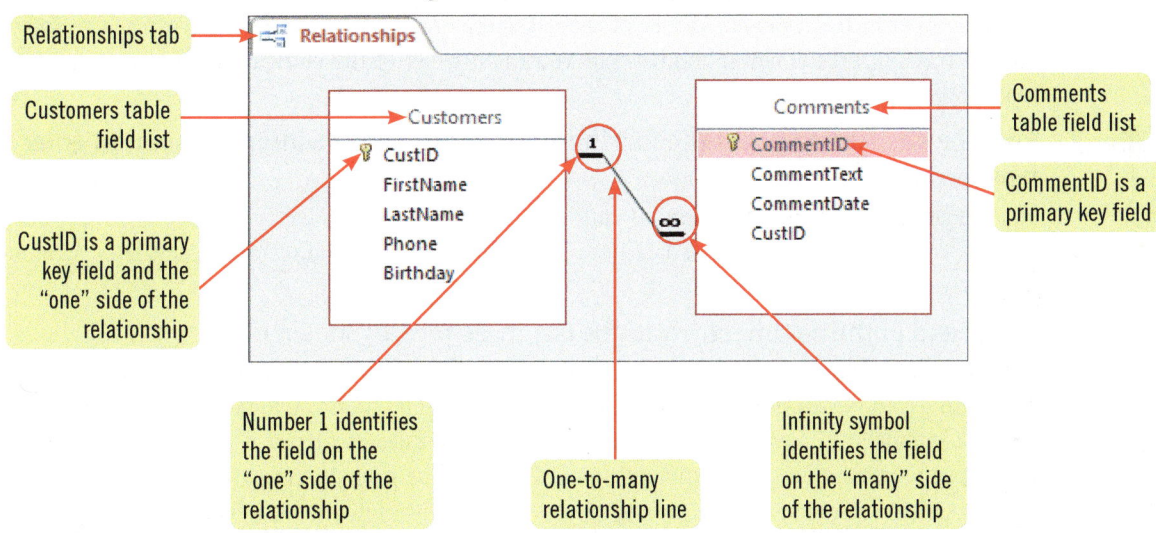

- Relationships tab
- Customers table field list
- CustID is a primary key field and the "one" side of the relationship
- Number 1 identifies the field on the "one" side of the relationship
- One-to-many relationship line
- Infinity symbol identifies the field on the "many" side of the relationship
- Comments table field list
- CommentID is a primary key field

FIGURE 1-14: Entering comments using the subdatasheet

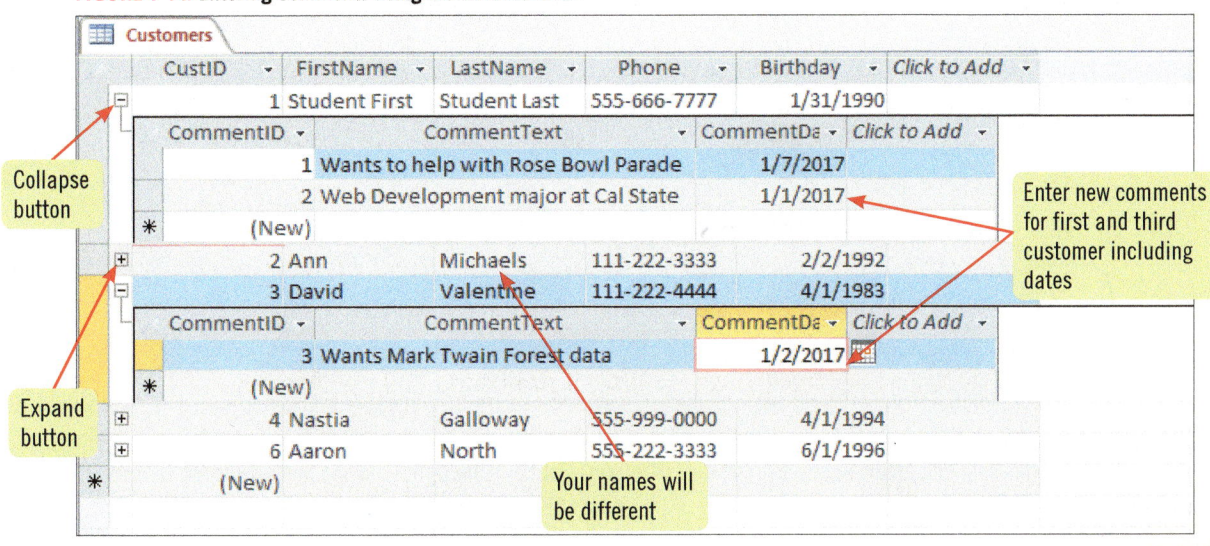

- Collapse button
- Expand button
- Enter new comments for first and third customer including dates
- Your names will be different

Enter Data

Learning Outcomes
- Navigate records in a datasheet
- Enter records in a datasheet

Your skill in navigating and entering new records is a key to your success with a relational database. You can use many techniques to navigate through the records in the table's datasheet. **CASE** ▶ *Even though you have already successfully entered some records, Julia Rice asks you to master this essential skill by entering several more customers in the R2G database.*

STEPS

1. **Double-click the Customers table in the Navigation Pane to open it, press [Tab] three times, then press [Enter] three times**

   The Customers table reopens. The Comments subdatasheets are collapsed. Both the [Tab] and [Enter] keys move the focus to the next field. The **focus** refers to which data you would edit if you started typing. When you navigate to the last field of the record, pressing [Tab] or [Enter] advances the focus to the first field of the next record. You can also use the Next record ▶ and Previous record ◀ **navigation buttons** on the navigation bar in the lower-left corner of the datasheet to navigate through the records. The **Current record** text box on the navigation bar tells you the number of the current record as well as the total number of records in the datasheet.

   QUICK TIP
   Press [Tab] in the CustID AutoNumber field.

2. **Click the FirstName field of the fourth record to position the insertion point to enter a new record**

   You can also use the New (blank) record button ▶✱ on the navigation bar to move to a new record. You enter new records at the end of the datasheet. You learn how to sort and reorder records later. A complete list of navigation keystrokes is shown in **TABLE 1-5**.

   QUICK TIP
   Access databases are multiuser with one important limitation: Two users cannot edit the same record at the same time. In that case, a message explains that the second user must wait until the first user moves to a different record.

3. **At the end of the datasheet, enter the last three records shown in FIGURE 1-15**

   The **edit record symbol** 🖉 appears to the left of the record you are currently editing. When you move to a different record, Access saves the data. Therefore, Access never prompts you to save data because it performs that task automatically. Saving data automatically allows Access databases to be **multiuser** databases, which means that more than one person can enter and edit data in the same database at the same time.

   Your CustID values might differ from those in **FIGURE 1-15**. Because the CustID field is an **AutoNumber** field, Access automatically enters the next consecutive number into the field as it creates the record. If you delete a record or are interrupted when entering a record, Access discards the value in the AutoNumber field and does not reuse it. Therefore, AutoNumber values do not represent the number of records in your table. Instead, they provide a unique value per record, similar to check numbers.

Changing from Navigation mode to Edit mode

If you navigate to another area of the datasheet by clicking with the mouse pointer instead of pressing [Tab] or [Enter], you change from **Navigation mode** to Edit mode. In **Edit mode**, Access assumes that you are trying to make changes to the current field value, so keystrokes such as [Ctrl][End], [Ctrl][Home], [←], and [→] move the insertion point within the field. To return to Navigation mode, press [Tab] or [Enter] (thus moving the focus to the next field), or press [↑] or [↓] (thus moving the focus to a different record).

FIGURE 1-15: New records in the Customers table

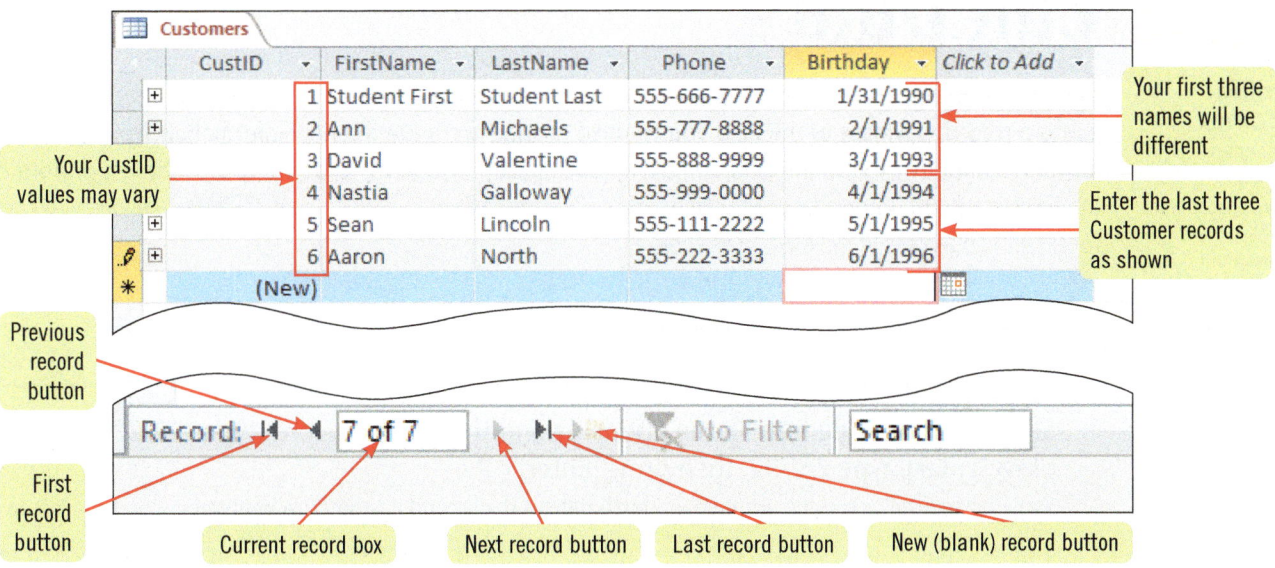

TABLE 1-5: Navigation mode keyboard shortcuts

shortcut key	moves to the
[Tab], [Enter], or [→]	Next field of the current record
[Shift][Tab] or [←]	Previous field of the current record
[Home]	First field of the current record
[End]	Last field of the current record
[Ctrl][Home] or [F5]	First field of the first record
[Ctrl][End]	Last field of the last record
[↑]	Current field of the previous record
[↓]	Current field of the next record

Cloud computing

Using **OneDrive**, a free service from Microsoft, you can store files in the "cloud" and retrieve them anytime you are connected to the Internet. Saving your files to the OneDrive is one example of cloud computing. **Cloud computing** means you are using an Internet resource to complete your work.

Edit Data

Learning Outcomes
- Edit data in a datasheet
- Delete records in a datasheet
- Preview and print a datasheet

Updating existing data in a database is another critical database task. To change the contents of an existing record, navigate to the field you want to change and type the new information. You can delete unwanted data by clicking the field and using [Backspace] or [Delete] to delete text to the left or right of the insertion point. Other data entry keystrokes are summarized in TABLE 1-6. **CASE** *Julia Rice asks you to correct two records in the Customers table.*

STEPS

1. **Select the phone number in the Phone field of the second record, type 111-222-3333, press [Enter], type 2/2/92, then press [Enter]**

   You changed the telephone number and birth date of the second customer. When you entered the last two digits of the year value, Access inserted the first two digits after you pressed [Enter]. You'll also update the third customer.

QUICK TIP
The ScreenTip for the Undo button ↩ displays the action you can undo.

2. **Press [Enter] enough times to move to the Phone field of the third record, type 111-222-4444, then press [Esc]**

   Pressing [Esc] once removes the current field's editing changes, so the Phone value changes back to the previous entry. Pressing [Esc] twice removes all changes to the current record. When you move to another record, Access saves your edits, so you can no longer use [Esc] to remove editing changes to the current record. You can, however, click the Undo button ↩ on the Quick Access Toolbar to undo changes to a previous record.

3. **Retype 111-222-4444, press [Enter], type 3/1/83 in the Birthday field, press [Enter], click the 3/1/83 date you just entered, click the Calendar icon 📅, then click April 1, 1983, as shown in FIGURE 1-16**

   When you are working in the Birthday field, which has a Date/Time data type, you can enter a date from the keyboard or use the **Calendar Picker**, a pop-up calendar, to find and select a date.

4. **Click the record selector for the fifth record (Sean Lincoln), click the Delete button in the Records group on the Home tab, then click Yes**

   A message warns that you cannot undo a record deletion. The Undo button ↩ is dimmed, indicating that you cannot use it. The Customers table now has five records, as shown in FIGURE 1-17. Keep in mind that your CustID values might differ from those in the figure because they are controlled by Access.

QUICK TIP
If requested to print the Customers datasheet by your instructor, click the Print button, then click OK.

5. **Click the File tab, click Print, then click Print Preview to review the printout of the Customers table before printing**

6. **Click the Close Print Preview button, then click the Close button ✕ in the upper-right corner of the window to close the R2G.accdb database and Access 2016**

FIGURE 1-16: Editing customer records

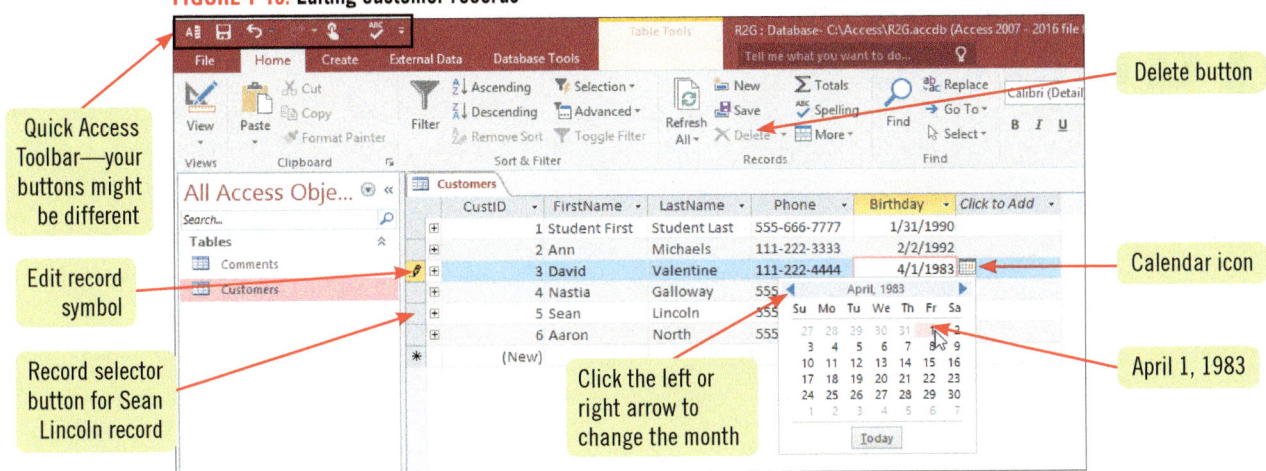

FIGURE 1-17: Final Customers datasheet

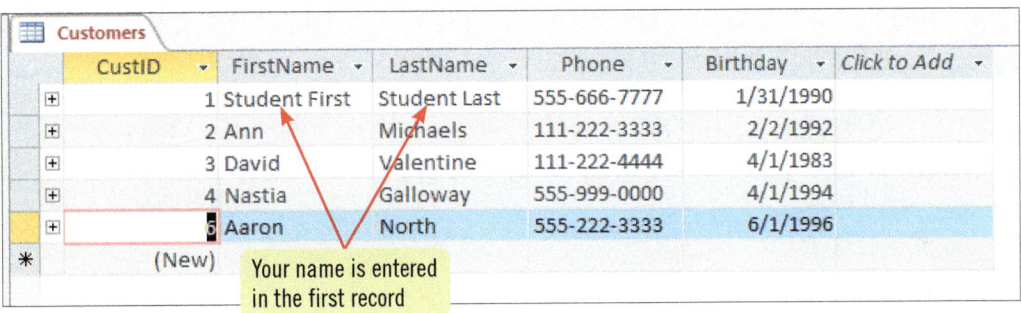

TABLE 1-6: Edit mode keyboard shortcuts

editing keystroke	action
[Backspace]	Deletes one character to the left of the insertion point
[Delete]	Deletes one character to the right of the insertion point
[F2]	Switches between Edit and Navigation mode
[Esc]	Undoes the change to the current field
[Esc][Esc]	Undoes all changes to the current record
[F7]	Starts the spell-check feature
[Ctrl][']	Inserts the value from the same field in the previous record into the current field
[Ctrl][;]	Inserts the current date in a Date field

Resizing and moving datasheet columns

You can resize the width of a field in a datasheet by dragging the column separator, the thin line that separates the field names to the left or right. The pointer changes to ↔ as you make the field wider or narrower. Release the mouse button when you have resized the field. To adjust the column width to accommodate the widest entry in the field, double-click the column separator. To move a column, click the field name to select the entire column, then drag the field name left or right.

Practice

Concepts Review

Label each element of the Access window shown in FIGURE 1-18**.**

FIGURE 1-18

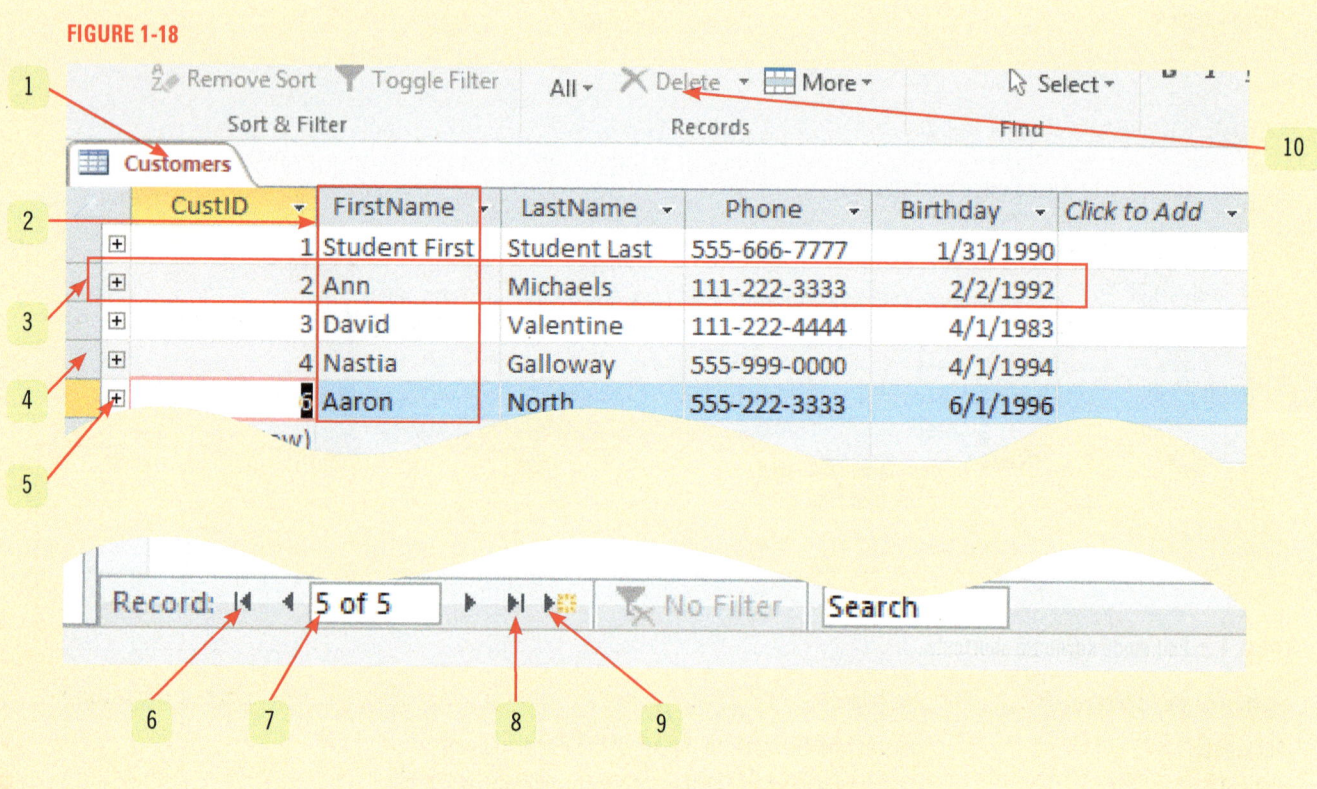

Match each term with the statement that best describes it.

11. Field	**a.** A subset of data from one or more tables
12. Record	**b.** A collection of records for a single subject, such as all the customer records
13. Table	**c.** A professional printout of database information
14. Datasheet	**d.** A spreadsheet-like grid that displays fields as columns and records as rows
15. Query	**e.** A group of related fields for one item, such as all of the information for one
16. Form	customer
17. Report	**f.** A category of information in a table, such as a company name, city, or state
	g. An easy-to-use data entry screen

Select the best answer from the list of choices.

18. **When you create a new database, which object is created first?**
    - **a.** Module
    - **b.** Query
    - **c.** Table
    - **d.** Form

19. **Which of the following is *not* a typical benefit of relational databases?**
    - **a.** Minimized duplicate data entry
    - **b.** More accurate data
    - **c.** Tables automatically create needed relationships
    - **d.** More consistent data

20. **Which of the following is *not* an advantage of managing data with relational database software such as Access versus spreadsheet software such as Excel?**
    - **a.** Allows multiple users to enter data simultaneously
    - **b.** Uses a single table to store all data
    - **c.** Provides data entry forms
    - **d.** Reduces duplicate data entry

Skills Review

1. **Understand relational databases.**
   - **a.** Write down five advantages of managing database information in Access versus using a spreadsheet.
   - **b.** Write a sentence to explain how the terms field, record, table, and relational database relate to one another.

2. **Explore a database.**
   - **a.** Start Access.
   - **b.** Open the LakeHomes-1.accdb database from the location where you store your Data Files. Click Enable Content if a yellow Security Warning message appears.
   - **c.** Open each of the four tables to study the data they contain. Complete the following table:

table name	number of records	number of fields

   - **d.** Double-click the ListingsByRealtor query in the Navigation Pane to open it. Change any occurrence of Gordon Bono to *your* name. Move to another record to save your changes.
   - **e.** Double-click the RealtorsMainForm in the Navigation Pane to open it. Use the navigation buttons to navigate through the 13 realtors to observe each realtor's listings.
   - **f.** Double-click the RealtorListingReport in the Navigation Pane to open it. The records are listed in ascending order by realtor last name. Scroll through the report to make sure your name is positioned correctly.
   - **g.** Close the LakeHomes-1 database, then close Access 2016.

3. **Create a database.**
   - **a.** Start Access, click the Blank desktop database icon, use the Browse button to navigate to the location where you store your Data Files, type **LakeHomeMarketing** as the filename, click OK, and then click Create to create a new database named LakeHomeMarketing.accdb.

Skills Review (continued)

b. Switch to Table Design View, name the table **Prospects**, then enter the following fields and data types:

field name	data type
ProspectID	AutoNumber
ProspectFirst	Short Text
ProspectLast	Short Text
Phone	Short Text
Email	Hyperlink
Street	Short Text
City	Short Text
State	Short Text
Zip	Short Text

c. Save the table, switch to Datasheet View, and enter two records using your name in the first record and your instructor's name in the second. Tab through the ProspectID field, an AutoNumber field.

d. Enter **TN** (Tennessee) as the value in the State field for both records. Use school or fictitious (rather than personal) data for all other field data, and be sure to fill out each record completely.

e. Widen each column in the Prospects table so that all data is visible, then save and close the Prospects table.

4. Create a table.

a. Click the Create tab on the Ribbon, click the Table Design button in the Tables group, then create a new table with the following two fields and data types:

field name	data type
State2	Short Text
StateName	Short Text

b. Save the table with the name **States**. Click No when asked if you want Access to create the primary key field.

5. Create primary keys.

a. In Table Design View of the States table, set the State2 field as the primary key field.

b. Save the States table and open it in Datasheet View.

c. Enter one state record, using **TN** for the State2 value and **Tennessee** for the StateName value to match the State value of TN that you entered for both records in the Prospects table.

d. Close the States table.

6. Relate two tables.

a. From the Database Tools tab, open the Relationships window.

b. Add the States, then the Prospects table to the Relationships window.

c. Drag the bottom edge of the Prospects table to expand the field list to display all of the fields.

FIGURE 1-19

d. Drag the State2 field from the States table to the State field of the Prospects table.

e. In the Edit Relationships dialog box, click the Enforce Referential Integrity check box, then click Create. Your Relationships window should look like **FIGURE 1-19**. If you connect the wrong fields by mistake, right-click the line connecting the two fields, click Delete, then try again.

f. Close the Relationships window, and save changes when prompted.

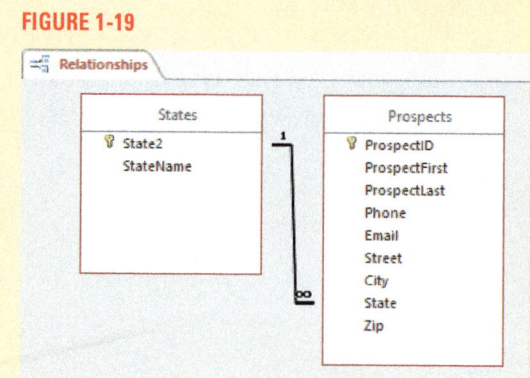

Skills Review (continued)

7. Enter data.

a. Open the States table and enter the following records:

State2 field	StateName field
CO	Colorado
IA	Iowa
KS	Kansas
MO	Missouri
NE	Nebraska
OK	Oklahoma
WI	Wisconsin
TX	Texas

b. Add three more state records of your choice for a total of 12 records in the States table using the correct two-character abbreviation for the state and the correctly spelled state name.

c. Close and reopen the States table. Notice that Access automatically sorts the records by the values in the primary key field, the State2 field.

8. Edit data.

a. Click the Expand button for the TN record to see the two related records from the Prospects table.

b. Enter two more prospects in the TN subdatasheet using any fictitious but realistic data, as shown in **FIGURE 1-20**. Notice that you are not required to enter a value for the State field, the foreign key field in the subdatasheet.

c. If required by your instructor, print the States datasheet and the Prospects datasheet.

d. Click the Close button in the upper-right corner of the Access window to close all open objects as well as the LakeHomeMarketing.accdb database and Access 2016. If prompted to save any design changes, click Yes.

FIGURE 1-20

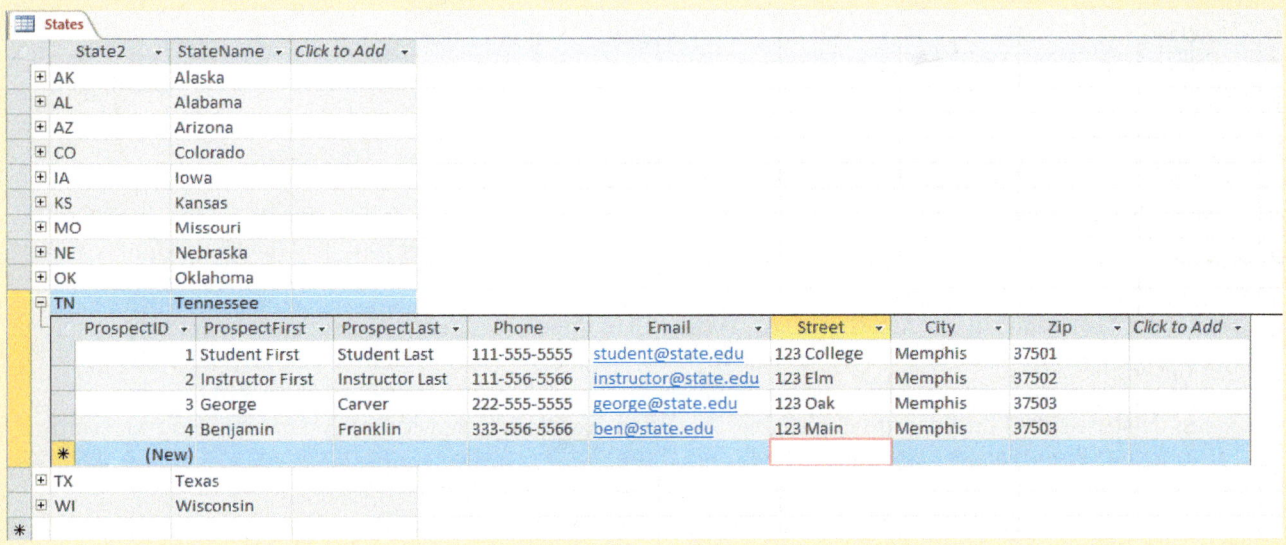

Independent Challenge 1

Consider the following twelve subject areas:

- Telephone directory
- Islands of the Caribbean
- Members of the U.S. House of Representatives
- College course offerings
- Physical activities
- Ancient wonders of the world
- Restaurant menu
- Shopping catalog items
- Vehicles
- Conventions
- Party guest list
- Movie listings

a. For each subject, build a Word table with 4–7 columns and three rows. In the first row, enter field names that you would expect to see in a table used to manage that subject.

b. In the second and third rows of each table, enter two realistic records. The first table, Telephone Directory, is completed as an example to follow.

TABLE: Telephone Directory

FirstName	LastName	Street	Zip	Phone
Marco	Lopez	100 Main Street	88715	555-612-3312
Christopher	Stafford	253 Maple Lane	77824	555-612-1179

c. Consider the following guidelines as you build the table:

Make sure each record represents one item in that table. For example, in the Restaurant Menu table, the following table is a random list of categories of food. The records do not represent one item in a restaurant menu.

Beverage	Appetizer	Meat	Vegetable	Dessert
Milk	Chicken wings	Steak	Carrots	Chocolate cake
Tea	Onion rings	Salmon	Potato	Cheesecake

A better example of records that describe an item in the restaurant menu would be the following:

Category	Description	Price	Calories	Spicy
Appetizer	Chicken wings	$10	800	Yes
Beverage	Milk	$2	250	No

Do not put first and last names in the same field. This prevents you from easily sorting, filtering, or searching on either part of the name later.

For the same reasons, break street, city, state, zip, and country data into separate fields as well.

Do not put values and units of measure such as 5 minutes, 4 lbs, or 6 sq. miles in the same field. This also prevents you from sorting and calculating on the numeric part of the information. Make your field names descriptive such as TimeInMinutes or AreaInSquareMiles so that each record's entries are consistent.

Do not put these tables in one Access database. Putting all of these tables in one Access database would be analogous to putting a letter to your Congressman, a creative poem, and a cover letter to a future employer all in the same Word file. Just as that wouldn't make organizational sense, these tables do not belong together in the same Access database either. Create your sample tables in a Word document to stay focused on proper field and record construction versus the task of building Access tables.

Independent Challenge 2

You are working with several civic groups to coordinate a community-wide recycling effort. You have started a database called Salvage-1, which tracks the clubs, their recyclable material deposits, and the collection centers that are participating.

a. Start Access, then open the Salvage-1.accdb database from the location where you store your Data Files. Enable content if prompted.

b. Open each table's datasheet to study the number of fields and records per table. Notice that there are no expand buttons to the left of any records because relationships have not yet been established between these tables.

c. In a Word document, re-create the following table and fill in the blanks:

table name	number of records	number of fields

d. Close all table datasheets, then open the Relationships window and create the following one-to-many relationships. Drag the tables from the Navigation Pane to the Relationships window, and drag the title bars and borders of the field lists to position them as shown in **FIGURE 1-21**.

field on the "one" side of the relationship	field on the "many" side of the relationship
ClubNumber in Clubs table	ClubNumber in Deposits table
CenterNumber in Centers table	CenterNumber in Deposits table

e. Be sure to enforce referential integrity on all relationships. If you create an incorrect relationship, right-click the line linking the fields, click Delete, and try again. Your final Relationships window should look like **FIGURE 1-21**.

f. Click the Relationship Report button on the Design tab, and if required by your instructor, click Print to print a copy of the Relationships for Salvage-1 report. To close the report, right-click the Relationships for Salvage-1 tab and click Close. Click Yes when prompted to save changes to the report with the name **Relationships for Salvage-1**. Save and close the Relationships window.

g. Open the Clubs table and add a new record with fictitious but realistic data in all of the fields. Enter **8** as the ClubNumber value and your name in the FName (first name) and LName (last name) fields.

h. Expand the subdatasheets for each record in the Clubs table to see the related records from the Deposits table. Which club made the most deposits? Be ready to answer in class. Close the Clubs table.

i. Open the Centers table and add a new record with fictitious but realistic data in all of the fields. Enter your first and last names in the CenterName field and enter **5** as the CenterNumber.

j. Expand the subdatasheets for each record in the Centers table to see the related records from the Deposits table. Which center made the most deposits? Be ready to answer in class. Close the Centers table.

k. Close the Salvage-1.accdb database, then exit Access 2016.

FIGURE 1-21

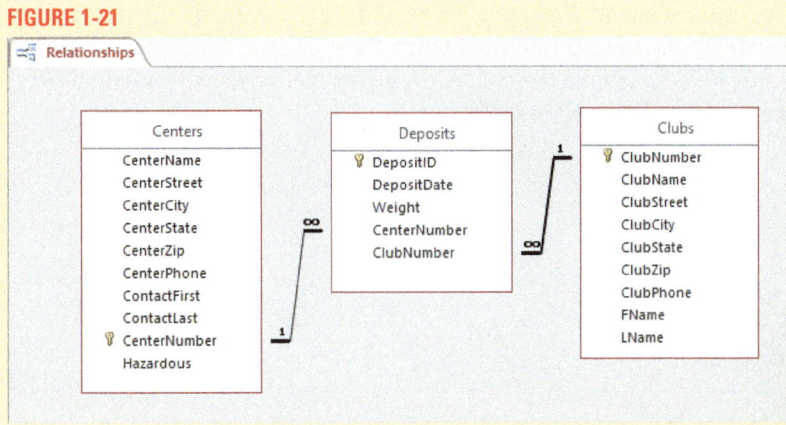

Independent Challenge 3

You are working for an advertising agency that provides social media consulting for small and large businesses in the midwestern United States. You have started a database called Contacts-1, which tracks your company's customers. (*Note*: To complete this Independent Challenge, make sure you are connected to the Internet.)

a. Start Access and open the Contacts-1.accdb database from the location where you store your Data Files. Enable content if prompted.

b. Add a new record to the Customers table, using any local business name, your first and last names, **$10,500** in the YTDSales field, and fictitious but reasonable entries for the rest of the fields.

c. Edit the Sprint Systems record (ID 1). Change the Company name to **A1 Cellular**, and change the Street value to **4455 Mastin St**.

d. Delete the record for EBC (ID 18), then close the Customers table.

e. Create a new table with two fields, **State2** and **StateName**. Assign both fields a Short Text data type. The State2 field will contain the two-letter abbreviation for state names. The StateName field will contain the Set the State2 field as the primary key field, then save the table as **States**.

f. Enter at least three records into the States table, making sure that all of the states used in the Customers datasheet are entered in the States table. This includes **KS Kansas**, **MO Missouri**, and any other state you entered in Step b when you added a new record to the Customers table.

g. Close all open tables. Open the Relationships window, add both the States and Customers field lists to the window, then expand the size of the Customers field list so that all fields are visible. (*Hint*: The field list will not show a vertical scroll bar when all fields in the list are visible.)

h. Build a one-to-many relationship between the States and Customers tables by dragging the State2 field from the States table to the State field of the Customers table to create a one-to-many relationship between the two tables. Enforce referential integrity on the relationship. If you are unable to enforce referential integrity, it means that a value in the State field of the Customers table doesn't have a perfect match in the State2 field of the States table. Open both table datasheets, making sure every state in the State field of the Customers table is also represented in the State2 field of the States table, close all datasheets, then reestablish the one-to-many relationship between the two tables with referential integrity.

i. Click the Relationship Report button on the Design tab, then if requested by your instructor, click Print to print the report.

j. Right-click the Relationships for Contacts-1 tab, then click Close. Click Yes when prompted to save the report with the name **Relationships for Contacts-1**.

k. Close the Relationships window, saving changes as prompted.

l. Close the Contacts-1.accdb database, then exit Access 2016.

Independent Challenge 4: Explore

Now that you've learned about Microsoft Access and relational databases, brainstorm how you might use an Access database in your daily life or career. Start by visiting the Microsoft website, and explore what's new in Access 2016.

(*Note*: To complete this Independent Challenge, make sure you are connected to the Internet.)

a. Using your favorite search engine, look up the keywords *benefits of a relational database* or *benefits of Microsoft Access* to find articles that discuss the benefits of organizing data in a relational database.

b. Read several articles about the benefits of organizing data in a relational database such as Access, identifying three distinct benefits. Use a Word document to record those three benefits. Also, copy and paste the website address of the article you are referencing for each benefit you have identified.

c. In addition, as you read the articles that describe relational database benefits, list any terminology unfamiliar to you, identifying at least five new terms.

d. Using a search engine or a website that provides a computer glossary such as www.whatis.com or www.webopedia.com, look up the definition of the new terms, and enter both the term and the definition of the term in your document as well as the website address where your definition was found.

e. Finally, based on your research and growing understanding of Access 2016, list three ways you could use an Access database to organize, enhance, or support the activities and responsibilities of your daily life or career. Type your name at the top of the document, and submit it to your instructor as requested.

Visual Workshop

Open the Basketball-1.accdb database from the location where you store your Data Files, then enable content if prompted. Open the Offense query datasheet, which lists offensive statistics by player by game. Modify any of the Matthew Douglas records to contain your first and last names, then move to a different record, observing the power of a relational database to modify every occurrence of that name throughout the database. Close the Offense query, then open the Players table. Note that there are no expand buttons to the left of the records, indicating that this table does not participate on the "one" side of a one-to-many relationship. Close the Players table and open the Relationships window. Drag the tables from the Navigation Pane and create the relationships with referential integrity, as shown in FIGURE 1-22. Note the one-to-many relationship between the Players and Stats table. Print the Relationships report if requested by your instructor and save it with the name **Relationships for Basketball-1**. Close the report and close and save the Relationships window. Now reopen the Players table noting the expand buttons to the left of each record. Expand the subdatasheet for your name and for several other players to observe the "many" records from the Stats table that are now related to each record in the Players table.

FIGURE 1-22

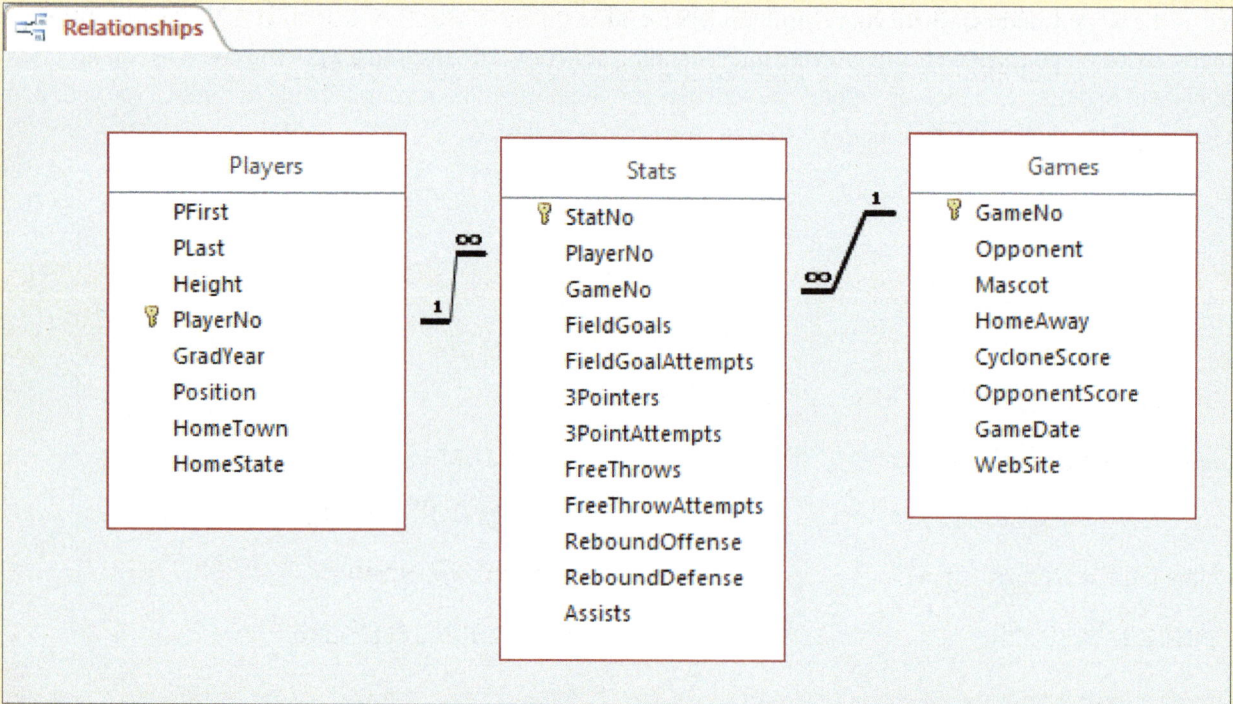

Building and Using Queries

CASE Julia Rice, trip developer for U.S. group travel at Reason 2 Go, has several questions about the customer and trip information in the R2G database. You'll develop queries to provide Julia with up-to-date answers.

Module Objectives

After completing this module, you will be able to:

- Use the Query Wizard
- Work with data in a query
- Use Query Design View
- Sort and find data

- Filter data
- Apply AND criteria
- Apply OR criteria
- Format a datasheet

Files You Will Need

R2G-2.accdb	HouseOfReps-2.accdb
Salvage-2.accdb	VetClinic-2.accdb
Service-2.accdb	Baseball-2.accdb

Use the Query Wizard

Learning Outcomes
- Describe the purpose for a query
- Create a query with the Simple Query Wizard

A **query** answers a question about the information in the database. A query allows you to select a subset of fields and records from one or more tables and then present the selected data as a single datasheet. A major benefit of working with data through a query is that you can focus on only the specific information you need, rather than navigating through all the fields and records from one or more large tables. You can enter, edit, and navigate data in a query datasheet just like a table datasheet. However, keep in mind that Access data is physically stored only in tables, even though you can select, view, and edit it through other Access objects such as queries and forms. Because a query doesn't physically store the data, a query datasheet is sometimes called a **logical view** of the data. A query stores a set of **SQL (Structured Query Language)** instructions, but because you can use Access query tools such as Query Design View to create and modify the query, you are not required to write SQL statements to build or use Access queries. Access provides several tools to create a new query, one of which is the Simple Query Wizard. **CASE** ▸ *Julia Rice suggests that you use the Simple Query Wizard to create a query that displays fields from the Trips and Customers tables in one datasheet.*

STEPS

1. **Start Access, open the R2G-2.accdb database, enable content if prompted, then maximize the window**

   Access provides several tools to create a new query. One way is to use the **Simple Query Wizard**, which prompts you for the information it needs to create the query.

2. **Click the Create tab on the Ribbon, click the Query Wizard button in the Queries group, then click OK to start the Simple Query Wizard**

   The first Simple Query Wizard dialog box opens, prompting you to select the fields you want to view in the new query. You can select fields from one or more existing tables or queries.

3. **Click the Tables/Queries list arrow, click Table: Trips, double-click TripName, double-click City, double-click Category, then double-click Price**

   So far, you've selected four fields from the Trips table to display basic trip information in this query. You also want to add the first and last name information from the Customers table so you know which customers purchased each trip.

4. **Click the Tables/Queries list arrow, click Table: Customers, double-click FName, then double-click LName**

   You've selected four fields from the Trips table and two from the Customers table for your new query, as shown in **FIGURE 2-1**.

5. **Click Next, click Next to select Detail, select Trips Query in the title text box, type TripCustomerList as the name of the query, then click Finish**

   The TripCustomerList datasheet opens, displaying four fields from the Trips table and two from the Customers table, as shown in **FIGURE 2-2**. The query can show which customers have purchased which Trips because of the one-to-many table relationships established in the Relationships window.

Simple Query Wizard

The **Simple Query Wizard** is a series of dialog boxes that prompt you for the information needed to create a Select query. A **Select query** selects fields from one or more tables in your database and is by far the most common type of query. The other query wizards—Crosstab, Find Duplicates, and Find Unmatched—are used to create queries that do specialized types of data analysis and are covered in Module 10 on advanced queries.

FIGURE 2-1: Selecting fields using the Simple Query Wizard

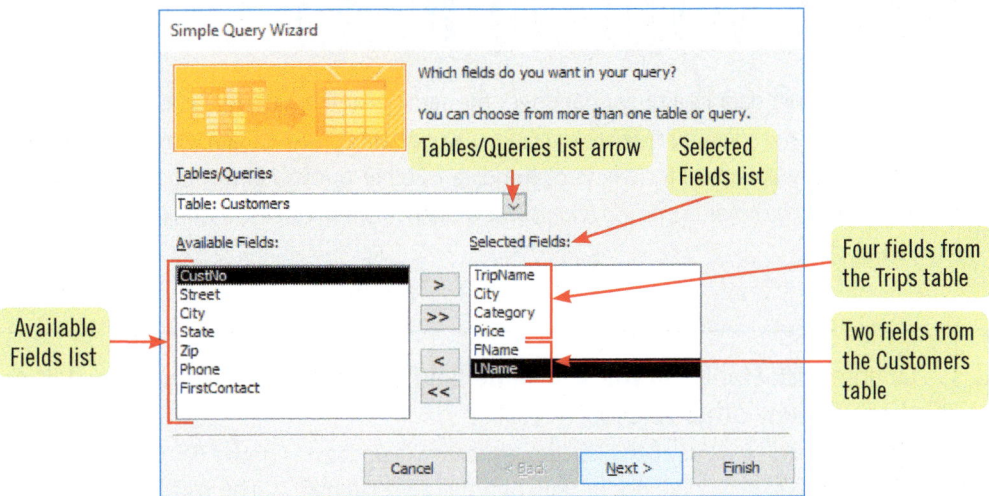

FIGURE 2-2: TripCustomerList datasheet

TripName	City	Category	Price	FName	LName
Stanley Bay Cleanup	Captiva	Eco	$750	Ralph	Stewart
Stanley Bay Cleanup	Captiva	Eco	$750	Lisa	Gomez
Breckenridge Reconstruction	Breckenridge	Eco	$850	Kristen	Collins
Stanley Bay Cleanup	Captiva	Eco	$750	Kris	Shaw
Stanley Bay Cleanup	Captiva	Eco	$750	Lois	Gordon
Stanley Bay Cleanup	Captiva	Eco	$750	Naresh	Blackwell
Coastal Shore Cleanup	Captiva	Family	$1,000	Julia	Bouchart
Breckenridge Reconstruction	Breckenridge	Eco	$850	Tom	Camel
Golden Hands Venture	Orlando	Family	$900	Shirley	Cruz
Golden Hands Venture	Orlando	Family	$900	Zohra	Bell
Golden Hands Venture	Orlando	Family	$900	Kathryn	Hall
Golden Hands Venture	Orlando	Family	$900	Jose	Edwards
Red Reef Cleanup	Islamadora	Eco	$1,500	Jane	Taylor
Stanley Bay Cleanup	Captiva	Eco	$750	Kori	James
American Heritage Tour	Philadelphia	Educational	$1,200	Sharol	Wood
American Heritage Tour	Philadelphia	Educational	$1,200	Lois	Gordon
American Heritage Tour	Philadelphia	Educational	$1,200	Tim	Hayes
American Heritage Tour	Philadelphia	Educational	$1,200	Frank	Torres
Yosemite Park Cleanup	Sacramento	Eco	$1,250	Tom	Camel
American Heritage Tour	Philadelphia	Educational	$1,200	Jane	Taylor
Yosemite Park Cleanup	Sacramento	Eco	$1,250	Kristen	Collins
American Heritage Tour	Philadelphia	Educational	$1,200	Kris	Shaw
American Heritage Tour	Philadelphia	Educational	$1,200	Ralph	Stewart
American Heritage Tour	Philadelphia	Educational	$1,200	Nancy	Cole
American Heritage Tour	Philadelphia	Educational	$1,200	Brad	Long

Record: 1 of 106 | No Filter | Search

106 records

Access 2016

Work with Data in a Query

You enter and edit data in a query datasheet the same way you do in a table datasheet. Because all data is stored in tables, any edits you make to data in a query datasheet are actually stored in the underlying tables and are automatically updated in all views of the data in other queries, forms, and reports. **CASE** ▸ *Julia Rice wants to change the name of one trip and update a city name. You can use the TripCustomerList query datasheet to make these edits.*

STEPS

1. **Double-click Stanley in the TripName field of the first or second record, type Captiva, then click any other record**

   All occurrences of Stanley Bay Cleanup automatically update to Captiva Bay Cleanup because this TripName field value is stored only once in the Trips table. See **FIGURE 2-3**. The TripName is selected from the Trips table and displayed in the TripCustomerList query for each customer who purchased this trip.

2. **Double-click Orlando in the City field of any record for the Golden Hands Venture trip, type College Park, then click any other record**

   All occurrences of Orlando automatically update to College Park for the Golden Hands Venture trip because this value is stored only once in the City field of the Trips table for the Golden Hands Venture record. The Golden Hands Venture trip is displayed in the TripCustomerList query for each customer who purchased that trip.

3. **Click the record selector button to the left of the first record, click the Home tab, click the Delete button in the Records group, then click Yes**

   You can delete records from a query datasheet the same way you delete them from a table datasheet. Notice that the navigation bar now indicates you have 105 records in the datasheet, as shown in **FIGURE 2-4**.

4. **Right-click the TripCustomerList query tab, then click Close**

   Each time a query is opened, it shows a current view of the data. This means that as new trips, customers, or sales are recorded in the database, the next time you open this query, the information will include all updates.

Hiding and unhiding fields in a datasheet

To hide a field in a datasheet, right-click the field name at the top of the datasheet and click the Hide Fields option on the shortcut menu. To unhide a field, right-click any field name, click Unhide Fields, and check the hidden field's check box in the Unhide Columns dialog box.

Freezing and unfreezing fields in a datasheet

In large datasheets, you may want to freeze certain fields so that they remain on the screen at all times. To freeze a field, right-click its field name in the datasheet, and then click Freeze Fields. To unfreeze a field, right-click any field name and click Unfreeze All Fields.

FIGURE 2-3: Working with data in a query datasheet

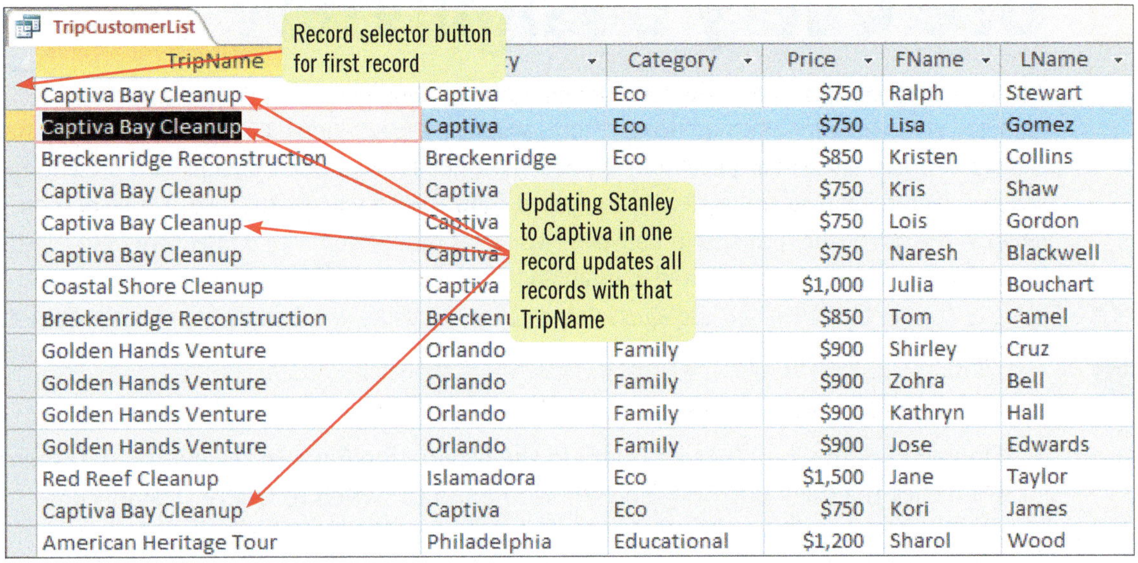

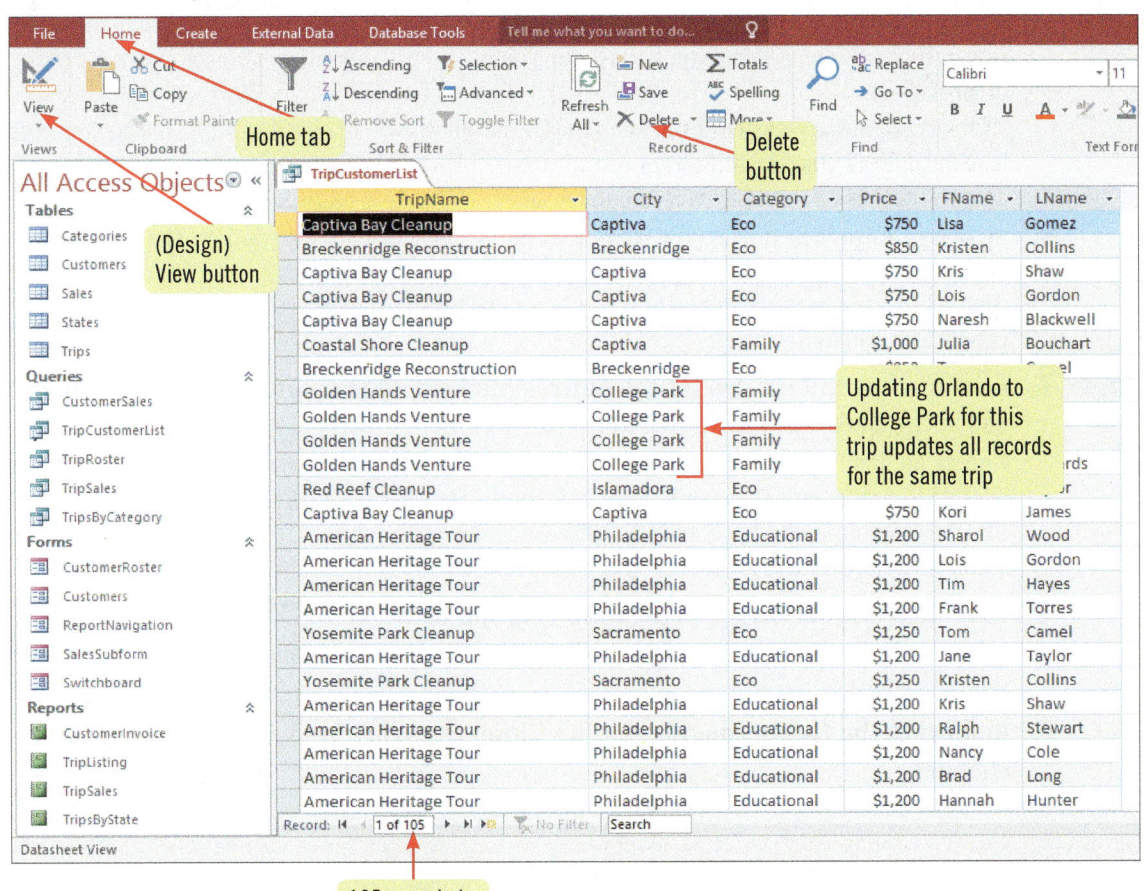

FIGURE 2-4: Final TripCustomerList datasheet

Use Query Design View

You use **Query Design View** to add, delete, or move the fields in an existing query; to specify sort orders; or to add **criteria** to limit the number of records shown in the resulting datasheet. You can also use Query Design View to create a new query from scratch. In the upper pane, Query Design View presents the fields you can use for that query in small windows called **field lists**. If you use the fields of two or more related tables in the query, the relationship between two tables is displayed with a **join line** (also called a **link line**) identifying which fields are used to establish the relationship. **CASE** ▸ *Julia Rice asks you to produce a list of trips in California. You use Query Design View to modify the existing TripsByState query to meet her request.*

STEPS

1. **Double-click the TripsByState query in the Navigation Pane to review the datasheet, then click the View button ☑ on the Home tab to switch to Query Design View**

   The TripsByState query contains the StateName field from the States table and the TripName, TripStartDate, and Price fields from the Trips table. This query contains two ascending sort orders: StateName and TripName. All records in California, for example, are further sorted by the TripName value.

QUICK TIP
Drag the lower edge of the field list to resize it to view all fields.

2. **Click the File tab, click Save As, click Save Object As, click the Save As button, type CATrips to replace Copy of TripsByState, then click OK**

   If you want to build a new query starting from an existing query, use the Save As command and give the new query a new name before you start working on it. This will prevent you from accidentally changing the original query.

   In Access, the **Save As command** on the File tab allows you to save the *entire database* (the entire database includes all objects within it) or just the *current object* with a new name. Recall that Access saves *data* automatically as you move from record to record.

   Query Design View displays the tables used in the upper pane of the window. The link line shows that one record in the States table may be related to many records in the Trips table. The lower pane of the window, called the **query design grid** (or **query grid** for short), displays the field names, sort orders, and criteria used within the query.

QUICK TIP
Query criteria are not case sensitive, so "California" equals "CALIFORNIA" equals "california".

3. **Click the first Criteria cell for the StateName field, type California, then click any other cell in the query grid as shown in FIGURE 2-5**

   Criteria are limiting conditions you set in the query design grid. In this case, the condition limits the selected records to only those with "California" in the StateName field. Criteria for a field with a Short Text data type are surrounded by "quotation marks" though you do not need to type the quotation marks. Access automatically adds them for you.

4. **Click the View button ▦ in the Results group to switch to Datasheet View**

   Now only 15 records are selected, because only 15 of the trips have "California" in the StateName field, as shown in FIGURE 2-6.

5. **Right-click the CATrips query tab, click Close, then click Yes when prompted to save changes**

Adding or deleting a table in a query

You might want to add a table's field list to the upper pane of Query Design View to select fields from that table for the query. To add a new table to Query Design View, drag it from the Navigation Pane to Query Design View, or click the Show Table button on the Design tab, then add the desired table(s). To delete an unneeded table from Query Design View, click its title bar, then press [Delete].

FIGURE 2-5: CATrips query in Design View

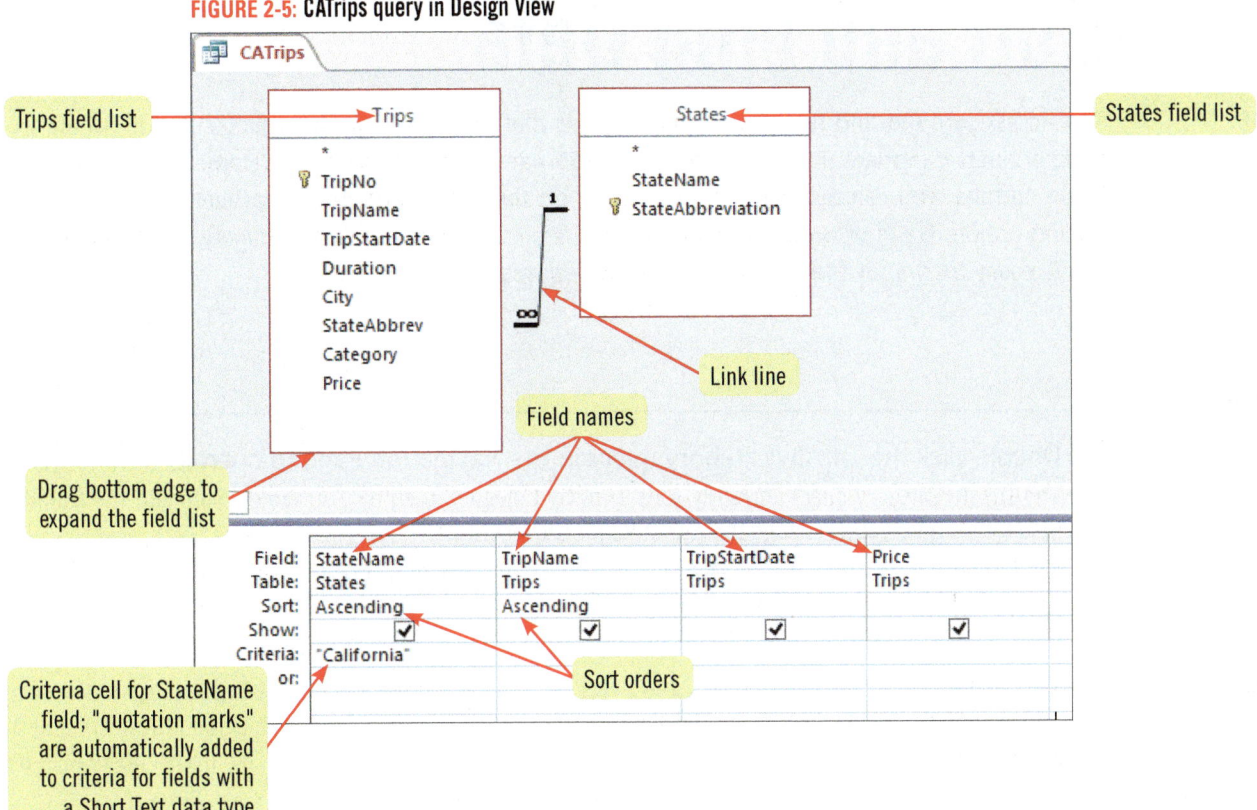

Trips field list

States field list

Trips field list → Trips

States ← States field list

Link line

Field names

Drag bottom edge to expand the field list

Field:	StateName	TripName	TripStartDate	Price
Table:	States	Trips	Trips	Trips
Sort:	Ascending	Ascending		
Show:	☑	☑	☑	☑
Criteria:	"California"			
or:				

Sort orders

Criteria cell for StateName field; "quotation marks" are automatically added to criteria for fields with a Short Text data type

FIGURE 2-6: CATrips query with California criterion

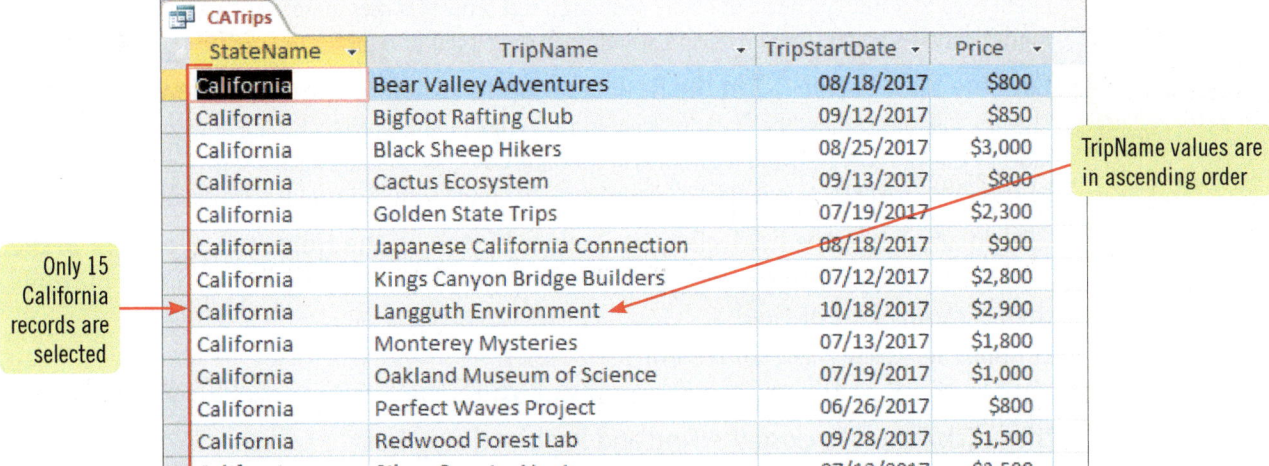

StateName	TripName	TripStartDate	Price
California	Bear Valley Adventures	08/18/2017	$800
California	Bigfoot Rafting Club	09/12/2017	$850
California	Black Sheep Hikers	08/25/2017	$3,000
California	Cactus Ecosystem	09/13/2017	$800
California	Golden State Trips	07/19/2017	$2,300
California	Japanese California Connection	08/18/2017	$900
California	Kings Canyon Bridge Builders	07/12/2017	$2,800
California	Langguth Environment	10/18/2017	$2,900
California	Monterey Mysteries	07/13/2017	$1,800
California	Oakland Museum of Science	07/19/2017	$1,000
California	Perfect Waves Project	06/26/2017	$800
California	Redwood Forest Lab	09/28/2017	$1,500
California	Silver Country Venture	07/12/2017	$3,500
California	Water Education Foundation	09/20/2017	$1,300
California	Yosemite Park Cleanup	07/19/2017	$1,250

TripName values are in ascending order

Only 15 California records are selected

Sort and Find Data

The Access sort and find features are handy tools that help you quickly organize and find data in a table or query datasheet. TABLE 2-1 describes the Sort and Find buttons on the Home tab. Besides using these buttons, you can also click the list arrow on the field name in a datasheet, and then click a sorting option. **CASE** *Julia asks you to provide a list of trips sorted by Category, and then by Price. You'll modify the TripsByCategory query to answer this request.*

STEPS

1. **Double-click the TripsByCategory query in the Navigation Pane to open its datasheet**

   The TripsByCategory query currently sorts Trips by Category, then by TripName. You'll add the Duration field to this query, then change the sort order for the records.

2. **Click the View button** ⬕ **in the Views group to switch to Design View, then double-click the Duration field in the Trips field list**

   When you double-click a field in a field list, Access inserts it in the next available column in the query grid. You can also drag a field from a field list to a specific column of the query grid. To select a field in the query grid, you click its field selector. The **field selector** is the thin gray bar above each field in the query grid. To delete a field from a query, click its field selector, then press [Delete]. Deleting a field from a query does not delete it from the underlying table; the field is only deleted from the query.

   Currently, the TripsByCategory query is sorted by Category and then by TripName. Access evaluates sort orders from left to right. You want to change the sort order so that the records sort first by Category then by Price.

3. **Click Ascending in the TripName Sort cell, click the list arrow, click (not sorted), double-click the Price Sort cell, click the list arrow, then click Descending**

   The records are now set to be sorted in ascending order by Category, and within each Category, in a descending order by the Price field, as shown in **FIGURE 2-7**. Because sort orders always work from left to right, you might need to rearrange the fields before applying a sort order that uses more than one field. To move a field in the query design grid, click its field selector, then drag it left or right.

4. **Click the View button** ▦ **in the Results group to switch to Datasheet View**

   The new datasheet shows the Duration field in the fifth column. The records are now sorted in ascending order by the Category field, but for records in the same Category, they are further sorted in descending order by Price. Your next task is to replace all occurrences of "Tour" with "Trip" in the TripName field.

5. **Click in any TripName field, click the Replace button on the Home tab, type Tour in the Find What box, click in the Replace With box, type Trip, click the Match arrow button, then click Any Part of Field**

   The Find and Replace dialog box is shown in **FIGURE 2-8**.

6. **Click the Replace All button in the Find and Replace dialog box, click Yes to continue, then click Cancel to close the Find and Replace dialog box**

   Access replaced both occurrences of "Tour" with "Trip" in the TripName field, as shown in **FIGURE 2-9**.

7. **Right-click the TripsByCategory query tab, click Close, then click Yes if prompted to save changes**

FIGURE 2-7: Changing sort orders for the TripsByCategory query

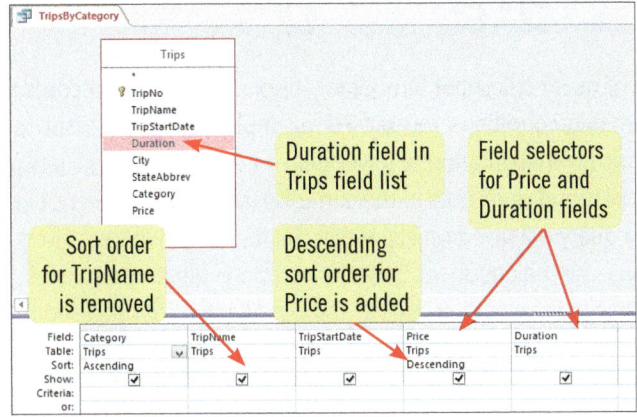

Duration field in Trips field list

Field selectors for Price and Duration fields

Sort order for TripName is removed

Descending sort order for Price is added

FIGURE 2-8: Find and Replace dialog box

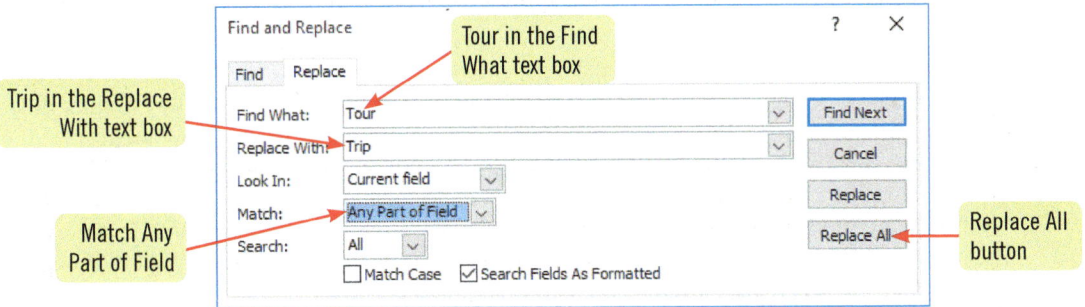

Tour in the Find What text box

Trip in the Replace With text box

Match Any Part of Field

Replace All button

FIGURE 2-9: Final TripsByCategory datasheet with new sort orders

Trip replaces Tour in the TripName field

Records with the same Category are further sorted in descending order by the Price field

TABLE 2-1: Sort and Find buttons

name	button	purpose
Ascending		Sorts records based on the selected field in ascending order (0 to 9, A to Z)
Descending		Sorts records based on the selected field in descending order (Z to A, 9 to 0)
Remove Sort		Removes the current sort order
Find		Opens the Find and Replace dialog box to find data
Replace		Opens the Find and Replace dialog box to find and replace data
Go To		Helps you navigate to the first, previous, next, last, or new record
Select		Helps you select a single record or all records in a datasheet

Filter Data

Filtering a table or query datasheet temporarily displays only those records that match given criteria. Recall that criteria are limiting conditions you set. For example, you might want to show only trips in the state of Missouri, or only trips with a duration of fewer than 14 days. Although filters provide a quick and easy way to display a temporary subset of records in the current datasheet, they are not as powerful or flexible as queries. Most important, a query is a saved object within the database, whereas filters are temporary. Access removes all filters when you close the datasheet. **TABLE 2-2** compares filters and queries. **CASE** *Julia asks you to find all Family trips offered in the month of August. You can filter the Trips table datasheet to provide this information.*

STEPS

1. **Double-click the Trips table to open it, click any occurrence of Family in the Category field, click the Selection button in the Sort & Filter group on the Home tab, then click Equals "Family"**

   Six records are selected as shown in **FIGURE 2-10**. A filter icon appears to the right of the Category field. Filtering by the selected field value, called **Filter By Selection**, is a fast and easy way to filter the records for an exact match. To filter for comparative data (for example, where TripStartDate is equal to or greater than 7/1/2017), you must use the **Filter By Form** feature. Filter buttons are summarized in **TABLE 2-3**.

2. **Click the Advanced button in the Sort & Filter group, then click Filter By Form**

   The Filter by Form window opens. The previous Filter By Selection criterion, "Family" in the Category field, is still in the grid. Access places "quotation marks" around text criteria.

3. **Click the TripStartDate cell, then type 8/*/2017 as shown in FIGURE 2-11**

   Filter By Form also allows you to apply two or more criteria at the same time. An asterisk (*) in the day position of the date criterion works as a wildcard, selecting any date in the month of August in the year 2017.

4. **Click the Toggle Filter button in the Sort & Filter group**

   The datasheet selects one record that matches both filter criteria, as shown in **FIGURE 2-12**. Note that filter icons appear next to the TripStartDate and Category field names as both fields are involved in the filter.

5. **Close the Trips datasheet, then click Yes when prompted to save the changes**

   Saving changes to the datasheet saves the last sort order and column width changes. *Filters are not saved.*

Using wildcard characters

To search for a pattern, you can use a **wildcard** character to represent any character in the condition entry. Use a question mark (?) to search for any single character and an asterisk (*) to search for any number of characters. Wildcard characters are often used with the **Like** operator. For example, the criterion Like "12/*/17" would find all dates in December of 2017, and the criterion Like "F*" would find all entries that start with the letter F.

FIGURE 2-10: Filtering the Trips table

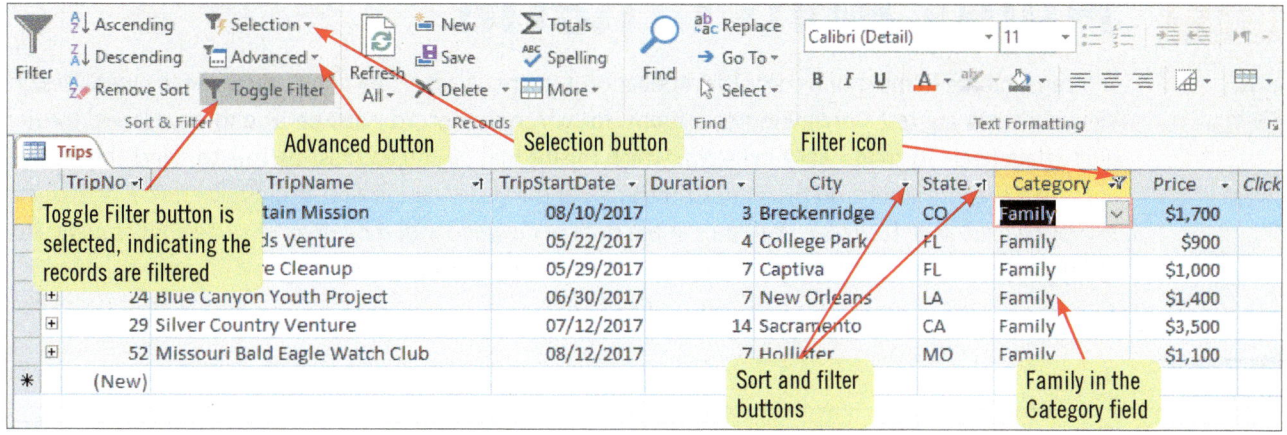

FIGURE 2-11: Filtering by Form criteria

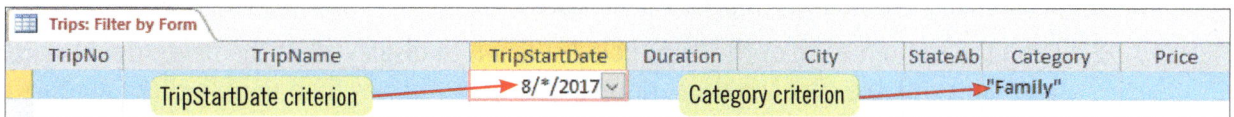

FIGURE 2-12: Results of filtering by form

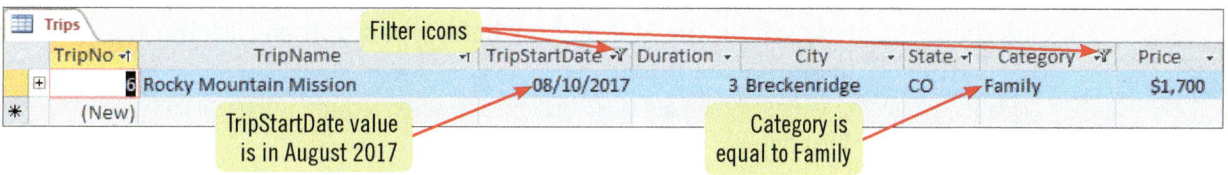

TABLE 2-2: Filters vs. queries

characteristics	filters	queries
Are saved as an object in the database		•
Can be used to select a subset of records in a datasheet	•	•
Can be used to select a subset of fields in a datasheet		•
Resulting datasheet used to enter and edit data	•	•
Resulting datasheet used to sort, filter, and find records	•	•
Commonly used as the source of data for a form or report		•
Can calculate sums, averages, counts, and other types of summary statistics across records		•
Can be used to create calculated fields		•

TABLE 2-3: Filter buttons

name	button	purpose
Filter		Provides a list of values in the selected field that can be used to customize a filter
Selection		Filters records that equal, do not equal, or are otherwise compared with the current value
Advanced		Provides advanced filter features such as Filter By Form, Save As Query, and Clear All Filters
Toggle Filter		Applies or removes the current filter

Apply AND Criteria

You can limit the number of records that appear on a query datasheet by entering criteria in Query Design View. **Criteria** are tests, or limiting conditions, for which the record must be true to be selected for the query datasheet. To create **AND criteria**, which means that *all* criteria must be true to select the record, enter two or more criteria on the *same* Criteria row of the query design grid. **CASE** *Julia Rice asks you to provide a list of all Eco (ecological) trips in the state of Colorado with a duration of seven days or more. Use Query Design View to create the query with AND criteria to meet her request.*

STEPS

1. **Click the Create tab on the Ribbon, click the Query Design button, double-click Trips, then click Close in the Show Table dialog box**

   You want four fields from the Trips table in this query.

2. **Drag the bottom edge of the Trips field list down to display all of the fields, double-click TripName, double-click Duration, double-click StateAbbrev, then double-click Category to add these fields to the query grid**

   First add criteria to select only those records in Colorado. Because you are using the StateAbbrev field, you need to use the two-letter state abbreviation for Colorado, CO, as the Criteria entry.

3. **Click the first Criteria cell for the StateAbbrev field, type CO, then click the View button [ ] to display the results**

   Querying for only those trips in the state of Colorado selects seven records. Next, you add criteria to select only the trips in the Eco category.

4. **Click the View button [ ], click the first Criteria cell for the Category field, type Eco, then click the View button [ ] in the Results group**

   Criteria added to the same line of the query design grid are AND criteria. When entered on the same line, each criterion must be true for the record to appear in the resulting datasheet. Querying for both CO and Eco trips narrows the selection to three records. Every time you add AND criteria, you narrow the number of records that are selected because the record must be true for all criteria.

5. **Click the View button [ ], click the first Criteria cell for the Duration field, then type >=7, as shown in FIGURE 2-13**

   Access assists you with **criteria syntax**, rules that specify how to enter criteria. Access automatically adds "quotation marks" around text criteria in Short Text and Long Text fields ("CO" and "Eco") and pound signs (#) around date criteria in Date/Time fields. The criteria in the Number, Currency, and Yes/No fields are not surrounded by any characters. See **TABLE 2-4** for more information about comparison operators such as >= (greater than or equal to).

6. **Click the View button [ ] in the Results group**

   The third AND criterion further narrows the number of records selected to two, as shown in **FIGURE 2-14**.

7. **Click the Save button [ ] on the Quick Access Toolbar, type EcoCO7 as the query name, click OK, then close the query**

   The query is saved with the new name, EcoCO7, as a new object in the R2G-2 database. Criteria entered in Query Design View are permanently saved with the query (as compared to filters in the previous lesson, which are temporary and not saved with the object).

FIGURE 2-13: Query Design View with AND criteria

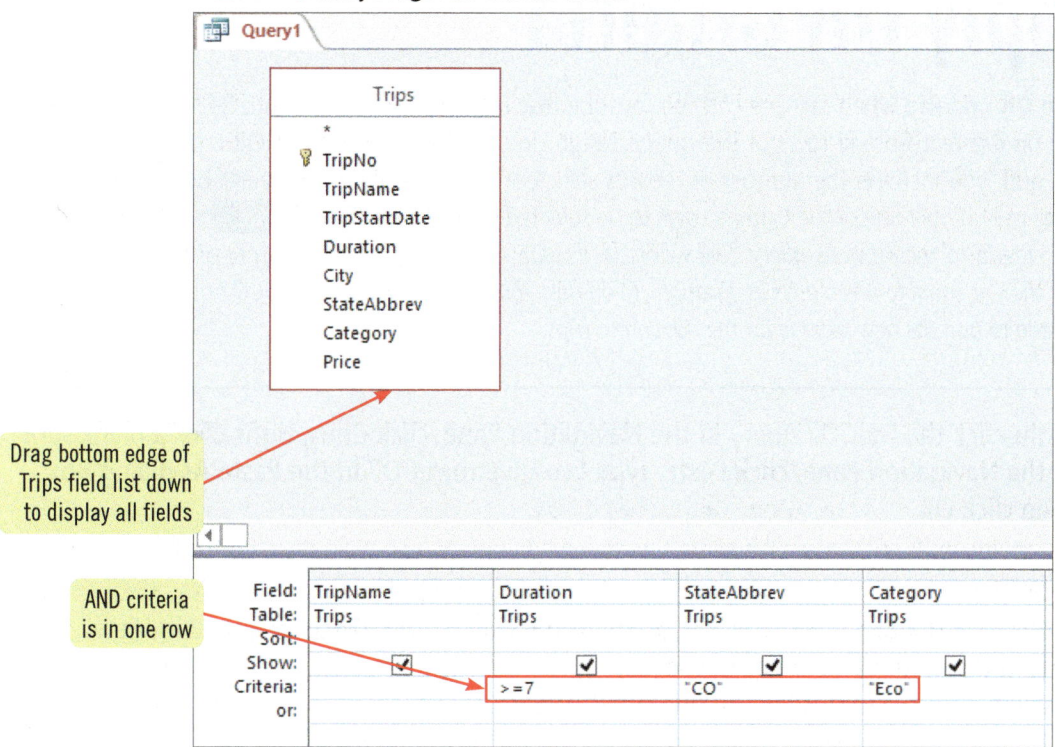

FIGURE 2-14: Final datasheet of EcoCO7 query

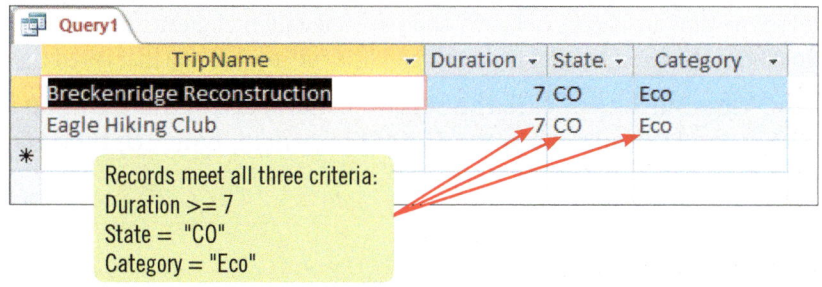

TABLE 2-4: Comparison operators

operator	description	expression	meaning
>	Greater than	>500	Numbers greater than 500
>=	Greater than or equal to	>=500	Numbers greater than or equal to 500
<	Less than	<"Elder"	Names from A to Elder, but not Elder
<=	Less than or equal to	<="Buehler"	Names from A through Buehler, inclusive
<>	Not equal to	<>"Bridgewater"	Any name except for Bridgewater

Searching for blank fields

Is Null and Is Not Null are two other types of common criteria. The **Is Null** criterion finds all records where no entry has been made in the field. **Is Not Null** finds all records where there is any entry in the field, even if the entry is 0. Primary key fields cannot have a null entry.

Apply OR Criteria

Learning Outcomes
- Enter OR criteria in a query
- Rename a query

You use **OR criteria** when *any one criterion* must be true in order for the record to be selected. Enter OR criteria on *different* Criteria rows of the query design grid. As you add rows of OR criteria to the query design grid, you increase the number of records selected for the resulting datasheet because the record needs to match only one of the Criteria rows to be selected for the datasheet. **CASE** *Julia Rice asks you to add criteria to the previous query. She wants to include Adventure trips in the state of Colorado that are greater than or equal to seven days in duration. To do this, you make a copy of the EcoCO7 query to modify with OR criteria to add the new records for the Adventure trips.*

STEPS

1. **Right-click the EcoCO7 query in the Navigation Pane, click Copy, right-click a blank spot in the Navigation Pane, click Paste, type EcoAdventureCO7 in the Paste As dialog box, then click OK**

   By copying the EcoCO7 query before starting your modifications, you avoid changing the EcoCO7 query by mistake.

2. **Right-click the EcoAdventureCO7 query in the Navigation Pane, click Design View, click the second Criteria cell in the Category field, type Adventure, then click the View button [icon] to display the query datasheet**

   The query selected 11 records including all of the trips with Adventure in the Category field. Note that some of the Duration values are less than seven and some of the StateAbbrev values are not CO. Because each row of the query grid is evaluated separately, *all* Adventure trips are selected regardless of criteria in any other row. In other words, the criteria in one row have no effect on the criteria of other rows. To make sure that the Adventure trips are also in Colorado and have a duration of greater than or equal to seven days, you need to modify the second row of the query grid (the "or" row) to add that criteria.

3. **Click the View button [icon], click the second Criteria cell in the Duration field, type >=7, click the second Criteria cell in the StateAbbrev field, type CO, then click in any other cell of the grid**

   Query Design View should look like **FIGURE 2-15**.

4. **Click the View button [icon]**

   Three records are selected that meet all three criteria as entered in row one or row two of the query grid, as shown in **FIGURE 2-16**.

5. **Right-click the EcoAdventureCO7 query tab, click Close, then click Yes to save and close the query datasheet**

FIGURE 2-15: Query Design View with OR criteria

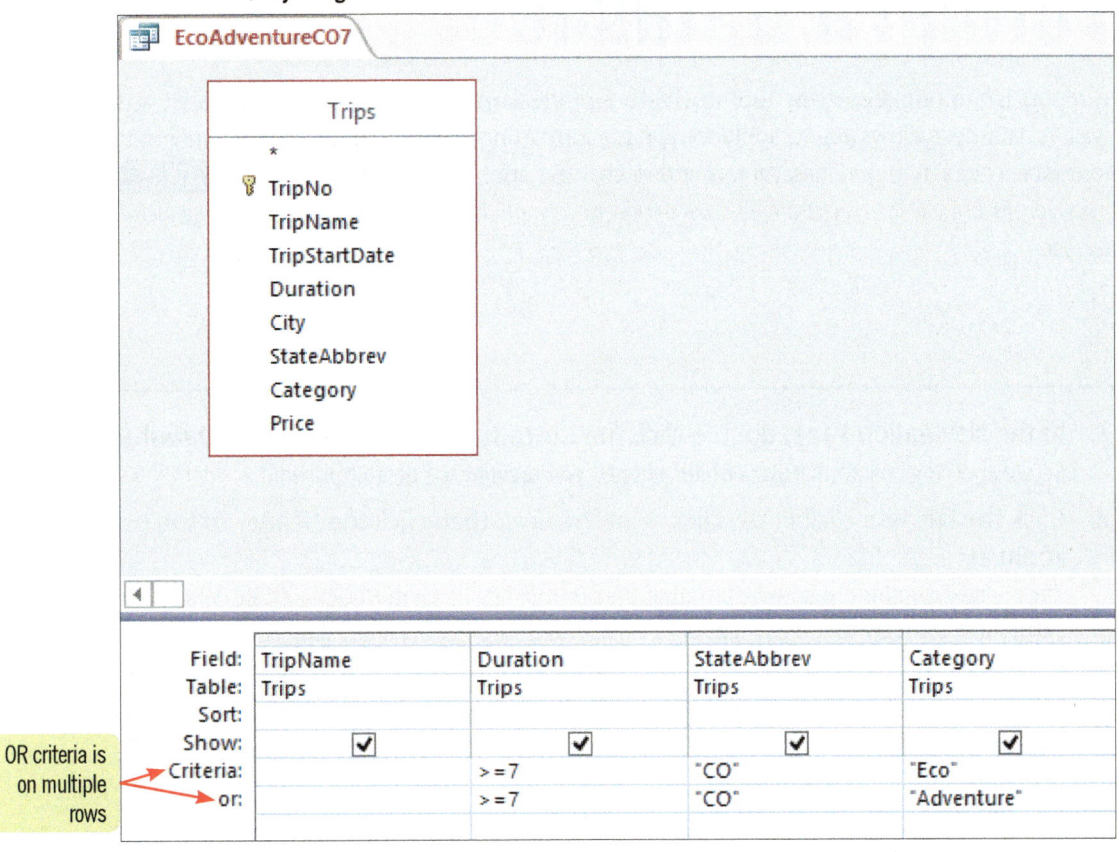

FIGURE 2-16: Final datasheet of EcoAdventureCO7 query

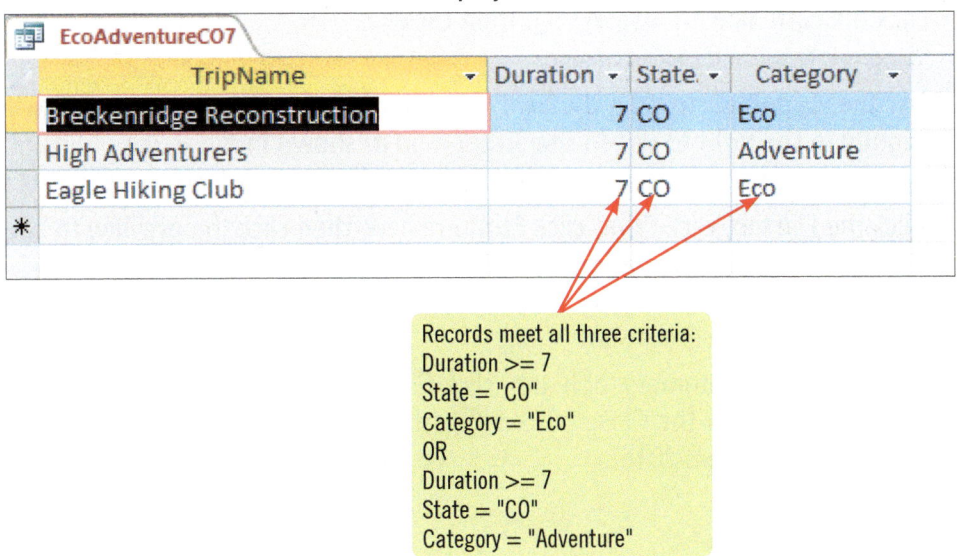

Access 2016

Format a Datasheet

Learning Outcomes
- Zoom in print preview
- Format a datasheet
- Change page orientation

A report is the primary Access tool to create a professional printout, but you can print a datasheet as well. A datasheet allows you to apply some basic formatting modifications such as changing the font size, font face, colors, and gridlines. All formatting changes apply to the entire datasheet. **CASE** *Julia Rice asks you to print a list of customers. You decide to format the Customers table datasheet before printing it for her.*

STEPS

1. **In the Navigation Pane, double-click the Customers table to open it in Datasheet View**
   Before applying new formatting enhancements, you preview the default printout.

2. **Click the File tab, click Print, click Print Preview, then click the header of the printout to zoom in**
   The preview window displays the layout of the printout, as shown in **FIGURE 2-17**. By default, the printout of a datasheet contains the object name and current date in the header. The page number is in the footer.

3. **Click the Next Page button ▶ in the navigation bar to move to the next page of the printout**
   The last two fields, Phone and FirstContact, print on the second page because the first is not wide enough to accommodate them. You decide to switch the report to landscape orientation so that all of the fields print on one page, and then increase the size of the font before printing to make the text easier to read.

4. **Click the Landscape button on the Print Preview tab to switch the report to landscape orientation, then click the Close Print Preview button**
   You return to Datasheet View where you can make font face, font size, font color, gridline color, and background color choices.

5. **Click the Font list arrow** Calibri (Detail) **in the Text Formatting group, click Arial Narrow, click the Font Size list arrow** 11 ▾ **, then click 12**
   You decide to widen the Street column.

6. **Use the ⁺↔ pointer to drag the field separator between the Street and City field names slightly to the right to widen the Street field as shown in FIGURE 2-18**
   Double-clicking the field separators widens the columns as needed to display every entry in those fields.

QUICK TIP
If you need a printout of this datasheet, add your name as a new record to the Customers table, then print it.

7. **Click the File tab, click Print, click Print Preview, then click the preview to zoom in and out to review the information**
   All of the fields now fit across a page in landscape orientation. The preview of the printout is two pages, and in landscape orientation, it is easier to read.

8. **Right-click the Customers table tab, click Close, click Yes when prompted to save changes, then click the Close button ✖ on the title bar to close the R2G-2.accdb database and Access 2016**

FIGURE 2-17: Preview of Customers datasheet

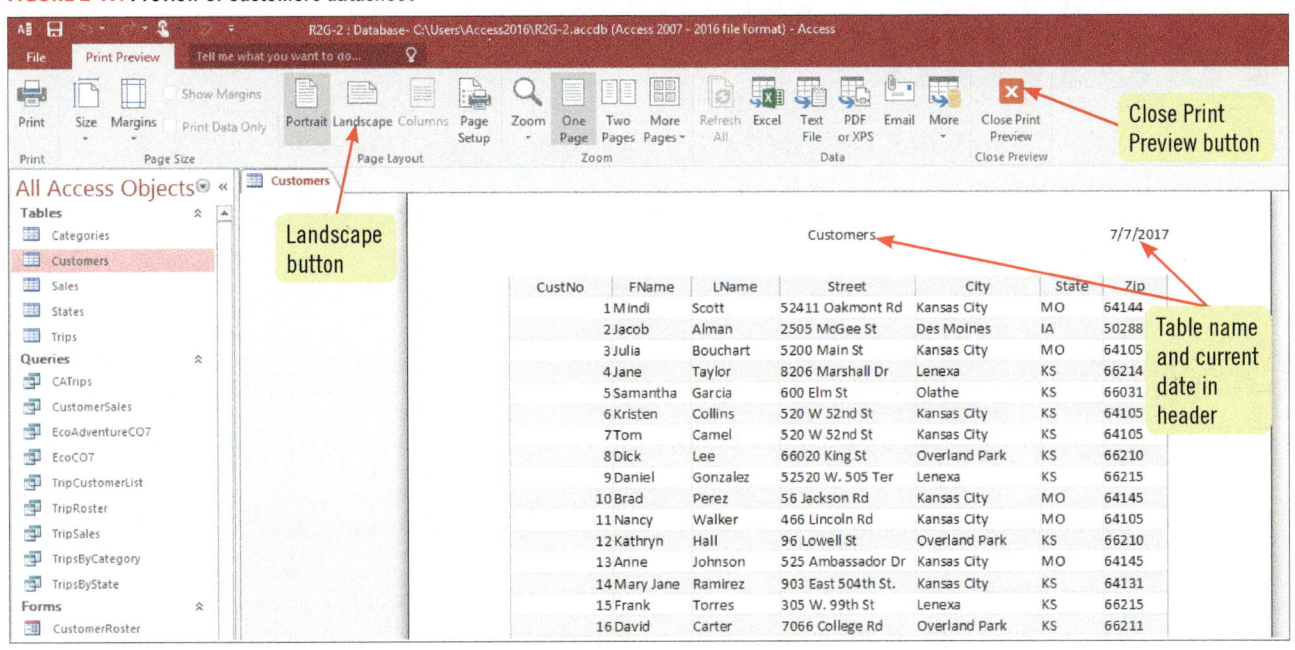

FIGURE 2-18: Formatting the Customers datasheet

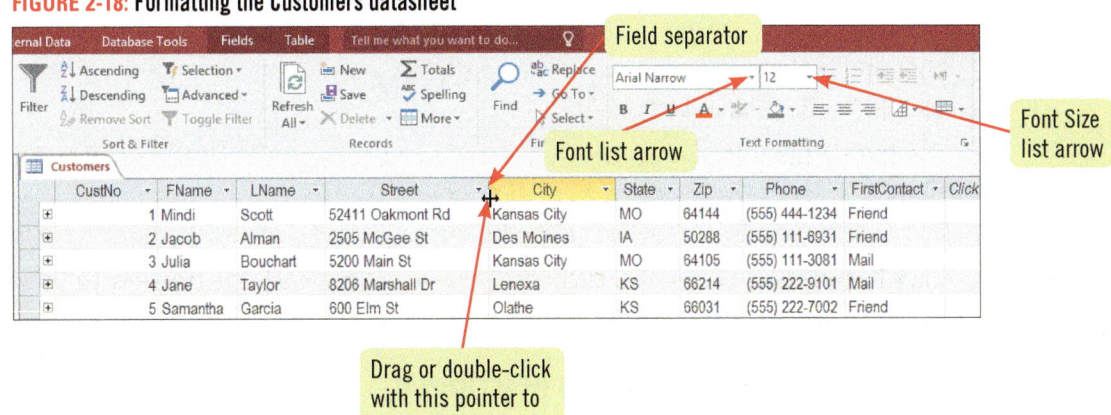

Access 2016

Practice

Concepts Review

Label each element of the Access window shown in FIGURE 2-19.

FIGURE 2-19

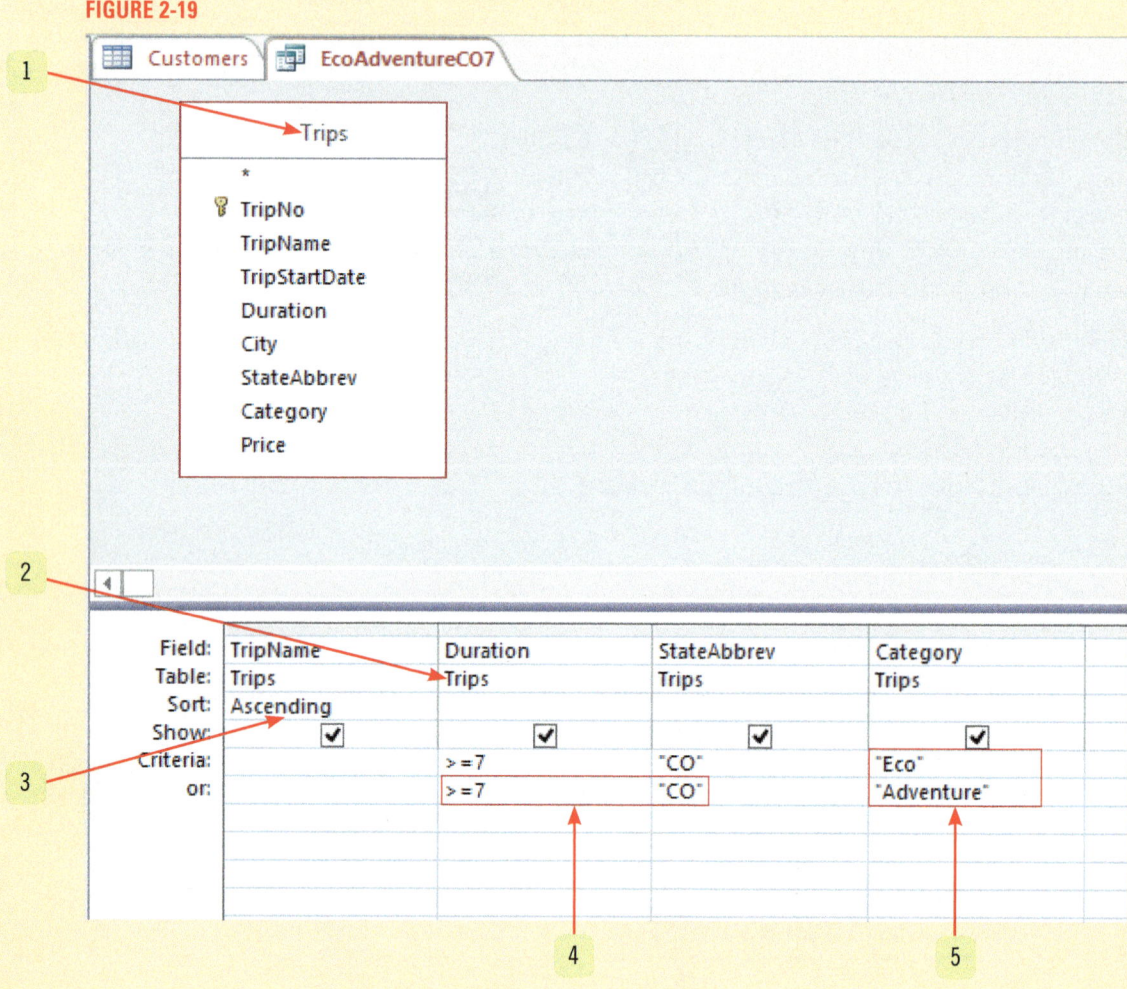

Match each term with the statement that best describes it.

6. **Query grid**   a. Putting records in ascending or descending order based on the values of a field

7. **Field selector**   b. Limiting conditions used to restrict the number of records that are selected in a query

8. **Filter**   c. The thin gray bar above each field in the query grid

9. **Filter By Selection**   d. Creates a temporary subset of records

10. **Field lists**   e. Small windows that display field names

11. **Sorting**   f. Rules that determine how criteria are entered

12. **Join line**   g. Used to search for a pattern of characters

13. **Criteria**   h. The lower pane in Query Design View

14. **Syntax**   i. Identifies which fields are used to establish a relationship between two tables

15. **Wildcard**   j. A fast and easy way to filter the records for an exact match

Select the best answer from the list of choices.

16. AND criteria:
- **a.** determine sort orders.
- **b.** must all be true for the record to be selected.
- **c.** determine fields selected for a query.
- **d.** help set link lines between tables in a query.

17. SQL stands for which of the following?
- **a.** Structured Query Language
- **b.** Standard Query Language
- **c.** Special Query Listing
- **d.** Simple Query Listing

18. A query is sometimes called a logical view of data because:
- **a.** you can create queries with the Logical Query Wizard.
- **b.** queries contain logical criteria.
- **c.** query naming conventions are logical.
- **d.** queries do not store data—they only display a view of data.

19. Which of the following describes OR criteria?
- **a.** Selecting a subset of fields and/or records to view as a datasheet from one or more tables
- **b.** Using two or more rows of the query grid to select only those records that meet given criteria
- **c.** Reorganizing the records in either ascending or descending order based on the contents of one or more fields
- **d.** Using multiple fields in the query design grid

20. Which of the following is *not* true about a query?
- **a.** A query is the same thing as a filter.
- **b.** A query can select fields from one or more tables in a relational database.
- **c.** A query can be created using different tools.
- **d.** An existing query can be modified in Query Design View.

Skills Review

1. **Use the Query Wizard.**
   a. Open the Salvage-2.accdb database from the location where you store your Data Files. Enable content if prompted.
   b. Create a new query using the Simple Query Wizard. Select the CenterName field from the Centers table, the DepositDate and Weight fields from the Deposits table, and the ClubName field from the Clubs table. Select Detail, and enter **CenterDeposits** as the name of the query.
   c. Open the query in Datasheet View, then change any record with the Johnson Recycling value to a center name that includes your last name.

2. **Work with data in a query.**
   a. Delete the first record (A1 Salvage Center with a DepositDate value of 2/4/2014).
   b. Change any occurrence of JavaScript KC in the ClubName field to **Bootstrap Club**.
   c. Click any value in the DepositDate field, then click the Descending button on the Home tab to sort the records in descending order on the DepositDate field.
   d. Use the Calendar Picker to choose the date of **1/30/17** for the first record.
   e. Save and close the CenterDeposits query.

3. **Use Query Design View.**
   a. Click the Create tab, click the Query Design button, double-click Clubs, double-click Deposits, and then click Close to add the Clubs and Deposits tables to Query Design View.
   b. Drag the bottom edge of both field lists down as needed to display all of the field names in both tables.
   c. Add the following fields from the Clubs table to the query design grid in the following order: FName, LName, ClubName. Add the following fields from the Deposits table in the following order: DepositDate, Weight. View the results in Datasheet View, observing the number of records that are selected in the record navigation bar at the bottom of the datasheet.
   d. In Design View, enter criteria to display only those records with a Weight value of **>=100**, then observe the number of records that are selected in Datasheet View.
   e. Save the query with the name **100PlusDeposits**.

4. **Sort and find data.**
   a. In Query Design View of the 100PlusDeposits query, choose an ascending sort order for the ClubName field and a descending sort order for the Weight field.
   b. Display the query in Datasheet View, noting how the records have been resorted.
   c. In the ClubName field, change any occurrence of Boy Scout Troop 324 to Boy Scout Troop **6**.
   d. In the FName field, change any occurrence of Trey to *your* initials and save the query.

5. **Filter data.**
   a. Filter the 100PlusDeposits datasheet for only those records where the ClubName equals **Access Users Group**.
   b. Apply an advanced Filter By Form and use the >= operator to further narrow the records so that only the deposits with a DepositDate value on or after 1/1/2015 are selected.
   c. Apply the filter to see the datasheet and, if requested by your instructor, print the filtered 100PlusDeposits datasheet.
   d. Save and close the 100PlusDeposits query. Reopen the 100PlusDeposits query to confirm that filters are temporary (not saved), and then close the 100PlusDeposits query again.

Skills Review (continued)

6. **Apply AND criteria.**
   a. Right-click the 100PlusDeposits query, copy it, and then paste it as **100PlusDeposits2016**.
   b. Open the 100PlusDeposits2016 query in Query Design View.
   c. Modify the criteria to select all of the records with a DepositDate in **2016** and a Weight value **greater than or equal to 100**. (*Hint*: To select all records with a DepositDate in 2016, use a wildcard character for the month and day positions of the date criterion.)
   d. Display the results in Datasheet View. If requested by your instructor, print the 100PlusDeposits2016 datasheet, then save and close it.

7. **Apply OR criteria.**
   a. Right-click the 100PlusDeposits query, copy it, then paste it as **100PlusDeposits2Clubs**.
   b. Open the 100PlusDeposits2Clubs query in Design View, then add criteria to select the records with a ClubName of **Social Media Club** and a Weight value **greater than or equal to 100**.
   c. Add criteria to also include the records with a ClubName of **Access Users Group** with a Weight value **greater than or equal to 100**. FIGURE 2-20 shows the results.
   d. If requested by your instructor, print the 100PlusDeposits2Clubs datasheet, then save and close it.

FIGURE 2-20

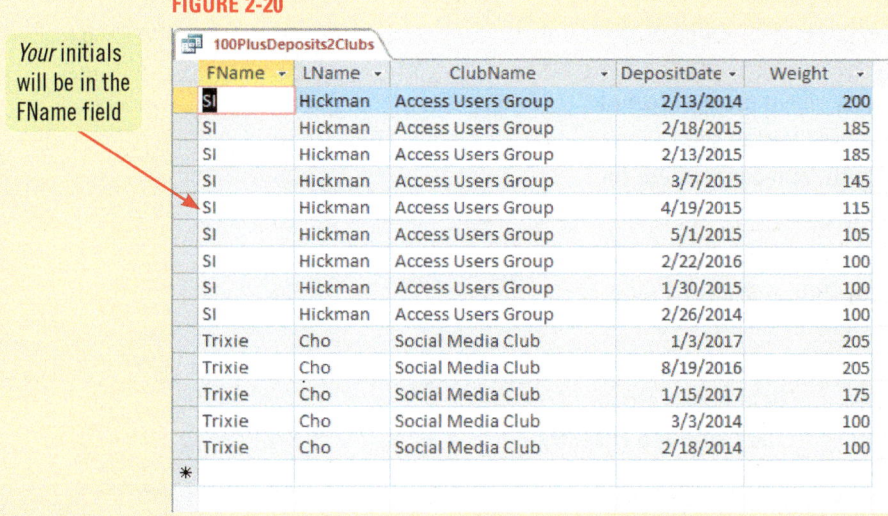

Your initials will be in the FName field

FName	LName	ClubName	DepositDate	Weight
SI	Hickman	Access Users Group	2/13/2014	200
SI	Hickman	Access Users Group	2/18/2015	185
SI	Hickman	Access Users Group	2/13/2015	185
SI	Hickman	Access Users Group	3/7/2015	145
SI	Hickman	Access Users Group	4/19/2015	115
SI	Hickman	Access Users Group	5/1/2015	105
SI	Hickman	Access Users Group	2/22/2016	100
SI	Hickman	Access Users Group	1/30/2015	100
SI	Hickman	Access Users Group	2/26/2014	100
Trixie	Cho	Social Media Club	1/3/2017	205
Trixie	Cho	Social Media Club	8/19/2016	205
Trixie	Cho	Social Media Club	1/15/2017	175
Trixie	Cho	Social Media Club	3/3/2014	100
Trixie	Cho	Social Media Club	2/18/2014	100

8. **Format a datasheet.**
   a. In the Centers table datasheet, apply the Times New Roman font and a 14-point font size.
   b. Resize all columns so that all data and field names are visible.
   c. Display the Centers datasheet in Print Preview, switch the orientation to landscape, click the Margins button in the Page Size group, then click Narrow.
   d. If requested by your instructor, print the Centers datasheet.
   e. Save and close the Centers table, then close Access 2016.

Independent Challenge 1

You have built an Access database to track membership in a community service club. The database tracks member names and addresses as well as their community service hours.

a. Open the Service-2.accdb database from the location where you store your Data Files, enable content if prompted, then open the Activities, Members, and Zips tables to review their datasheets.

b. In the Zips table, click the expand button to the left of the 64111, Kansas City, MO record to display the two members linked to that zip code. Click the expand button to the left of the Jeremiah Hopper record to display the three activity records linked to Jeremiah.

c. Close all three datasheets, click the Database Tools tab, then click the Relationships button. The Relationships window shows you that one record in the Zips table is related to many records in the Members table through the common ZipCode field, and that one record in the Members table is related to many records in the Activities table through the common MemberNo field.

d. Click the Relationship Report button, then if requested by your instructor, print the Relationship report. Close and save the report with the default name **Relationships for Service-2**. Close the Relationships window.

e. Using Query Design View, build a query with the following fields: FirstName and LastName from the Members table and ActivityDate and HoursWorked from the Activities table.

f. View the datasheet, observe the number of records selected, then return to Query Design View.

g. Add criteria to select only those records where the ActivityDate is in March of 2017.

h. In Query Design View, apply an ascending sort order to the LastName and a descending sort order to the ActivityDate field, then view the datasheet.

i. Change the name Quentin Garden to your name, widen all columns so that all data and field names are visible, and save the query with the name **March2017**, as shown in FIGURE 2-21.

j. If requested by your instructor, print the March2017 datasheet, then close the March2017 query and close Access 2016.

FIGURE 2-21

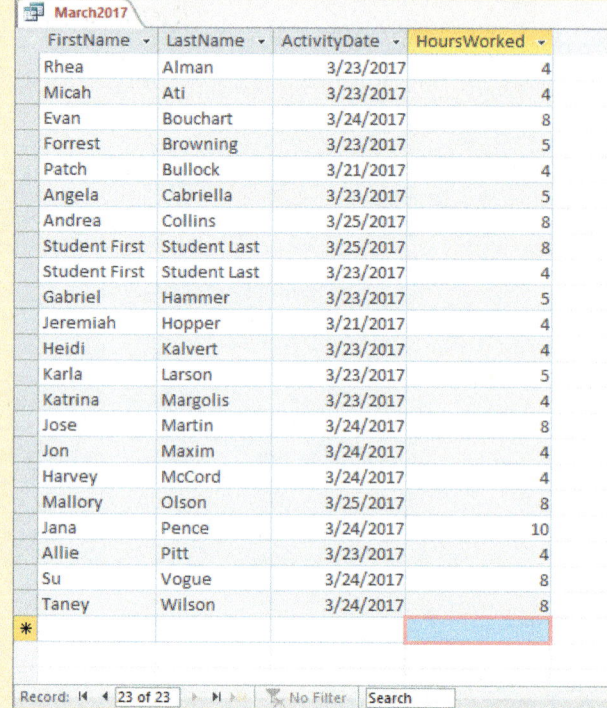

FirstName	LastName	ActivityDate	HoursWorked
Rhea	Alman	3/23/2017	4
Micah	Ati	3/23/2017	4
Evan	Bouchart	3/24/2017	8
Forrest	Browning	3/23/2017	5
Patch	Bullock	3/21/2017	4
Angela	Cabriella	3/23/2017	5
Andrea	Collins	3/25/2017	8
Student First	Student Last	3/25/2017	8
Student First	Student Last	3/23/2017	4
Gabriel	Hammer	3/23/2017	5
Jeremiah	Hopper	3/21/2017	4
Heidi	Kalvert	3/23/2017	4
Karla	Larson	3/23/2017	5
Katrina	Margolis	3/23/2017	4
Jose	Martin	3/24/2017	8
Jon	Maxim	3/24/2017	4
Harvey	McCord	3/24/2017	4
Mallory	Olson	3/25/2017	8
Jana	Pence	3/24/2017	10
Allie	Pitt	3/23/2017	4
Su	Vogue	3/23/2017	8
Taney	Wilson	3/24/2017	8

Record: 23 of 23   No Filter   Search

Independent Challenge 2

You work for a nonprofit agency that tracks voting patterns. You have developed an Access database with contact information for members of the House of Representatives. The director of the agency has asked you to create several state lists of representatives. You will use queries to extract this information.

a. Open the HouseOfReps-2.accdb database from the location where you store your Data Files, then enable content if prompted.

b. Open the Representatives and the States tables. Notice that one state is related to many representatives as evidenced by the expand buttons to the left of the records in the States tables.

c. Close both datasheets, then using Query Design View, create a query with the StateAbbrev, StateName, and Capital fields from the States table (in that order) as well as the FName and LName fields from the Representatives table.

d. Sort the records in ascending order on the StateName field, then in ascending order on the LName field.

e. Add criteria to select the representatives from Ohio or Pennsylvania. Use the StateAbbrev field to enter your criteria, using the two-character state abbreviations of **OH** and **PA**.

f. Save the query with the name **OhioAndPenn**, view the results, shown in FIGURE 2-22, then change the last name of Butterfield in the second record to *your* last name. Resize the columns as needed to view all the data and field names.

g. Print the OhioAndPenn datasheet if requested by your instructor, then close it and exit Access 2016.

FIGURE 2-22

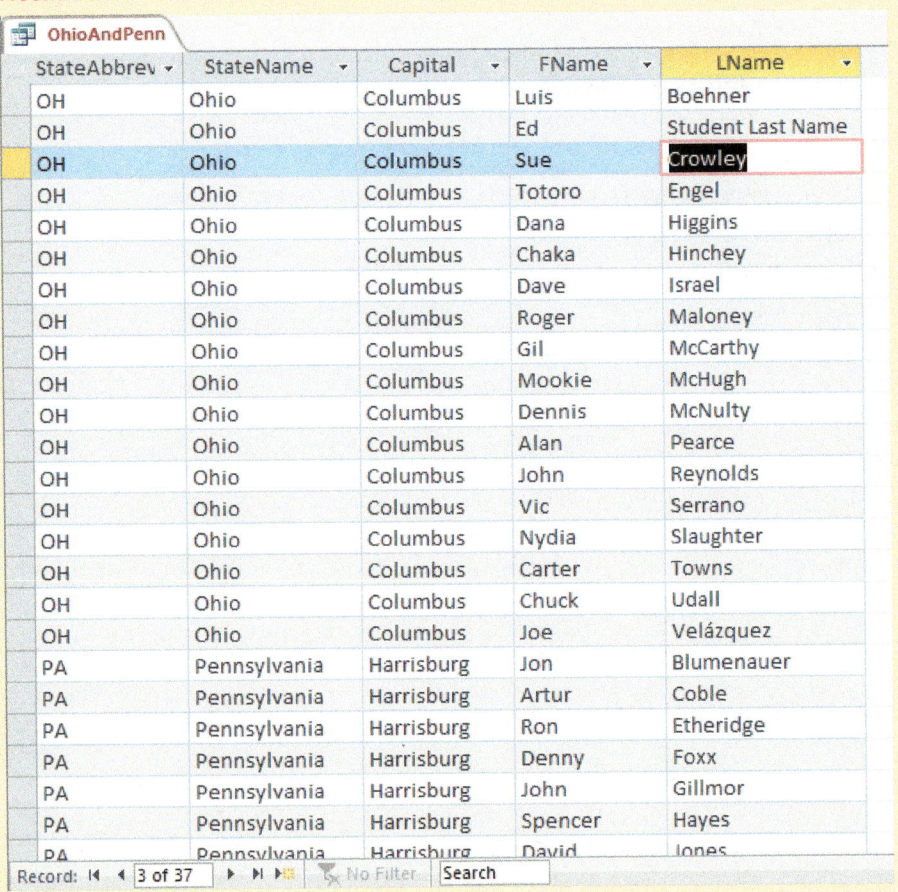

Independent Challenge 3

You have built an Access database to track the veterinarian clinics in your area.

a. Open the VetClinic-2.accdb database from the location where you store your Data Files, then enable content if prompted.

b. Open the Vets table and then the Clinics table to review the data in both datasheets.

c. Click the expand button next to the Animal Haven record in the Clinics table, then add your name as a new record to the Vets subdatasheet.

d. Close both datasheets.

e. Using the Simple Query Wizard, select the VetLast and VetFirst fields from the Vets table, and select the ClinicName and Phone fields from the Clinics table. Title the query **ClinicVetListing**, then view the datasheet.

f. Update any occurrence of Animal Haven in the ClinicName field to **Animal Emergency Shelter**.

g. In Query Design View, add criteria to select only **Animal Emergency Shelter** or **Veterinary Specialists** in the ClinicName field, then view the datasheet.

h. In Query Design View, move the ClinicName field to the first column, then add an ascending sort order on the ClinicName and VetLast fields.

i. Display the ClinicVetListing query in Datasheet View, resize the fields as shown in FIGURE 2-23, then print the datasheet if requested by your instructor.

j. Save and close the ClinicVetListing datasheet, then exit Access 2016.

FIGURE 2-23

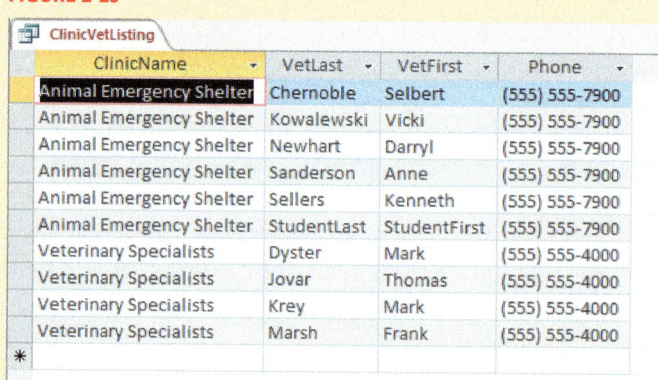

ClinicName	VetLast	VetFirst	Phone
Animal Emergency Shelter	Chernoble	Selbert	(555) 555-7900
Animal Emergency Shelter	Kowalewski	Vicki	(555) 555-7900
Animal Emergency Shelter	Newhart	Darryl	(555) 555-7900
Animal Emergency Shelter	Sanderson	Anne	(555) 555-7900
Animal Emergency Shelter	Sellers	Kenneth	(555) 555-7900
Animal Emergency Shelter	StudentLast	StudentFirst	(555) 555-7900
Veterinary Specialists	Dyster	Mark	(555) 555-4000
Veterinary Specialists	Jovar	Thomas	(555) 555-4000
Veterinary Specialists	Krey	Mark	(555) 555-4000
Veterinary Specialists	Marsh	Frank	(555) 555-4000

Independent Challenge 4: Explore

An Access database is an excellent tool to help record and track job opportunities. For this exercise, you'll create a database from scratch that you can use to enter, edit, and query data in pursuit of a new job or career.

a. Create a new desktop database named **Jobs.accdb**.

b. Create a table named **Positions** with the following field names, data types, and descriptions:

Field name	Data type	Description
PositionID	AutoNumber	Primary key field
Title	Short Text	Title of position such as Accountant, Assistant Court Clerk, or Web Developer
CareerArea	Short Text	Area of the career field such as Accounting, Government, or Information Systems
AnnualSalary	Currency	Annual salary
Desirability	Number	Desirability rating of 1 = low to 5 = high to show how desirable the position is to you
EmployerID	Number	Foreign key field to the Employers table

c. Create a table named **Employers** with the following field names, data types, and descriptions:

Field name	Data type	Description
EmployerID	AutoNumber	Primary key field
CompanyName	Short Text	Company name of the employer
EmpStreet	Short Text	Employer's street address
EmpCity	Short Text	Employer's city
EmpState	Short Text	Employer's state
EmpZip	Short Text	Employer's zip code
EmpPhone	Short Text	Employer's phone, such as 111-222-3333

d. Be sure to set EmployerID as the primary key field in the Employers table and the PositionID as the primary key field in the Positions table.

e. Link the Employers and Positions tables together in a one-to-many relationship using the common EmployerID field. One employer record will be linked to many position records. Be sure to enforce referential integrity.

f. Using any valid source of potential employer data, enter five records into the Employers table.

g. Using any valid source of job information, enter five records into the Positions table by using the subdatasheets from within the Employers datasheet.

Because one employer may have many positions, all five of your Positions records may be linked to the same employer, you may have one position record per employer, or any other combination.

h. Build a query that selects CompanyName from the Employers table, and the Title, CareerArea, AnnualSalary, and Desirability fields from the Positions table. Sort the records in descending order based on Desirability. Save the query as **JobList**, and print it if requested by your instructor.

i. Close the JobList datasheet, then exit Access 2016.

Visual Workshop

Open the Baseball-2.accdb database from the location where you store your Data Files, and enable content if prompted. Create a query in Query Design View based on the Players and Teams tables, as shown in **FIGURE 2-24**. Add criteria to select only those records where the PlayerPosition field values are equal to 1 or 2 (representing pitchers and catchers). In Query Design View, set an ascending sort order on the TeamName and PlayerPosition fields. In the results, change the name of Aaron Campanella to your name. Save the query with the name **PitchersAndCatchers**, then compare the results with **FIGURE 2-24**, making changes and widening columns to display all of the data. Print the datasheet if requested by your instructor. Save and close the query and the Baseball-2.accdb database, then exit Access 2016.

FIGURE 2-24

PitchersAndCatchers			
TeamName	PlayerFirst	PlayerLast	Positi
Brooklyn Beetles	Student First	Student Last	1
Brooklyn Beetles	Cy	Young	2
Mayfair Monarchs	Luis	Durocher	1
Mayfair Monarchs	Carl	Mathewson	2
Rocky's Rockets	Andrew	Spalding	1
Rocky's Rockets	Sanford	Koufax	2
Snapping Turtles	Charles	Ford	1
Snapping Turtles	Greg	Perry	2

Using Forms

CASE Julia Rice, a trip developer at Reason 2 Go, asks you to create forms to make trip information easier to access, enter, and update.

Module Objectives

After completing this module, you will be able to:

- Use the Form Wizard
- Create a split form
- Use Form Layout View
- Add fields to a form

- Modify form controls
- Create calculations
- Modify tab order
- Insert an image

Files You Will Need

R2G-3.accdb

R2GLogo.jpg

LakeHomes-3.accdb

LakeHome.jpg

Scuba-3.accdb

Service-3.accdb

Salvage-3.accdb

Jobs-3.accdb

Baseball-3.accdb

Use the Form Wizard

Learning Outcomes
- Create a form with the Form Wizard
- Sort data in a form
- Describe form terminology and views

A **form** is an easy-to-use data entry and navigation screen. A form allows you to arrange the fields of a record in any layout so a database **user** can quickly and easily find, enter, edit, and analyze data. The database **designer** or **application developer** is the person responsible for building and maintaining tables, queries, forms, and reports for all of the users. **CASE** ▶ *Julia Rice asks you to build a form to enter and maintain trip information.*

STEPS

1. **Start Access, open the R2G-3.accdb database from the location where you store your Data Files, then enable content if prompted**

   You can use many methods to create a new form, but the Form Wizard is a fast and popular tool that helps you get started. The **Form Wizard** prompts you for information it needs to create a form, such as the fields, layout, and title for the form.

2. **Click the Create tab on the Ribbon, then click the Form Wizard button in the Forms group**

   The Form Wizard starts, prompting you to select the fields for this form. You want to create a form to enter and update data in the Trips table.

3. **Click the Tables/Queries list arrow, click Table: Trips, then click the Select All Fields button** `>>`

   You could now select fields from other tables, if necessary, but in this case, you have all of the fields you need.

4. **Click Next, click the Columnar option button, click Next, type Trips Entry Form as the title, then click Finish**

   The Trips Entry Form opens in **Form View**, as shown in **FIGURE 3-1**. Access provides three different views of forms, as summarized in **TABLE 3-1**. Each item on the form is called a **control**. A **label control** is used to describe the data shown in other controls such as text boxes. A label is also used for the title of the form, Trips Entry Form. A **text box** is used to display the data as well as enter, edit, find, sort, and filter the data. A **combo box** is a combination of two controls: a text box and a list. The Category data is displayed in a combo box control. You click the arrow button on a combo box control to display a list of values, or you can edit data directly in the combo box itself.

QUICK TIP
Click in the text box of the field you want to sort before clicking a sort button.

5. **Click Stanley Bay Cleanup in the TripName text box, click the Ascending button in the Sort & Filter group, then click the Next record button** ▶ **in the navigation bar to move to the second record**

   The Bass Habitat Project trip is the second record when the records are sorted in ascending order on the TripName data. Information about the current record number and total number of records appears in the navigation bar, just as it does in a datasheet.

6. **Click the Previous record button** ◀ **in the navigation bar to move back to the first record, click the TripName text box, then change American Legacy Project to American Heritage Project**

   Your screen should look like **FIGURE 3-2**. Forms displayed in Form View are the primary tool for database users to enter, edit, and delete data in an Access database.

7. **Right-click the Trips Entry Form tab, then click Close**

   When a form is closed, Access automatically saves any edits made to the current record.

FIGURE 3-1: Trips Entry Form in Form View

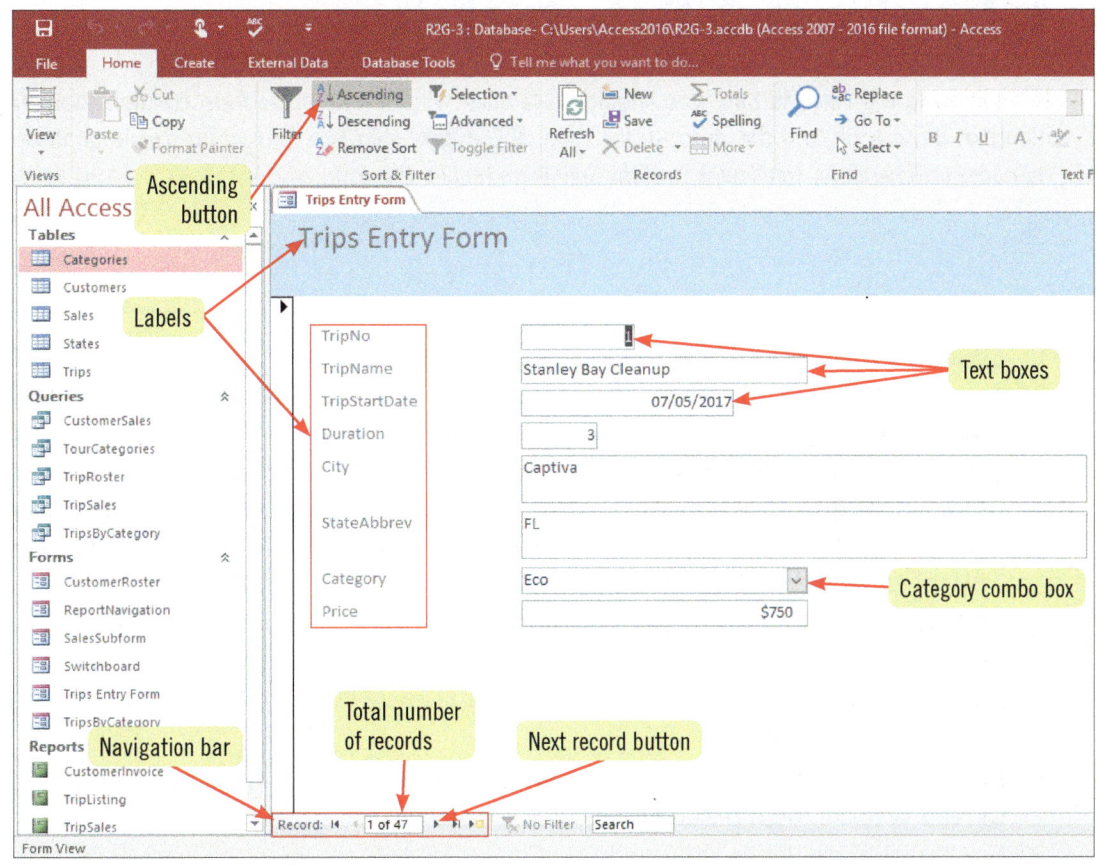

FIGURE 3-2: Editing data in Form View

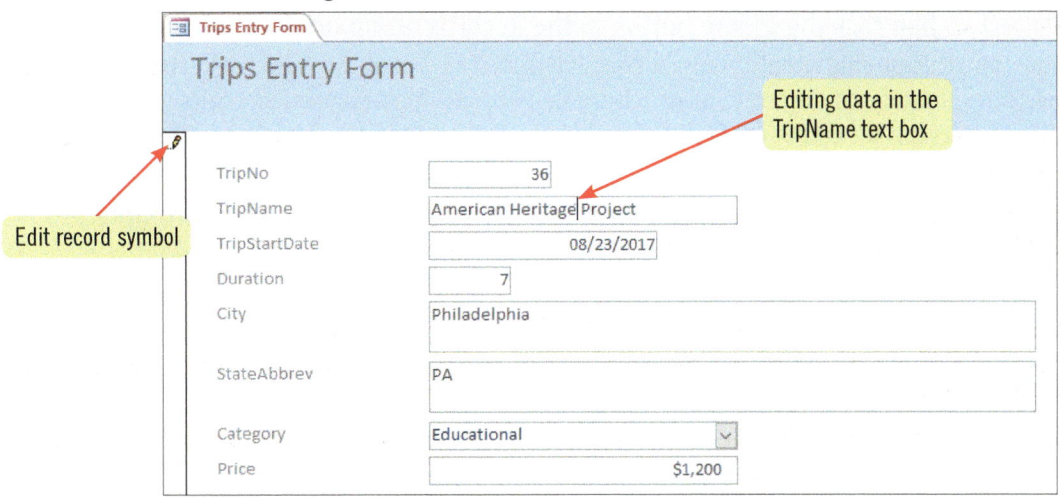

TABLE 3-1: Form views

view	primary purpose
Form	To find, sort, enter, and edit data
Layout	To modify the size, position, or formatting of controls; shows data as you modify the form, making it the tool of choice when you want to change the appearance and usability of the form while viewing data
Design	To modify the Form Header, Detail, and Footer section, or to access the complete range of controls and form properties; Design View does not display data

Create a Split Form

Learning
Outcomes
• Create a split form
• Enter and edit
data in a form

In addition to the Form Wizard, you should be familiar with several other form creation tools. **TABLE 3-2** identifies those tools and the purpose for each. **CASE** *Julia Rice asks you to create another form to manage customer data. You'll work with the Split Form tool for this task.*

STEPS

QUICK TIP
Layout View allows you to view and filter the data, but not edit it.

1. **Click the Customers table in the Navigation Pane, click the Create tab, click the More Forms button, click Split Form, then click the Add Existing Fields button in the Tools group on the Design tab to close the Field List if it opens**

   The Customers data appears in a split form with the top half in **Layout View**. The benefit of a **split form** is that the upper pane allows you to display the fields of one record in any arrangement, and the lower pane maintains a datasheet view of the first few records. If you edit, sort, or filter records in the upper pane, the lower pane is automatically updated, and vice versa.

2. **Click MO in the State text box in the upper pane, click the Home tab, click the Selection button in the Sort & Filter group, then click Does Not Equal "MO"**

   Thirty-seven records are filtered where the State field is not equal to MO. You also need to change a value in the Jacob Alman record.

TROUBLE
Make sure you edit the record in the datasheet in the lower pane.

3. **In the lower pane, select Des Moines in the City field of the first record, edit the entry to read Waukee, then press [Enter]**

   Note that "Waukee" is now the entry in the City field in both the upper and lower panes, as shown in **FIGURE 3-3**.

4. **Click the record selector for the Kristen Collins record in the lower pane as shown in FIGURE 3-4, then click the Delete button in the Records group on the Home tab**

   You cannot delete this record because it contains related records in the Sales table. This is a benefit of referential integrity on the one-to-many relationship between the Customers and Sales tables. Referential integrity prevents the creation of **orphan records**, records on the many side of a relationship that do not have a match on the one side.

5. **Click OK, right-click the Customers form tab, click Close, click Yes when prompted to save changes, then click OK to save the form with Customers as the name**

TABLE 3-2: Form creation tools

tool	icon	creates a form
Form		with one click based on the selected table or query
Form Design		from scratch in Form Design View
Blank Form		from scratch in Form Layout View
Form Wizard		by answering a series of questions provided by the Form Wizard dialog boxes
Navigation		used to navigate or move between different areas of the database
More Forms		based on Multiple Items, Datasheet, Split Form, or Modal Dialog arrangements
Split Form		with two panes, the upper showing one record at a time and the lower displaying a datasheet of many records

FIGURE 3-3: Customers table in a split form

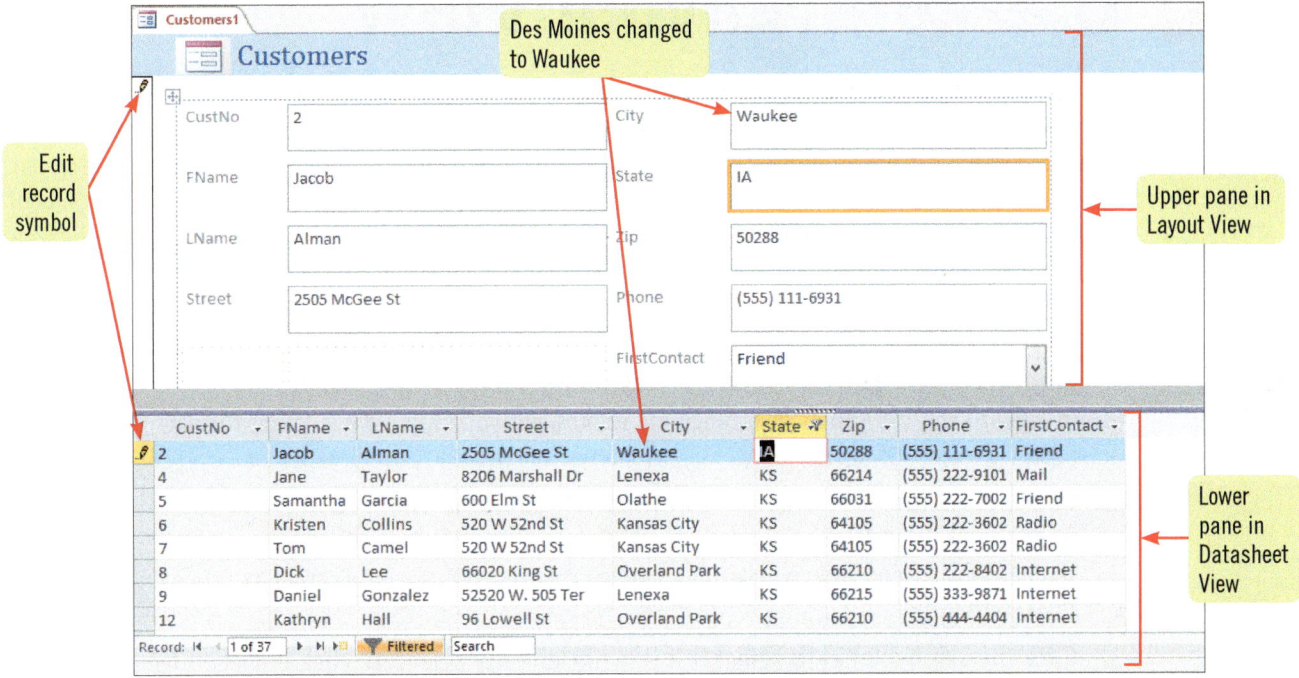

FIGURE 3-4: Editing data in a split form

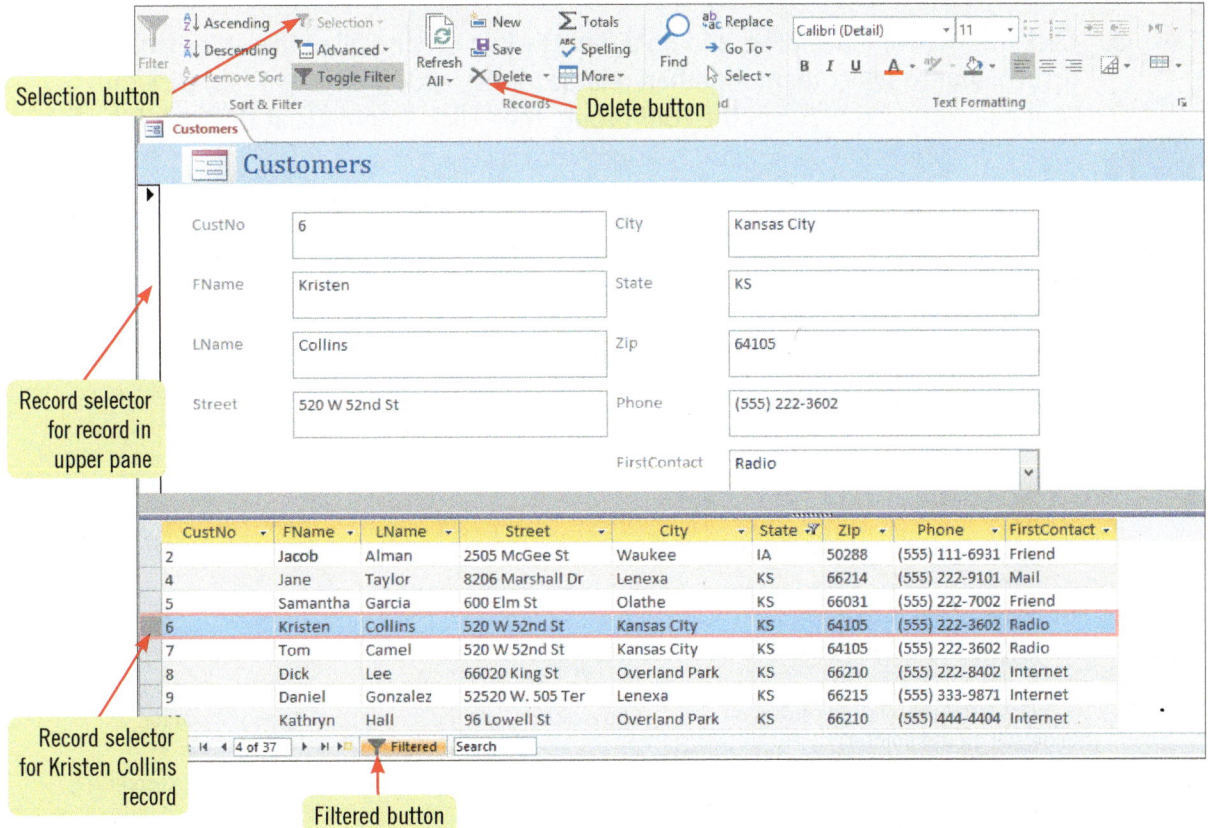

Use Form Layout View

Learning Outcomes
- Resize controls in Layout View
- Format controls in Layout View

Layout View lets you make some design changes to a form while you are browsing the data. For example, you can move and resize controls, add or delete a field on the form, filter and sort data, or change formatting characteristics, such as fonts and colors. **TABLE 3-4** lists several of the most popular formatting commands found on the Format tab when you are working in Layout or Form Design View. **CASE** *Julia Rice asks you to make several design changes to the Trips Entry Form. You can make these changes in Layout View.*

STEPS

1. **Right-click Trips Entry Form in the Navigation Pane, then click Layout View**

   In Layout View, you can move through the records, but you cannot enter or edit the data as you can in Form View.

   TROUBLE
   If your third record is not Bear Valley Adventures, sort the records in ascending order on the TripName field.

2. **Click the Next record button ▶ in the navigation bar twice to move to the third record, Bear Valley Adventures**

   You often use Layout View to make minor design changes, such as editing labels and changing formatting characteristics.

3. **Click the TripNo label to select it if it is not already selected, click between the words Trip and No, then press [Spacebar]**

   You also want to edit a few more labels.

   TROUBLE
   Be sure to modify the labels in the left column instead of the text boxes on the right.

4. **Continue editing the labels, as shown in FIGURE 3-5**

   You also want to change the text color of the labels to black to make them more noticeable.

5. **Click the Trip No label, press and hold [Shift] while clicking all of the other labels in the first column to select them together, release [Shift], click the Format tab, click the Font Color list arrow A ⋅ in the Font group, then click Automatic at the top of the list**

   You also decide to narrow the City and StateAbbrev text boxes.

   TROUBLE
   Be sure to modify the text boxes in the right column instead of the labels on the left.

6. **Click Sacramento in the City text box, press and hold [Shift], click CA in the StateAbbrev text box to select the two text boxes at the same time, release [Shift], then use the ↔ pointer to drag the right edge of the selection to the left to make the text boxes approximately half as wide**

   Layout View for the Trips Entry Form should look like **FIGURE 3-5**. Mouse pointers in Form Layout and Form Design View are very important as they indicate what happens when you drag the mouse. Mouse pointers are described in **TABLE 3-3**.

TABLE 3-3: Mouse pointer shapes

shape	when does this shape appear?	action
▱	When you point to any unselected control on the form (the default mouse pointer)	Single-clicking with this mouse pointer selects a control
✥	When you point to the upper-left corner or edge of a selected control in Form Design View or the middle of the control in Form Layout View	Dragging with this mouse pointer moves the selected control(s)
↕ ↔ ⤢ ⤡	When you point to any sizing handle (except the larger one in the upper-left corner in Form Design View)	Dragging with one of these mouse pointers resizes the control

FIGURE 3-5: Using Layout View to modify controls on the Trips Entry Form

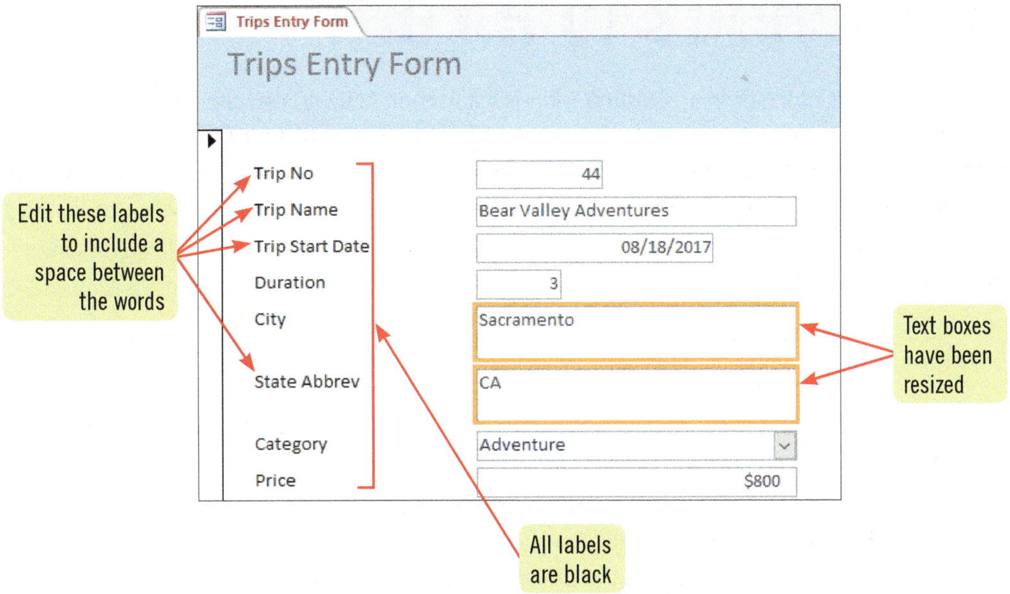

TABLE 3-4: Useful formatting commands

button	button name	description
B	Bold	Toggles bold on or off for the selected control(s)
I	Italic	Toggles italic on or off for the selected control(s)
U	Underline	Toggles underline on or off for the selected control(s)
A	Font Color	Changes the text color of the selected control(s)
	Background Color or Shape Fill	Changes the background color of the selected control(s)
	Align Left	Left-aligns the selected control(s) within its own border
	Center	Centers the selected control(s) within its own border
	Align Right	Right-aligns the selected control(s) within its own border
	Alternate Row Color	Changes the background color of alternate records in the selected section
	Shape Outline	Changes the border color, thickness, or style of the selected control(s)
	Shape Effects	Changes the special visual effect of the selected control(s)

Table layouts

Layouts provide a way to group several controls together on a form or report to more quickly add, delete, rearrange, resize, or align controls. To insert a layout into a form or report, select the controls you want to group together, then choose the Stacked or Tabular button on the Arrange tab in Layout View. Each option applies a table layout to the controls so that you can insert, delete, merge, or split the cells in the layout to quickly rearrange or edit the controls in the layout. To remove a layout, use the Remove Layout button on the Arrange tab in Form Design View.

Access 2016

Add Fields to a Form

Adding and deleting fields in an existing form is a common activity. You can add or delete fields in a form in either Layout View or Design View using the Field List. The **Field List** lists the database tables and the fields they contain. To add a field to the form, drag it from the Field List to the desired location on the form. To delete a field on a form, click the field to select it, then press the [Delete] key. Deleting a field from a form does not delete it from the underlying table or have any effect on the data contained in the field. You can toggle the Field List on and off using the Add Existing Fields button on the Design tab in Layout or Design View. **CASE** ▸ *Julia Rice asks you to add the Trip description from the Categories table to the Trips Entry Form. You can use Layout View and the Field List to accomplish this goal.*

STEPS

TROUBLE
If you don't see the Design tab on the Ribbon, switch to Layout View.

1. **Click the Design tab on the Ribbon, click the Add Existing Fields button in the Tools group, then click the Show all tables link in the Field List**

   The Field List opens in Layout View, as shown in **FIGURE 3-6**. Notice that the Field List is divided into sections. The upper section shows the tables currently used by the form, the middle section shows directly related tables, and the lower section shows other tables in the database. The expand/collapse button to the left of the table names allows you to expand (show) the fields within the table or collapse (hide) them. The Description field is in the Categories table in the middle section.

   To move the Field List, drag its title bar. Double-click the title bar of the Field List to dock it to the right.

TROUBLE
In Design View, adding the Description field creates a text box instead of a combo box.

2. **Click the expand button ➕ to the left of the Categories table, drag the Description field to the form, then use the 🕀 pointer to drag the new Description combo box and label below the Price text box**

   When you add a new field to a form, two controls are usually created: a label and a text box. The label contains the field name and the text box displays the data in the field. The Categories table moved from the middle to the top section of the Field List. You also want to align and format the new controls with others already on the form.

QUICK TIP
If you make a mistake, click the Undo button ↶ and try again.

3. **Click the Description label, click the Format tab on the Ribbon, then click the Font color button ⓐ ▾ to change the text color from gray to black**

   With the new controls in position and formatted, you want to enter a new record. You must switch to Form View to edit, enter, or delete data.

TROUBLE
Your Trip No value might not match **FIGURE 3-7**. As an AutoNumber value, the value is inserted automatically and is controlled by Access.

4. **Click the Home tab, click the View button 🖼 to switch to Form View, click the New (blank) record button ▶* in the navigation bar, click the TripName text box, then enter a new record in the updated form, as shown in FIGURE 3-7**

   Be sure to enter the correct value for each field and note that when you select a value in the Category combo box, the Description is automatically updated. This is due to the one-to-many relationship between the Categories and Trips tables in the Relationships window.

FIGURE 3-6: Field List in Form Layout View

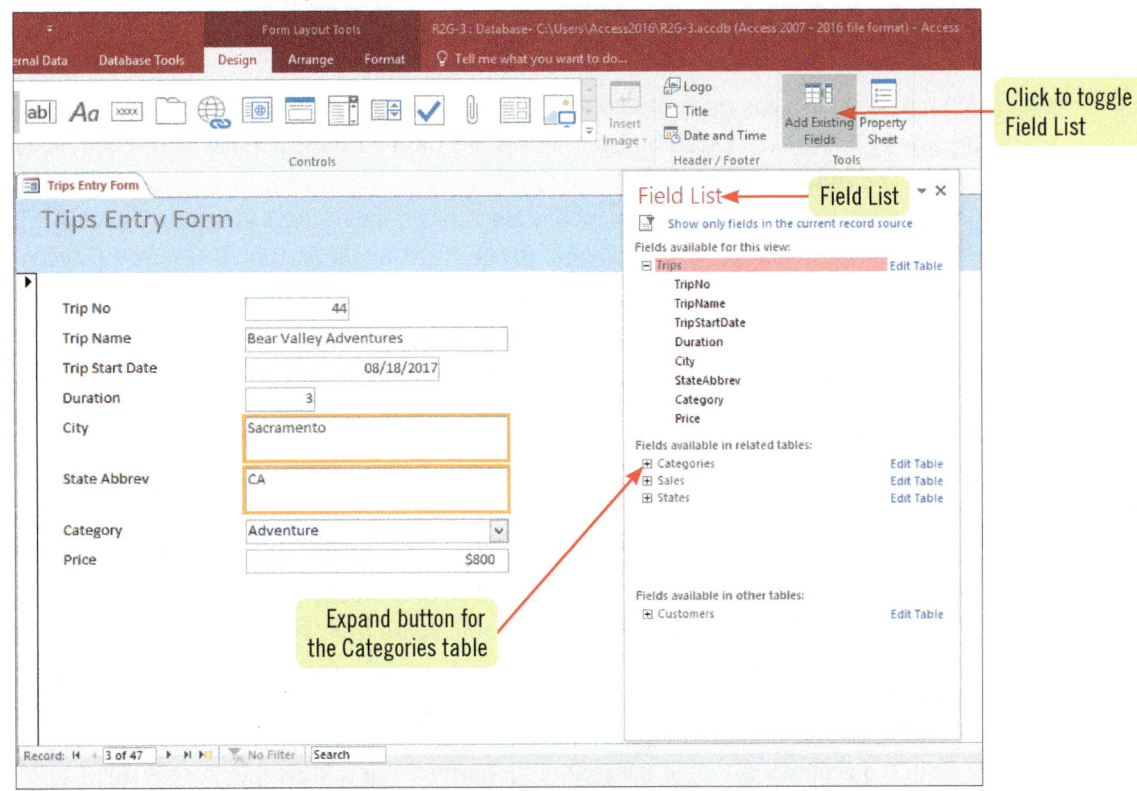

FIGURE 3-7: Entering a record in the updated Trips Entry Form in Form View

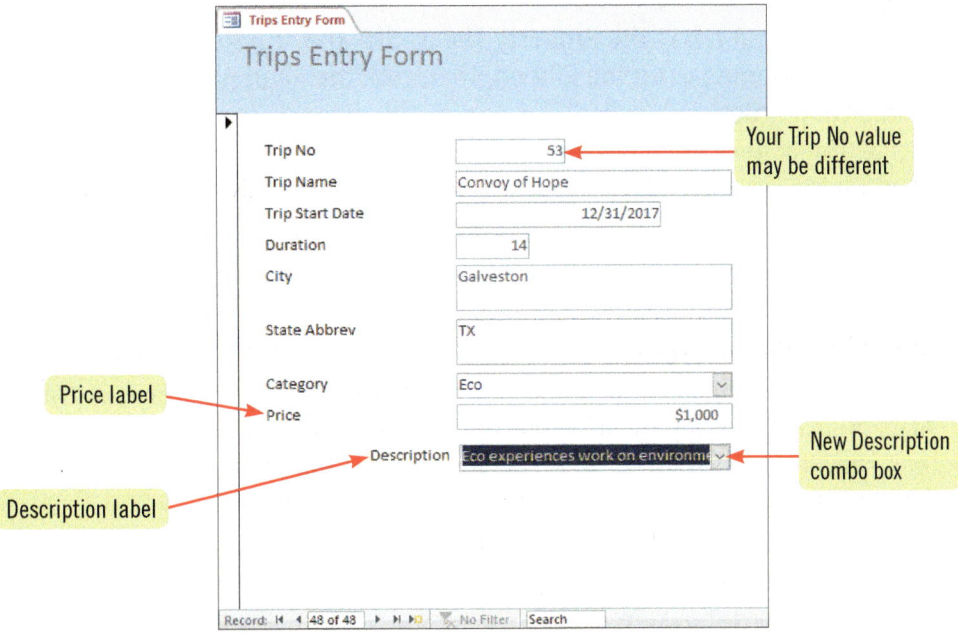

Bound versus unbound controls

Controls are either bound or unbound. **Bound controls** display values from a field such as text boxes and combo boxes. **Unbound controls** do not display data; unbound controls describe data or enhance the appearance of the form. Labels are the most common type of unbound control, but other types include lines, images, tabs, and command buttons. Another way

to distinguish bound from unbound controls is to observe the form as you move from record to record. Because bound controls display data, their contents change as you move through the records, displaying data from the field of the current record. Unbound controls such as labels and lines do not change as you move through the records in a form.

Modify Form Controls

You have already made many modifications to form controls, such as changing the font color of labels and the size of text boxes. Labels and text boxes are the two most popular form controls. Other common controls are listed in **TABLE 3-5**. When you modify controls, you change their **properties** (characteristics). All of the control characteristics you can modify are stored in the control's **Property Sheet.** **CASE** *Because R2G is now focused on Eco (ecological) trips, you decide to use the Property Sheet of the Category field to modify the default value to be "Eco." Julia asks you to use the Property Sheet to make other control modifications to better size and align the controls.*

STEPS

1. **Right-click the Trips Entry Form tab, click Layout View, then click the Property Sheet button in the Tools group**

   The Property Sheet opens, replacing the Field List and showing you all of the properties for the selected item. Drag the title bar of the Property Sheet to move it. Double-click the title bar to dock it to the right.

2. **Click the Category combo box on the form, click the Data tab in the Property Sheet (if it is not already selected), click the Default Value box, type Eco, then press [Enter]**

   The Property Sheet should look like **FIGURE 3-8**. Access often helps you with the **syntax** (rules) of entering property values. In this case, Access added quotation marks around "Eco" to indicate that the default entry is text. Properties are categorized in the Property Sheet with the Format, Data, Event, and Other tabs. The All tab is a complete list of all the control's properties. You can use the Property Sheet to make all control modifications, although you'll probably find that some changes are easier to make using the Ribbon. The property values change in the Property Sheet as you modify a control using the Ribbon and vice versa.

3. **Click the Format tab in the Property Sheet, click the Trip No label in the form to select it, click the Home tab on the Ribbon, then click the Align Right button ≡ in the Text Formatting group**

   Notice that the **Text Align property** on the Format tab in the Property Sheet is automatically updated from Left to Right even though you changed the property using the Ribbon instead of the Property Sheet.

4. **Click the Trip Name label, press and hold [Shift], then click each other label in the first column on the form**

   With all the labels selected, you can modify their Text Align property at the same time.

5. **Click ≡ in the Text Formatting group**

   Don't be overwhelmed by the number of properties available for each control on the form or the number of ways to modify each property. Over time, you will learn about most of these properties. At this point, it's only important to know the purpose of the Property Sheet and understand that properties are modified in various ways.

6. **Click the Save button 🔲 on the Quick Access Toolbar, click the Form View button 🔲 to switch to Form View, click the New (blank) record button ▶⁎ in the navigation bar, then enter the record shown in FIGURE 3-9**

   For new records, "Eco" is provided as the default value for the Category combo box, but you can change it by typing a new value or selecting one from the list. With the labels right-aligned, they are much closer to the data in the text boxes that they describe.

FIGURE 3-8: Using the Property Sheet

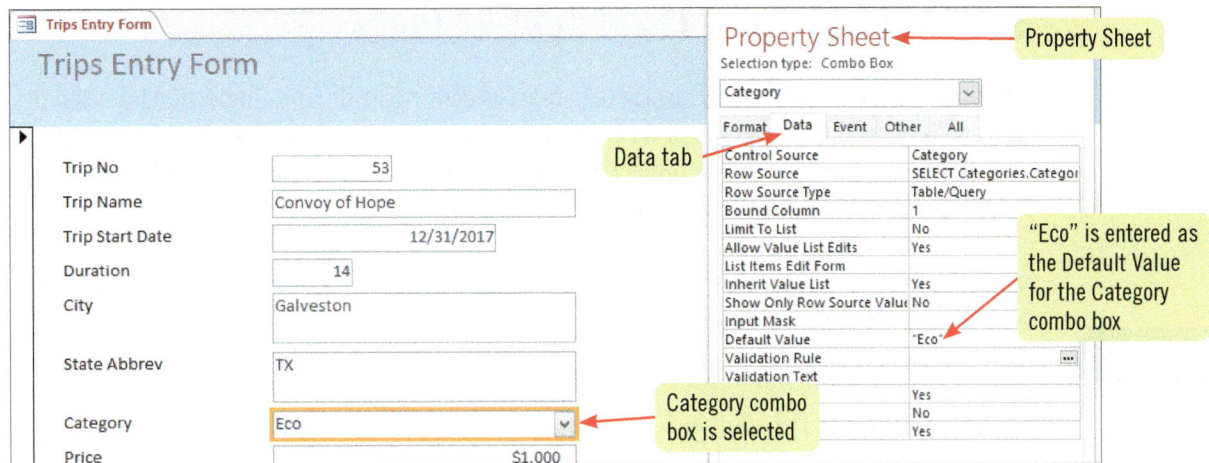

FIGURE 3-9: Modified Trips Entry Form

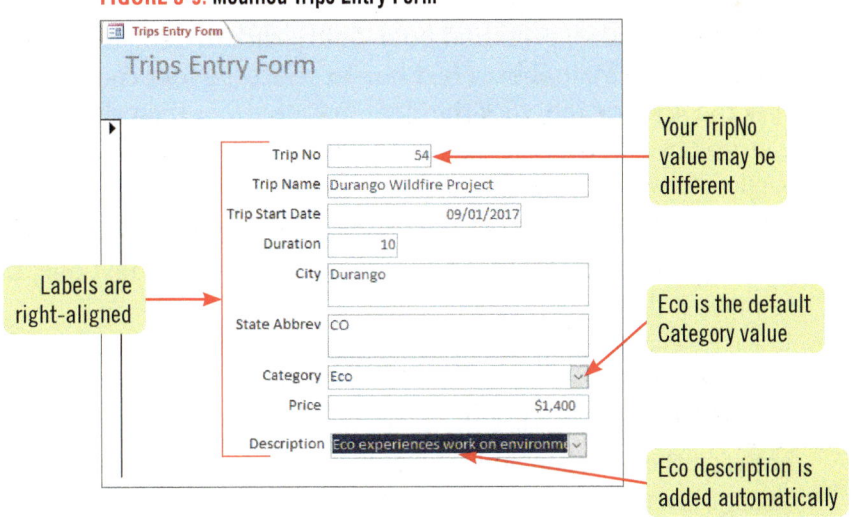

TABLE 3-5: Common form controls

name	used to	bound	unbound
Label	Provide consistent descriptive text as you navigate from record to record; the label is the most common type of unbound control and can also be used as a hyperlink to another database object, external file, or webpage		•
Text box	Display, edit, or enter data for each record from an underlying record source; the text box is the most common type of bound control	•	
List box	Display a list of possible data entries	•	
Combo box	Display a list of possible data entries for a field, and provide a text box for an entry from the keyboard; combines the list box and text box controls	•	
Tab control	Create a three-dimensional aspect on a form		•
Check box	Display "yes" or "no" answers for a field; if the box is checked, it means "yes"	•	
Toggle button	Display "yes" or "no" answers for a field; if the button is pressed, it means "yes"	•	
Option button	Display a choice for a field	•	
Option group	Display and organize choices (usually presented as option buttons) for a field	•	
Line and Rectangle	Draw lines and rectangles on the form		•
Command button	Provide an easy way to initiate a command or run a macro		•

Create Calculations

Text boxes are generally used to display data from underlying fields. The connection between the text box and field is defined by the **Control Source property** on the Data tab of the Property Sheet for that text box. A text box control can also display a calculation. To create a calculation in a text box, you enter an expression instead of a field name in the Control Source property. An **expression** is a combination of field names, operators (such as +, −, /, and *), and functions (such as Sum, Count, or Avg) that results in a single value. Sample expressions are shown in **TABLE 3-6**. **CASE** ▶ *Julia Rice asks you to add a text box to the Trips Entry Form to calculate the trip end date. You can add a text box in Form Design View to accomplish this.*

STEPS

1. **Right-click the Trips Entry Form tab, then click Design View**

   You want to add the trip end date calculation just below the Duration text box. First, you'll resize the City and State Abbrev fields.

2. **Click the City label, press and hold [Shift], click the City text box, click the State Abbrev label, click the StateAbbrev text box to select the four controls together, release [Shift], click the Arrange tab, click the Size/Space button, then click To Shortest**

   With the City and StateAbbrev fields resized, you're ready to move them to make room for the new control to calculate the tour end date.

3. **Click a blank spot on the form to deselect the four controls, click the StateAbbrev text box, use the ⬚ pointer to move it down, click the City text box, then use the ⬚ pointer to move it down**

   To add the calculation to determine the trip end date (the trip start date plus the duration), start by adding a new text box to the form between the Duration and City text boxes.

4. **Click the Design tab, click the Text Box button [ab] in the Controls group, then click between the Duration and City text boxes to insert the new text box**

   Adding a new text box automatically adds a new label to the left of the text box.

5. **Double-click Text23, type Trip End Date, click the Home tab, click the Font Color button [A ▾], then press [Enter]**

   With the label updated to correctly identify the text box to the right, you're ready to enter the expression to calculate the tour end date.

6. **Click the new text box to select it, click the Data tab in the Property Sheet, click the Control Source property, type =[TripStartDate]+[Duration], then press [Enter] to update the form as shown in FIGURE 3-10**

   All expressions entered in a control must start with an equal sign (=). When referencing a field name within an expression, [square brackets]—(not parentheses) and not {curly braces}—surround the field name. In an expression, you must type the field name exactly as it was created in Table Design View, but you do not need to match the capitalization.

7. **Click the View button [▦] to switch to Form View, tab three times to the Duration field, type 5, then press [Enter]**

   Note that the trip end date, calculated by an expression, automatically changed to five days after the trip start date to reflect the new duration value. The updated Trips Entry Form with the trip end date calculation for the Bikers for Ecology is shown in **FIGURE 3-11**.

FIGURE 3-10: Adding a text box to calculate a value

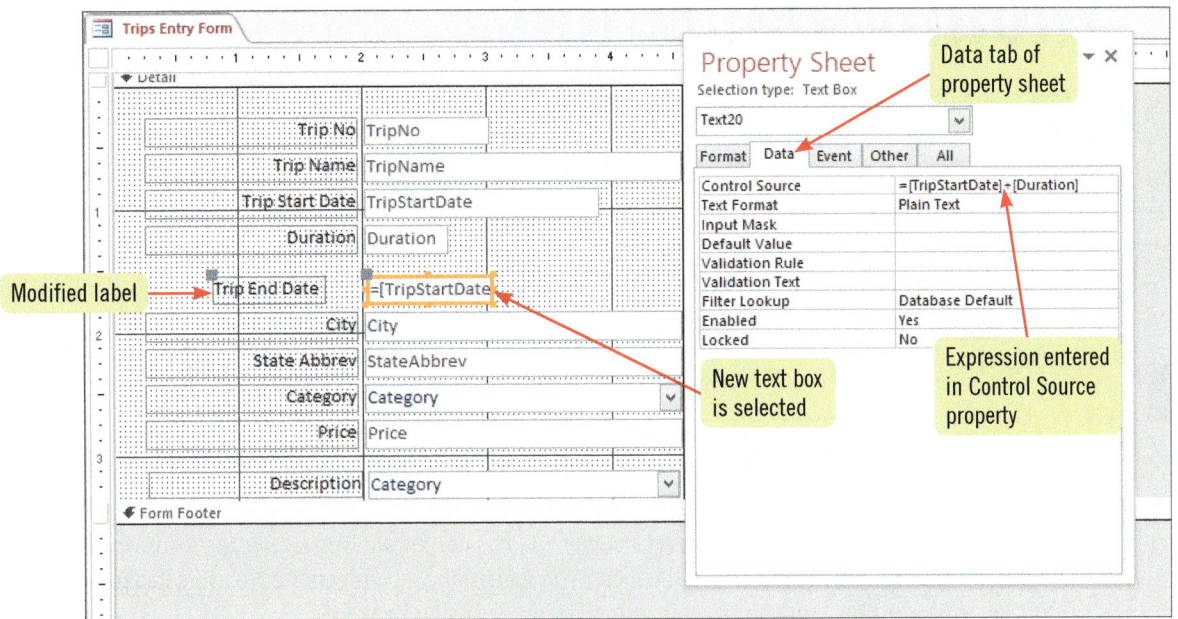

FIGURE 3-11: Displaying the results of a calculation in Form View

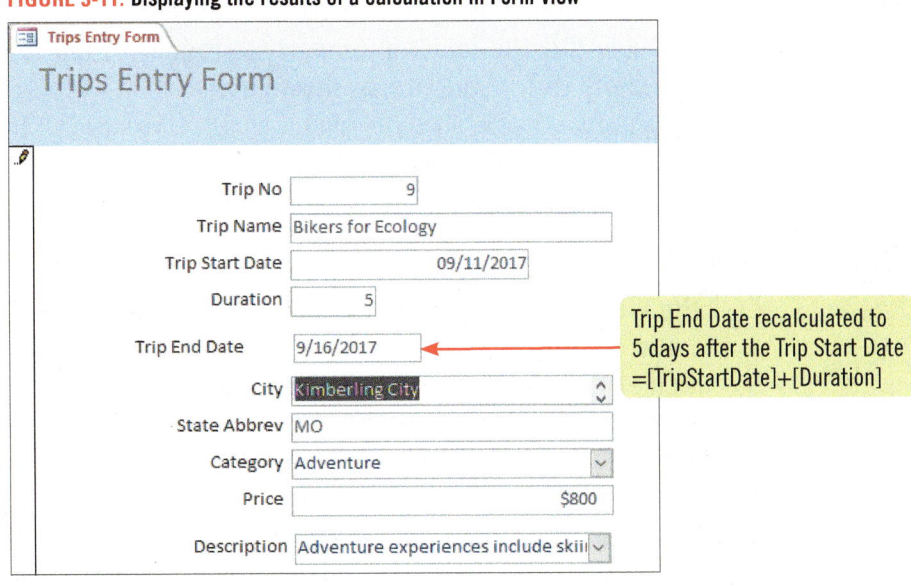

TABLE 3-6: Sample expressions

sample expression	description
=Sum([Salary])	Uses the **Sum** function to add the values in the Salary field
=[Price] * 1.05	Multiplies the Price field by 1.05 (adds 5% to the Price field)
=[Subtotal] + [Shipping]	Adds the value of the Subtotal field to the value of the Shipping field
=Avg([Freight])	Uses the **Avg** function to display an average of the values in the Freight field
=Date()	Uses the **Date** function to display the current date in the form of mm-dd-yy
="Page " &[Page]	Displays the word Page, a space, and the result of the [Page] field, an Access field that contains the current page number
=[FirstName]& " " &[LastName]	Displays the value of the FirstName and LastName fields in one control, separated by a space
=Left([ProductNumber],2)	Uses the **Left** function to display the first two characters in the ProductNumber field

Modify Tab Order

Learning
Outcomes
• Modify tab order
properties

After positioning all of the controls on the form, you should check the tab order and tab stops. **Tab order** is the order the focus moves as you press [Tab] in Form View. A **tab stop** refers to whether a control can receive the focus in the first place. By default, the Tab Stop property for all text boxes and combo boxes is set to Yes, but some text boxes, such as those that contain expressions, will not be used for data entry. Therefore, the Tab Stop property for a text box that contains a calculation should be set to No. Unbound controls such as labels and lines do not have a Tab Stop property because they cannot be used to enter or edit data. **CASE** ▶ *Julia suggests that you check the tab order of the Trips Entry Form, then change tab stops and tab order as necessary.*

STEPS

1. **Press [Tab] enough times to move through several records, watching the focus move through the bound controls of the form**

   Because the Trip End Date text box is a calculated field, you don't want it to receive the focus. To prevent the Trip End Date text box from receiving the focus, you set its Tab Stop property to No using its Property Sheet. You can work with the Property Sheet in either Layout or Design View.

QUICK TIP

You can also switch between views using the View buttons in the lower-right corner of the window.

2. **Right-click the Trips Entry Form tab, click Design View, click the text box with the Trip End Date calculation if it is not already selected, click the Other tab in the Property Sheet, double-click the Tab Stop property to toggle it from Yes to No, then change the Name property to TripEndDate, as shown in FIGURE 3-12**

   The Other tab of the Property Sheet contains the properties you need to change the tab stop and tab order. The **Tab Stop property** determines whether the field accepts focus, and the **Tab Index property** indicates the numeric tab order for all controls on the form that have the Tab Stop property set to Yes. The **Name property** on the Other tab is also important as it identifies the name of the control, which is used in other areas of the database. To review your tab stop changes, return to Form View.

QUICK TIP

In Form Design View, press [Ctrl][.] to switch to Form View. In Form View, press [Ctrl][,] to switch to Form Design View.

3. **Click the View button ▦ to switch to Form View, then press [Tab] nine times to move to the next record**

   Now that the tab stop has been removed from the TripEndDate text box, the tab order flows correctly from the top to the bottom of the form, skipping the calculated field. To review the tab order for the entire form in one dialog box, you must switch to Form Design View.

4. **Right-click the Trips Entry Form tab, click Design View, then click the Tab Order button in the Tools group to open the Tab Order dialog box**

   The Tab Order dialog box allows you to view and change the tab order by dragging fields up or down using the **field selector** to the left of the field name. Moving fields up and down in this list also renumbers the Tab Index property for the controls in their respective Property Sheets. If you want Access to create a top-to-bottom and left-to-right tab order, click **Auto Order**.

TROUBLE

If the order of your fields does not match those in FIGURE 3-13, move a field by clicking the field selector and then dragging the field up or down.

5. **Click the Auto Order button to make sure your tab order goes top to bottom as shown in FIGURE 3-13, click OK to close the Tab Order dialog box, click the Property Sheet button to toggle it off, click the Save button 🔲 on the Quick Access Toolbar to save your work, then click a blank spot on the form to deselect the text box**

FIGURE 3-12: Using the Property Sheet to set tab properties

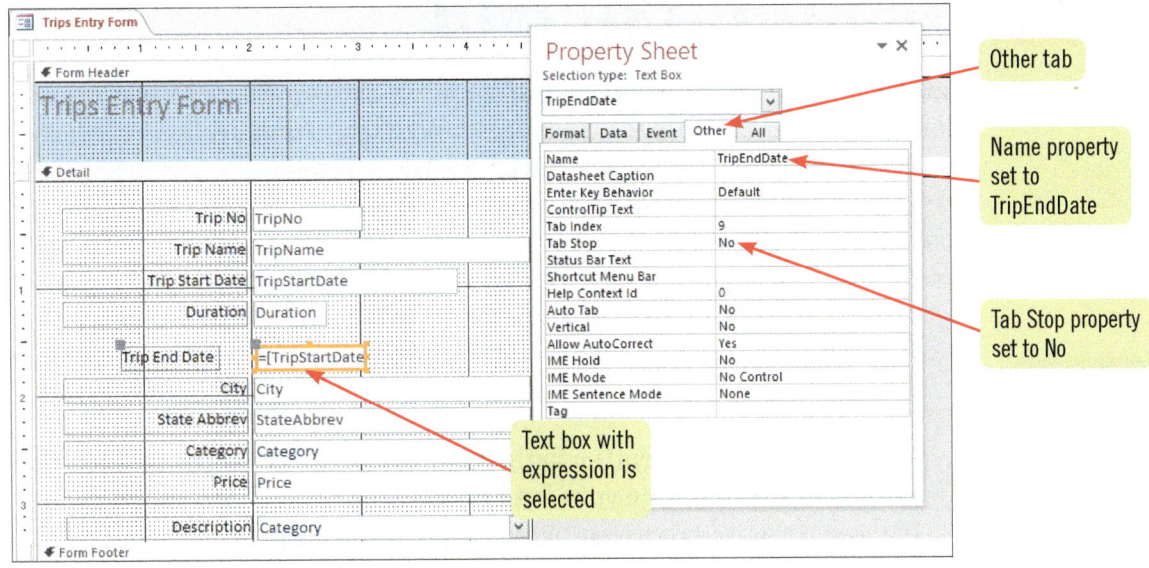

FIGURE 3-13: Tab Order dialog box

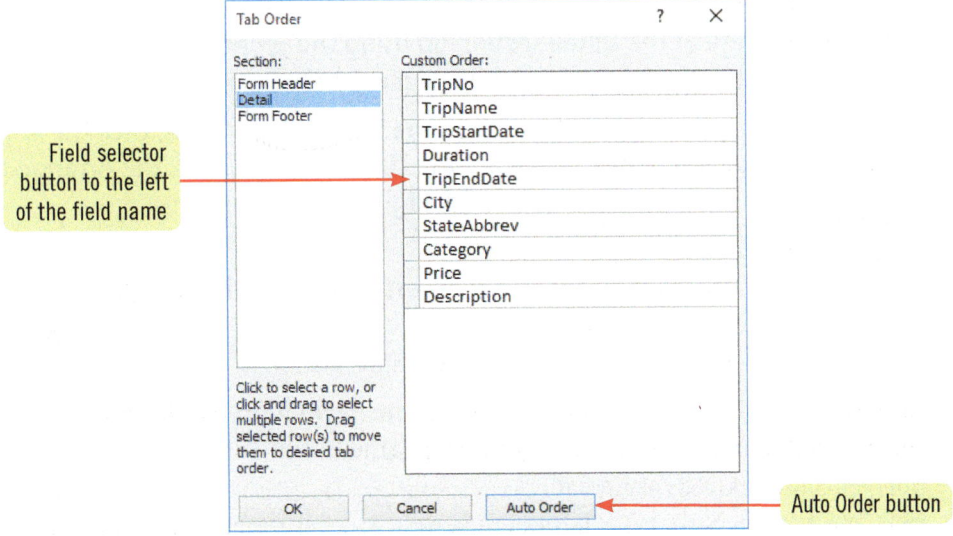

Form layouts

A **layout** helps you keep the controls on a form organized as a group. You can apply a stacked or tabular layout to the controls on your form by clicking the Stacked or Tabular buttons on the Arrange tab in Form Design View. Remove a layout by clicking the Remove Layout button. You can also modify a layout by modifying the margins, padding, and anchoring options of the layout using buttons found in the Position group on the Arrange tab in Form Design View. **Margin** refers to the space between the outer edge of the control and the data displayed inside the control. **Padding** is the space between the controls. **Anchoring** allows you to tie controls together so you can work with them as a group. Some of the Form Wizards automatically apply a layout to the controls that you can modify or remove as needed.

Insert an Image

Learning Outcomes
- Insert an image on a form
- Modify form sections
- Print a selected record

Graphic images, such as pictures, logos, or clip art, can add style and professionalism to a form. The form section in which you place the images is significant. **Form sections** determine where controls are displayed and printed; they are described in TABLE 3-7. For example, if you add a company logo to the Form Header section, the image appears at the top of the form in Form View as well as at the top of a printout. If you add the same image to the Detail section, it prints next to each record in the printout because the Detail section is printed for every record. **CASE** *Julia Rice suggests that you add the R2G logo to the top of the Trips Entry Form. You can add the control in either Layout or Design View, but if you want to place it in the Form Header section, you have to work in Design View.*

STEPS

1. **Click the Insert Image button in the Controls group, click Browse, then navigate to the location where you store your Data Files**
   The Insert Picture dialog box opens, prompting you for the location of the image.

2. **Click the Web-Ready Image Files button, click All Files, double-click R2GLogo.jpg, then click at the top of the Form Header section at about the 3" mark on the ruler**
   The R2GLogo image is added to the right side of the Form Header section. When an image or control is selected in Design View, you can use **sizing handles**, which are small squares at the corners of the selection box. Drag a handle to resize the image or control. You use the ⊹ pointer to move a control.

3. **Use the ⊹ pointer to move the logo to the top edge of the Form Header section, then drag the top edge of the Detail section up using the ➕ pointer**
   You also want to align the Trip End Date label with the other labels in the first column.

   TROUBLE
   You may need to continue to move or slightly adjust the controls to fit them all on the screen.

4. **Click the Trip End Date label, click the Home tab on the Ribbon, click the Align Right button ▤, press and hold [Shift], click the Duration label, click the Arrange tab on the Ribbon, click the Align button, then click Right as shown in FIGURE 3-14**
   With the form completed, you open it in Form View to observe the changes.

5. **Click the Save button 🖫 on the Quick Access Toolbar, click the Home tab, then click the View button ▤ to switch to Form View**
   You decide to add one more record with your final Trips Entry Form.

6. **Click the New (blank) record button ▶* in the navigation bar, then enter the new record shown in FIGURE 3-15, using your last name in the Trip Name field**
   Now print only this single new record.

   TROUBLE
   If you do not click the Selected Record(s) option button, you will print all records, which creates a very long printout.

7. **Click the File tab, click Print in the navigation bar, click Print, click the Selected Record(s) option button, then click OK**

8. **Close the Trips Entry Form, click Yes if prompted to save it, close the R2G-3.accdb database, then exit Access 2016**

FIGURE 3-14: Adding an image to the Form Header section

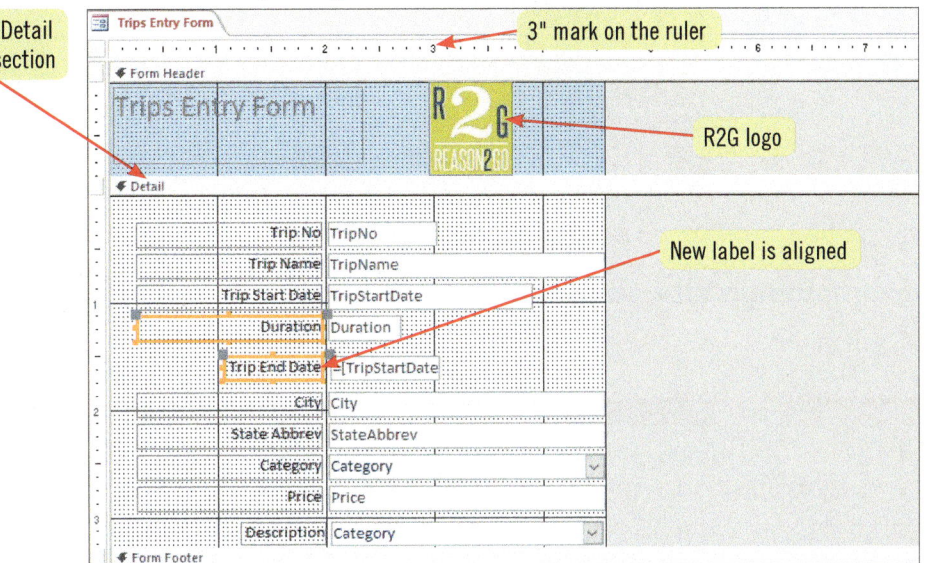

FIGURE 3-15: Final Trips Entry Form with new record

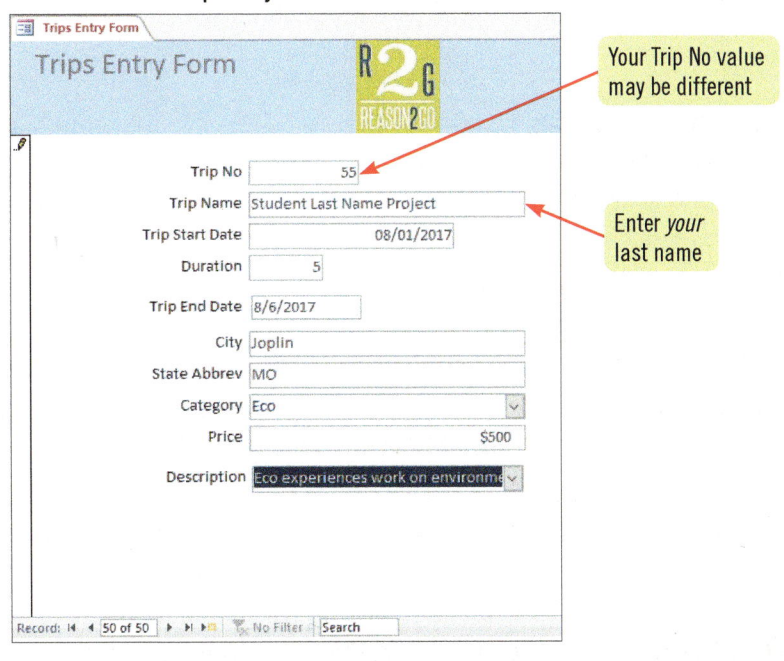

TABLE 3-7: Form sections

section	controls placed in this section print
Form Header	Only once at the top of the first page of the printout
Detail	Once for every record
Form Footer	Only once at the end of the last page of the printout

Applying a background image

A **background image** is an image that fills the entire form or report, appearing "behind" the other controls. A background image is sometimes called a watermark image. To add a background image, use the Picture property for the form or report to browse for the image that you want to use in the background.

Practice

Concepts Review

Label each element of Form Design View shown in FIGURE 3-16.

FIGURE 3-16

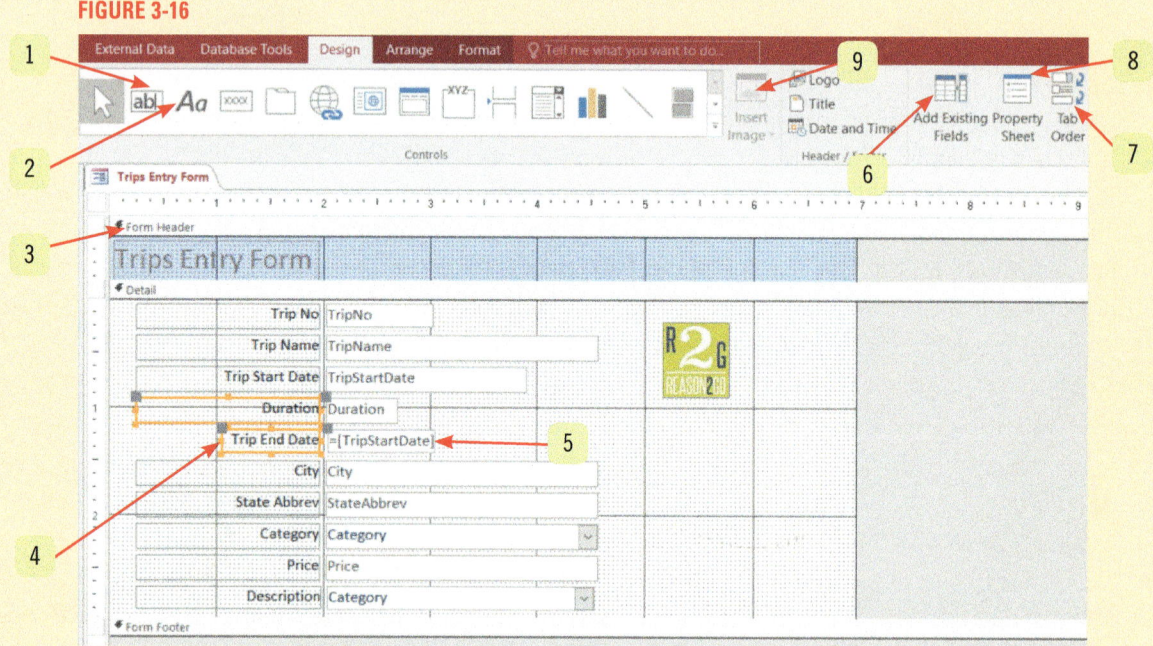

Match each term with the statement that best describes it.

10. Tab order
11. Calculated control
12. Detail section
13. Form Footer section
14. Bound control
15. Database designer

a. Created by entering an expression in a text box
b. Controls placed here print once for every record in the underlying record source
c. Used on a form to display data from a field
d. Controls placed here print only once at the end of the printout
e. The way the focus moves from one bound control to the next in Form View
f. Responsible for building and maintaining tables, queries, forms, and reports

Select the best answer from the list of choices.

16. Every element on a form is called a(n):
   a. property.
   b. item.
   c. control.
   d. tool.

17. Which of the following is probably *not* a graphic image?
   a. Logo
   b. Clip art
   c. Calculation
   d. Picture

18. The most common bound control is the:
- **a.** combo box.
- **b.** label.
- **c.** list box.
- **d.** text box.

19. The most common unbound control is the:
- **a.** text box.
- **b.** combo box.
- **c.** label.
- **d.** command button.

20. Which form view cannot be used to view data?
- **a.** Layout
- **b.** Design
- **c.** Datasheet
- **d.** Preview

Skills Review

1. Use the Form Wizard.
- **a.** Start Access and open the LakeHomes-3.accdb database from the location where you store your Data Files. Enable content if prompted.
- **b.** Click the Create tab, then use the Form Wizard to create a form based on all of the fields in the Realtors table. Use a Columnar layout and type **Realtor Entry Form** to title the form.
- **c.** Add a *new record* with your name in the RFirst and RLast text boxes. Note that the RealtorNo field is an AutoNumber field that is automatically incremented as you enter your first and last names. Enter your school's telephone number for the RPhone field value, and enter **4** as the AgencyNo field value.
- **d.** Save and close the Realtor Entry Form.

2. Create a split form.
- **a.** Click the Agencies table in the Navigation Pane, click the Create tab, click the More Forms button, then click Split Form.
- **b.** Close the Property Sheet if it opens then switch to Form View.
- **c.** Click the record selector in the lower pane for AgencyNo 3, Green Mountain Realty, then click the Delete button in the Records group to delete this realtor. Click OK when prompted that you cannot delete this record because there are related records in the Realtors table.
- **d.** Navigate to the AgencyNo 4 record, Shepherd of the Hills Realtors, in either the upper or lower pane of the split form. Change 7744 Pokeberry Lane to **800 Lake Shore Drive**.
- **e.** Right-click the Agencies form tab, click Close, click Yes when prompted to save changes, type **Agencies Split Form** as the name of the form, then click OK.

3. Use Form Layout View.
- **a.** Open the Realtor Entry Form in Layout View.
- **b.** Modify the labels on the left to read: **Realtor Number**, **Realtor First Name**, **Realtor Last Name**, **Realtor Cell**, **Agency Number**.
- **c.** Modify the text color of the labels to be black.
- **d.** Resize all of the text boxes on the right to be the same width as the RealtorNo text box.
- **e.** Save the Realtor Entry Form.

4. Add fields to a form.
- **a.** Open the Field List, show all the tables, then expand the Agencies table to display its fields.
- **b.** Drag the AgencyName field to the form, then move the AgencyName label and combo box below the Agency Number controls.
- **c.** Modify the AgencyName label to read **Agency Name**.
- **d.** Modify the text color of the Agency Name label to black.
- **e.** Close the Field List and save and close the Realtor Entry Form.

Skills Review (continued)

5. Modify form controls.

a. Reopen the Realtor Entry Form in Layout View, then select all of the labels in the left column and use the Align Right button on the Home tab to right-align them.

b. Save the form, switch to Form View, navigate to Realtor No 5 (Jane Ann Welch), then use the Agency Name combo box to change the Agency Name to **Big Cedar Realtors**.

c. In Layout View, resize and align all controls so that the labels are lined up on the left and the text boxes are lined up on the right, as shown in **FIGURE 3-17**.

FIGURE 3-17

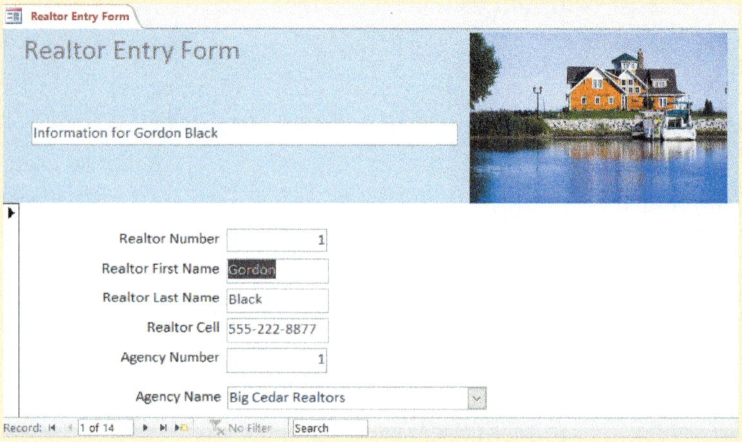

6. Create calculations.

a. Switch to Form Design View, expand the size of the Form Header section by dragging the top edge of the Detail section down about 0.5", then add a text box at about the 1" mark below the Realtor Entry Form label in the Form Header section.

b. Delete the Text14 label that is created when you add a new text box. The number in your label is based on previous work done to the form, so it might vary.

c. Widen the text box to be almost as wide as the entire form, then enter the following expression into the text box, which will add the words *Information for* to the realtor's first name, a space, and then the realtor's last name.

  ="Information for "&[RFirst]&" "&[RLast]

d. Save the form, then view it in Form View. Be sure the new text box correctly displays a space before and after the realtor's first name. If #Name? appears, which indicates that the expression was entered incorrectly, return to Design View to correct the expression.

e. In Form View, change the Realtor Last Name for Realtor Number 1 from Bono to **Black**. Tab to the RPhone text box to observe how the expression in the Form Header automatically updates.

f. Tab through several records, observing the expression in the Form Header section.

7. Modify tab order.

a. Switch to Form Design View, then open the Property Sheet.

b. Select the new text box with the expression in the Form Header section, then change the Tab Stop property from Yes to **No**.

c. Select the RealtorNo text box in the Detail section, then change the Tab Stop property from Yes to **No**. (AutoNumber fields cannot be edited, so they do not need to have a tab stop.)

d. Close the Property Sheet.

e. Open the Tab Order dialog box and click the Auto Order button to make sure the focus moves from top to bottom through the form.

f. Save the form and view it in Form View. Tab through the form to make sure that the tab order is sequential and skips the expression in the Form Header as well as the Realtor Number text box. Use the Tab Order button on the Design tab in Form Design View to modify the tab order, if necessary.

Skills Review (continued)

8. **Insert an image.**

   a. Switch to Design View, then click the Form Header section bar.

   b. Add the LakeHome.jpg image to the right side of the Form Header, then resize the image to be about 2.5" × 1.5". Remember to search for All files.

   c. Remove the extra blank space in the Form Header section by dragging the top edge of the Detail section up as far as possible.

   d. Drag the right edge of the form as far as possible to the left.

   e. Save the form, then switch to Form View as shown in **FIGURE 3-17**. Move through the records, observing the calculated field from record to record to make sure it is calculating correctly.

   f. Find the record with your name, and if requested by your instructor, print only that record.

   g. Close the Realtor Entry Form, close the LakeHomes-3.accdb database, then exit Access.

Independent Challenge 1

As a volunteer for a scuba divers' club, you have developed a database to help manage scuba dives. In this exercise, you'll create a data entry form to manage the dive trips.

   a. Start Access, then open the Scuba-3.accdb database from the location where you store your Data Files. Enable content if prompted.

   b. Using the Form Wizard, create a form that includes all the fields in the DiveTrips table and uses the Columnar layout, then type **Dive Trip Entry** as the title of the form.

   c. Switch to Layout View, then delete the ID text box and label.

   d. Using Form Design View, use the [Shift] key to select all of the text boxes except the last one for TripReport, then resize them to the shortest size using the To Shortest option on the Size/Space button on the Arrange tab.

   e. Using Form Design View, resize the Location, City, State/Province, Country, and Lodging text boxes to be no wider than the Rating text box.

   f. Using Form Design View, move and resize the controls, as shown in **FIGURE 3-18**. This will require several steps. Once the controls are resized, drag the top of the Form Footer section up to remove the extra blank space in the Detail section.

   g. Using Form Layout View, modify the labels and alignment of the labels, as shown in **FIGURE 3-18**. Note that there are spaces between the words in the labels, the labels are right-aligned, and the text boxes are left-aligned.

FIGURE 3-18

   h. In Form View, sort the records in ascending order on the Dive Master ID field, which will order the Great Barrier Reef tour as the first record. Edit the Certification Diving and Trip Report fields, as shown in **FIGURE 3-18** for the TripReport field using your name.

   i. Save the form, then if requested by your instructor, print only the record with your name.

   j. Close the Dive Trip Entry form, close the Scuba-3.accdb database, then exit Access 2016.

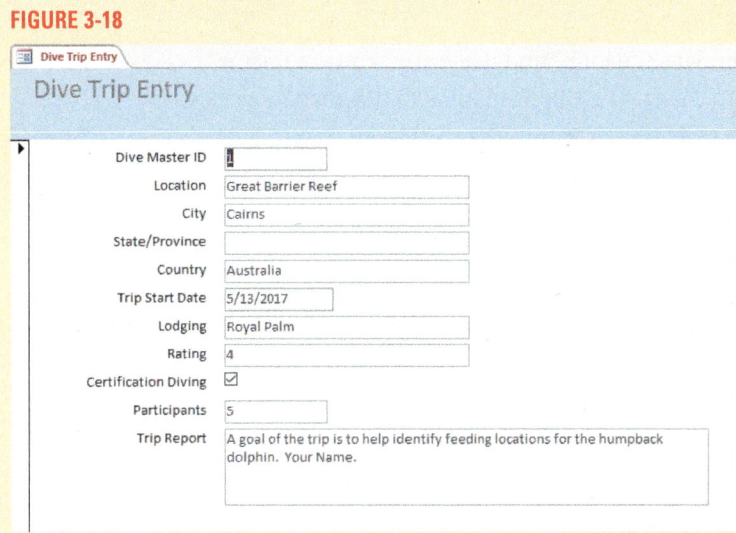

Dive Trip Entry	
Dive Master ID	1
Location	Great Barrier Reef
City	Cairns
State/Province	
Country	Australia
Trip Start Date	5/13/2017
Lodging	Royal Palm
Rating	4
Certification Diving	☑
Participants	5
Trip Report	A goal of the trip is to help identify feeding locations for the humpback dolphin. Your Name.

Independent Challenge 2

You have built an Access database to track membership in a community service club. The database tracks member names and addresses as well as their status in the club.

a. Start Access, then open the Service-3.accdb database from the location where you store your Data Files. Enable content if prompted.

b. Using the Form Wizard, create a form based on all of the fields of the Members table and the DuesOwed field in the Status table.

c. View the data by Members, use a Columnar layout, then enter **Member Information** as the title of the form.

d. Enter a new record with your name and the school name, and address of your school for the Company and address fields. Give yourself a StatusNo entry of **1**. In the DuesPaid field, enter **50**. The DuesOwed field automatically displays 100 because that value is pulled from the Status table and is based on the entry in the StatusNo field, which links the Members table to the Status table.

e. In Layout View, add a text box to the form and move it below the DuesOwed text box.

f. Open the Property Sheet for the new text box, display the Data tab, and in the Control Source property of the new text box, enter **=[DuesOwed]-[DuesPaid]**, the expression that calculates the balance between DuesOwed and DuesPaid.

g. Open the Property Sheet for the new label, and change the Caption property on the Format tab for the new label to **Balance**. Resize the label to be as wide as the labels above it.

h. Right-align all of the labels in the first column.

i. Set the Tab Stop property for the text box that contains the calculated Balance to **No**.

j. In Layout or Design View, resize DuesPaid and DuesOwed text boxes to be the same width as the new Balance text box, then right-align all data within the three text boxes because numbers are clearer when they align on the decimal point.

k. Make sure that the Format property on the Format tab is Currency for the DuesPaid, DuesOwed, and Balance expression text boxes. Close the Property Sheet.

l. In Form Design View, make sure that the right edge of the form is at or less than the 7" mark on the horizontal ruler. The horizontal ruler is located just above the Form Header section.

m. Save the form, find the record with your name, change the DuesPaid value to **60**, then move and resize controls as necessary to match **FIGURE 3-19**.

n. If requested by your instructor, print only the record with your name.

o. Save and close the Member Information form, then close the Service-3.accdb database and exit Access 2016.

FIGURE 3-19

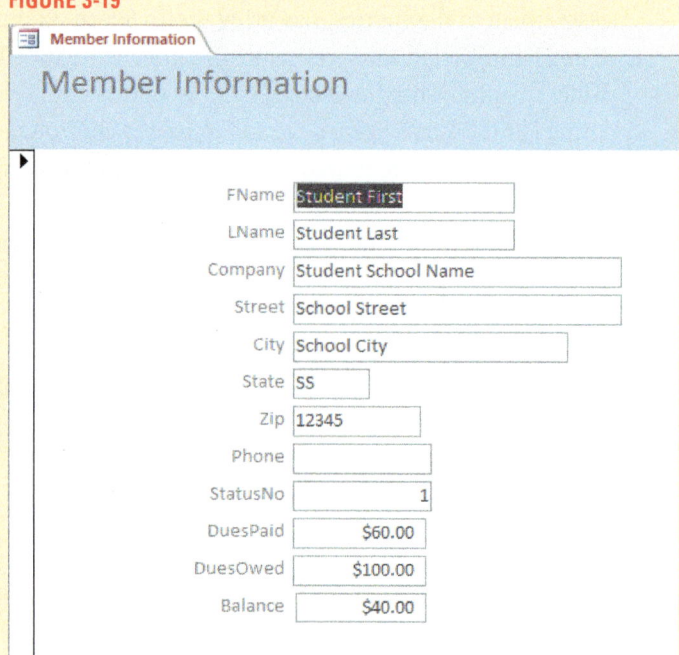

Independent Challenge 3

You have built an Access database to organize the deposits at a salvage and recycling center. Various clubs regularly deposit recyclable material, which is measured in pounds when the deposits are made.

a. Open the Salvage-3.accdb database from the location where you store your Data Files. Enable content if prompted.

b. Using the Form Wizard, create a form based on all of the fields in the CenterDeposits query. View the data by Deposits, use the Columnar layout, and title the form **Deposit Listing**.

c. Switch to Layout View, then make each label bold.

d. Modify the labels so that CenterName is **Center Name**, DepositDate is **Deposit Date**, and ClubName is **Club Name**.

e. Switch to Form Design View and resize the CenterName and ClubName text boxes so they are the same height and width as the Weight text box, as shown in FIGURE 3-20.

f. Switch to Form View, find and change any entry of A1 Salvage Center to *your* last name, then print one record with your name if requested by your instructor.

g. Using Form View of the Deposit Listing form, filter for all records with your last name in the CenterName field.

h. Using Form View of the Deposit Listing form, sort the filtered records in descending order on the DepositDate field.

i. In Form Design View, narrow the form by dragging the right edge as far left as possible.

j. Preview the first record, as shown in FIGURE 3-20. If requested by your instructor, print the first record.

k. Save and close the Deposit Listing form, close the Salvage-3.accdb database, then exit Access.

FIGURE 3-20

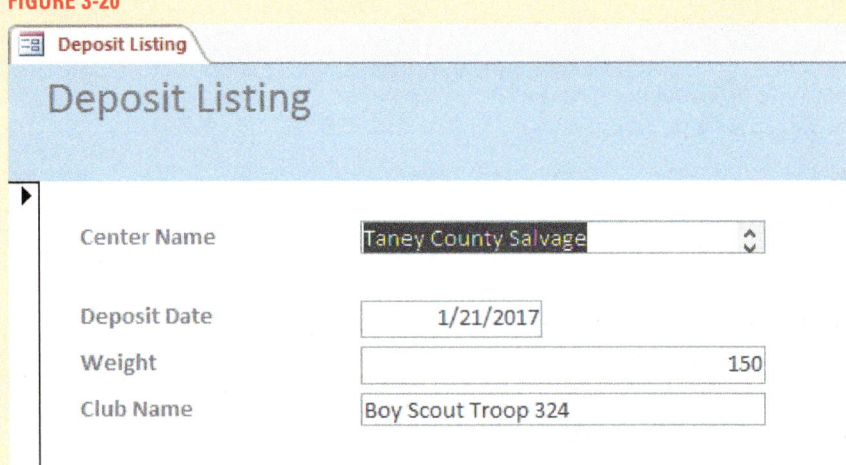

Access 2016

Independent Challenge 4: Explore

One way you can use an Access database on your own is to record and track your job search efforts. In this exercise, you will develop a form to help you enter data into your job-tracking database.

a. Start Access and open the Jobs-3.accdb database from the location where you store your Data Files. Enable content if prompted.

b. Click the Create tab, then use the Form Wizard to create a new form based on all the fields of both the Employers and Positions tables.

c. View the data by Employers, use a Datasheet layout for the subform, accept the default names for the form and subform, then open the form to view information.

d. Use Layout View and Design View to modify the form labels, text box positions, alignment, and sizes, as shown in FIGURE 3-21. Also note that the columns within the subform have been resized to display all of the data in the subform.

FIGURE 3-21

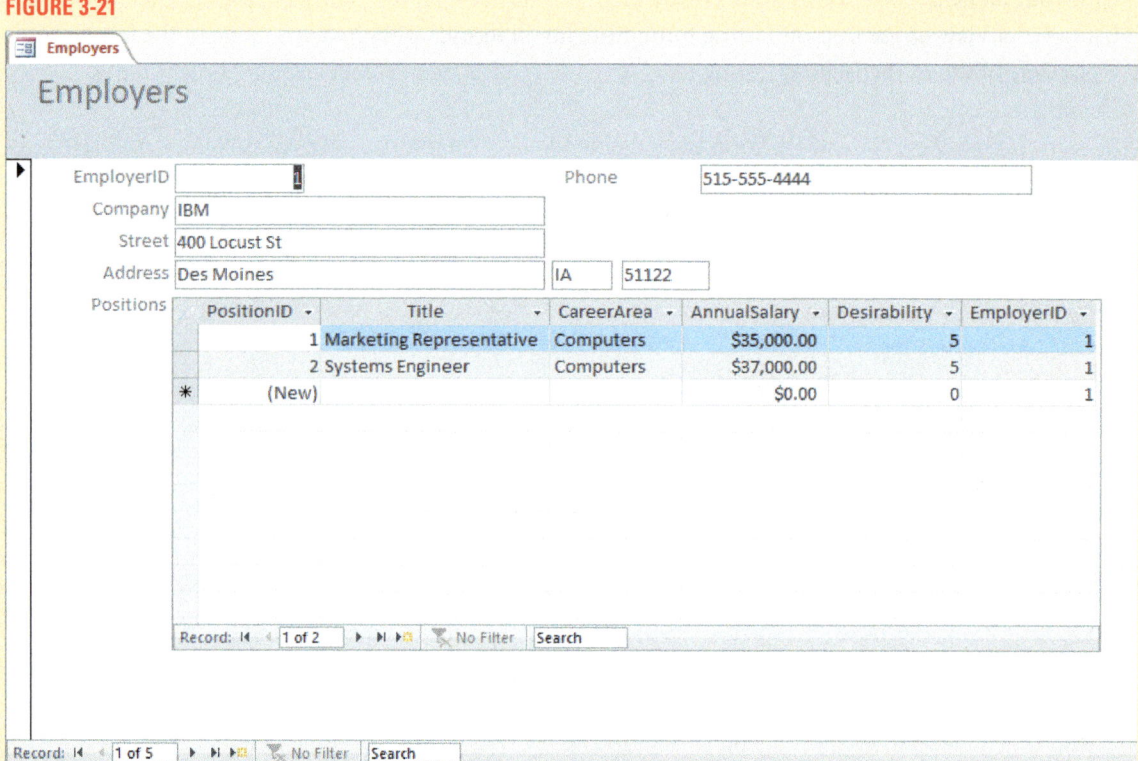

Independent Challenge 4: Explore (continued)

e. Change the CompanyName of IBM in the first record to *Your* **Last Name Software**, and if instructed to create a printout, print only that record. Close the Employers form.

f. Click the Employers table in the Navigation Pane, then use the Split Form option on the More Forms button of the Create tab to create a split form on the Employers table. Close and save the split form with the name **Employers Split Form**.

g. Open the Employers Split Form in Form View, change the address and phone number information for EmployerID 1 to your school's address and phone information, as shown in FIGURE 3-22.

h. Navigate through all five records, then back to EmployerID 1, observing both the upper and lower panes of the split form as you move from record to record.

i. Open the Employers form and navigate forward and backward through all five records to study the difference between the Employers form, which uses a form/subform versus the Employers Split Form. Even though both the Employers form and Employers Split Form show datasheets in the bottom halves of the forms, they are fundamentally very different. The split form is displaying the records of only the Employers table, whereas the Employers form is using a subform to display related records from the Positions table in the lower datasheet. You will learn more about forms and subforms in later modules.

j. Close the Jobs-3.accdb database, then exit Access.

FIGURE 3-22

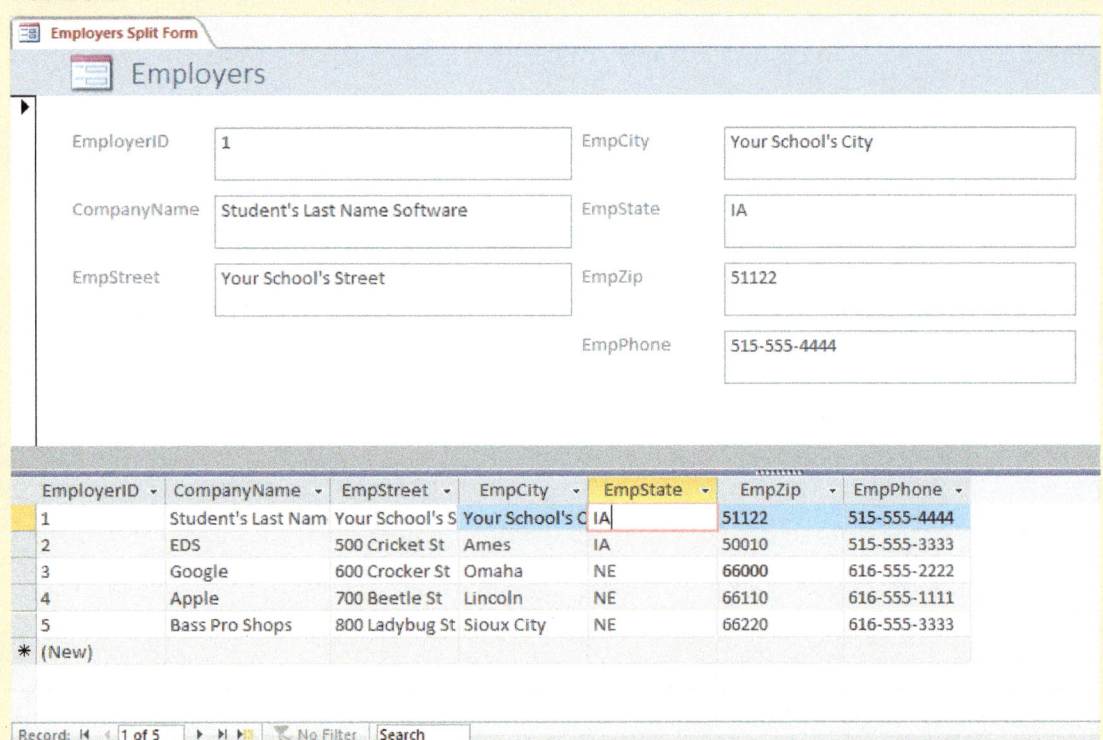

Visual Workshop

Open the Baseball-3.accdb database, enable content if prompted, then use the Split Form tool to create a form named **Players**, as shown in FIGURE 3-23, based on the Players table. Switch to Form Design View, remove the layout, and resize the controls as shown. Modify the labels as shown and note that they are all right-aligned. View the data in Form View, and sort the records in ascending order by last name. Change the first, last, and nickname of the John Bench record in the first record to your name, and if instructed to create a printout, print only that record. Save and close the Players form, close the Baseball-3.accdb database, then exit Access.

FIGURE 3-23

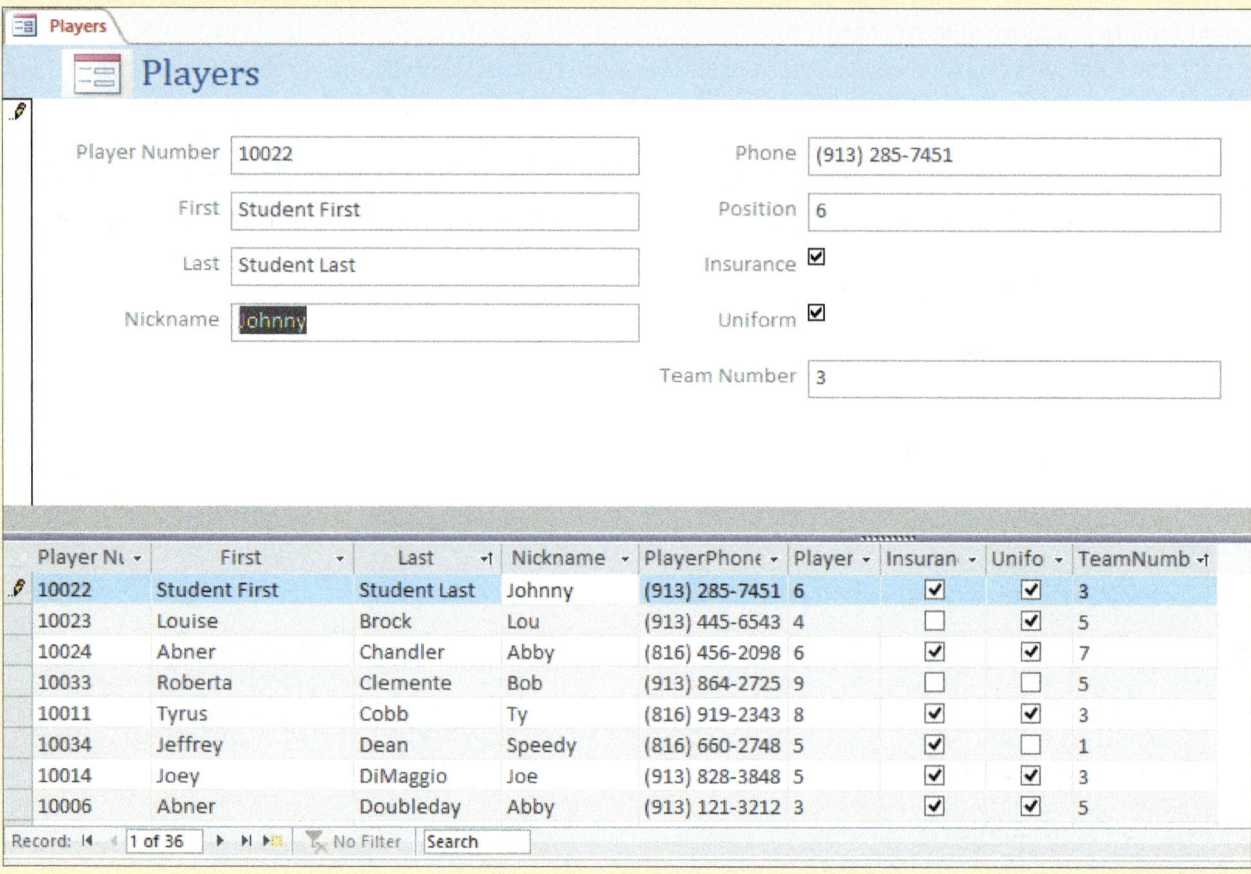

Using Reports

CASE Julia Rice, a trip developer at Reason 2 Go, asks you to produce some reports to help her share and analyze data. A report is an Access object that creates a professional-looking printout.

Module Objectives

After completing this module, you will be able to:

- Use the Report Wizard
- Use Report Layout View
- Review report sections
- Apply group and sort orders
- Add subtotals and counts
- Resize and align controls
- Format a report
- Create mailing labels

Files You Will Need

R2G-4.accdb

LakeHomes-4.accdb

Conventions-4.accdb

Service-4.accdb

Salvage-4.accdb

JobSearch-4.accdb

Basketball-4.accdb

Use the Report Wizard

Learning Outcomes
- Create a report with the Report Wizard
- Change page orientation

A **report** is the primary object you use to print database content because it provides the most formatting, layout, and summary options. A report may include various fonts and colors, clip art and lines, and multiple headers and footers. A report can also calculate subtotals, averages, counts, and other statistics for groups of records. You can create reports in Access by using the **Report Wizard**, a tool that asks questions to guide you through the initial development of the report. Your responses to the Report Wizard determine the record source, style, and layout of the report. The **record source** is the table or query that defines the fields and records displayed on the report. The Report Wizard also helps you sort, group, and analyze the records. **CASE** ▶ *Julia Rice asks you to use the Report Wizard to create a report to display the trips within each state.*

STEPS

1. **Start Access, open the** R2G-4.accdb database**, enable content if prompted, click the Create tab on the Ribbon, then click the Report Wizard button in the Reports group**

   The Report Wizard starts, prompting you to select the fields you want on the report. You can select fields from one or more tables or queries.

TROUBLE
If you select a field by mistake, click the unwanted field in the Selected Fields list, then click the Remove Field button `<` .

2. **Click the Tables/Queries list arrow, click Table: States, double-click the StateName field, click the Tables/Queries list arrow, click Table: Trips, click the Select All Fields button `>>` , click StateAbbrev in the Selected Fields list, then click the Remove Field button `<`**

   By selecting the StateName field from the States table, and all fields from the Trips table except the StateAbbrev field, you have all of the fields you need for the report, as shown in FIGURE 4-1.

3. **Click Next, then click by States if it is not already selected**

   Choosing "by States" groups the records for each state. In addition to record-grouping options, the Report Wizard later asks if you want to sort the records within each group. You can use the Report Wizard to specify up to four fields to sort in either ascending or descending order.

QUICK TIP
Click Back to review previous dialog boxes within a wizard.

4. **Click Next, click Next again to include no additional grouping levels, click the first sort list arrow, click TripName, then click Next**

   The last questions in the Report Wizard deal with report appearance and the report title.

5. **Click the Stepped option button, click the Landscape option button, click Next, type State Trips for the report title, then click Finish**

   The State Trips report opens in **Print Preview**, which displays the report as it appears when printed, as shown in FIGURE 4-2. The records are grouped by state, the first state being California, and then sorted in ascending order by the TripName field within each state. Reports are **read-only** objects, meaning you can use them to read and display data but not to change (write to) data. As you change data using tables, queries, or forms, reports constantly display those up-to-date edits just like all of the other Access objects.

6. **Scroll down to see the second grouping section on the report for the state of Colorado, then click the Next Page button ▶ in the navigation bar to see the second page of the report**

   Even in **landscape orientation** (11" wide by 8.5" tall as opposed to **portrait orientation**, which is 8.5" wide by 11" tall), the fields on the State Trips report may not fit on one sheet of paper. The labels in the column headings and the data in the columns need to be resized to improve the layout. Depending on your monitor, you might need to scroll to the right to display all the fields on this page.

FIGURE 4-1: Selecting fields for a report using the Report Wizard

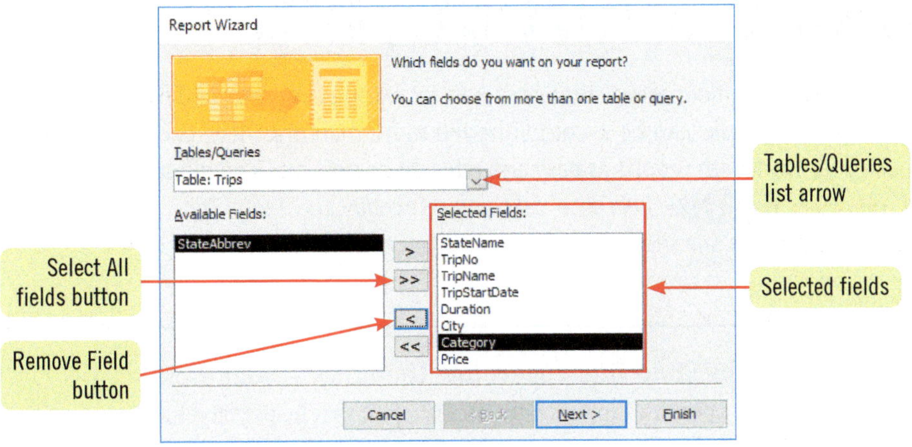

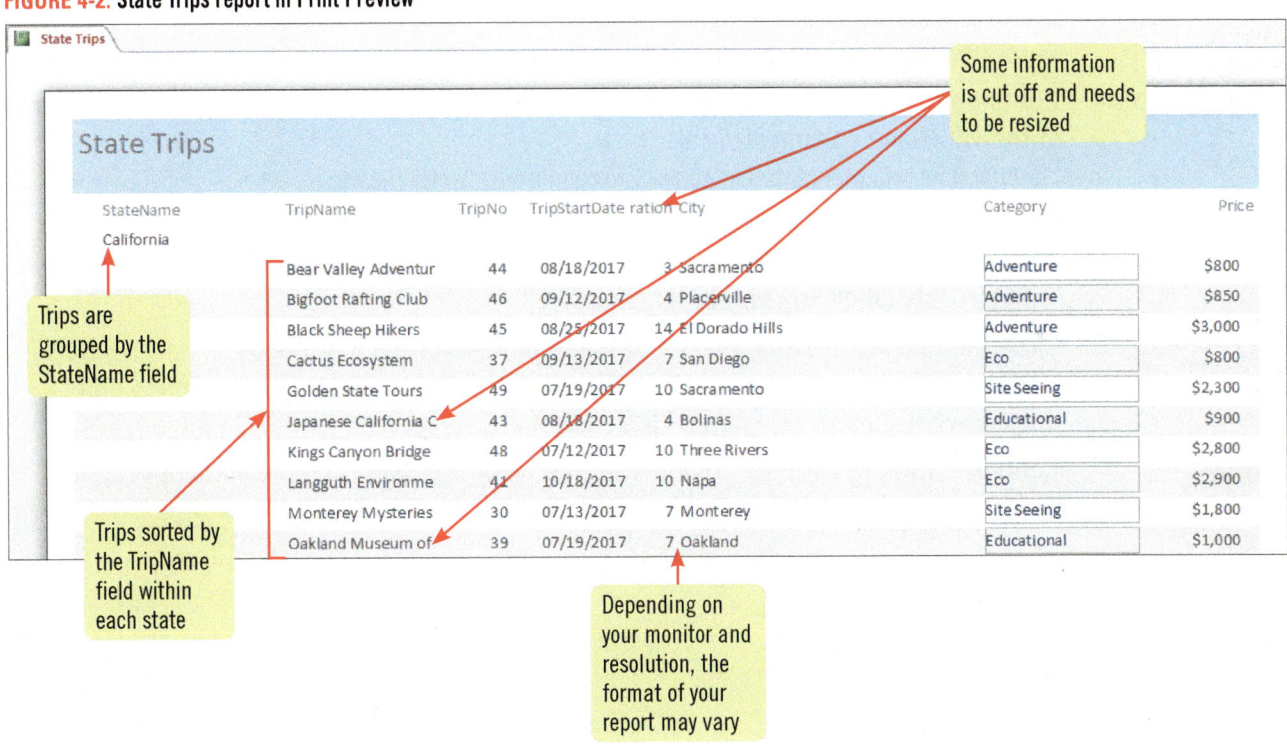

FIGURE 4-2: State Trips report in Print Preview

Changing page orientation

To change page orientation from Portrait (8.5" wide by 11" tall) to Landscape (11" wide by 8.5" tall) and vice versa, click the Portrait or Landscape button on the Print Preview tab when viewing the report in Print Preview. To switch to Print Preview, right-click the report in the Navigation Pane, and then choose Print Preview on the shortcut menu.

Use Report Layout View

Learning
Outcomes
• Move and resize
controls in Layout
View
• Modify labels

Reports have multiple views that you use for various report-building and report-viewing activities. Although some tasks can be accomplished in more than one view, each view has a primary purpose to make your work with reports as easy and efficient as possible. The different report views are summarized in TABLE 4-1. **CASE** *Julia Rice asks you to modify the State Trips report so that all of the fields fit comfortably across one sheet of paper in landscape orientation.*

STEPS

TROUBLE
If the Field List or Property Sheet window opens,, close it.

1. **Right-click the State Trips report tab, then click Layout View**

   Layout View opens and applies a grid to the report that helps you resize, move, and position controls. You decide to narrow the City column to make room for the Price data.

2. **Click Sacramento (or any value in the City column), then use the ↔ pointer to drag the left edge of the City column to the right to narrow it to about half of its current size, as shown in FIGURE 4-3**

   By narrowing the City column, you create extra space in the report.

QUICK TIP
If you select the entire row, just click again directly on the label to select it.

3. **Click the City label, then use ↔ to drag the left edge to the right to position it above the column of City data**

   You use the extra room to better display the data on the report.

QUICK TIP
You can use the Undo button ↻ to undo multiple actions in Layout View.

4. **Continue to use ↔ to resize the columns of data and labels so that the entire trip name in the TripName column is visible**

   The TripName column now has more space to completely display the trip names.

5. **Click the StateName label, click between the words State and Name, press the [Spacebar] so that the label reads State Name, then modify the TripName, TripNo, and TripStartDate labels to contain spaces as well**

6. **Click the StateName label, press and hold [Shift], click each of the other seven labels to select them as a group, release [Shift], click the Format tab, click the Font Color drop-down list arrow A , then click Automatic**

7. **Continue working with the columns so that all of the data is visible and your report looks like FIGURE 4-4**

FIGURE 4-3: Modifying the column width in Report Layout View

FIGURE 4-4: Final State Trips report in Report Layout View

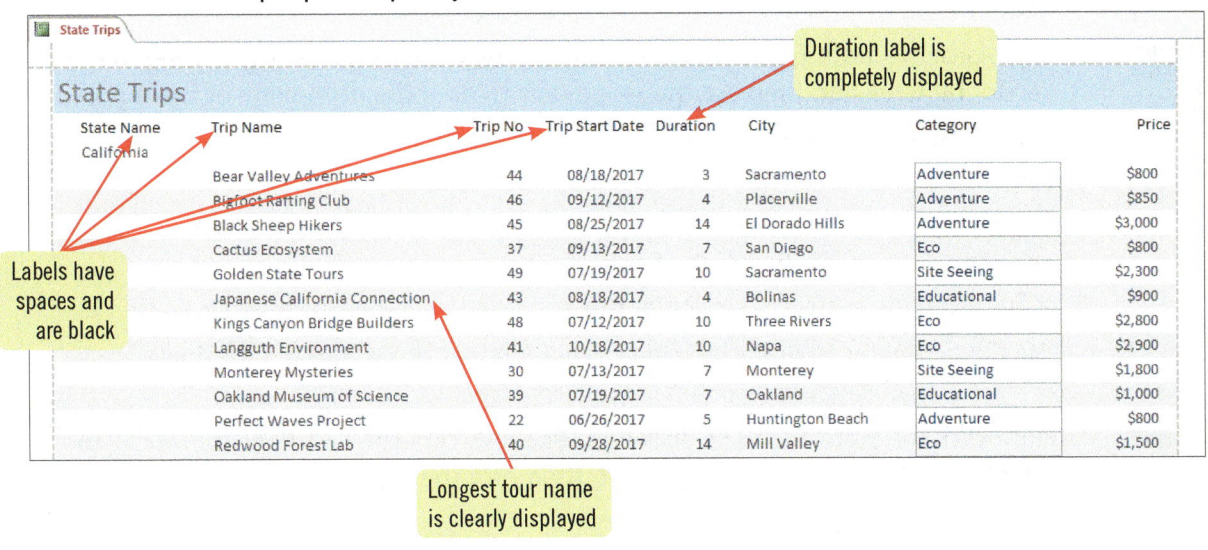

TABLE 4-1: Report views

view	primary purpose
Report View	To quickly review the report without page breaks
Print Preview	To review each page of an entire report as it will appear if printed
Layout View	To modify the size, position, or formatting of controls; shows live data as you modify the report, making it the tool of choice when you want to change the appearance and positioning of controls on a report while also reviewing live data
Design View	To work with report sections or to access the complete range of controls and report properties; Design View does not display data

Review Report Sections

Learning Outcomes
- Navigate through report sections and pages
- Resize the width of the report
- Work with error indicators

Report **sections** determine where and how often controls in that section print in the final report. For example, controls in the Report Header section print only once at the beginning of the report, but controls in the Detail section print once for every record the report displays. **TABLE 4-2** describes report sections. **CASE** ▶ *You and Julia Rice preview the State Trips report to review and understand report sections.*

STEPS

1. **Right-click the State Trips tab, click Print Preview, then scroll up as needed and click the light blue bar at the top of the report above the Trip Start Date label until you display the first page of the report, as shown in FIGURE 4-5**

   The first page shows four report sections: Report Header, Page Header, StateAbbreviation Header, and Detail.

2. **Click the Next Page button ▶ on the navigation bar to move to the second page of the report**

   If the second page of the report does not contain data, it means that the report may be too wide to fit on a single sheet of paper. You fix that problem in Report Design View.

   QUICK TIP
   If your report is too wide, you will see a green error indicator in the upper-left corner of the report. Pointing to the error icon ⚠ ▾ displays a message about the error.

3. **Right-click the State Trips tab, click Design View, scroll to the far right using the bottom horizontal scroll bar, then use the ↔ pointer to drag the right edge of the report as far as you can to the left, as shown in FIGURE 4-6**

   In Report Design View, you can work with the report sections and make modifications to the report that you cannot make in other views, such as narrowing the width. Report Design View does not display any data, however. For your report to fit on one page in landscape orientation, you need to move all of the controls to the left of the 10.5" mark on the horizontal **ruler** using the default 0.25" left and right margins. You will practice fixing this problem by moving the page calculation in the Page Footer section.

4. **Use the ⬚ pointer to drag the page calculation text box about 0.5" to the left**

   To review your modifications, show the report in Print Preview.

   QUICK TIP
   You can also use the View buttons in the lower-right corner of a report to switch views.

5. **Right-click the State Trips tab, click Print Preview, click the Last Page button ▶| to navigate to the last page of the report, then click the report to zoom in and out to examine the page, as shown in FIGURE 4-7**

   Previewing each page of the report helps you confirm that no blank pages are created and allows you to examine how the different report sections print on each page.

TABLE 4-2: Report sections

section	where does this section print?
Report Header	At the top of the first page
Page Header	At the top of every page (but below the Report Header on the first page)
Group Header	Before every group of records
Detail	Once for every record
Group Footer	After every group of records
Page Footer	At the bottom of every page
Report Footer	At the end of the report

FIGURE 4-5: State Trips in Print Preview

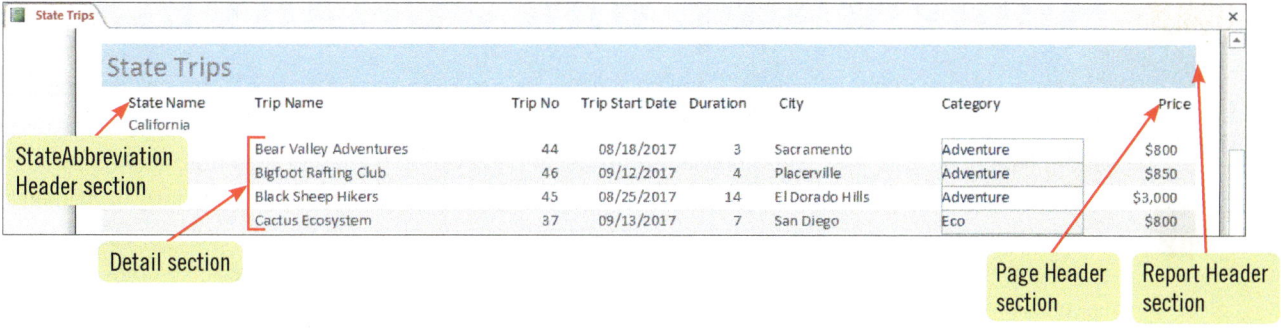

FIGURE 4-6: State Trips report in Design View

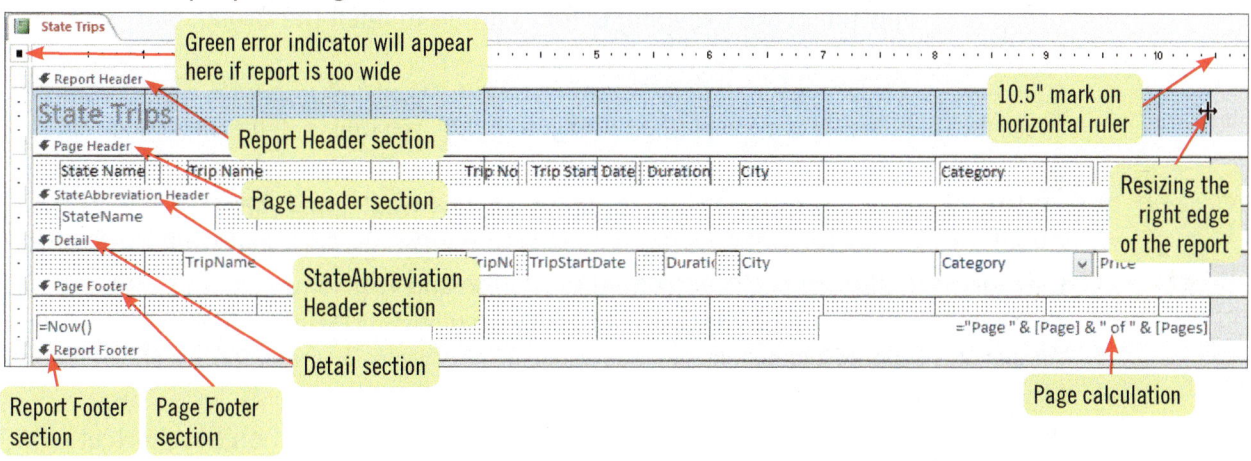

FIGURE 4-7: Last page of State Trips report in Print Preview

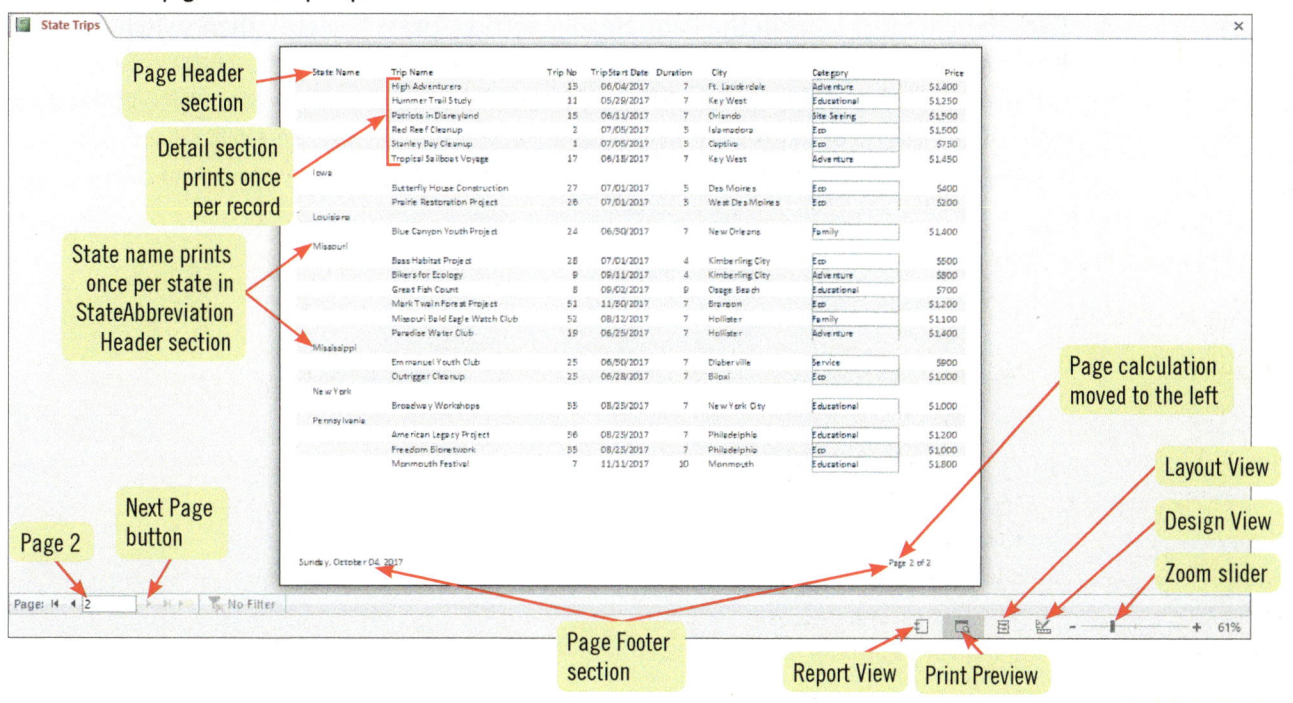

Access 2016

Apply Group and Sort Orders

Learning
Outcomes
• Group and sort
  records in a report
• Cut and paste
  controls

Grouping means to sort records by a particular field plus provide a header and/or footer section before or after each group of sorted records. For example, if you group records by the StateAbbreviation field, the Group Header is called the StateAbbreviation Header and the Group Footer is called the StateAbbreviation Footer. The StateAbbreviation Header section appears once for each state in the report, immediately before the records in that state. The StateAbbreviation Footer section also appears once for each state in the report, immediately after the records for that state. **CASE** *The records in the State Trips report are currently grouped by the StateAbbreviation field. Julia Rice asks you to further group the records by the Category field (Adventure, Eco, Educational, and Family, for example) within each state.*

STEPS

1. **Click the Close Print Preview button to return to Report Design View, then click the Group & Sort button in the Grouping & Totals group to open the Group, Sort, and Total pane**

   Currently, the records are grouped by the StateAbbreviation field and further sorted by the TripName field. To add the Category field as a grouping field within each state, you work with the Group, Sort, and Total pane in Report Design View.

2. **Click the Add a group button in the Group, Sort, and Total pane, click Category, then click the Move up button on the right side of the Group, Sort, and Total pane so that Category is positioned between StateAbbreviation and TripName**

   A Category Header section is added to Report Design View just below the StateAbbreviation Header section. You move the Category control from the Detail section to the Category Header section so it prints only once for each new Category instead of once for each record in the Detail section.

3. **Right-click the Category combo box in the Detail section, click Cut on the shortcut menu, right-click the Category Header section, click Paste, then use the pointer to drag the Category combo box to the right to position it as shown in FIGURE 4-8**

   Now that you've moved the Category combo box to the Category Header, it will print only once per category within each state. You no longer need the Category label in the Page Header section.

4. **Click the Category label in the Page Header section, press [Delete], then switch to Print Preview and zoom to 100%**

   The State Trips report should look like FIGURE 4-9. Notice that the records are now grouped by category within state. Detail records are further sorted in ascending order by the TripName field value.

FIGURE 4-8: Group, Sort, and Total pane and new Category Header section

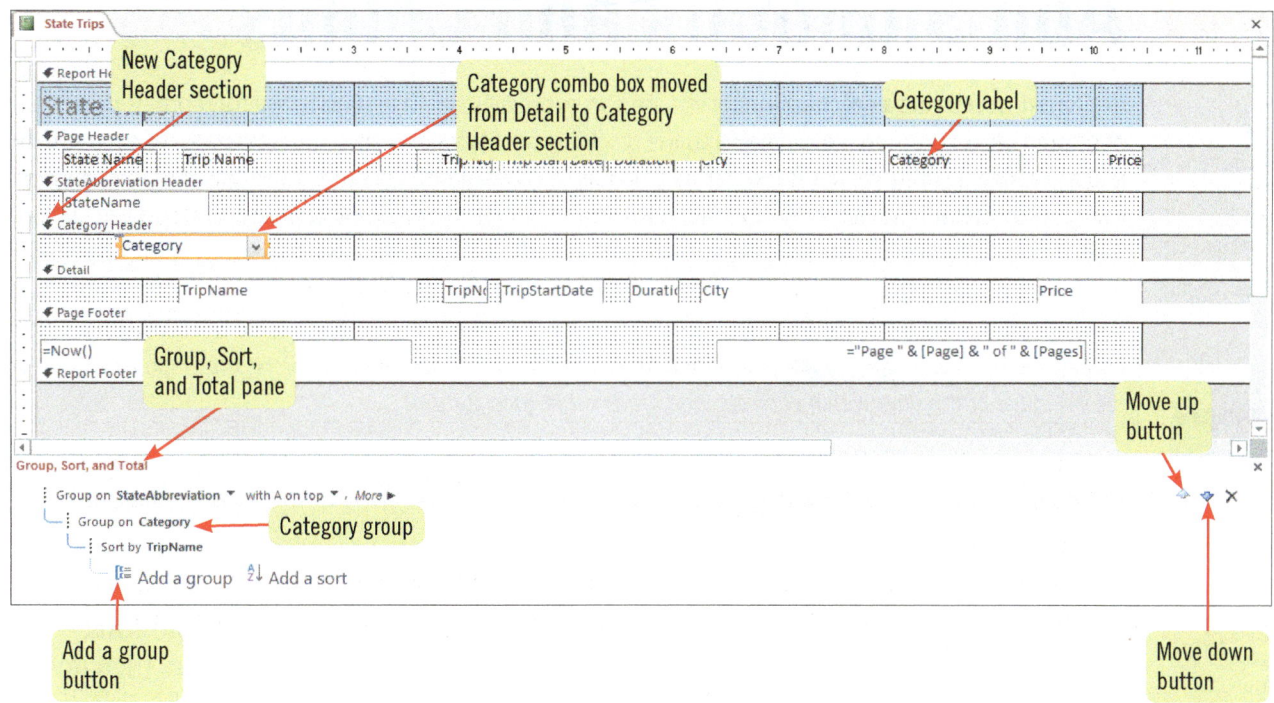

FIGURE 4-9: State Trips report grouped by category within state

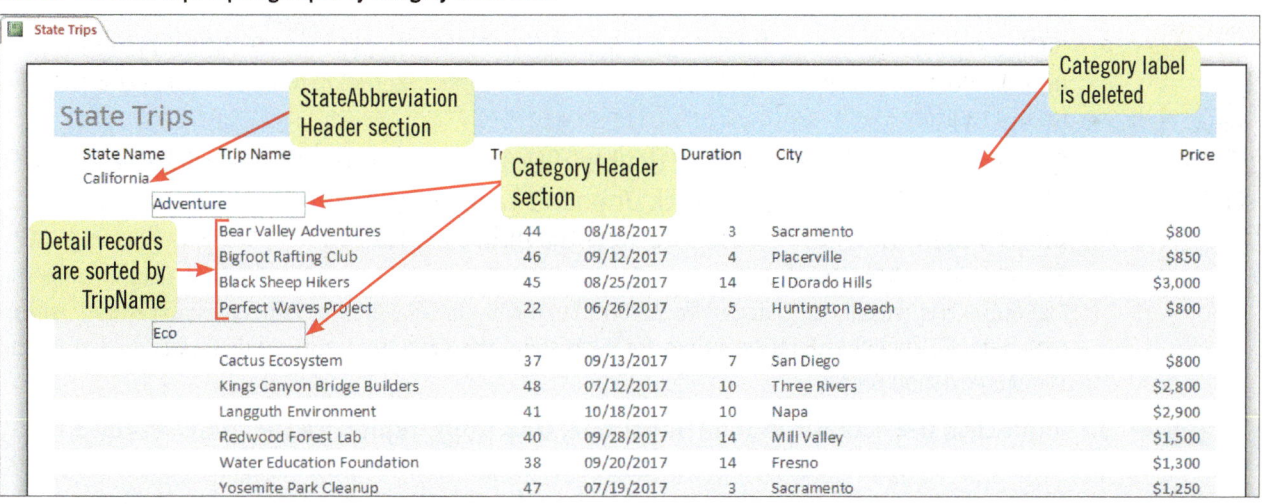

Record Source Property

The **Record Source property** of a report or form determines what fields and records that report or form will display. It is the first property on the Data tab of the Property Sheet for a report or form. The value of the Record Source property may be the name of a table or query. The Record Source property can also be a SELECT statement, which is SQL (Structured Query Language) code. In the Property Sheet for a report, click the Record Source property, and then click the Build button ... to enter Query Design View, where you can change the Record Source property or save it as a query object within the database.

Add Subtotals and Counts

Learning Outcomes
- Create calculations to subtotal and count records
- Copy and paste controls

In a report, you create a **calculation** by entering an expression into a text box. When a report is previewed or printed, the expression is evaluated and the resulting calculation is placed on the report. An **expression** is a combination of field names, operators (such as +, –, /, and *), and functions that results in a single value. A **function** is a built-in formula, such as Sum or Count, that helps you quickly create a calculation. Notice that every expression starts with an equal sign (=), and when it uses a function, the arguments for the function are placed in (parentheses). **Arguments** are the pieces of information that the function needs to create the final answer. When an argument is a field name, the field name must be surrounded by [square brackets]. **CASE** ▶ *Julia Rice asks you to add a calculation to the State Trips report to sum the total number of trip days within each category and within each state.*

STEPS

1. **Switch to Report Design View**

   A logical place to add subtotals for each group is right after that group of records prints, in the Group Footer section. You use the Group, Sort, and Total pane to open Group Footer sections.

2. **Click the More button for the StateAbbreviation field in the Group, Sort, and Total pane, click the without a footer section list arrow, click with a footer section, then do the same for the Category field, as shown in FIGURE 4-10**

   With the StateAbbreviation Footer and Category Footer sections open, you're ready to add controls to calculate the total number of trip days within each category and within each state. You use a text box control with an expression to make this calculation.

3. **Click the Text Box button 🔲 in the Controls group, then click just below the Duration text box in the Category Footer section**

   Adding a new text box automatically adds a new label to its left. First, you modify the label to identify the information; then you modify the text box to contain the correct expression to sum the number of trip days for that category.

4. **Click the Text20 label to select it, double-click Text20, type Total days:, click the Unbound text box to select it, click Unbound again, type =Sum([Duration]), press [Enter], then widen the text box to view the entire expression**

   The expression =Sum([Duration]) uses the Sum function to add the days in the Duration field. Because the expression is entered in the Category Footer section, it will sum all Duration values for that category within that state. To sum the Duration values for each state, the expression also needs to be inserted in the StateAbbreviation Footer.

5. **Right-click the =Sum([Duration]) text box, click Copy, right-click the StateAbbreviation Footer section, click Paste, then press [→] enough times to position the controls in the StateAbbreviation Footer section just below those in the Category Footer section, as shown in FIGURE 4-11**

   With the expression copied to the StateAbbreviation Footer section, you're ready to preview your work.

6. **Switch to Print Preview, navigate to the last page of the report, then click to zoom so you can see all of the Pennsylvania trips**

   As shown in FIGURE 4-12, seven trip days are totaled for the Eco category, and 17 for the Educational category, which is a total of 24 trip days for the state of Pennsylvania. The summary data would look better if it were aligned more directly under the trip Duration values. You resize and align controls in the next lesson.

FIGURE 4-10: Opening group footer sections

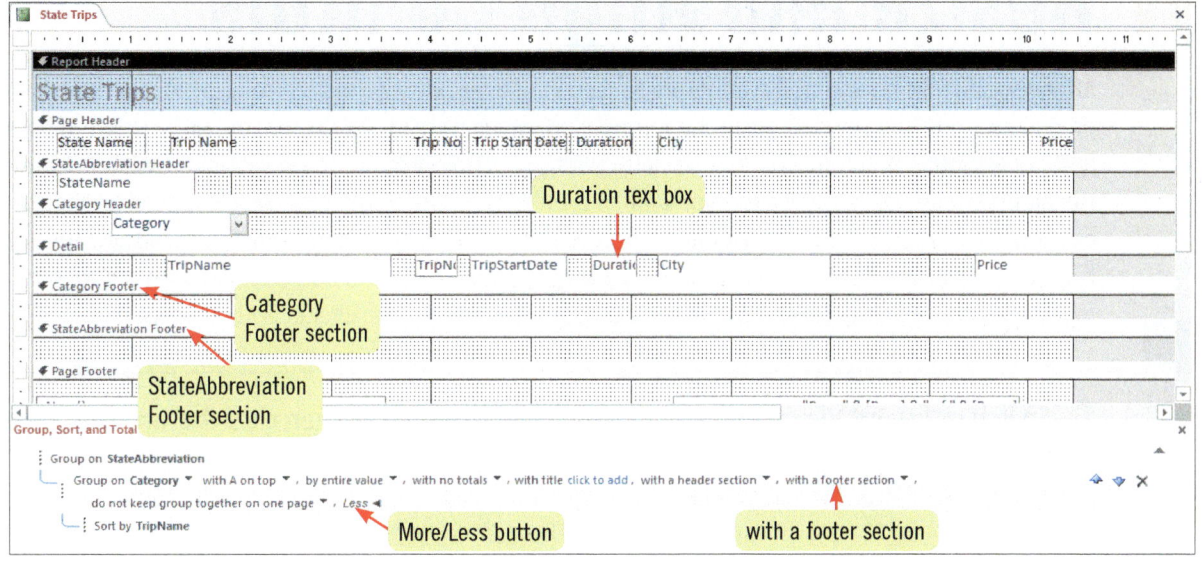

FIGURE 4-11: Adding subtotals to group footer sections

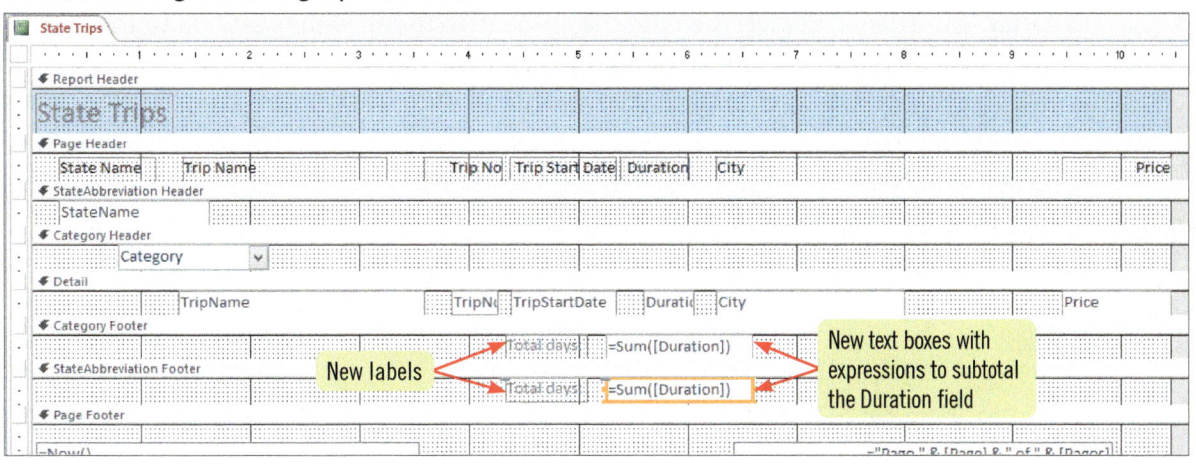

FIGURE 4-12: Previewing the new group footer calculations

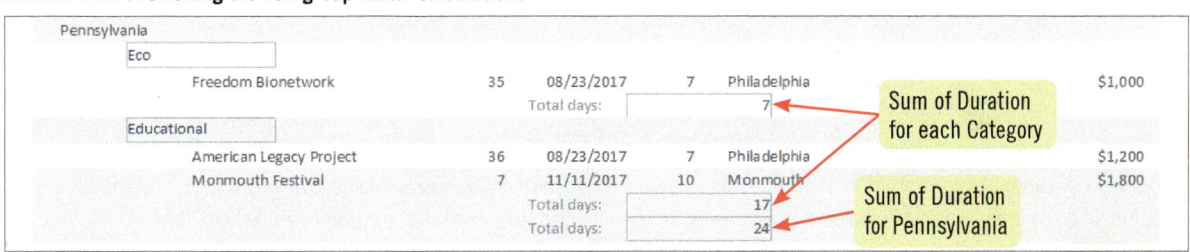

Resize and Align Controls

Learning
Outcomes
• Align data within a
  control
• Align the borders
  of controls

After you add information to the appropriate section of a report, you might also want to align the data in precise columns and rows to make the information easier to read. To do so, you can use two different types of **alignment** commands. You can left-, right-, or center-align a control within its own border using the Align Left ▤, Center ▤, and Align Right ▤ buttons on the Home tab. You can also align the edges of controls with respect to one another using the Left, Right, Top, and Bottom commands on the Align button of the Arrange tab in Report Design View. **CASE** ▸ *You decide to resize and align several controls to improve the readability of the State Trips report. Layout View is a good choice for these tasks.*

STEPS

1. **Switch to Layout View, click the Design tab on the Ribbon, then click the Group & Sort button to toggle off the Group, Sort, and Total pane**

   You decide to align the expressions that subtotal the number of trip days for each category within the Duration column to make the report easier to read and more professional.

QUICK TIP
You can also use the buttons on the Format tab to align and format text, including applying number formats and increasing or decreasing decimals.

2. **Click the Total days text box in the Category Footer, then use the ↔ pointer to resize the text box so that the data is aligned in the Duration column, as shown in FIGURE 4-13**

   If the value in your Total days text box is not right-aligned, click the Align Right button (shown in **FIGURE 4-13**). With the calculation formatted as desired in the Category Footer, you can quickly apply those modifications to the calculation in the StateAbbreviation Footer as well.

TROUBLE
If you make a mistake, click the Undo button ↶ on the Quick Access toolbar. You can click ↶ multiple times in Report or Form Design View.

3. **Scroll down the report far enough to find and then click the Total days text box in the StateAbbreviation Footer, then use the ↔ pointer to resize the text box so that it is the same width as the text box in the Category Footer section**

   With both expressions resized so they line up under the Duration values in the Detail section, they are easier to read on the report.

4. **Scroll the report so you can see all of the Colorado trips, as shown in FIGURE 4-14**

   You can apply resize, alignment, or formatting commands to more than one control at a time. **TABLE 4-3** provides techniques for selecting more than one control at a time in Report Design View.

Precisely moving and resizing controls

You can move and resize controls using the mouse or other pointing device, but you can move controls more precisely using the keyboard. Pressing the arrow keys while holding [Ctrl] moves selected controls one **pixel** (picture element) at a time in the direction of the arrow. Pressing the arrow keys while holding [Shift] resizes selected controls one pixel at a time.

FIGURE 4-13: Resizing controls in Layout View

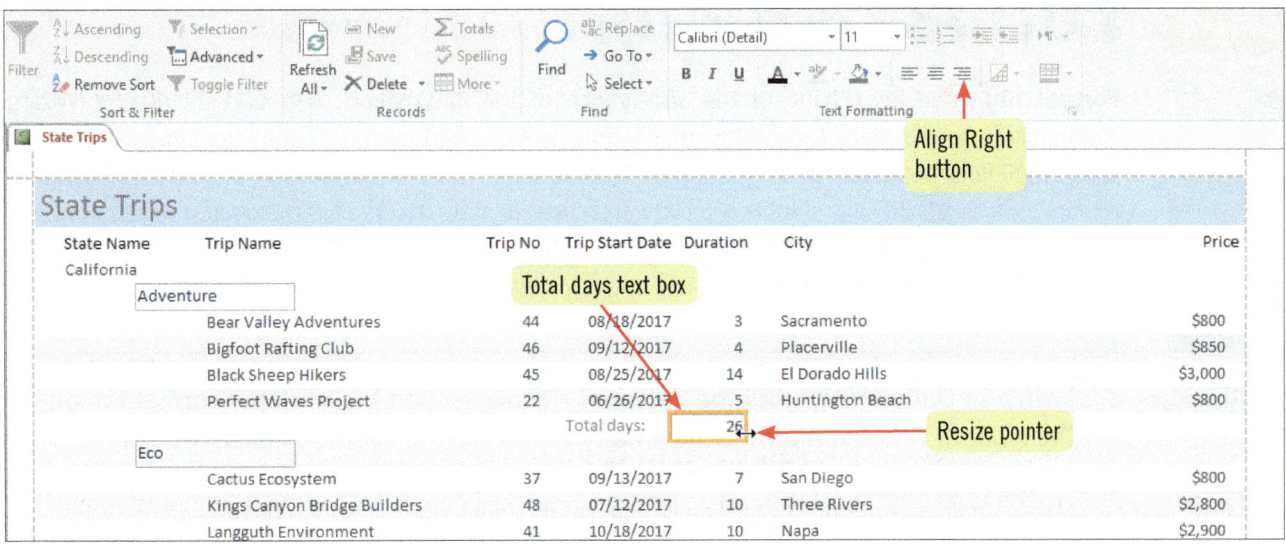

FIGURE 4-14: Reviewing the aligned and resized controls

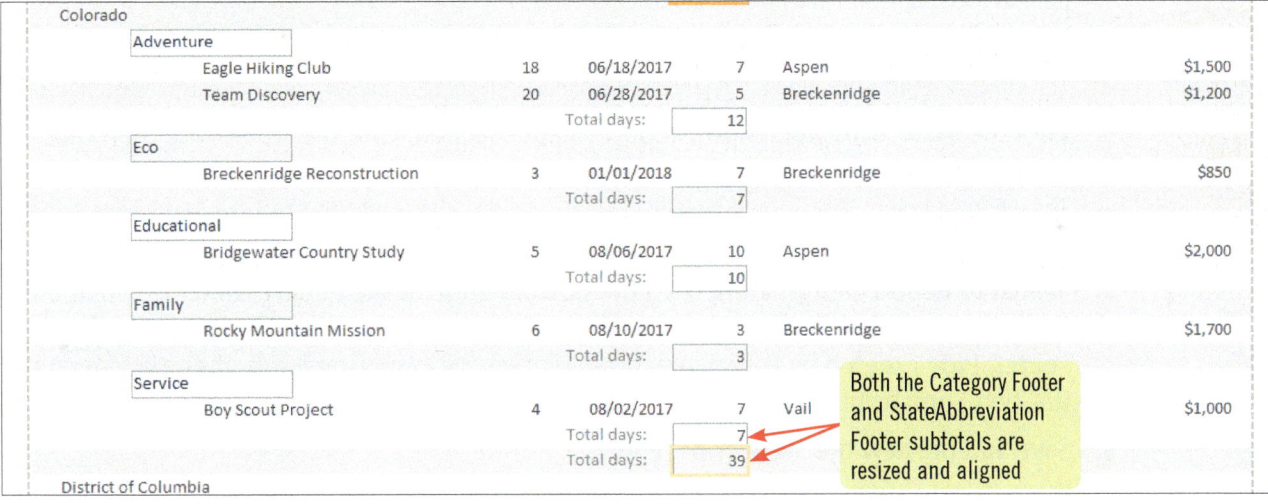

TABLE 4-3: Selecting more than one control at a time in Report Design View

technique	description
Click, [Shift]+click	Click a control, and then press and hold [Shift] while clicking other controls; each one is selected
Drag a selection box	Drag a selection box (an outline box you create by dragging the pointer in Report Design View); every control that is in or is touched by the edges of the box is selected
Click in the ruler	Click in either the horizontal or vertical ruler to select all controls that intersect the selection line
Drag in the ruler	Drag through either the horizontal or vertical ruler to select all controls that intersect the selection line as it is dragged through the ruler

Format a Report

Learning Outcomes
- Format controls and sections of a report
- Add labels to a report

Formatting refers to enhancing the appearance of the information. Although the Report Wizard automatically applies many formatting embellishments, you often want to change the appearance of the report to fit your particular needs. **CASE** ▶ *When reviewing the State Trips report with Julia, you decide to change the background color of some of the report sections to make the data easier to read. The Report Wizard applied alternating formats, which you want to change. You want to shade each Category Header and Category Footer section using the same color. To make changes to entire report sections, you work in Report Design View.*

STEPS

QUICK TIP
The quick keystroke for Undo is [Ctrl][Z]. The quick keystroke for Redo is [Ctrl][Y].

1. **Switch to Design View, click the Category Header section bar, click the Format tab on the Ribbon, click the Alternate Row Color button arrow, click the Maroon 2 color square as shown in FIGURE 4-15, click the Shape Fill button, then click the Maroon 2 color square**

   Make a similar modification by applying a different fill color to the Category Footer section.

2. **Click the Category Footer section bar, click the Alternate Row Color button arrow, click the Maroon 1 color square (just above Maroon 2 in the Standard Colors section), click the Shape Fill button, then click the Maroon 1 color square**

   When you use the Alternate Row Color and Shape Fill buttons, you're actually modifying the **Back Color** and **Alternate Back Color** properties in the Property Sheet of the section or control you selected. Background shades can help differentiate parts of the report, but be careful with dark colors, as they may print as solid black on some printers and fax machines.

3. **Switch to Layout View to review your modifications**

   The category sections are clearer, but you decide to make one more modification to emphasize the report title.

4. **Click the State Trips label in the Report Header section, click the Home tab, then click the Bold button B in the Text Formatting group**

   The report in Layout View should look like FIGURE 4-16. You also want to add a label to the Report Footer section to identify yourself.

5. **Switch to Report Design View, drag the bottom edge of the Report Footer down about 0.5", click the Label button Aa in the Controls group, click at the 1" mark in the Report Footer, type Created by *your* name, press [Enter], click the Home tab, then click B in the Text Formatting group**

6. **Save and preview the State Trips report**

7. **If required by your instructor, print the report, and then close it**

FIGURE 4-15: Formatting section backgrounds

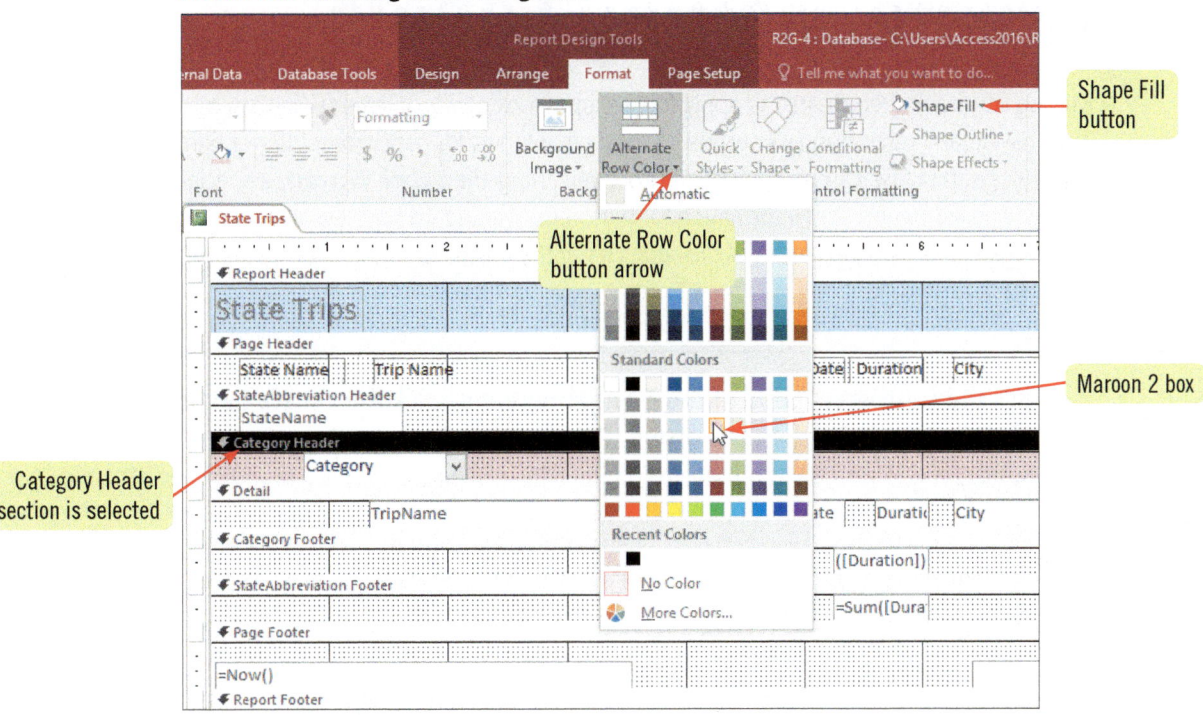

FIGURE 4-16: Final formatted State Trips report

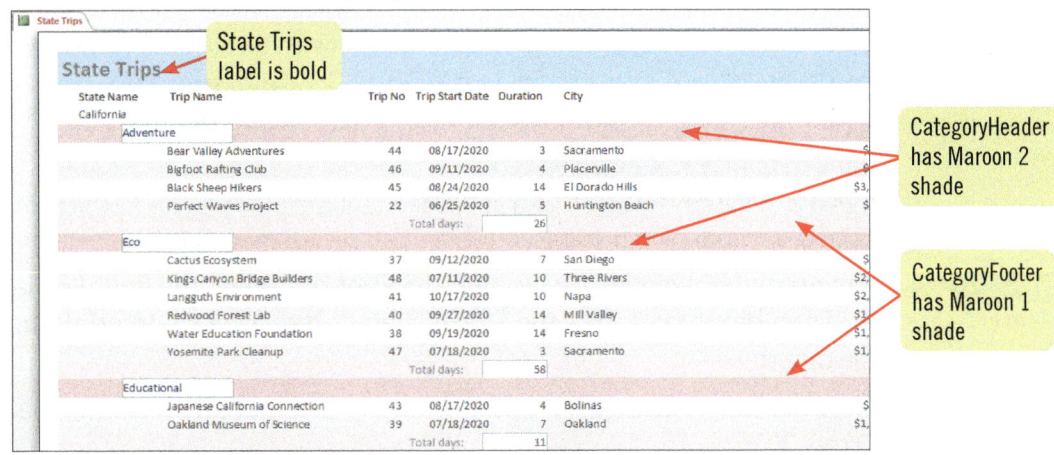

Create Mailing Labels

Mailing labels are often created to apply to envelopes, postcards, or letters when assembling a mass mailing. They have many other business purposes too, such as labels for paper file folders or name tags. Any data in your Access database can be converted into labels using the **Label Wizard**, a special report wizard that precisely positions and sizes information for hundreds of standard business labels. **CASE** *Julia Rice asks you to create mailing labels for all of the addresses in the Customers table. You use the Label Wizard to handle this request.*

STEPS

1. **Click the Customers table in the Navigation Pane, click the Create tab, then click the Labels button in the Reports group**

   The first Label Wizard dialog box opens. The Filter by manufacturer list box provides over 30 manufacturers of labels. Avery is the default choice. With the manufacturer selected, your next task is to choose the product number of the labels you will feed through the printer. The cover on the box of labels you are using provides this information. In this case, you'll be using Avery 5160 labels, a common type of sheet labels used for mailings and other purposes.

2. **Scroll through the Product number list, then click 5160 as shown in FIGURE 4-17**

   Note that by selecting a product number, you also specify the dimensions of the label and number of columns.

3. **Click Next, then click Next again to accept the default font and color choices**

   The third question of the Label Wizard asks how you want to construct your label. You'll add the fields from the Customers table with spaces and line breaks to pattern a standard mailing format.

4. **Double-click FName, press [Spacebar], double-click LName, press [Enter], double-click Street, press [Enter], double-click City, type a comma (,) and press [Spacebar], double-click State, press [Spacebar], then double-click Zip**

   If your prototype label doesn't look exactly like FIGURE 4-18, delete the fields in the Prototype label box and try again. Be careful to put a space between the FName and LName fields in the first row, a comma and a space between the City and State fields, and a space between the State and Zip fields.

5. **Click Next, double-click LName to select it as a sorting field, click Next, click Finish to accept the name Labels Customers for the new report, then click OK if prompted that some data may not be displayed**

   A portion of the new report is shown in FIGURE 4-19. It is generally a good idea to print the first page of the report on standard paper to make sure everything is aligned correctly before printing on labels.

6. **If requested by your instructor, click the Print button on the Print Preview tab, click the From box, type 1, click the To box, type 1, then click OK to print the first page of the report**

7. **Close the Labels Customers report, close the R2G-4.accdb database, then exit Access 2016**

FIGURE 4-17: Label Wizard dialog box

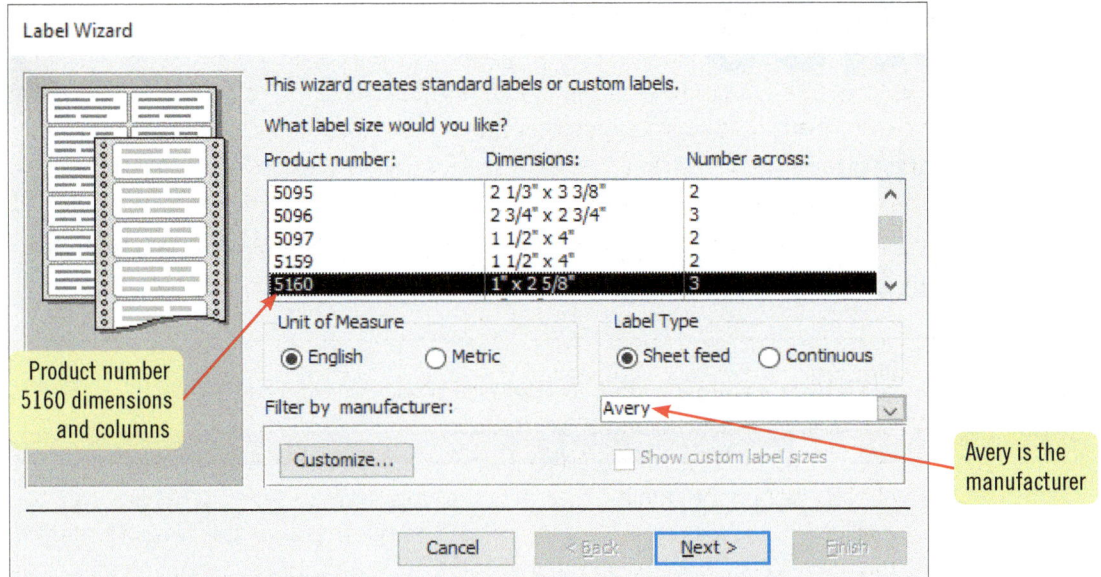

Product number 5160 dimensions and columns

Avery is the manufacturer

FIGURE 4-18: Building a prototype label

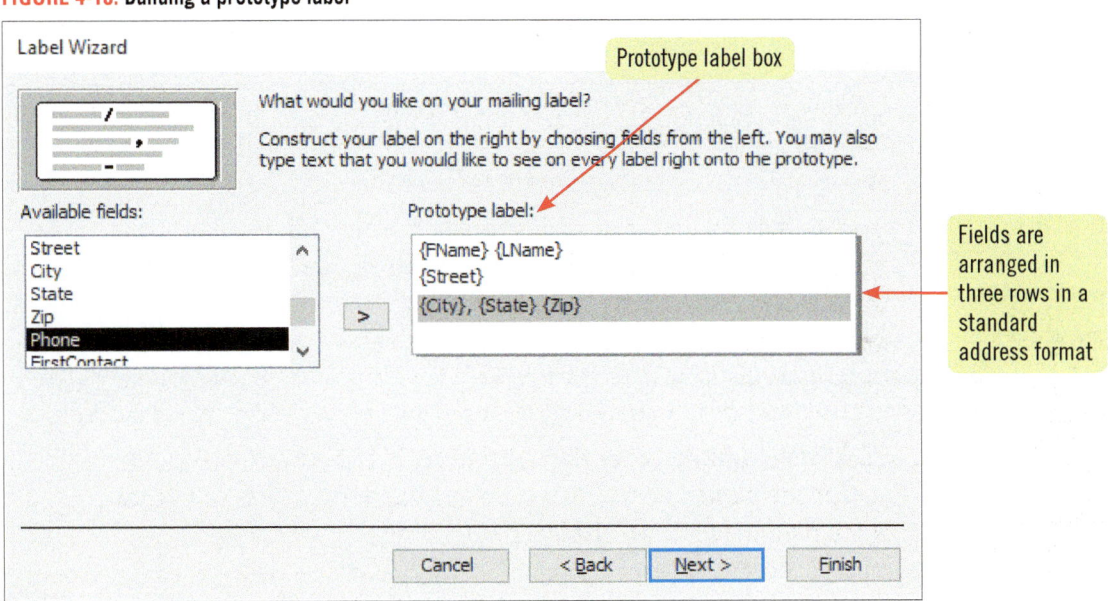

Prototype label box

Fields are arranged in three rows in a standard address format

FIGURE 4-19: Labels Customers report

Jacob Alman
2505 McGee St
Des Moines, IA 50288

Maria Armstrong
7722 Mastin St
Mission, KS 63552

Zohra Bell
506 Lowell St
Point Lookout, MO 65727

Orlando Berry
7722 Mastin St
Mission, KS 63552

Naresh Blackwell
2345 Grand Blvd
Kansas City, KS 64108

Julia Bouchart
5200 Main St
Kansas City, MO 64105

Tom Camel
520 W 52nd St
Kansas City, KS 64105

David Carter
7066 College Rd
Overland Park, KS 66211

Jaele Clark
620 King St
Overland Park, KS 66210

Data is merged to a 3-column Avery 5160 label format

Practice

Concepts Review

Label each element of the Report Design View window shown in FIGURE 4-20.

FIGURE 4-20

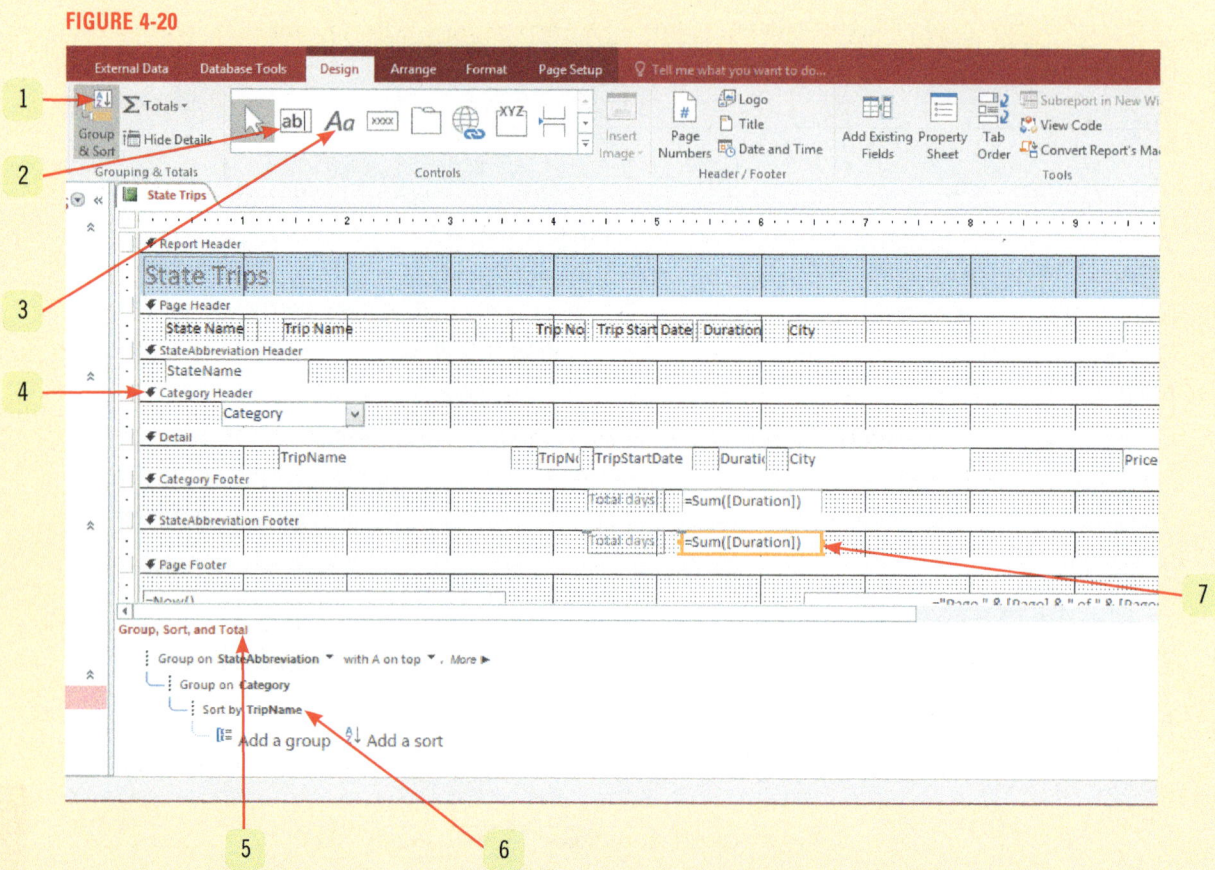

Match each term with the statement that best describes it.

8. Record source
9. Alignment
10. Detail section
11. Expression
12. Grouping
13. Section
14. Formatting

a. Left, center, or right are common choices
b. Prints once for every record
c. Used to identify which fields and records are passed to the report
d. Sorting records *plus* providing a header or footer section
e. Determines how controls are positioned on the report
f. A combination of field names, operators, and functions that results in a single value
g. Enhancing the appearance of information displayed in the report

Select the best answer from the list of choices.

15. **Which type of control is most commonly placed in the Detail section?**
    a. Image
    b. Line
    c. Text box
    d. Label

16. **Which of the following is not a valid report view?**
    a. Print Preview
    b. Section View
    c. Layout View
    d. Design View

17. **A title for a report would most commonly be placed in which report section?**
    a. Group Footer
    b. Detail
    c. Report Header
    d. Report Footer

18. **A calculated expression that presents page numbering information would probably be placed in which report section?**
    a. Report Header
    b. Detail
    c. Group Footer
    d. Page Footer

19. **To align the edges of several controls with each other, you use the alignment commands on the:**
    a. Formatting tab.
    b. Design tab.
    c. Print Preview tab.
    d. Arrange tab.

20. **Which of the following expressions counts the number of records using the FirstName field?**
    a. =Count([FirstName])
    b. =Count[FirstName]
    c. =Count((FirstName))
    d. =Count{FirstName}

21. **What is the difference between grouping and sorting in a report?**
    a. Grouping allows you to add a Group Header and/or Group Footer section to a report.
    b. Grouping means to sort in ascending order.
    c. Grouping means to sort by more than one field.
    d. You can have more than one grouping field, but you can only have one sorting field.

Skills Review

1. **Use the Report Wizard.**
   a. Start Access and open the LakeHomes-4.accdb database from the location where you store your Data Files. Enable content if prompted.
   b. Use the Report Wizard to create a report based on the RLast and RPhone fields from the Realtors table and the Type, SqFt, BR, Bath, and Asking fields from the Listings table. (*Hint*: Make sure your fields are added in the order listed.)
   c. View the data by Realtors, do not add any more grouping levels, and sort the records in descending order by the Asking field. (*Hint*: Click the Ascending button to toggle it to Descending.)
   d. Use a Stepped layout and a Landscape orientation. Title the report **Listings by Realtor**.
   e. Preview the first and second pages of the new report.

2. **Use Report Layout View.**
   a. Switch to Layout View and close the Field List and Property Sheet if they are open.
   b. Drag the right edge of the Asking column and label to the left to provide a little more space between the Asking column and Type column.
   c. Modify the RLast label to read **Realtor**, the RPhone label to read **Cell**, the SqFt label to read **Square Ft**, the BR label to read **Bedrooms**, and the Bath label to read **Baths**.
   d. Switch to Print Preview to review your changes.

Skills Review (continued)

3. Review report sections.

   a. Switch to Report Design View.

   b. Drag the text box that contains the Page calculation in the lower-right corner of the Page Footer section to the left so that it is to the left of the 9" mark on the horizontal ruler.

   c. Drag the right edge of the entire report to the left as far as possible.

   d. Preview the report and make sure there are no blank pages between printed pages. You may need to move or narrow more controls and narrow the report again in order to accomplish this.

4. Apply group and sort orders.

   a. Open the Group, Sort, and Total pane.

   b. Add the Type field as a grouping field between the RealtorNo grouping field and Asking sort field. Make sure the sort order on the Asking field is in descending order (from largest to smallest). (*Hint*: Use the Move up button to move the Type field between the RealtorNo and Asking fields in the Group, Sort, and Total pane.)

   c. Cut and paste the Type combo box from its current position in the Detail section to the Type Header section.

   d. Move the Type combo box in the Type Header section so its left edge is at about the 1" mark on the horizontal ruler.

   e. Delete the Type label in the Page Header section.

   f. Switch to Layout View, and resize the Asking, Square Ft, Bedrooms, and Baths columns as needed so they are more evenly spaced across the page.

5. Add subtotals and counts.

   a. Switch to Report Design View, then open the RealtorNo Footer section. (*Hint*: Use the More button on the RealtorNo field in the Group, Sort, and Total pane.)

   b. Add a text box control to the RealtorNo Footer section, just below the Asking text box in the Detail section. Change the label to read **Subtotal:**, and enter the expression **=Sum([Asking])** in the text box.

   c. Drag the bottom edge of the Report Footer section down about 0.25" to add space to the Report Footer.

   d. Copy and paste the new expression in the RealtorNo Footer section to the Report Footer section. Position the new controls in the Report Footer section directly below the controls in the RealtorNo Footer section.

   e. Modify the Subtotal: label in the Report Footer section to read **Grand Total:**.

   f. Preview the last page of the report to view the new subtotals in the RealtorNo Footer and Report Footer sections.

6. Resize and align controls.

   a. Switch to Design View, then click the Group & Sort button on the Design tab to close the Group, Sort, and Total pane if it is open.

   b. Click the Asking text box in the Detail section, press and hold [Shift], and then click the expression in the RealtorNo Footer as well as the Report Footer sections to select the three text boxes at the same time. Click the Arrange tab on the Ribbon, click the Align button, then click Right to right-align the edges of the three text boxes.

   c. With all three text boxes still selected, click the Format tab on the Ribbon, click the Apply Comma Number Format button, and click the Decrease Decimals button twice so that the values appear as whole dollar amounts without cents.

   d. Preview the report to view the alignment and format on the Asking data and subtotals.

7. Format a report.

   a. In Report Design View, change the Alternate Row Color of the Detail section to No Color.

   b. Change the Alternate Row Color of the Type Header, the RealtorNo Header, and the RealtorNo Footer sections to No Color.

   c. Change the Shape Fill color of the RealtorNo Header section to Green 2. (*Hint*: The Shape Fill button will change the Back Color property in the Property Sheet.)

Skills Review (continued)

d. Select the RLast and RPhone text boxes in the RealtorNo Header section, and change the Shape Fill color to Green 2 to match the RealtorNo Header section.

e. Bold the title of the report, which is the **Listings by Realtor** label in the Report Header, and resize it to make it a little wider to accommodate the bold text.

f. Change the font color of each label in the Page Header section to Automatic (black).

g. Save and preview the report in Print Preview. It should look like **FIGURE 4-21**. The report should fit on three pages, and the grand total for all Asking values should be 7,957,993. If there are blank pages between printed pages, return to Report Design View and drag the right edge of the report to the left.

FIGURE 4-21

h. In Report Design View, add a label to the left side of the Report Footer section with your name. Be sure to add a label and not a text box control. Make sure that your name is displayed clearly on the last page only in Print Preview.

i. Print the report if requested by your instructor, then save and close the Listings by Realtor report.

8. Create mailing labels.

a. Click the Agencies table in the Navigation Pane, then start the Label Wizard.

b. Choose Avery 5160 labels and the default text appearance choices.

c. Build a prototype label with the AgencyName on the first line, Street on the second line, and City, State, and Zip on the third line with a comma and space between City and State, and a space between State and Zip.

d. Sort by AgencyName, and name the report **Labels Agencies**.

e. Preview then save and close the report. Click OK if a warning dialog box appears regarding horizontal space. The data in your label report does not exceed the dimensions of the labels.

f. Open the Agencies table and change the name of Big Cedar Realtors to **Your Last Name Realtors**. Close the Agencies table, reopen the Labels Agencies report, then print it if requested by your instructor.

g. Close the Labels Agencies report, close the LakeHomes-4.accdb database, then exit Access 2016.

Independent Challenge 1

As the office manager of an international convention planning company, you have created a database to track convention, enrollment, and company data. Your goal is to create a report of up-to-date attendee enrollments.

a. Start Access, then open the Conventions-4.accdb database from the location where you store your Data Files. Enable content if prompted.

b. Use the Report Wizard to create a report with the AttendeeLast and AttendeeFirst fields from the Attendees table, the CompanyName field from the Companies table, and the ConventionName and CountryName from the Conventions table. Add the fields in the order listed.

c. View your data by Conventions, add the CompanyName as a second grouping field, then sort in ascending order by AttendeeLast.

d. Use the Block layout and Portrait orientation, then name the report **Convention Attendees**.

e. In Layout View, change the labels in the Page Header section from ConventionName to **Convention** and CompanyName to **Company**. Delete the CountryName, AttendeeLast, and AttendeeFirst labels in the Page Header section.

f. In Report Design View, open the Group, Sort, and Total pane, then open the ConventionNo Footer section.

g. In Report Design View, add a text box to the ConventionNo Footer section just below the AttendeeLast text box in the Detail section. The purpose of the text box is to count the number of people enrolled for each convention. The label should read **Count of Attendees:**, and the expression in the text box should be **=Count([AttendeeLast])**.

h. Resize the new label and text box as needed to make their contents clearly visible.

i. Copy and paste the new label and expression to the Report Footer section. Move and align the controls so they are at the same horizontal position on the page.

j. Change the text color of all labels to Automatic (black). (*Hint:* There are labels in the Report Header, Page Header, ConventionNo Footer, and Report Footer sections.)

k. Preview the report and make sure there are no blank pages between pages. Resize controls in Layout View and narrow the report in Report Design view as needed to remove blank pages.

l. Preview the last page of the report to make sure the subtotal count for each convention and grand total count for the report are aligned as shown in FIGURE 4-22.

m. Add a label with your name to the left side of the Report Footer section, change the text color to Automatic (black), and then print the last page if required by your instructor.

n. Save and close the Convention Attendees report, close the Conventions-4.accdb database, then exit Access 2016.

FIGURE 4-22

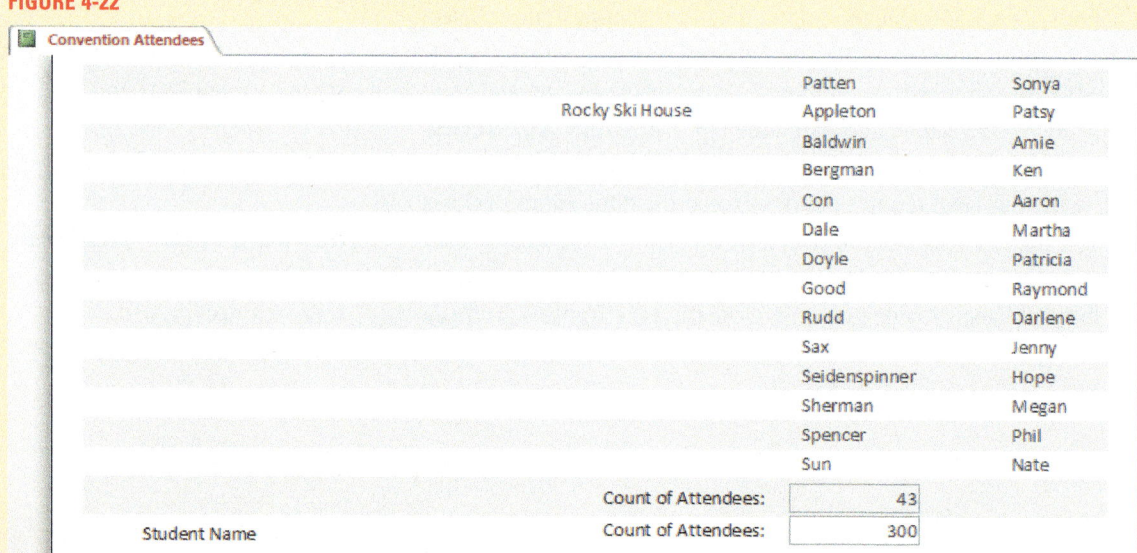

Independent Challenge 2

You have built an Access database to track membership in a community service club. The database tracks member names and addresses as well as their status and rank in the club and their hours of service to the community.

a. Start Access and open the Service-4.accdb database from the location where you store your Data Files. Enable content if prompted.

b. Open the Members table, find and change the name of Micah Ati to *your* name, then close the Members table.

c. Use the Report Wizard to create a report using the FirstName, LastName, and Dues fields from the Members table and the ActivityDate and HoursWorked fields from the Activities table, all in that order.

d. View the data by Members. Do not add any more grouping fields, and sort the records in ascending order by ActivityDate.

e. Use a Stepped layout and Portrait orientation, title the report **Activity Log**, then preview the report.

f. Use Report Layout View to resize the controls to fit the available space and display all data clearly.

g. Change the FirstName label to **First Name**. Change the LastName label to **Last Name**. Change the ActivityDate label to **Date**. Change the HoursWorked label to **Hours**.

h. Switch to Report Design View, then use the Group, Sort, and Total pane to open the MemberNo Footer section.

i. Add a text box to the MemberNo Footer section, just below the HoursWorked text box in the Detail section. Change the label to **Total:** and the expression in the text box to **=Sum([HoursWorked])**.

j. Open the Report Footer section, then copy and paste the **=Sum([HoursWorked])** text box to the Report Footer section. Change the label in the Report Footer section to read **Grand Total:**.

k. Align the HoursWorked text box in the Detail section and the two expressions in the MemberNo Footer and Report Footer sections so that the numbers are perfectly aligned. Be sure to preview the last page of the report to make sure all three controls are aligned as shown in FIGURE 4-23.

l. Add a label to the left edge of the Report Footer section with your name.

m. Preview each page of the report to make sure there are no blank pages. If there are, narrow the controls and the right edge of the report in Report Design View to fix this problem.

n. Print the last page of the report if requested to do so by your instructor.

o. Close the Activity Log report, close the Service-4.accdb database, then exit Access.

FIGURE 4-23

Total:	13
Grand Total:	476

Independent Challenge 3

You have built an Access database to organize the deposits at a salvage center. Various clubs regularly deposit material, which is measured in pounds when the deposits are made.

a. Start Access and open the Salvage-4.accdb database from the location where you store your Data Files. Enable content if prompted.

b. Open the Centers table, change **A1 Salvage Center** to **Your Last Name Salvage**, then close the table.

c. Use the Report Wizard to create a report with the CenterName field from the Centers table, the DepositDate and Weight fields from the Deposits table, and the ClubName field from the Clubs table.

d. View the data by Centers, do not add any more grouping levels, and sort the records in ascending order by DepositDate.

e. Use a Stepped layout and a Portrait orientation, then title the report **Deposit Log**.

f. In Layout View, resize the Weight label and Weight data to better position the data across the report. Rename the DepositDate label to **Date**.

g. Add spaces to the labels so that CenterName becomes **Center Name**, and ClubName becomes **Club Name**.

h. In Report Design View, open the Group, Sort, and Total pane and then open the CenterNumber Footer section.

i. Add a text box to the CenterNumber Footer section just below the Weight text box with the expression **=Sum([Weight])**.

j. Rename the new label to be **Subtotal:**.

k. Copy the new text box and paste it back to the CenterNumber Footer section. Change the new label to **Count:** and the expression to **=Count([Weight])**. Align the new controls directly below the Subtotal and =Sum([Weight]) expression.

l. Paste the controls a second time to the CenterNumber Footer section, and change the new label to **Average:** and the expression to **=Avg([Weight])**.

m. Change the Format property of the =Avg([Weight]) expression to **Standard**, and change the Decimal Places property to **0**. (*Hint*: Open the Property Sheet for the text box and click the Format tab to find the Format and Decimal Places properties.)

n. Expand the Report Footer section, then copy and paste the three text boxes from the CenterNumber Footer section to the Report Footer section.

o. Move and align the text boxes in the CenterNumber Footer and Report Footer sections to be positioned directly under the Weight text box in the Detail section. (*Hint*: You may need to both right-align the text boxes as well as align the right edges of the text boxes.)

p. Change the Subtotal label in the Report Footer section to **Total Sum:**. Change the Count label in the Report Footer section to **Total Count:** and also left-align the labels in the CenterNumber Footer and Report Footer sections.

q. Add a label to the left edge of the Report Footer section with your name and preview the last page of the report, a portion of which is shown in FIGURE 4-24. Your numbers should match.

r. Continue to improve the report as needed to align all numbers and labels and to remove any extra blank space in the report by making your sections as vertically short as possible in Report Design View.

s. Save and close the Deposit Log report, close the Salvage-4.accdb database, then exit Access.

FIGURE 4-24

1/16/2017	85	Access Users Group
1/21/2017	150	Boy Scout Troop 324
Subtotal:	3315	
Count:	36	
Average:	92	
Total Sum:	11360	
Total Count:	118	
Average:	96	

Student Name

Independent Challenge 4: Explore

One way you can use an Access database on your own is to record and track your job search efforts. In this exercise, you create a report to help read and analyze data in your job-tracking database.

a. Start Access and open the JobSearch-4.accdb database from the location where you store your Data Files. Enable content if prompted.

b. Open the Employers table, and enter five more records to identify five more potential employers.

c. Use subdatasheets in the Employers table to enter five more potential jobs. You may enter all five jobs for one employer, one job for five different employers, or any combination thereof. Be sure to check the spelling of all data entered. For the Desirability field, enter a value from **1** to **5**, 1 being the least desirable and 5 being the most desirable. Close the Employers table.

d. Use the Report Wizard to create a report that lists the CompanyName, EmpCity, and EmpState fields from the Employers table, and the Title, AnnualSalary, and Desirability fields from the Positions table.

e. View the data by Employers, do not add any more grouping levels, and sort the records in descending order by Desirability.

f. Use an Outline layout and a Portrait orientation, then title the report **Jobs**.

g. In Design View, revise the labels in the EmployerID Header section from CompanyName to **Company**, EmpCity to **City**, EmpState to **State**, and AnnualSalary to **Salary**.

h. Right-align the text within the Company, City, and State labels so they are closer to the text boxes they describe.

i. In Report Layout View, resize the Desirability, Title, and Salary labels and text boxes to space the controls evenly across the report.

j. Preview the report, then switch to Report Design View to remove any extra space in the report sections. This will involve moving the controls in the EmployerID Header section as far to the top of that section as possible, then dragging the top edge of the Detail section up.

k. Preview the report, making sure all controls fit within the width of portrait orientation. If not, switch to Report Design View and fix this problem.

l. Print the first page if requested by your instructor.

m. Close the Jobs report, close the JobSearch-4.accdb database, then exit Access 2016.

Visual Workshop

Open the Basketball-4.accdb database from the location where you store your Data Files and enable content if prompted. Open the Players table, change the name of Matthew Douglas to *your* name, then close the table. Your goal is to create the report shown in FIGURE 4-25. Use the Report Wizard, and select the PFirst, PLast, HomeTown, and HomeState fields from the Players table. Select the FieldGoals, 3Pointers, and FreeThrows fields from the Stats table. View the data by Players, do not add any more grouping levels, and do not add any more sorting levels. Use a Block layout and a Portrait orientation, then title the report **Scoring Report**. In Layout View, resize all of the columns so that they fit on a single piece of portrait paper, and change the labels in the Page Header section as shown. In Design View, open the PlayerNo Footer section and add text boxes with expressions to sum the FieldGoals, 3Pointers, and FreeThrows fields and bold those controls. Drag the top edge of the Page Footer section down a little to add a little space between the subtotals in the PlayerNo Footer section and the next set of records for the next player. Move, modify, align, and resize all controls as needed to match FIGURE 4-25. (*Hint*: Change the Shape Outline of the text boxes in the PlayerNo Footer section to Transparent to remove the outline.) Be sure to print preview the report to make sure that it fits within the width of one sheet of paper. Modify the report to narrow it in Report Design View if needed.

FIGURE 4-25

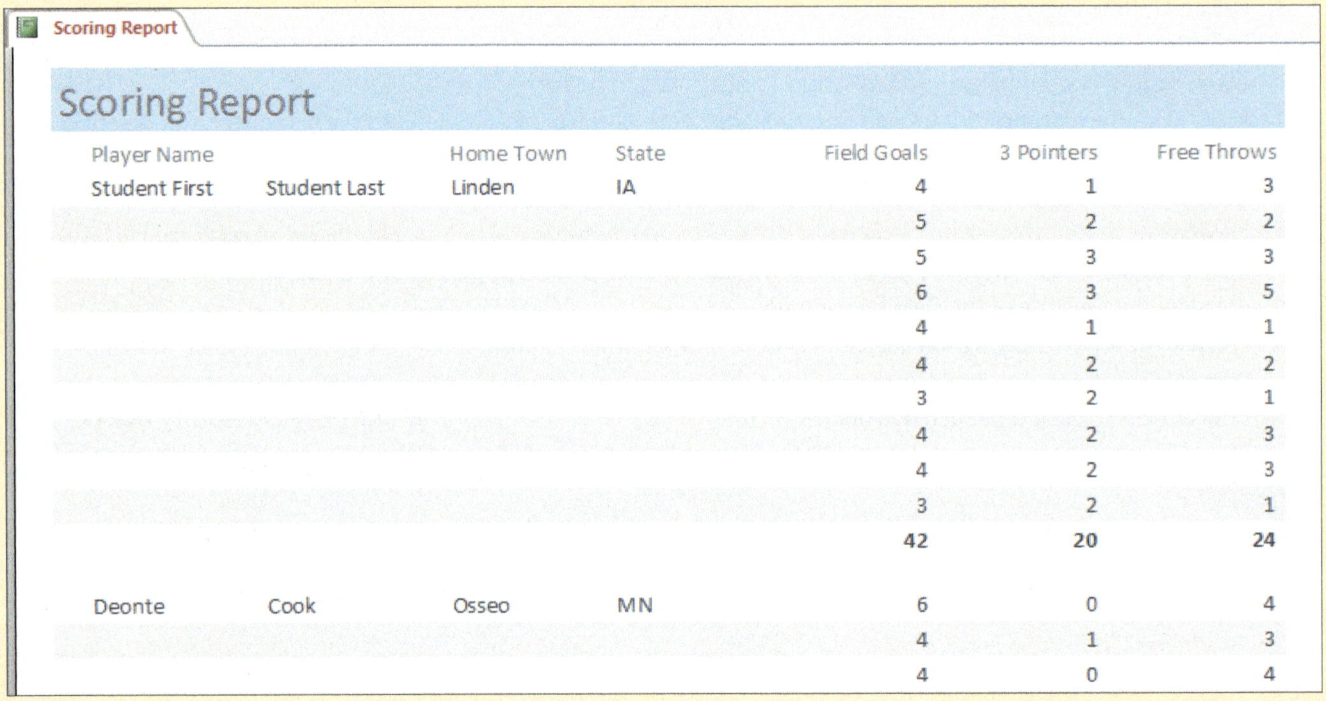

				Field Goals	3 Pointers	Free Throws
Player Name		**Home Town**	**State**			
Student First	Student Last	Linden	IA	4	1	3
				5	2	2
				5	3	3
				6	3	5
				4	1	1
				4	2	2
				3	2	1
				4	2	3
				4	2	3
				3	2	1
				42	**20**	**24**
Deonte	Cook	Osseo	MN	6	0	4
				4	1	3
				4	0	4

Modifying the Database Structure

CASE ▶ Working with Julia Rice, the trip developer for U.S. travel at Reason 2 Go, you are developing an Access database to track trips, customers, sales, and payments. The database consists of multiple tables that you link, modify, and enhance to create a relational database.

Module Objectives

After completing this module, you will be able to:

- Examine relational databases
- Design related tables
- Create one-to-many relationships
- Create Lookup fields
- Modify Short Text fields

- Modify Number and Currency fields
- Modify Date/Time fields
- Modify validation properties
- Create Attachment fields

Files You Will Need

R2G-5.accdb
JAlman.jpg
Member1.jpg

Jobs-5.accdb
Training-5.accdb

Examine Relational Databases

Learning Outcomes
- Design tables and fields
- Design primary and foreign key fields
- Analyze one-to-many relationships

The purpose of a relational database is to organize and store data in a way that minimizes redundancy and maximizes your flexibility when querying and analyzing data. To accomplish these goals, a relational database uses related tables rather than a single large table of data. At one time, the Sales Department at Reason 2 Go tracked information about its trip sales and payments using a single Access table called Sales, shown in **FIGURE 5-1**. This created data redundancy problems because of the duplicate trip, customer, and payment information entered into a single table. **CASE** ▶ *You decide to study the principles of relational database design to help R2G reorganize these fields into a correctly designed relational database.*

DETAILS

To redesign a list into a relational database, follow these principles:

- **Design each table to contain fields that describe only one subject**

  Currently, the table in **FIGURE 5-1** contains four subjects—trips, sales, customers, and payments—which creates redundant data. For example, the trip name must be duplicated for each sale of that trip. The customer's name must be reentered every time that customer purchases a trip or makes a payment. The problems of redundant data include extra data entry work; more data entry inconsistencies and errors; larger physical storage requirements; and limitations on your ability to search for, analyze, and report on the data. You minimize these problems by implementing a properly designed relational database.

- **Identify a primary key field for each table**

  A **primary key field** is a field that contains unique information for each record. For example, in a customer table, the customer number field usually serves this purpose. Although using the customer's last name as the primary key field might work in a small database, names are generally a poor choice for a primary key field because the primary key cannot accommodate two customers who have the same name.

- **Build one-to-many relationships**

  To tie the information from one table to another, a field must be common to each table. This linking field is the primary key field on the "one" side of the relationship and the **foreign key field** on the "many" side of the relationship. Recall that a primary key field stores unique information for each record in that table. For example, a CustomerNo field acting as the primary key field in the Customers table would link to a CustomerNo foreign key field in a Sales table to join one customer to many sales. You are not required to give the primary and foreign key fields the same name, although doing so does clarify which fields are used to link two tables in a one-to-many relationship.

  The revised design for the database is shown in **FIGURE 5-2**. One customer can purchase many trips, so the Customers and Sales tables have a one-to-many relationship based on the linking CustNo field. One trip can be purchased many times, so the Trips and Sales tables have a one-to-many relationship (TripNo in the Sales table and TripNo in the Trips table). One sale may have many payments, creating a one-to-many relationship between the Sales and Payments tables based on the common SalesNo field.

Using many-to-many relationships

As you design your database, you might find that two tables have a **many-to-many relationship**, which means that a record in one table may be related to many records in the other table and vice versa. To join them, you must establish a third table called a **junction table**, which contains two foreign key fields to serve on the "many" side of separate one-to-many relationships with the two original tables. The Customers and Trips tables have a many-to-many relationship because one customer can purchase many trips and one trip can have many customers purchase it. The Sales table serves as the junction table to link the three tables together.

FIGURE 5-1: Single Sales table results in duplicate data

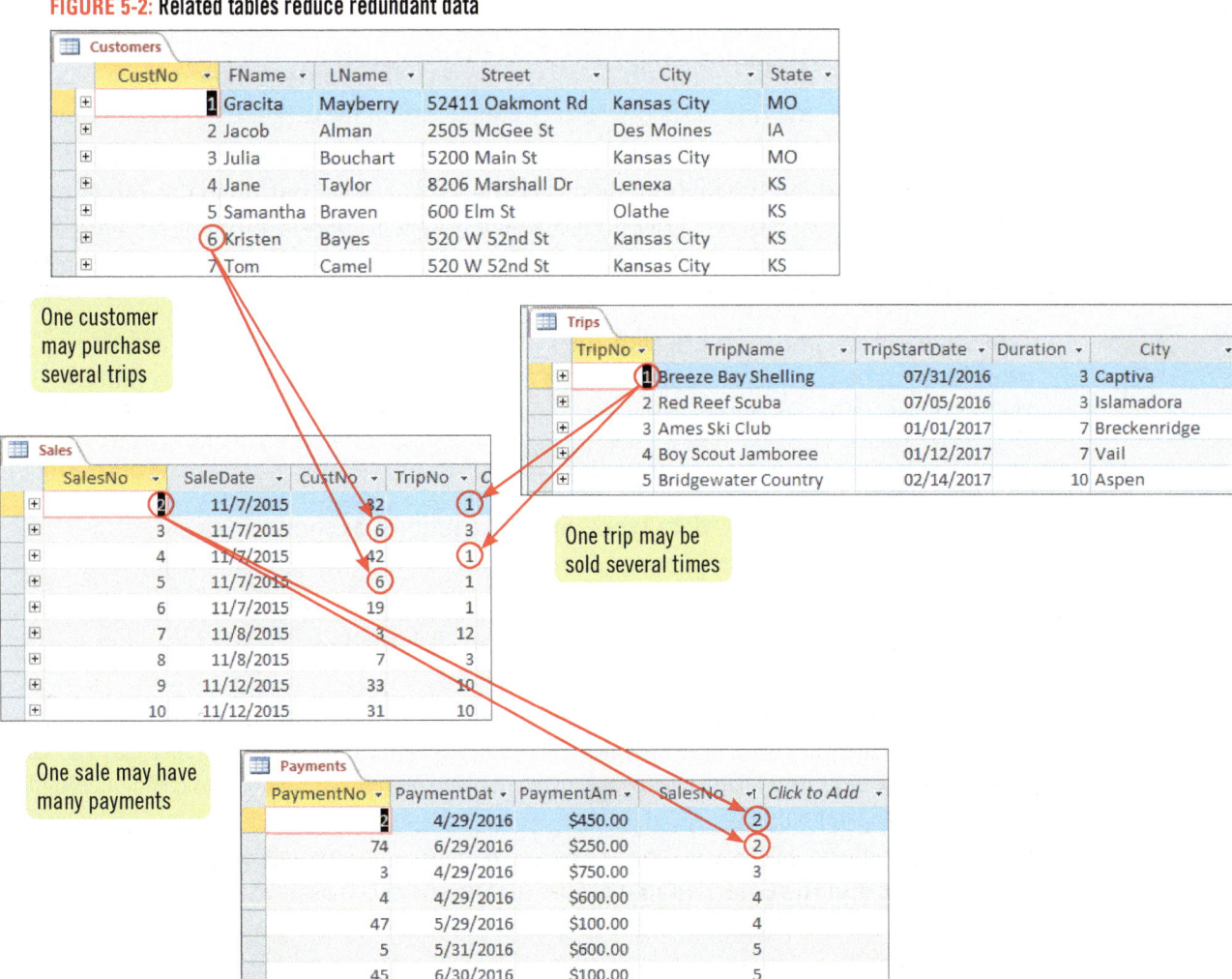

FIGURE 5-2: Related tables reduce redundant data

Enforcing referential integrity

Referential integrity is a set of rules that helps reduce invalid entries and orphan records. An **orphan record** is a record in the "many" table that doesn't have a matching entry in the linking field of the "one" table. With **referential integrity** enforced on a one-to-many relationship, you cannot enter a value in a foreign key field of the "many" table that does not have a match in the linking field of the "one" table. Referential integrity also prevents you from deleting a record in the "one" table if a matching entry exists in the foreign key field of the "many" table. You should enforce referential integrity on all one-to-many relationships if possible. If you are working with a database that already contains orphan records, you cannot enforce referential integrity on that relationship until the orphan records are either corrected or deleted, a process called **scrubbing** the database.

Design Related Tables

Learning Outcomes
- Set field data types in Table Design View
- Set field descriptions in Table Design View

After you develop a valid relational database design, you are ready to create the tables in Access. Using **Table Design View**, you can specify all characteristics of a table, including field names, data types, field descriptions, field properties, Lookup properties, and primary key field designations. **CASE** *Using the new database design, Julia Rice asks you to create the Payments table for Reason 2 Go.*

STEPS

1. **Start Access, open the R2G-5.accdb database, then enable content if prompted**

   The Customers, Sales, and Trips tables have already been created in the database. You need to create the Payments table.

2. **Click the Create tab on the Ribbon, then click the Table Design button in the Tables group**

   Table Design View opens, where you can enter field names and specify data types and field properties for the new table. Field names should be as short as possible but long enough to be descriptive. The field name you enter in Table Design View is used as the default name for the field in all later queries, forms, and reports.

   > **QUICK TIP**
   > When specifying field data types, you can type the first letter of the data type to quickly select it.

3. **Type PaymentNo, press [Enter], click the Data Type list arrow, click AutoNumber, press [Tab], type Unique payment number and primary key field, then press [Enter]**

   The AutoNumber data type automatically assigns the next available integer in the sequence to each new record. The AutoNumber data type is often used as the primary key field for a table because it always contains a unique value for each record.

4. **Type the other field names, data types, and descriptions, as shown in FIGURE 5-3**

   Field descriptions entered in Table Design View are optional, but they provide a way to add helpful information about the field.

   > **TROUBLE**
   > If you set the wrong field as the primary key field, click the Primary Key button again to toggle it off.

5. **Click PaymentNo in the Field Name column, then click the Primary Key button in the Tools group**

   A **key symbol** appears to the left of PaymentNo to indicate that this field is defined as the primary key field for this table. Primary key fields have two roles: They uniquely define each record, and they may also serve as the "one" side of a one-to-many relationship between two tables. **TABLE 5-1** describes common examples of one-to-many relationships.

   > **QUICK TIP**
   > To delete or rename an existing table, right-click it in the Navigation Pane, then click Delete or Rename.

6. **Click the Save button 🖫 on the Quick Access Toolbar, type Payments in the Table Name text box, click OK, then close the table**

   The Payments table is now displayed as a table object in the R2G-5.accdb database Navigation Pane, as shown in **FIGURE 5-4**.

Specifying the foreign key field data type

A foreign key field in the "many" table must have the same data type (Short Text or Number) as the primary key it is related to in the "one" table. An exception to this rule is when the primary key field in the "one" table has an AutoNumber data type. In this case, the linking foreign key field in the "many" table must have a Number data type. Also note that a Number field used as a foreign key field must have a Long Integer Field Size property to match the Field Size property of the AutoNumber primary key field.

FIGURE 5-3: Table Design View for the new Payments table

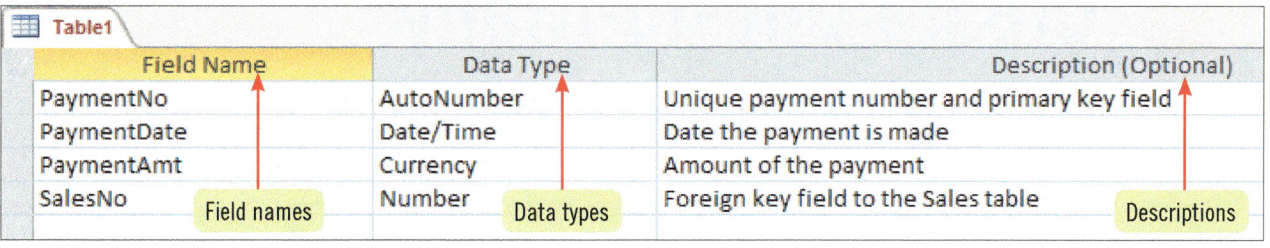

Field Name	Data Type	Description (Optional)
PaymentNo	AutoNumber	Unique payment number and primary key field
PaymentDate	Date/Time	Date the payment is made
PaymentAmt	Currency	Amount of the payment
SalesNo	Number	Foreign key field to the Sales table

FIGURE 5-4: Payments table in R2G-5 database Navigation Pane

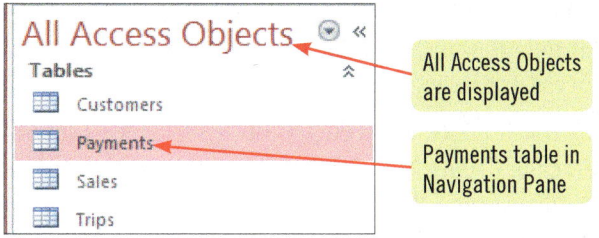

TABLE 5-1: Common one-to-many relationships

table on "one" side	table on "many" side	linking field	description
Products	Sales	ProductID	A ProductID field must have a unique entry in a Products table, but it is listed many times in a Sales table
Students	Enrollments	StudentID	A StudentID field must have a unique entry in a Students table, but it is listed many times in an Enrollments table as the student enrolls in multiple classes
Employees	Promotions	EmployeeID	An EmployeeID field must have a unique entry in an Employees table, but it is listed many times in a Promotions table as the employee is promoted over time

Learning Outcomes
- Enforce referential integrity on a one-to-many relationship
- Create a Relationship report

Create One-to-Many Relationships

After creating the tables you need, you link them together in appropriate one-to-many relationships using the primary key field in the "one" table and the foreign key field in the "many" table. To avoid time-consuming rework, be sure that your table relationships are finished before building queries, forms, or reports using fields from multiple tables. **CASE** ▸ *Julia asks you to define the one-to-many relationships between the tables of the R2G-5.accdb database.*

STEPS

QUICK TIP
Drag the table's title bar to move the field list.

1. **Click the Database Tools tab on the Ribbon, click the Relationships button, click the Show Table button, double-click Customers, double-click Sales, double-click Trips, double-click Payments, then click Close in the Show Table dialog box**
   The four table field lists appear in the Relationships window. The primary key fields are identified with a small key symbol to the left of the field name. With all of the field lists in the Relationships window, you're ready to link them in proper one-to-many relationships.

QUICK TIP
Drag the bottom border of the field list to display all of the fields.

2. **Click CustNo in the Customers table field list, then drag it to the CustNo field in the Sales table field list**
   Dragging a field from one table to another in the Relationships window links the two tables by the selected fields and opens the Edit Relationships dialog box, as shown in **FIGURE 5-5**. Recall that referential integrity helps ensure data accuracy.

TROUBLE
Right-click a relationship line then click Delete if you need to delete a relationship and start over.

3. **Click the Enforce Referential Integrity check box in the Edit Relationships dialog box, then click Create**
   The **one-to-many line** shows the link between the CustNo field of the Customers table and the CustNo field of the Sales table. The "one" side of the relationship is the unique CustNo value for each record in the Customers table. The "many" side of the relationship is identified by an infinity symbol pointing to the CustNo field in the Sales table. You also need to link the Trips table to the Sales table.

4. **Click TripNo in the Trips table field list, drag it to TripNo in the Sales table field list, click the Enforce Referential Integrity check box, then click Create**
   Finally, you need to link the Payments table to the Sales table.

5. **Click SalesNo in the Sales table field list, drag it to SalesNo in the Payments table field list, click the Enforce Referential Integrity check box, click Create, then drag the Trips title bar down so all links are clear**
   The updated Relationships window should look like **FIGURE 5-6**.

TROUBLE
Click the Landscape button on the Print Preview tab if the report is too wide for portrait orientation.

6. **Click the Relationship Report button in the Tools group, click the Print button on the Print Preview tab, then click OK**
   A printout of the Relationships window, called the **Relationship report**, shows how your relational database is designed and includes table names, field names, primary key fields, and one-to-many relationship lines. This printout is helpful as you later create queries, forms, and reports that use fields from multiple tables. Note that it is not necessary to directly link each table to every other table.

7. **Right-click the Relationships for R2G-5 report tab, click Close, click Yes to save the report, then click OK to accept the default report name**
   The Relationships for R2G-5 report is saved in your database, as shown in the Navigation Pane.

8. **Close the Relationships window, then click Yes if prompted to save changes**

FIGURE 5-5: Edit Relationships dialog box

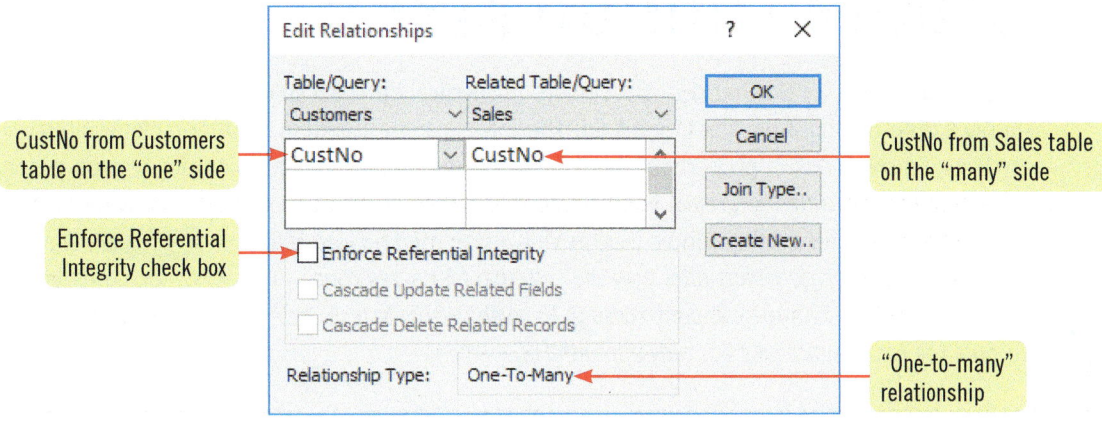

CustNo from Customers table on the "one" side

Enforce Referential Integrity check box

CustNo from Sales table on the "many" side

"One-to-many" relationship

FIGURE 5-6: Final Relationships window

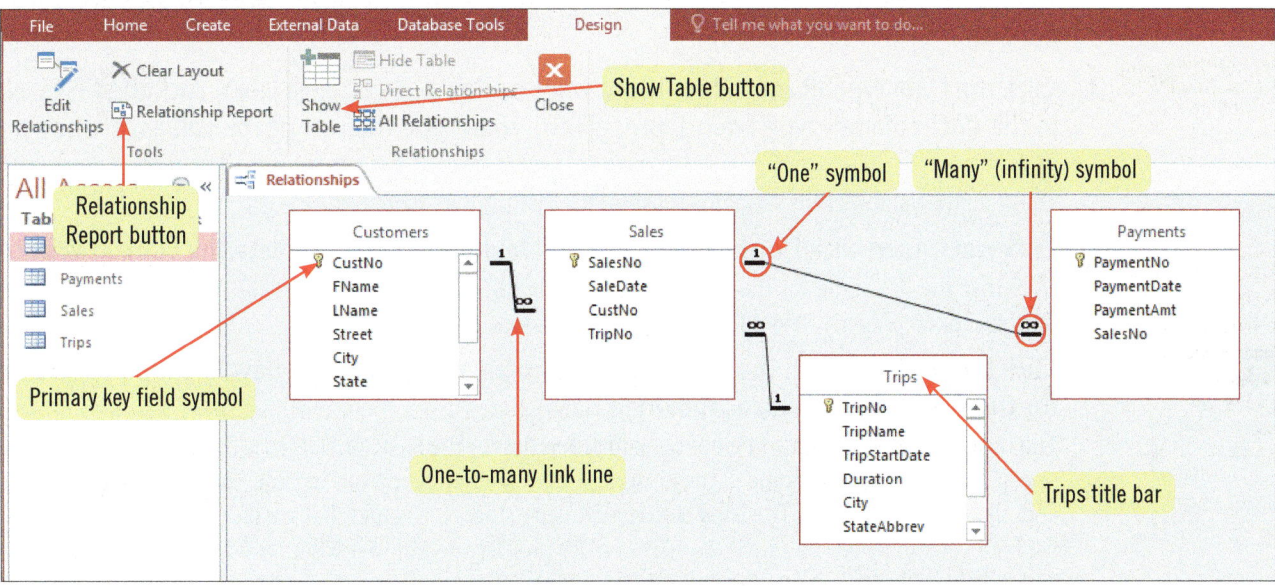

Show Table button

Relationship Report button

"One" symbol

"Many" (infinity) symbol

Primary key field symbol

One-to-many link line

Trips title bar

More on enforcing referential integrity

Recall that referential integrity is a set of rules to help ensure that no orphan records are entered or created in the database. An orphan record is a record in the "many" table (also called the **child table**) that doesn't have a matching entry in the linking field of the "one" table (also called the **parent table**). Referential integrity prevents orphan records in multiple ways. Referential integrity will not allow you to make an entry in the foreign key field of the child table that does not have a matching value in the linking field of the parent table. (So you can't make a sale to a customer who doesn't first exist in the Customers table, for example.) Referential integrity

also prevents you from deleting a record in the parent table that has related records in the child table. (So you can't delete a customer from the Customers table who already has related sales records in the Sales table, for example.) You should enforce referential integrity on all one-to-many relationships if possible. Unfortunately, if you are working with a database that already contains orphan records, you cannot enforce this powerful set of rules unless you find and fix the data so that orphan records no longer exist. The process of removing and fixing orphan records is commonly called **scrubbing data** or **data cleansing**.

Create Lookup Fields

A **Lookup field** is a field that contains Lookup properties. **Lookup properties** are field properties that supply a drop-down list of values for a field. The values can be stored in another table or directly stored in the **Row Source** Lookup property of the field. Fields that are good candidates for Lookup properties are those that contain a defined set of appropriate values such as State, Gender, or Department. You can set Lookup properties for a field in Table Design View using the **Lookup Wizard**. **CASE** *The FirstContact field in the Customers table identifies how the customer first made contact with R2G, such as being referred by a friend (Friend), finding the company through the web (Web), or responding to a radio advertisement (Radio). Because the FirstContact field has only a handful of valid entries, it is a good Lookup field candidate.*

STEPS

1. **Right-click the Customers table in the Navigation Pane, then click Design View**
   The Lookup Wizard is included in the Data Type list.

2. **Click the Short Text data type for the FirstContact field, click the Data Type list arrow, then click Lookup Wizard**
   The Lookup Wizard starts and prompts you for information about where the Lookup column will get its values.

3. **Click the I will type in the values that I want option button, click Next, click the first cell in the Col1 column, type Friend, press [Tab], then type the rest of the values, as shown in FIGURE 5-7**
   These are the values for the drop-down list for the FirstContact field.

4. **Click Next, then click Finish to accept the default label and complete the Lookup Wizard**
   Note that the data type for the FirstContact field is still Short Text. The Lookup Wizard is a process for setting Lookup property values for a field, not a data type itself.

5. **Click the Lookup tab in the Field Properties pane to observe the new Lookup properties for the FirstContact field, as shown in FIGURE 5-8**
   The Lookup Wizard helped you enter Lookup properties for the FirstContact field, but you can always enter or edit them directly, too. Some of the most important Lookup properties include Row Source, Limit To List, and Allow Value List Edits. The **Row Source** property stores the values that are provided in the drop-down list for a Lookup field. The **Limit To List** Lookup property determines whether you can enter a new value into a field with other Lookup properties, or whether the entries are limited to the drop-down list. The **Allow Value List Edits** property determines whether users can add or edit the list of items.

6. **Click the View button ▦ to switch to Datasheet View, click Yes when prompted to save the table, press [Tab] eight times to move to the FirstContact field, then click the FirstContact list arrow, as shown in FIGURE 5-9**
   The FirstContact field now provides a list of four values for this field. To edit the list in Datasheet View, click the **Edit List Items button** below the list.

7. **Close the Customers table**

Creating multivalued fields

Multivalued fields allow you to make more than one choice from a drop-down list for a field. As a database designer, multivalued fields allow you to select and store more than one choice without having to create a more advanced database design. To create a multivalued field, enter Yes in the **Allow Multiple Values** Lookup property.

FIGURE 5-7: Entering a list of values in the Lookup Wizard

Creating the drop-down list of values for a Lookup field

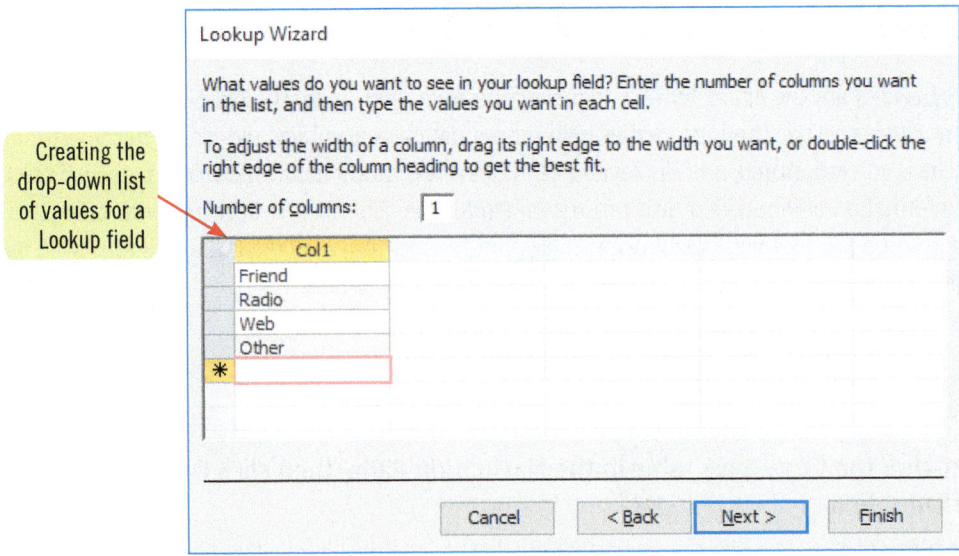

FIGURE 5-8: Viewing Lookup properties

Record selector

Data Type for FirstContact field is still Short Text

Lookup tab displays Lookup properties

Display Control property

Row Source property

Limit to List property

Allow Value List Edits property

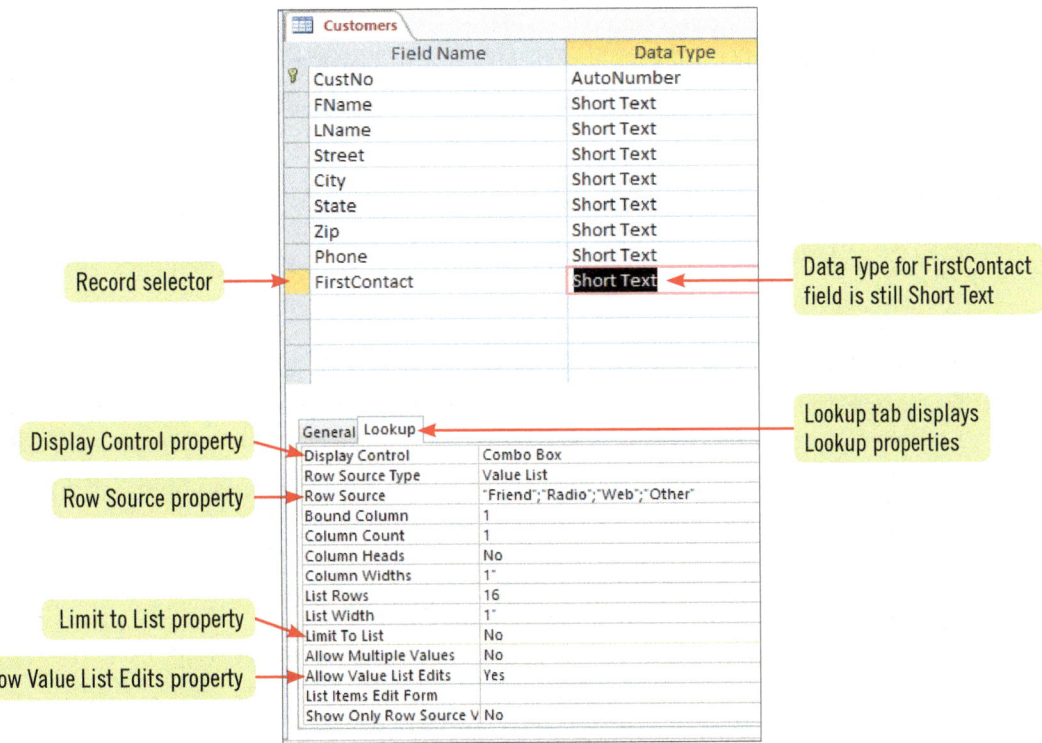

FIGURE 5-9: Using a Lookup field in a datasheet

Drop-down list for Lookup field

Edit List Items button

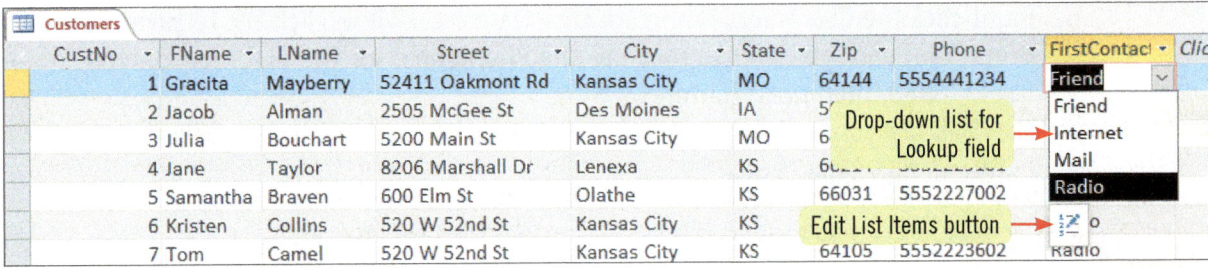

Modify Short Text Fields

Field properties are the characteristics that describe each field, such as Field Size, Format, Input Mask, Caption, or Default Value. These properties help ensure database accuracy and clarity because they restrict the way data is entered, stored, and displayed. You modify field properties in Table Design View. See **TABLE 5-2** for more information on Short Text field properties. (*Note:* The "Short Text" data type was called the "Text" data type in some previous versions of Access.) **CASE** *After reviewing the Customers table with Julia Rice, you decide to change field properties for several Short Text fields in that table.*

STEPS

1. **Right-click the Customers table in the Navigation Pane, then click Design View on the shortcut menu**

   Field properties appear on the General tab on the lower half of the Table Design View window called the **Field Properties pane**, and they apply to the selected field. Field properties change depending on the field's data type. For example, when you select a field with a Short Text data type, you see the **Field Size property**, which determines the number of characters you can enter in the field. However, when you select a field with a Date/Time data type, Access controls the size of the data, so the Field Size property is not displayed. Many field properties are optional, but for those that require an entry, Access provides a default value.

2. **Press [↓] to move through each field while viewing the field properties in the lower half of the window**

   The **field selector button** to the left of the field indicates which field is currently selected.

3. **Click the FirstContact field name, double-click 255 in the Field Size property text box, type 6, click the Save button 🖫 on the Quick Access Toolbar, then click Yes**

   The maximum and the default value for the Field Size property for a Short Text field is 255. In general, however, you want to make the Field Size property for Short Text fields only as large as needed to accommodate the longest reasonable entry. In some cases, shortening the Field Size property helps prevent typographical errors. For example, you should set the Field Size property for a State field that stores two-letter state abbreviations to 2 to prevent typos such as TXX. For the FirstContact field, your longest entry is "Friend"—6 characters.

4. **Change the Field Size property to 30 for the FName and LName fields, click 🖫, then click Yes**

   No existing entries are greater than 30 characters for either of these fields, so no data is lost. The **Input Mask** property provides a visual guide for users as they enter data. It also helps determine what types of values can be entered into a field.

5. **Click the Phone field name, click the Input Mask property text box, click the Build button ⋯, click the Phone Number input mask, click Next, click Next, click Finish, then click to the right of the Input Mask property value so you can read it**

   Table Design View of the Customers table should look like **FIGURE 5-10**, which shows the Input Mask property created for the Phone field by the Input Mask Wizard.

6. **Right-click the Customers table tab, click Datasheet View, click Yes to save the table, press [Tab] enough times to move to the Phone field for the first record, type 5551118888, then press [Enter]**

   The Phone Input Mask property creates an easy-to-use visual guide to facilitate accurate data entry.

7. **Close the Customers table**

FIGURE 5-10: Changing Short Text field properties

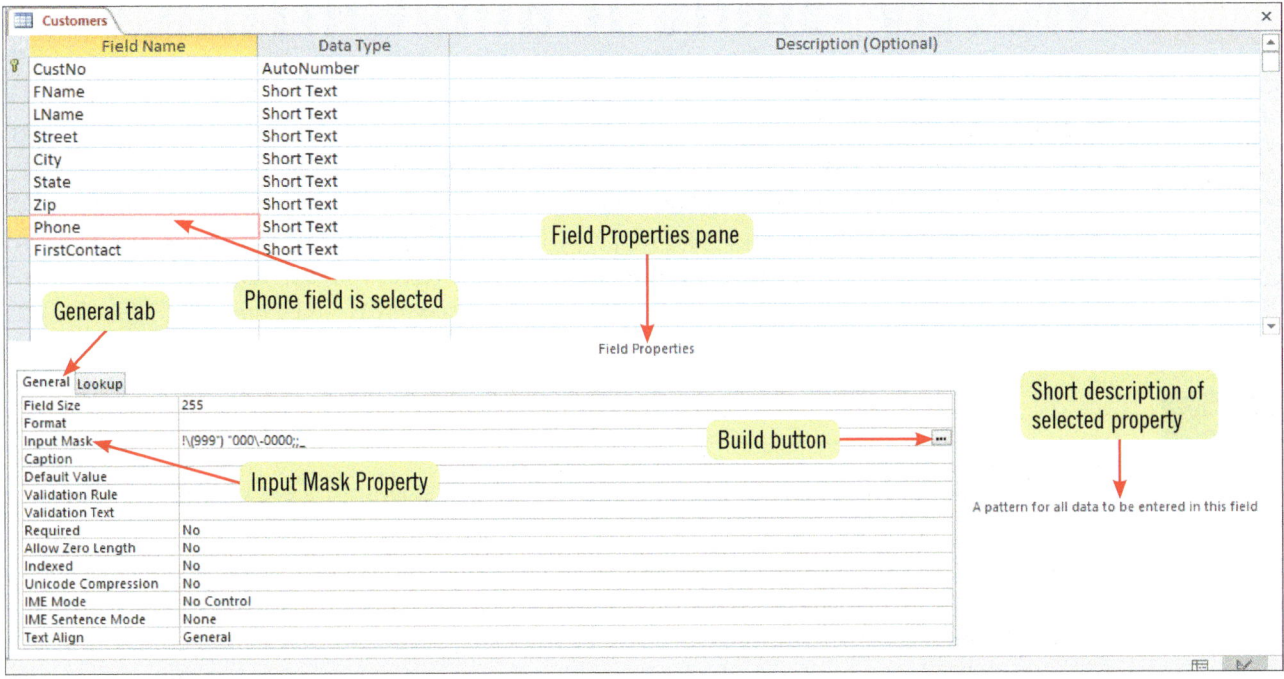

TABLE 5-2: Common Short Text field properties

property	description	sample field	sample property entry
Field Size	Controls how many characters can be entered into the field	State	2
Format	Controls how information will be displayed and printed	State	> (displays all characters in uppercase)
Input Mask	Provides a pattern for data to be entered	Phone	!(999) 000-0000;1;_
Caption	Describes the field in the first row of a datasheet, form, or report; if the Caption property is not entered, the field name is used to label the field	EmpNo	Employee Number
Default Value	Displays a value that is automatically entered in the given field for new records	City	Kansas City
Required	Determines if an entry is required for this field	LastName	Yes

Working with the Input Mask property

The Input Mask property provides a pattern for data to be entered, using three parts separated by semicolons. The first part provides a pattern for what type of data can be entered. For example, 9 represents an optional number, 0 a required number, ? an optional letter, and L a required letter. The second part determines whether all displayed characters (such as dashes in a phone number) are stored in the field. For the second part of the input mask, a 0 entry stores all characters, such as 555-1199, and a 1 entry stores only the entered data, 5551199. The third part of the input mask determines which character Access uses to guide the user through the mask. Common choices are the asterisk (*), underscore (_), or pound sign (#).

**Access 2016
Module 5**

**Learning
Outcomes**
• Modify the Field
Size property for
Number fields
• Modify the
Decimal Places
property

Modify Number and Currency Fields

Although some properties for Number and Currency fields are the same as the properties of Short Text fields, each data type has its own list of valid properties. Number and Currency fields have similar properties because they both contain numeric values. Currency fields store values that represent money, and Number fields store values that represent values such as quantities, measurements, and scores. **CASE** *The Trips table contains both a Number field (Duration) and a Currency field (Price). Julia wants you to modify the properties of these two fields.*

STEPS

QUICK TIP
The list arrow for
each property is on
the far right side of
the property box.

QUICK TIP
Double-click a
property name to
toggle through the
choices.

TROUBLE
If values appear as
#####, it means the
column needs to be
widened to see all of
the data.

1. **Right-click the Trips table in the Navigation Pane, click Design View on the shortcut menu, then click the Duration field name**

   The default Field Size property for a Number field is **Long Integer**. See **TABLE 5-3** for more information on the Field Size property and other common properties for a Number field. Access sets the size of Currency fields to control the way numbers are rounded in calculations, so the Field Size property isn't available for Currency fields.

2. **Click Integer in the Field Size property text box, click the Field Size list arrow, then click Byte**

   Choosing a **Byte** value for the Field Size property allows entries from 0 to 255, so it greatly restricts the possible values and the storage requirements for the Duration field.

3. **Click the Price field name, click Auto in the Decimal Places property text box, click the Decimal Places list arrow, click 0, then press [Enter]**

   Your Table Design View should look like **FIGURE 5-11**. Because all of R2G's trips are priced at a round dollar value, you do not need to display cents in the Price field.

4. **Save the table, then switch to Datasheet View**

   You won't lose any data because none of the current entries in the Duration field is greater than 255, the maximum value allowed by a Number field with a Byte Field Size property. You want to test the new property changes.

5. **Press [Tab] three times to move to the Duration field for the first record, type 300, then press [Tab]**

   Because 300 is larger than what the Byte Field Size property allows (0–255), an Access error message appears, indicating that the value isn't valid for this field.

6. **Click OK, press [Esc] to remove the inappropriate entry in the Duration field, then press [Tab] four times to move to the Price field**

   The Price field is set to display zero digits after the decimal point.

7. **Type 750.99 in the Price field of the first record, press [Tab], then click $751 in the Price field of the first record to see the full entry**

   Although the Decimal Places property for the Price field specifies that entries in the field are formatted to display zero digits after the decimal point, 750.99 is the actual value stored in the field. Modifying the Decimal Places property does not change the actual data. Rather, the Decimal Places property only changes the way the data is *presented*.

8. **Close the Trips table**

FIGURE 5-11: Changing Currency and Number field properties

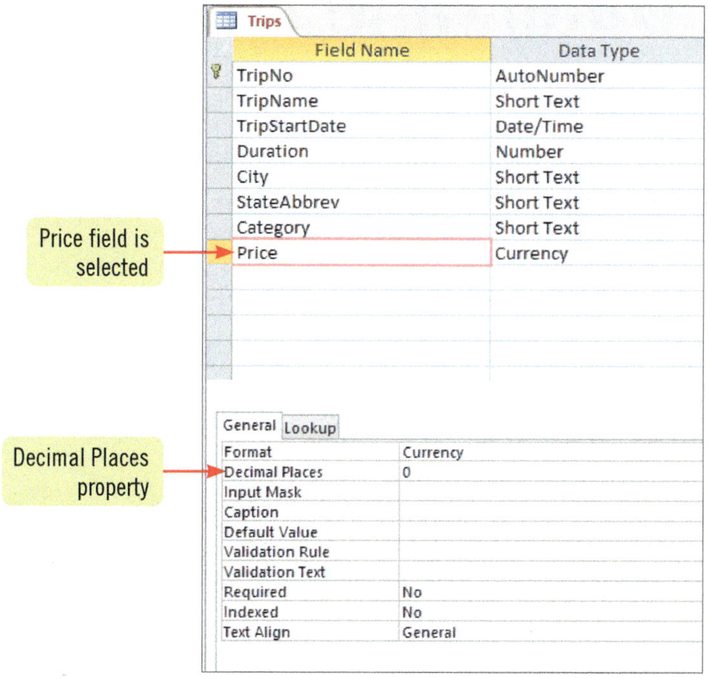

TABLE 5-3: Common Number field properties

property	description
Field Size	Determines the largest number that can be entered in the field, as well as the type of data (e.g., integer or fraction)
Byte	Stores numbers from 0 to 255 (no fractions)
Integer	Stores numbers from –32,768 to 32,767 (no fractions)
Long Integer	Stores numbers from –2,147,483,648 to 2,147,483,647 (no fractions)
Single	Stores numbers (including fractions with six digits to the right of the decimal point) times 10 to the –38th to +38th power
Double	Stores numbers (including fractions with more than 10 digits to the right of the decimal point) in the range of 10 to the –324th to +324th power
Decimal Places	The number of digits displayed to the right of the decimal point

Modifying fields in Datasheet View

When you work in Table Datasheet View, the Fields tab on the Ribbon provides many options to modify fields and field properties. For example, you can add and delete fields, change a field name or data type, and modify many field properties such as Caption, Default Value, and Format.

Table Design View, however, gives you full access to all field properties such as all of the Lookup properties. In Datasheet View, an **Autofilter** arrow is displayed to the right of each field name. Click the Autofilter arrow to quickly sort or filter by that field.

Modify Date/Time Fields

Many properties of the Date/Time field, such as Input Mask, Caption, and Default Value, work the same way as they do in fields with a Short Text or Number data type. One difference, however, is the **Format** property, which helps you format dates in various ways such as January 25, 2017; 25-Jan-17; or 01/25/2017. **CASE** ▸ *You want to change the format of Date/Time fields in the Trips table to display two digits for the month and day values and four digits for the year, as in 05/06/2017.*

STEPS

1. **Right-click the Trips table in the Navigation Pane, click Design View on the shortcut menu, then click the TripStartDate field name**

   You want the trip start dates to appear with two digits for the month and day, such as 07/05/2017, instead of the default presentation of dates, 7/5/2017.

2. **Click the Format property box, then click the Format list arrow**

   Although several predefined Date/Time formats are available, none matches the format you want. To define a custom format, enter symbols that represent how you want the date to appear.

3. **Type mm/dd/yyyy then press [Enter]**

   The updated Format property for the TripStartDate field shown in **FIGURE 5-12** sets the date to appear with two digits for the month, two digits for the day, and four digits for the year. The parts of the date are separated by forward slashes.

4. **Save the table, display the datasheet, then click the New (blank) record button ▸※ on the navigation bar**

   To test the new Format property for the TripStartDate field, you can add a new record to the table.

5. **Press [Tab] to move to the TripName field, type Mississippi Cleanup, press [Tab], type 5/6/17, press [Tab], type 7, press [Tab], type Dubuque, press [Tab], type IA, press [Tab], type Eco, press [Tab], type 1000, then press [Tab]**

   The new record you entered into the Trips table should look like **FIGURE 5-13**. The Format property for the TripStartDate field makes the entry appear as 05/06/2017, as desired.

FIGURE 5-12: Changing Date/Time field properties

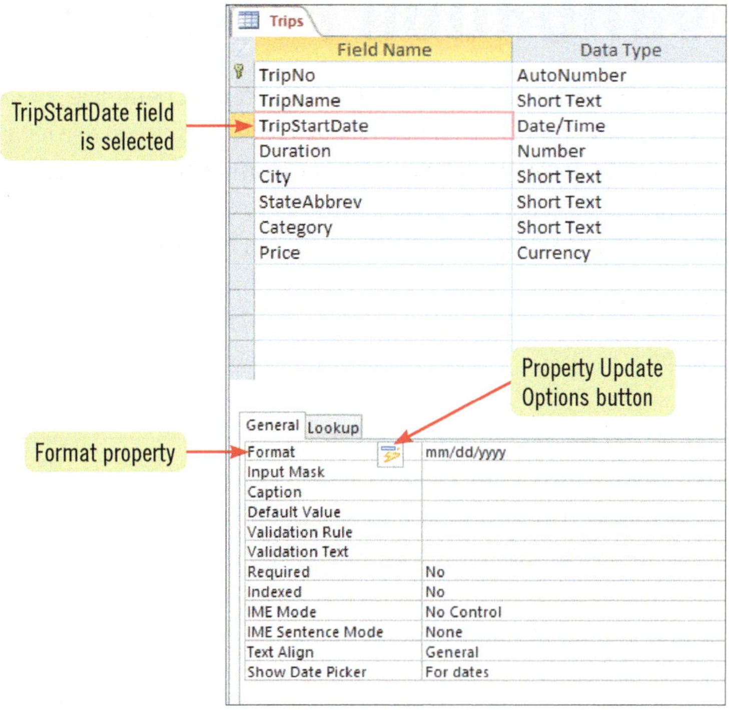

TripStartDate field is selected →

Property Update Options button

Format property →

Field Name	Data Type
TripNo	AutoNumber
TripName	Short Text
TripStartDate	Date/Time
Duration	Number
City	Short Text
StateAbbrev	Short Text
Category	Short Text
Price	Currency

General / Lookup

Format	mm/dd/yyyy
Input Mask	
Caption	
Default Value	
Validation Rule	
Validation Text	
Required	No
Indexed	No
IME Mode	No Control
IME Sentence Mode	None
Text Align	General
Show Date Picker	For dates

FIGURE 5-13: Testing the Format property

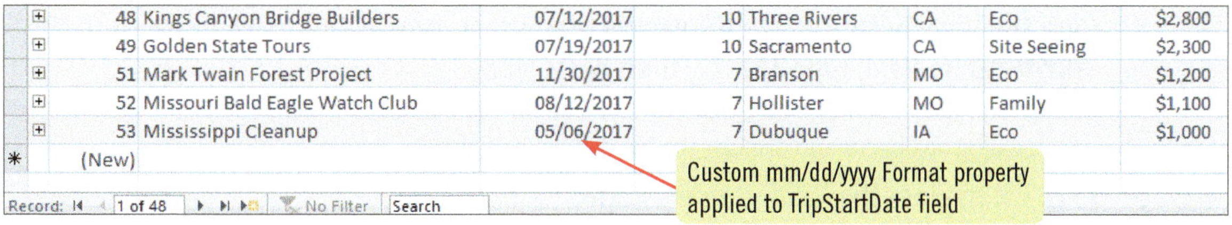

⊞	48	Kings Canyon Bridge Builders	07/12/2017	10	Three Rivers	CA	Eco	$2,800
⊞	49	Golden State Tours	07/19/2017	10	Sacramento	CA	Site Seeing	$2,300
⊞	51	Mark Twain Forest Project	11/30/2017	7	Branson	MO	Eco	$1,200
⊞	52	Missouri Bald Eagle Watch Club	08/12/2017	7	Hollister	MO	Family	$1,100
⊞	53	Mississippi Cleanup	05/06/2017	7	Dubuque	IA	Eco	$1,000
✱	(New)							

Record: ◄ ◄ 1 of 48 ► ►I ►⊞ No Filter Search

Custom mm/dd/yyyy Format property applied to TripStartDate field

Using Smart Tags

Smart Tags are buttons that automatically appear in certain conditions. They provide a small menu of options to help you work with the task at hand. Access provides the **Property Update Options** 📝 ▾ Smart Tag to help you quickly apply property changes to other objects of the database that use the field.

The **Error Indicator** ❗ ▾ Smart Tag helps identify potential design errors. For example, if you are working in Report Design View and the report is too wide for the paper, the Error Indicator appears in the upper-left corner by the report selector button to alert you to the problem.

Modify Validation Properties

Learning Outcomes
- Modify the Validation Rule property
- Modify the Validation Text property
- Define Validation Rule expressions

The **Validation Rule** property determines what entries a field can accept. For example, a validation rule for a Date/Time field might require date entries on or after a particular date. A validation rule for a Currency field might indicate that valid entries fall between a minimum and maximum value. You use the **Validation Text** property to display an explanatory message when a user tries to enter data that breaks the validation rule. Therefore, the Validation Rule and Validation Text field properties help you prevent unreasonable data from being entered into the database. **CASE** *Julia Rice reminds you that all new R2G trips must be scheduled to start before January 1, 2021. You can use the validation properties to establish this rule for the TripStartDate field in the Trips table.*

STEPS

1. **Right-click the Trips table tab, click Design View, click the TripStartDate field, click the Validation Rule property box, then type <1/1/2021**

   R2G is currently not scheduling any trips in the year 2021 or beyond. This entry forces all dates in the TripStartDate field to be less than 1/1/2021. See **TABLE 5-4** for more examples of Validation Rule expressions. The Validation Text property provides a helpful message to the user when the entry in the field breaks the rule entered in the Validation Rule property.

2. **Click the Validation Text box, then type Date must be before 1/1/2021**

   Design View of the Trips table should now look like **FIGURE 5-14**. Access modifies a property to include additional syntax by changing the entry in the Validation Rule property to <#1/1/2021#. Pound signs (#) are used to surround date criteria.

3. **Save the table, then click Yes when asked to test the existing data with new data integrity rules**

   Because no dates in the TripStartDate field are later than 1/1/2021, Access finds no date errors in the current data and saves the table. You now want to test that the Validation Rule and Validation Text properties work when entering data in the datasheet.

4. **Click the View button 🗐 to display the datasheet, press [Tab] twice to move to the TripStartDate field, type 1/1/21, then press [Tab]**

   Because you tried to enter a date that was not true for the Validation Rule property for the TripStartDate field, a dialog box opens and displays the Validation Text entry, as shown in **FIGURE 5-15**.

5. **Click OK to close the validation message**

   You now know that the Validation Rule and Validation Text properties work properly.

6. **Press [Esc] to reject the invalid date entry in the TripStartDate field**

7. **Close the Trips table**

FIGURE 5-14: Entering Validation properties

TripStartDate field
is selected →

Field Name	Data Type
TripNo	AutoNumber
TripName	Short Text
TripStartDate	Date/Time
Duration	Number
City	Short Text
StateAbbrev	Short Text
Category	Short Text
Price	Currency

General | Lookup

Validation Rule
property →

Validation Text
property →

Format	mm/dd/yyyy
Input Mask	
Caption	
Default Value	
Validation Rule	<#1/1/2021#
Validation Text	Date must be before 1/1/2021
Required	No
Indexed	No
IME Mode	No Control
IME Sentence Mode	None
Text Align	General
Show Date Picker	For dates

FIGURE 5-15: Validation Text message

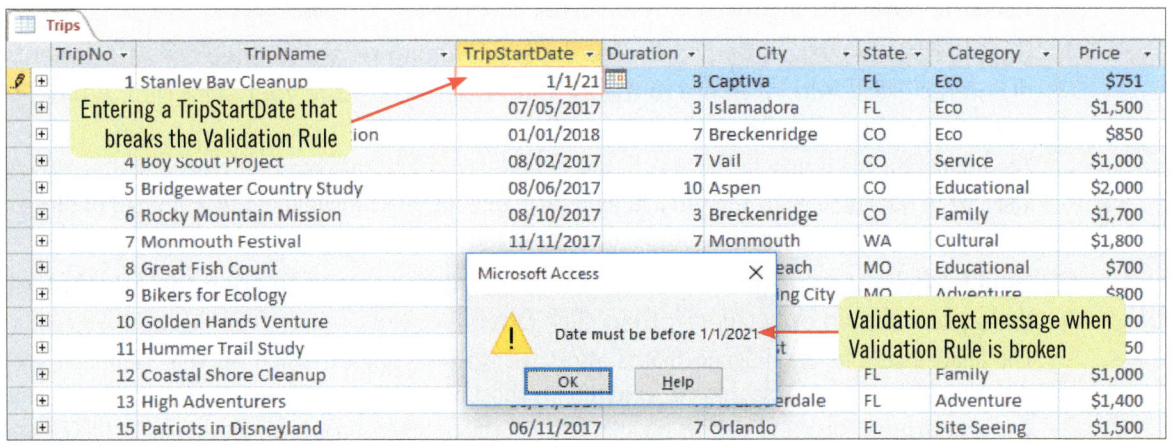

Entering a TripStartDate that breaks the Validation Rule

Validation Text message when Validation Rule is broken

TripNo	TripName	TripStartDate	Duration	City	State	Category	Price
1	Stanley Bay Cleanup	1/1/21	3	Captiva	FL	Eco	$751
		07/05/2017	3	Islamadora	FL	Eco	$1,500
	ion	01/01/2018	7	Breckenridge	CO	Eco	$850
4	Boy Scout Project	08/02/2017	7	Vail	CO	Service	$1,000
5	Bridgewater Country Study	08/06/2017	10	Aspen	CO	Educational	$2,000
6	Rocky Mountain Mission	08/10/2017	3	Breckenridge	CO	Family	$1,700
7	Monmouth Festival	11/11/2017	7	Monmouth	WA	Cultural	$1,800
8	Great Fish Count			each	MO	Educational	$700
9	Bikers for Ecology			ng City	MO	Adventure	$800
10	Golden Hands Venture						00
11	Hummer Trail Study						50
12	Coastal Shore Cleanup				FL	Family	$1,000
13	High Adventurers				FL	Adventure	$1,400
15	Patriots in Disneyland	06/11/2017	7	Orlando	FL	Site Seeing	$1,500

Microsoft Access — Date must be before 1/1/2021 — OK — Help

TABLE 5-4: Validation Rule expressions

data type	validation rule expression	description
Number or Currency	>0	The number must be positive
Number or Currency	>10 And <100	The number must be greater than 10 and less than 100
Number or Currency	10 Or 20 Or 30	The number must be 10, 20, or 30
Short Text	"AZ" Or "CO" Or "NM"	The entry must be AZ, CO, or NM
Date/Time	>=#7/1/17#	The date must be on or after 7/1/2017
Date/Time	>#1/1/10# And <#1/1/2030#	The date must be greater than 1/1/2010 and less than 1/1/2030

Create Attachment Fields

Learning Outcomes
- Create an Attachment field
- Attach and view a file in an Attachment field

An **Attachment field** allows you to attach an external file such as a picture, Word document, PowerPoint presentation, or Excel workbook to a record. Earlier versions of Access allowed you to link or embed external data using the **OLE** (object linking and embedding) data type. The Attachment data type stores more file formats such as JPEG images, requires no additional software to view the files from within Access, and allows you to attach more than one file to the Attachment field. **CASE** *You can use an Attachment field to store JPEG images for customer photo identification.*

STEPS

1. **Right-click the Customers table in the Navigation Pane, then click Design View**
   You can insert a new field anywhere in the list.

2. **Click the Street field selector, click the Insert Rows button on the Design tab, click the Field Name cell, type Photo, press [Tab], click the Data Type list arrow, then click Attachment, as shown in FIGURE 5-16**
   Now that you've created the new Attachment field named Photo, you're ready to add data to it in Datasheet View.

3. **Click the Save button 🖫 on the Quick Access Toolbar, click the View button ▦ on the Design tab to switch to Datasheet View, then press [Tab] three times to move to the new Photo field**
   An Attachment field cell displays a small paperclip icon with the number of files attached to the field in parentheses. You have not attached any files to this field yet, so each record shows zero (0) file attachments. You can attach files to this field directly from Datasheet View.

4. **Double-click the attachment icon 📎 for the Jacob Alman record to open the Attachments dialog box, click Add, navigate to the location where you store your Data Files, double-click JAlman.jpg, then click OK**
   The JAlman.jpg file is now included with the second record, and the datasheet reflects that one (1) file is attached to the Photo field. You can add more than one file attachment and different types of files to the same field. You can view file attachments directly from the datasheet, form, or report.

5. **Double-click the attachment icon for the Jacob Alman record to open the Attachments dialog box shown in FIGURE 5-17, then click Open**
   The image opens in the program that is associated with the .jpg extension on your computer such as Windows Photo Viewer. The **.jpg** file extension is short for **JPEG**, an acronym for **Joint Photographic Experts Group**. This group defines the standards for the compression algorithms that make JPEG files very efficient to use in databases and on webpages.

6. **Close the window that displays the JAlman.jpg image, click Cancel in the Attachments dialog box, close the Customers table, close the R2G-5.accdb database, then exit Access**

FIGURE 5-16: Adding an Attachment field

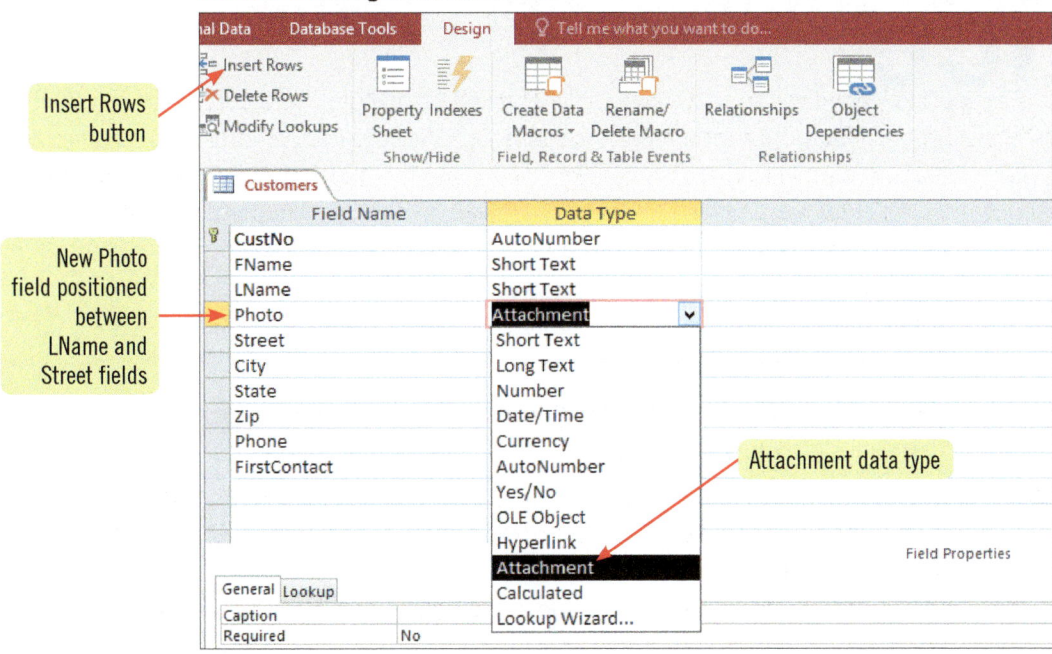

Insert Rows button

New Photo field positioned between LName and Street fields

Attachment data type

FIGURE 5-17: Opening an attached file

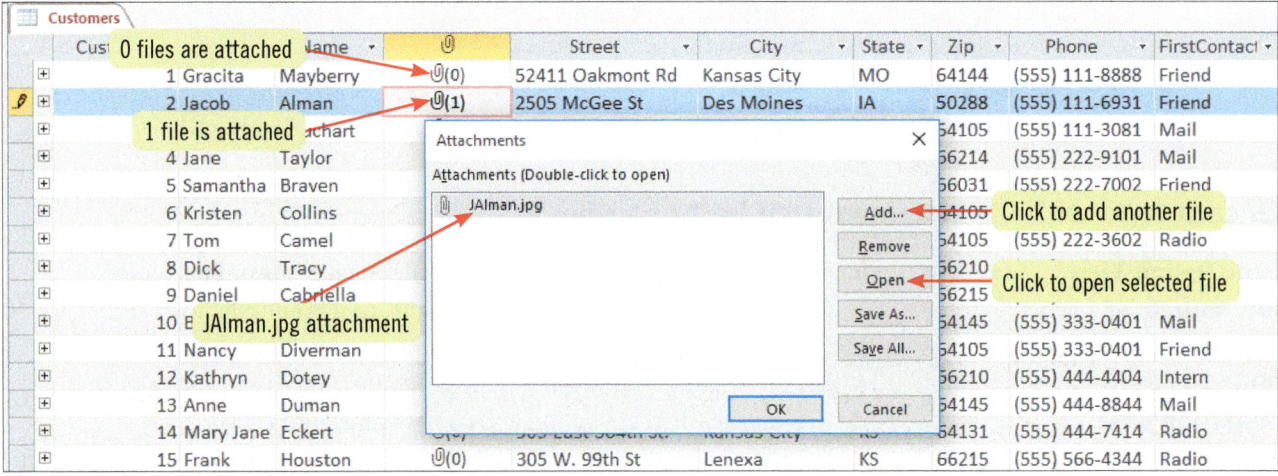

0 files are attached

1 file is attached

JAlman.jpg attachment

Click to add another file

Click to open selected file

Working with database file types

When you create a new database in Microsoft Access 2016, Access gives the file an **.accdb** extension and saves it as an Access 2007-2016 database file type as shown in the Access title bar. Saving the database as an Access 2007-2016 file type allows users of Access 2007, 2010, 2013, and 2016 to share the same database. Access 2007-2016 databases are not readable by earlier versions of Access such as Access 2000, Access 2002 (XP), or Access 2003. If you need to share your database with people using Access 2000, 2002, or 2003, you can use the Save As command on the File tab to save the database with an Access 2000 or 2002-2003 file type, which applies an **.mdb** file extension to the database. Databases with an Access 2000 file type can be used by any version of Access from Access 2000 through 2016, but some features, such as multivalued fields and Attachment fields, are only available when working with an Access 2007-2016 database.

Practice

Concepts Review

Identify each element of the Relationships window shown in FIGURE 5-18.

FIGURE 5-18

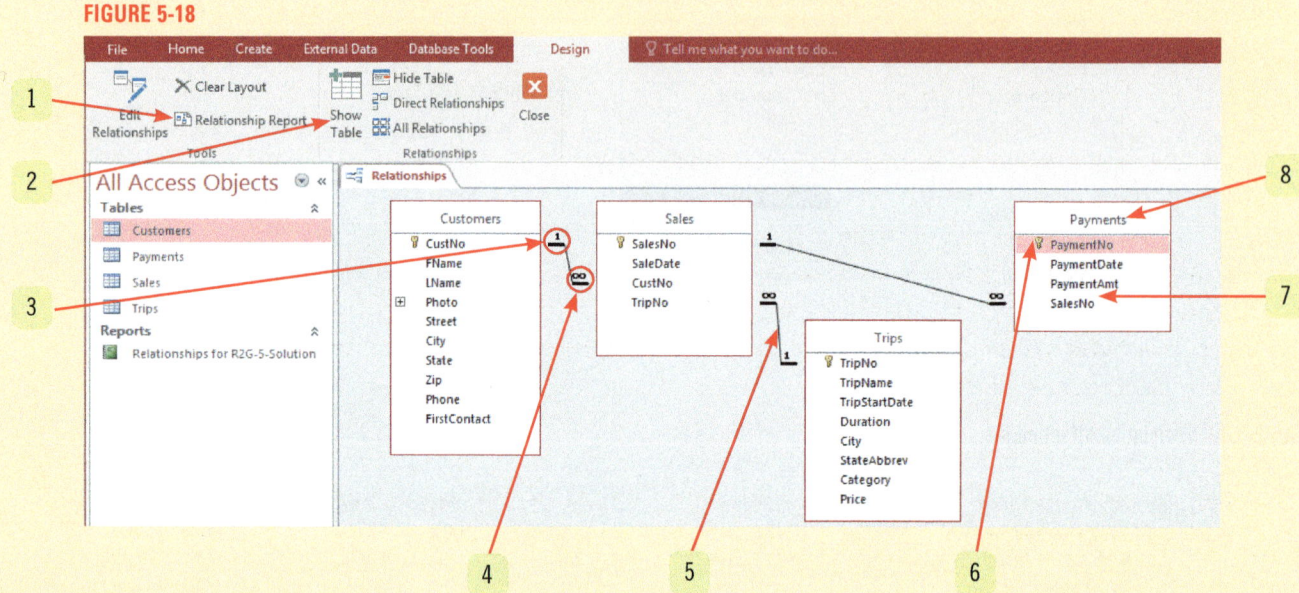

Match each term with the statement that best describes it.

9. **Table Design View**
10. **Row Source**
11. **Attachment field**
12. **Limit To List**
13. **Validation Rule**
14. **Input Mask**
15. **Lookup properties**
16. **Primary key field**
17. **Multivalued field**

a. Field that allows you to store external files such as a Word document, PowerPoint presentation, Excel workbook, or JPEG image

b. Field that holds unique information for each record in the table

c. Field that allows you to make more than one choice from a drop-down list

d. Determines whether you can enter a new value into a field

e. Field properties that allow you to supply a drop-down list of values for a field

f. Access window in which all characteristics of a table, such as field names and field properties, are defined

g. Field property that provides a visual guide as you enter data

h. Field property that prevents unreasonable data entries for a field

i. Lookup property that determines where the Lookup field gets its list of values

Modifying the Database Structure

Select the best answer from the list of choices.

18. **The linking field in the "many" table is called the:**
- **a.** Attachment field.
- **b.** Child field.
- **c.** Foreign key field.
- **d.** Primary key field.

19. **Which of the following problems most clearly indicates that you need to redesign your database?**
- **a.** Referential integrity is enforced on table relationships.
- **b.** The Input Mask Wizard has not been used.
- **c.** There is duplicated data in several records of a table.
- **d.** Not all fields have Validation Rule properties.

20. **Which of the following is not done in Table Design View?**
- **a.** Creating file attachments
- **b.** Defining field data types
- **c.** Specifying the primary key field
- **d.** Setting Field Size properties

21. **What is the purpose of enforcing referential integrity?**
- **a.** To require an entry for each field of each record
- **b.** To prevent incorrect entries in the primary key field
- **c.** To prevent orphan records from being created
- **d.** To force the application of meaningful validation rules

22. **To create a many-to-many relationship between two tables, you must create:**
- **a.** Foreign key fields in each table.
- **b.** A junction table.
- **c.** Two primary key fields in each table.
- **d.** Two one-to-one relationships between the two tables, with referential integrity enforced.

23. **The default filename extension for a database created in Access 2016 is:**
- **a.** .accdb.
- **b.** .acc16.
- **c.** .mdb.
- **d.** .mdb16.

24. **If the primary key field in the "one" table is an AutoNumber data type, the linking field in the "many" table will have which data type?**
- **a.** Number
- **b.** Short Text
- **c.** AutoNumber
- **d.** Attachment

25. **Which symbol is used to identify the "many" field in a one-to-many relationship in the Relationships window?**
- **a.** Arrow
- **b.** Triangle
- **c.** Key
- **d.** Infinity

26. **The process of removing and fixing orphan records is commonly called:**
- **a.** Relating tables.
- **b.** Designing a relational database.
- **c.** Scrubbing the database.
- **d.** Analyzing performance.

Skills Review

1. Examine relational databases.

   a. List the fields needed to create an Access relational database to manage volunteer hours for the members of a philanthropic club or community service organization.

   b. Identify fields that would contain duplicate values if all of the fields were stored in a single table.

   c. Group the fields into subject matter tables, then identify the primary key field for each table.

   d. Assume that your database contains two tables: Members and ServiceHours. If you did not identify these two tables earlier, regroup the fields within these two table names, then identify the primary key field for each table, the foreign key field in the ServiceHours table, and how the tables would be related using a one-to-many relationship.

2. Design related tables.

   a. Start Access 2016, then create a new blank desktop database named **Service-5** in the location where you store your Data Files.

   b. Use Table Design View to create a new table with the name **Members** and the field names, data types, descriptions, and primary key field, as shown in **FIGURE 5-19**. Close the Members table.

FIGURE 5-19

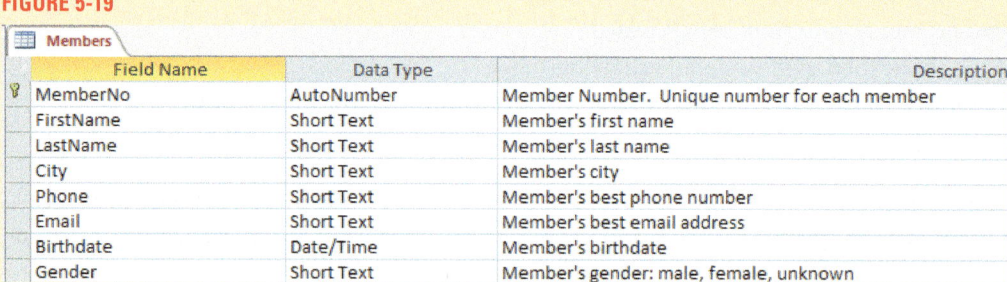

Field Name	Data Type	Description
MemberNo	AutoNumber	Member Number. Unique number for each member
FirstName	Short Text	Member's first name
LastName	Short Text	Member's last name
City	Short Text	Member's city
Phone	Short Text	Member's best phone number
Email	Short Text	Member's best email address
Birthdate	Date/Time	Member's birthdate
Gender	Short Text	Member's gender: male, female, unknown

   c. Use Table Design View to create a new table named **ServiceHours** with the field names, data types, descriptions, and primary key field shown in **FIGURE 5-20**. Close the ServiceHours table.

FIGURE 5-20

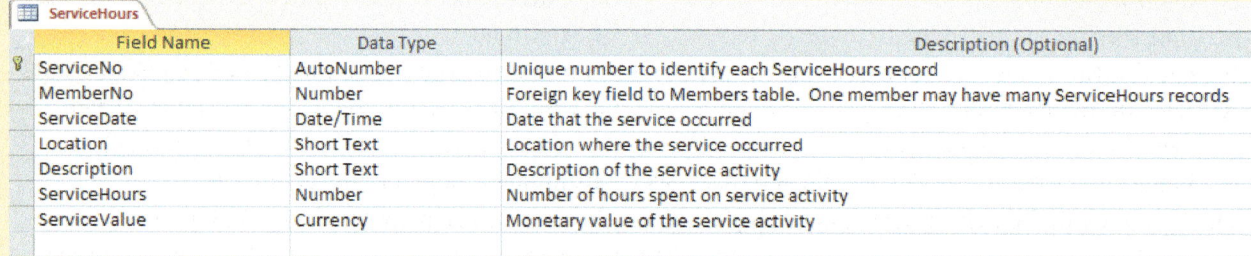

Field Name	Data Type	Description (Optional)
ServiceNo	AutoNumber	Unique number to identify each ServiceHours record
MemberNo	Number	Foreign key field to Members table. One member may have many ServiceHours records
ServiceDate	Date/Time	Date that the service occurred
Location	Short Text	Location where the service occurred
Description	Short Text	Description of the service activity
ServiceHours	Number	Number of hours spent on service activity
ServiceValue	Currency	Monetary value of the service activity

Skills Review (continued)

3. Create one-to-many relationships.

  a. Open the Relationships window, double-click Members, then double-click ServiceHours to add the two tables to the Relationships window. Close the Show Table dialog box.

  b. Resize all field lists by dragging the bottom border down so that all fields are visible, then drag the MemberNo field from the Members table to the MemberNo field in the ServiceHours table.

  c. Enforce referential integrity, and create the one-to-many relationship between Members and ServiceHours. See **FIGURE 5-21**.

FIGURE 5-21

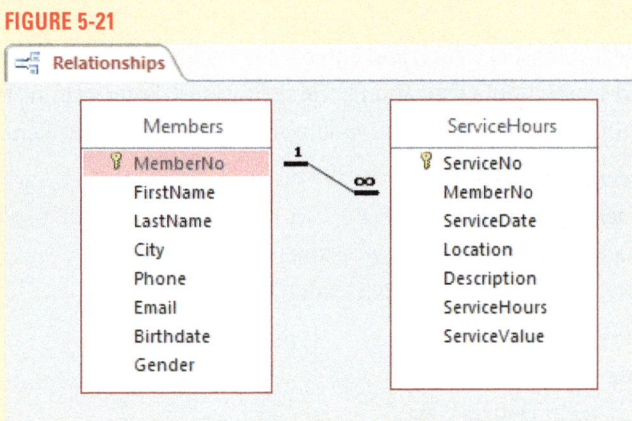

  d. Create a Relationship report for the Service-5 database, add your name as a label to the Report Header section of the report in Report Design View, save the Relationship report with the default name **Relationships for Service-5**, then preview it.

  e. Print the report if requested by your instructor, close the Relationship report, then save and close the Relationships window.

4. Create Lookup fields.

  a. Open the Members table in Design View, then start the Lookup Wizard for the Gender field.

  b. Select the option that allows you to enter your own values, then enter **Female**, **Male**, and **Unknown** as the values for the Lookup column in the Col1 list.

  c. Use the default **Gender** label, click the Limit To List check box, then click Finish to finish the Lookup Wizard.

  d. Save the Members table, display it in Datasheet View, and enter your name in the FirstName and LastName fields for the first record. Enter your school's city, **5551112233** in the Phone field, your school email address in the Email field, **1/1/1991** in the Birthdate field, and any valid choice in the Gender field.

  e. Type **Test** in the Gender field, then press [Tab] to test the Limit To List property. If it worked properly, you should receive an error message that states that the text you entered isn't an item on the list. Click OK in that dialog box, make a choice from the Gender drop-down list, then press [Tab] to finish the record. (*Hint*: If you were allowed to enter Test in the Gender field, it means that the Limit To List property is set to No instead of Yes. If that's the case, delete the Test entry, then switch to Table Design View. Modify the Limit To List Lookup property in the Lookup properties for the Gender field from No to Yes, save the table, then switch back to Datasheet View. Retest the property change by repeating Step e.)

  f. Resize fields in Datasheet View as needed to clearly see all entries.

Skills Review (continued)

5. Modify Short Text fields.

   a. Open the Members table in Design View.

   b. Use the Input Mask Wizard to create an Input Mask property for the Phone field. Choose the Phone Number Input Mask. Accept the other default options provided by the Input Mask Wizard. (*Hint*: If the Input Mask Wizard is not installed on your computer, type **!(999) 000-0000;;_** for the Input Mask property for the Phone field.)

   c. Change the Field Size property of the FirstName, LastName, and City fields to **25**. Change the Field Size property of the Phone field to **10**. Change the Field Size property of the Gender field to **7**. Save the Members table. None of these fields has data greater in length than the new Field Size properties, so click OK when prompted that some data may be lost.

   d. Open the Members table in Datasheet View, and enter a new record with your instructor's name in the FirstName and LastName fields and your school's City and Phone field values. Enter your instructor's email address, **1/1/1975** for the Birthdate field, and an appropriate choice for the Gender field. Close the Members table.

6. Modify Number and Currency fields.

   a. Open the ServiceHours table in Design View.

   b. Change the Decimal Places property of the ServiceHours field to **0**.

   c. Change the Decimal Places property of the ServiceValue field to **0**.

   d. Save and close the ServiceHours table.

7. Modify Date/Time fields.

   a. Open the ServiceHours table in Design View.

   b. Change the Format property of the ServiceDate field to Medium Date.

   c. Save and close the ServiceHours table.

   d. Open the Members table in Design View.

   e. Change the Format property of the Birthdate field to Medium Date.

   f. Save and close the Members table.

8. Modify validation properties.

   a. Open the Members table in Design View.

   b. Click the Birthdate field name, click the Validation Rule text box, then type **<Date()**. (Note that Date() is a built-in Access function that returns today's date.)

   c. Click the Validation Text box, then type **Birthdate must not be in the future**.

   d. Save and accept the changes, then open the Members table in Datasheet View.

   e. Test the Validation Text and Validation Rule properties by tabbing to the Birthdate field and entering a date in the future. (*Note*: You must enter dates in a m/d/yy pattern regardless of the Medium Date format property.) Click OK when prompted with the Validation Text message, press [Esc] to remove the invalid Birthdate field entry, then enter **1/1/91** as the Birthdate value for your record. (*Note*: Be sure your Validation Text message is spelled properly. If not, correct it in Table Design View.)

9. Create Attachment fields.

   a. Open the Members table in Design View, then add a new field after the Gender field with the field name **Photo** and an Attachment data type. Enter **Member's picture** for the Description. Save the Members table.

   b. Display the Members table in Datasheet View, then attach a .jpg file of yourself to the record. If you do not have a .jpg file of yourself, use the **Member1.jpg** file provided in the location where you store your Data Files.

   c. Close the Members table.

   d. Use the Form Wizard to create a form based on all of the fields in the Members table. Use a Columnar layout, and title the form **Member Entry Form**.

   e. If requested by your instructor, print the first record in the Members Entry Form that shows the picture you just entered in the Photo field, then close the form.

   f. Close the Service-5.accdb database, then exit Access.

Independent Challenge 1

As the manager of a music store's instrument rental program, you decide to create a database to track rentals to schoolchildren. The fields you need to track are organized with four tables: Instruments, Rentals, Students, and Schools.

a. Start Access, then create a new blank desktop database called **Rentals-5** in the location where you store your Data Files.

b. Use Table Design View or the Fields tab on the Ribbon of Table Datasheet View to create the four tables in the Rentals-5 database using the field names, data types, descriptions, and primary keys shown in **FIGURES 5-22**, **5-23**, **5-24**, and **5-25**.

FIGURE 5-22

Schools

Field Name	Data Type	Description
SchoolName	Short Text	Full name of school
🔑 SchoolID	Short Text	Unique three character id for each school

FIGURE 5-23

Students

Field Name	Data Type	Description (Optional)
FirstName	Short Text	Student's first name
LastName	Short Text	Student's last name
Street	Short Text	Student's street
City	Short Text	Student's city
State	Short Text	Student's state
Zip	Short Text	Student's zip code
🔑 StudentNo	AutoNumber	Unique number to identify each student
SchoolID	Short Text	Three character school id for that student

FIGURE 5-24

Instruments

Field Name	Data Type	Description
🔑 SerialNo	Short Text	Unique serial number on each instrument
Description	Short Text	Description of the instrument
MonthlyFee	Currency	Monthly rental fee

FIGURE 5-25

Rentals

Field Name	Data Type	Description (Optional)
🔑 RentalNo	AutoNumber	Unique rental number for each record
StudentNo	Number	Foreign key field to Students table. One student can be linked to many rentals
SerialNo	Short Text	Foreign key field to Instruments table. One instrument can be linked to many rentals
RentalStartDate	Date/Time	Date the rental starts

Independent Challenge 1 (continued)

  c. In Design View of the Rentals table, enter **>1/1/2016** as the Validation Rule property for the RentalStartDate field. This change allows only dates later than 1/1/2016, the start date for this business, to be entered into this field.

  d. Enter **Rental start dates must be after January 1, 2016** as the Validation Text property to the RentalStartDate field of the Rentals table. Note that Access adds pound signs (#) to the date criteria entered in the Validation Rule as soon as you tab out of the Validation Text property.

  e. Save and close the Rentals table.

  f. Open the Relationships window, then add the Schools, Students, Rentals, and Instruments tables to the window. Expand the Students field list to view all fields. Create one-to-many relationships, as shown in **FIGURE 5-26**. Be sure to enforce referential integrity on each relationship.

FIGURE 5-26

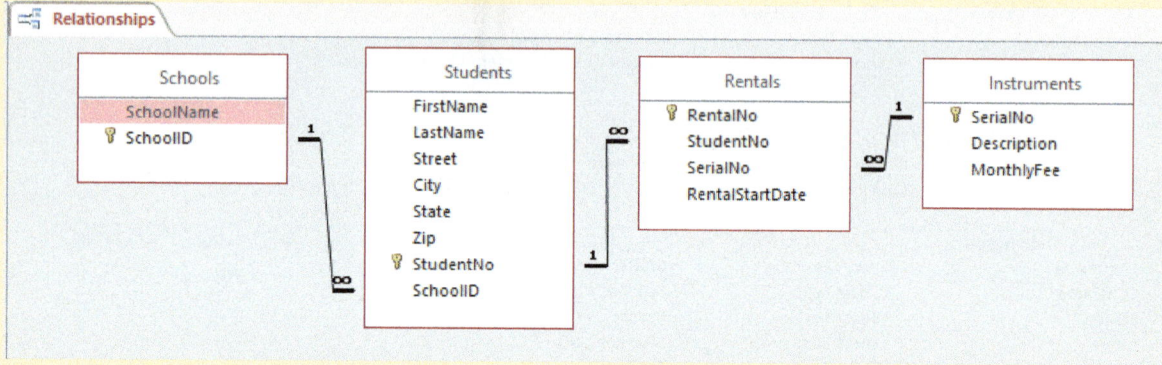

  g. Preview the Relationship report, add your name as a label to the Report Header section, then save the report with the default name **Relationships for Rentals-5**. If requested by your instructor, print the report and then close it.

  h. Save and close the Relationships window.

  i. Close the Rentals-5.accdb database, then exit Access.

Independent Challenge 2

You want to create a database that documents blood drive donations by the employees of your company. You want to track information such as employee name, blood type, date of donation, and the hospital where the employee chooses to send the donation. You also want to track basic hospital information, such as the hospital name and address.

a. Start Access, then create a new, blank desktop database called **BloodDrive-5** in the location where you store your Data Files.

b. Create an **Employees** table with appropriate field names, data types, and descriptions to record the automatic employee ID, employee first name, employee last name, and blood type. Make the EmployeeID field the primary key field. Use **FIGURE 5-27** as a guide for appropriate field names.

FIGURE 5-27

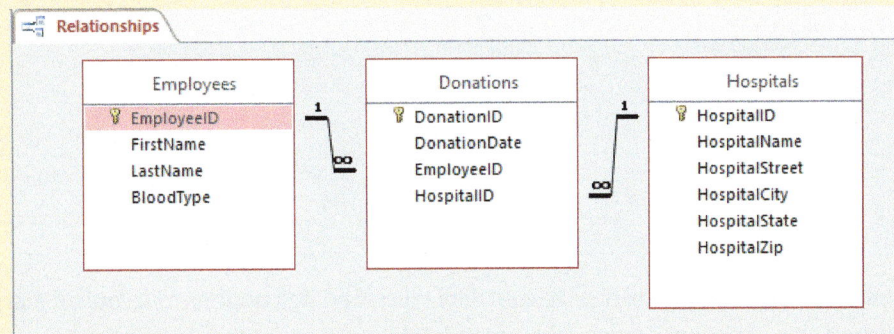

c. Add Lookup properties to the blood type field in the Employees table to provide only valid blood type entries of **A+, A–, B+, B–, O+, O–, AB+**, and **AB–** for this field.

d. Create a **Donations** table with appropriate field names, data types, and descriptions to record an automatic donation ID, date of the donation, employee ID field, and hospital ID field. Make the donation ID the primary key field. Use **FIGURE 5-27** as a guide for appropriate field names.

e. Create a **Hospitals** table with fields and appropriate field names, data types, and descriptions to record a hospital ID, hospital name, street, city, state, and zip. Make the hospital ID field the primary key field. Use **FIGURE 5-27** as a guide for appropriate field names.

f. In the Relationships window, create one-to-many relationships with referential integrity between the tables in the database, as shown in **FIGURE 5-27**. One employee may make several donations over time. Each donation is marked for a particular hospital, so each hospital may receive many donations over time.

g. Preview the Relationship report, add your name as a label to the Report Header section, then save the report with the default name **Relationships for BloodDrive-5**. If requested by your instructor, print the report and then close it.

h. Save and close the Relationships window.

i. Close the BloodDrive-5.accdb database, then exit Access.

Independent Challenge 3

You're a member and manager of a recreational baseball team and decide to create an Access database to manage player information, games, and batting statistics.

a. Start Access, then create a new, blank desktop database called **Baseball-5** in the location where you store your Data Files.

b. Create a **Players** table with appropriate field names, data types, and descriptions to record the uniform number, player first name, player last name, and position. Make the uniform number field the primary key field. Use **FIGURE 5-28** as a guide for appropriate field names.

FIGURE 5-28

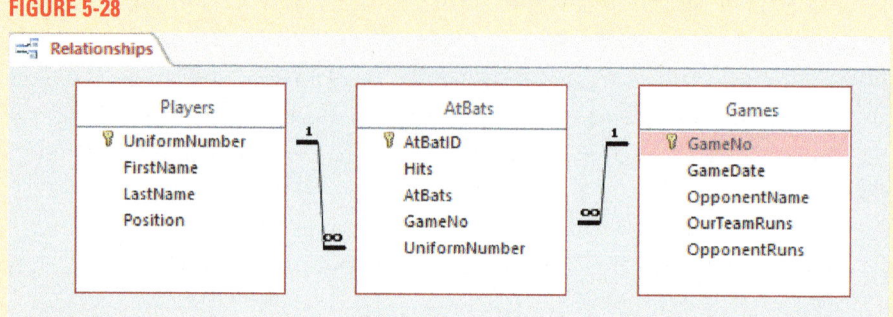

c. Create a **Games** table with appropriate field names, data types, and descriptions to record an automatic game number, date of the game, opponent's name, home team's total runs, and visitor team's total runs. Make the game number field the primary key field. Use **FIGURE 5-28** as a guide for appropriate field names.

d. Create an **AtBats** table with appropriate field names, data types, and descriptions to record hits, at bats, game number, and uniform number of each player. The game number and uniform number fields will both be foreign key fields. Create an AtBatID AutoNumber field to server as the primary key field. Use **FIGURE 5-28** as a guide for appropriate field names.

e. In the Relationships window, create one-to-many relationships with referential integrity between the tables shown in **FIGURE 5-28**. The AtBats table contains one record for each player that plays in each game to record his hitting statistics—hits and at bats—for each game. Therefore, one player record is related to many records in the AtBats table, and one game record is related to many records in the AtBats table.

f. Preview the Relationship report, add your name as a label to the Report Header section, then save the report with the default name **Relationships for Baseball-5**. If requested by your instructor, print the report and then close it.

g. Save and close the Relationships window.

h. Close the Baseball-5.accdb database, then exit Access.

Independent Challenge 4: Explore

An Access database can help record and track your job search efforts. In this exercise, you will modify two fields in the Positions table in your Jobs database with Lookup properties to make data entry easier, more efficient, and more accurate.

a. Start Access, open the Jobs-5.accdb database from the location where you store your Data Files, then enable content if prompted.

b. Open the Positions table in Design View. Click the EmployerID field, then start the Lookup Wizard.

c. In this situation, you want the EmployerID field in the Positions table to look up both the EmployerID and the CompanyName fields from the Employers table, so leave the "I want the lookup field to get the values from another table or query" option button selected.

d. The Employers table contains the fields you want to display in this Lookup field. Select both the EmployerID field and the CompanyName fields. Sort the records in ascending order by the CompanyName field.

e. Deselect the "Hide key column" check box so that you can see the data in both the EmployerID and CompanyName fields.

f. Choose EmployerID as the field in which to store values, choose **EmployerID** as the label for the Lookup field, click the Enable Data Integrity check box, then click Finish to finish the Lookup Wizard. Click Yes when prompted to save the table.

g. Switch to Datasheet View of the Positions table and tab to the EmployerID field for the first record. Click the EmployerID list arrow. You should see both the EmployerID value and the CompanyName in the drop-down list, as shown in **FIGURE 5-29**.

FIGURE 5-29

h. Return to Design View of the Positions table, click the Desirability field, and start the Lookup Wizard. This field stores the values 1 through 5 as a desirability rating. You will manually enter those values, so choose the "I will type in the values that I want" option button.

i. Enter **1**, **2**, **3**, **4**, and **5** in the Col1 column; accept the Desirability label for the Lookup field; click the Limit To List check box; then click Finish to finish the Lookup Wizard.

Independent Challenge 4: Explore (continued)

j. Save the table, and test the Desirability field for the first record in Datasheet View. You should see a drop-down list with the values 1, 2, 3, 4, and 5, as shown in **FIGURE 5-30**.

FIGURE 5-30

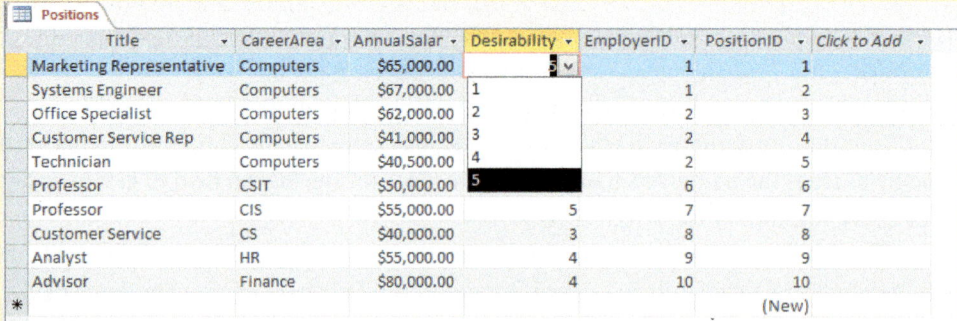

Title	CareerArea	AnnualSalar	Desirability	EmployerID	PositionID	Click to Add
Marketing Representative	Computers	$65,000.00		1	1	
Systems Engineer	Computers	$67,000.00	1	1	2	
Office Specialist	Computers	$62,000.00	2	2	3	
Customer Service Rep	Computers	$41,000.00	3	2	4	
Technician	Computers	$40,500.00	4	2	5	
Professor	CSIT	$50,000.00	5	6	6	
Professor	CIS	$55,000.00	5	7	7	
Customer Service	CS	$40,000.00	3	8	8	
Analyst	HR	$55,000.00	4	9	9	
Advisor	Finance	$80,000.00	4	10	10	
*					(New)	

k. Save the table, and test the Desirability and EmployerID fields. You should not be able to make any entries in those fields that are not presented in the list.

l. Close the Positions table, and open the Relationships window. Your Relationships window should look like **FIGURE 5-31**. The Lookup Wizard created the relationship between the Employers and Positions table when you completed Step f. Save and close the Relationships window.

FIGURE 5-31

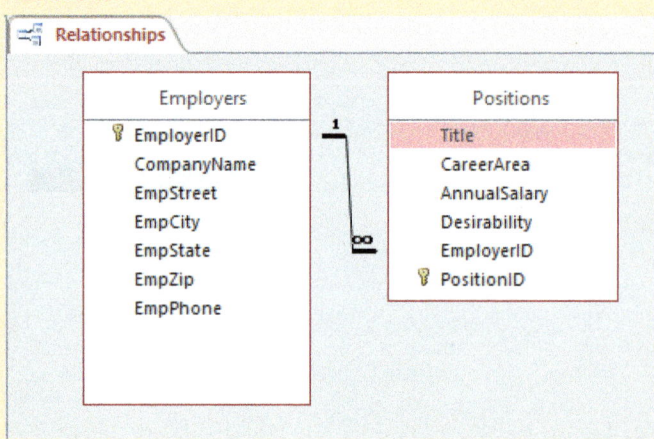

Independent Challenge 4: Explore (continued)

m. Use the Form Wizard and select all of the fields from both the Employers and Positions tables. View the data by Employers, and use a Datasheet layout for the subform.

n. Title the form **Job Entry Form** and the subform **Job Subform**. View the form in Form View.

o. In Form Design View, use your skills to move, resize, align, and edit the controls, and find the record for IBM as shown in FIGURE 5-32. Be sure to resize the columns of the subform as well. Enter a fictitious but realistic new job for IBM, and if requested by your instructor, print only that record in the Job Entry Form.

p. Save and close the Job Entry Form, close the Jobs-5.accdb database, and exit Access.

FIGURE 5-32

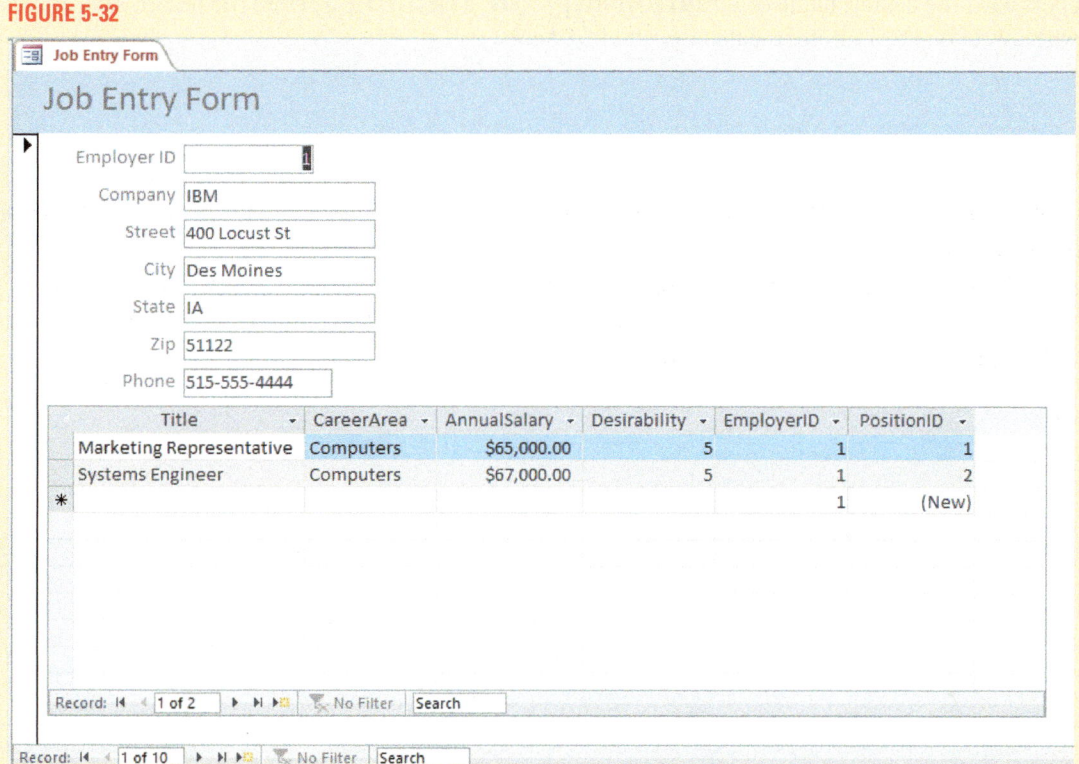

Visual Workshop

Open the Training-5.accdb database from the location where you store your Data Files, then enable content if prompted. Create a new table called **Textbooks** using the Table Design View shown in **FIGURE 5-33** to determine field names, data types, and descriptions. Make the following property changes: Change the Field Size property of the TextbookISBN field to **13**, the TextTitle field to **30**, and TextAuthorLastName field to **20**. Change the Field Size property of the TextEdition field to Byte. Be sure to specify that the TextbookISBN field is the primary key field. Relate the tables in the Training-5 database, as shown in **FIGURE 5-34**, which will require you to first add a foreign key field named **Textbook** with a Short Text data type to the Courses table. View the Relationship report in landscape orientation. Add your name as a label to the Report Header section to document the Relationship report, then print it if requested by your instructor. Save the Relationship report with the default name of **Relationships for Training-5**, close the report, save and close the Relationships window, close the Training-5 database, and exit Access.

FIGURE 5-33

Field Name	Data Type	
TextbookISBN	Short Text	Textbook 13-digit ISBN
TextTitle	Short Text	Textbook title
TextAuthorLastName	Short Text	Textbook author's last name
TextEdition	Number	Textbook edition

FIGURE 5-34

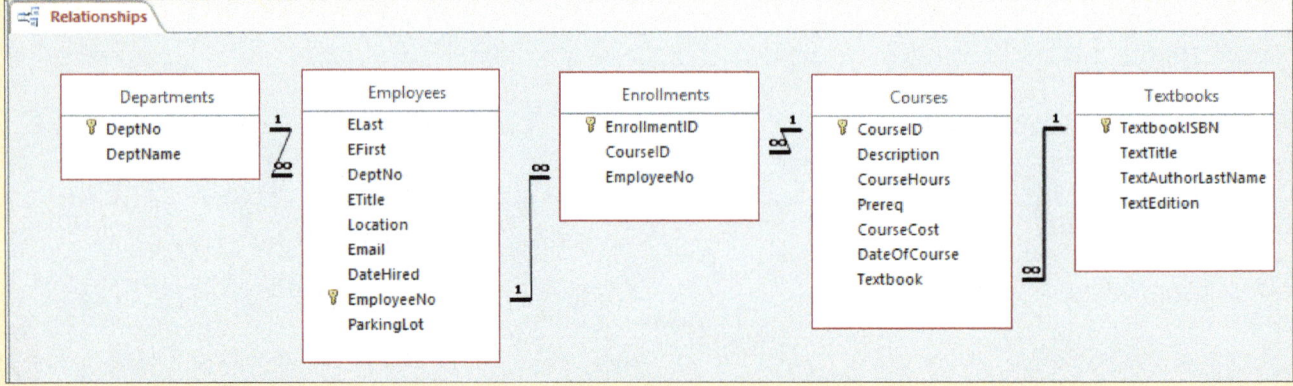

Modifying the Database Structure

Improving Queries

CASE ▶ The Reason 2 Go database has been updated to contain more customers, trips, and sales. You help Julia Rice, an R2G trip developer for U.S. travel, create queries to analyze this information.

Module Objectives

After completing this module, you will be able to:

- Create multitable queries
- Apply sorts and view SQL
- Develop AND criteria
- Develop OR criteria
- Create calculated fields
- Build summary queries
- Build crosstab queries
- Create a report on a query

Files You Will Need

R2G-6.accdb	LakeHomes-6.accdb
Service-6.accdb	Scholarships-6.accdb
Music-6.accdb	Training-6.accdb

Create Multitable Queries

Learning Outcomes
- Create a multitable query in Query Design View
- Add and delete fields in Query Design View

A **select query**, the most common type of query, selects fields from related tables and displays records in a datasheet where you can view, enter, edit, or delete data. You can create select queries by using the Simple Query Wizard, or you can start from scratch in Query Design View. **Query Design View** gives you more options for selecting and presenting information. When you open (or **run**) a query, the fields and records that you selected for the query are presented in **Query Datasheet View**, also called a **logical view** of the data. **CASE** ▸ *Julia Rice asks you to create a query to analyze customer payments. You select fields from the Customers, Trips, Sales, and Payments tables to complete this analysis.*

STEPS

1. **Start Access, open the R2G-6.accdb database from the location where you store your Data Files, then enable content if prompted**

2. **Click the Create tab on the Ribbon, then click the Query Design button in the Queries group**

   The Show Table dialog box opens and lists all the tables in the database.

   > **TROUBLE**
   > If you add a table to Query Design View twice by mistake, click the title bar of the extra field list, then press [Delete].

3. **Double-click Customers, double-click Sales, double-click Trips, double-click Payments, then click Close**

   Recall that the upper pane of Query Design View displays the fields for each of the selected tables in field lists. The name of the table is shown in the field list title bar. Primary key fields are identified with a small key icon. Relationships between tables are displayed with **one-to-many join lines** that connect the linking fields. You select the fields you want by adding them to the query design grid.

   > **TROUBLE**
   > Drag the bottom edge of the Trips field list down to resize it.

4. **Double-click the FName field in the Customers table field list to add this field to the first column of the query design grid, double-click LName, double-click TripName in the Trips field list, scroll then double-click Price in the Trips field list, double-click PaymentDate in the Payments field list, then double-click PaymentAmt, as shown in FIGURE 6-1**

   When you double-click a field in a field list, it is automatically added as the next field in the query grid. When you drag a field to the query design grid, any existing fields move to the right to accommodate the new field.

5. **Click the View button 📄 in the Results group to run the query and display the query datasheet**

   The resulting datasheet looks like FIGURE 6-2. The datasheet shows the six fields selected in Query Design View: FName and LName from the Customers table, TripName and Price from the Trips table, and PaymentDate and PaymentAmt from the Payments table. The datasheet displays 78 records because 78 different payments have been made. Some of the payments are from the same customer. For example, Kristen Collins has made payments on multiple trips (records 2 and 20). Kristen's last name has changed to Lang.

6. **Double-click Collins in the LName field of the second record, type Lang, then click any other record**

   Because Kristen's data is physically stored in only one record in the Customers table (but selected multiple times in this query because Kristen has made more than one payment), changing any occurrence of her last name updates all other selections of that data in this query and throughout all other queries, forms, and reports in the database, too. Note that Kristen's name has been updated to Kristen Lang in record 20, as shown in FIGURE 6-2.

FIGURE 6-1: Query Design View with six fields in the query design grid

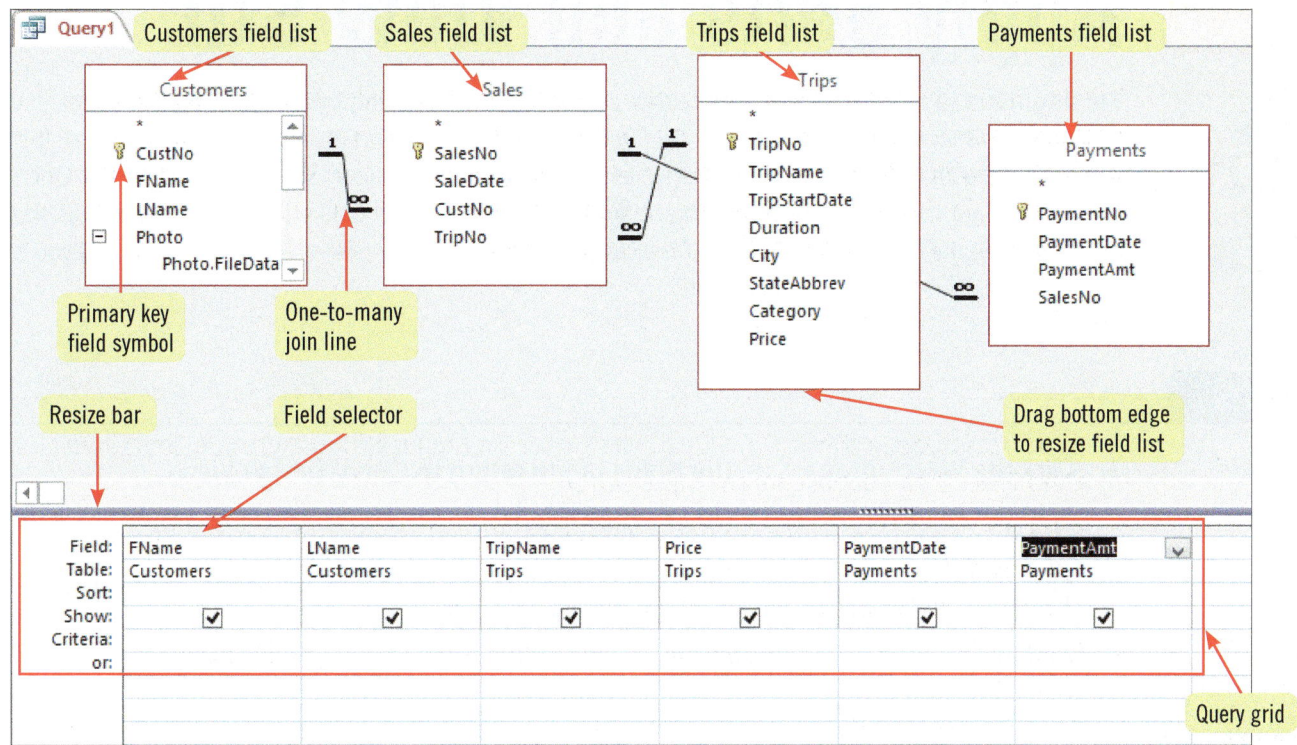

FIGURE 6-2: Query datasheet

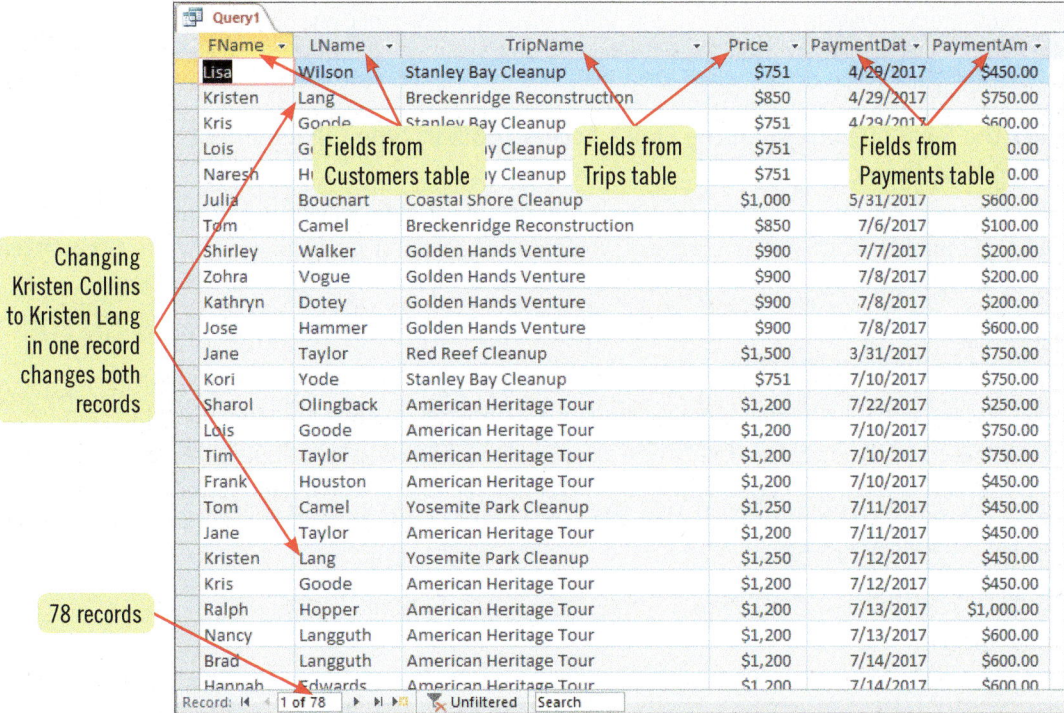

Deleting a field from the query grid

If you add the wrong field to the query design grid, you can delete it by clicking the **field selector**, the thin gray bar above each field name, then pressing [Delete]. Deleting a field from the query design grid removes it from the logical view of this query's datasheet, but does not delete the field from the database. A field is defined and the field's contents are stored in a table object only.

Apply Sorts and View SQL

Learning
Outcomes
• Apply sort orders
  in Query Design
  View
• View Structured
  Query Language
• Define SQL
  keywords

Sorting refers to reordering records in either ascending or descending order based on the values in a field. You can specify more than one sort field in Query Design View. Sort orders are evaluated from left to right, meaning that the sort field on the far left is the primary sort field. Sort orders defined in Query Design View are saved with the query object. **CASE** ▸ *Julia Rice wants to list the records in alphabetical order based on the customer's last name. If the customer has made more than one payment, Julia asks you to further sort the records by the payment date.*

STEPS

1. **Click the View button ⊻ on the Home tab to return to Query Design View**

   To sort the records by last name then by payment date, the LName field must be the primary sort field, and the PaymentDate field must be the secondary sort field.

2. **Click the LName field Sort cell in the query design grid, click the Sort list arrow, click Ascending, click the PaymentDate field Sort cell in the query design grid, click the Sort list arrow, then click Ascending**

   The resulting query design grid should look like **FIGURE 6-3**.

QUICK TIP

You can resize the columns of a datasheet by pointing to the right column border that separates the field names, then dragging left or right to resize the columns. Double-click to adjust the column width to fit the widest entry.

3. **Click the View button ⊞ in the Results group to display the query datasheet**

   The records of the datasheet are now listed in ascending order based on the values in the LName field. When the same value appears in the LName field, the records are further sorted by the secondary sort field, PaymentDate, as shown in **FIGURE 6-4**. Jacob Alman made two payments, one on 7/25/2017 and the next on 8/31/2017. Julia Bouchart made many payments and they are all listed in ascending order on the PaymentDate field.

4. **Click the Save button 🖫 on the Quick Access Toolbar, type CustPayments in the Save As dialog box, then click OK**

   When you save a query, you save a logical view of the data, a selection of fields and records from underlying tables. Technically, when you save a query, you are saving a set of instructions written in **Structured Query Language (SQL)**. You can view the SQL code for any query by switching to **SQL View**.

QUICK TIP

SQL keywords such as SELECT, FROM, or ORDER BY should not be used as field names.

5. **Click the View button list arrow, click SQL View, then click in the lower part of the SQL window to deselect the code**

   The SQL statements shown in **FIGURE 6-5** start with the **SELECT** keyword. Field names follow SELECT, and how the tables are joined follow the **FROM** keyword. The **ORDER BY** keyword determines how records are sorted. Fortunately, you do not have to write or understand SQL to use Access or select data from multiple tables. The easy-to-use Query Design View gives you a way to select and sort data from underlying tables without being an SQL programmer.

6. **Close the CustPayments query**

FIGURE 6-3: Specifying multiple sort orders in Query Design View

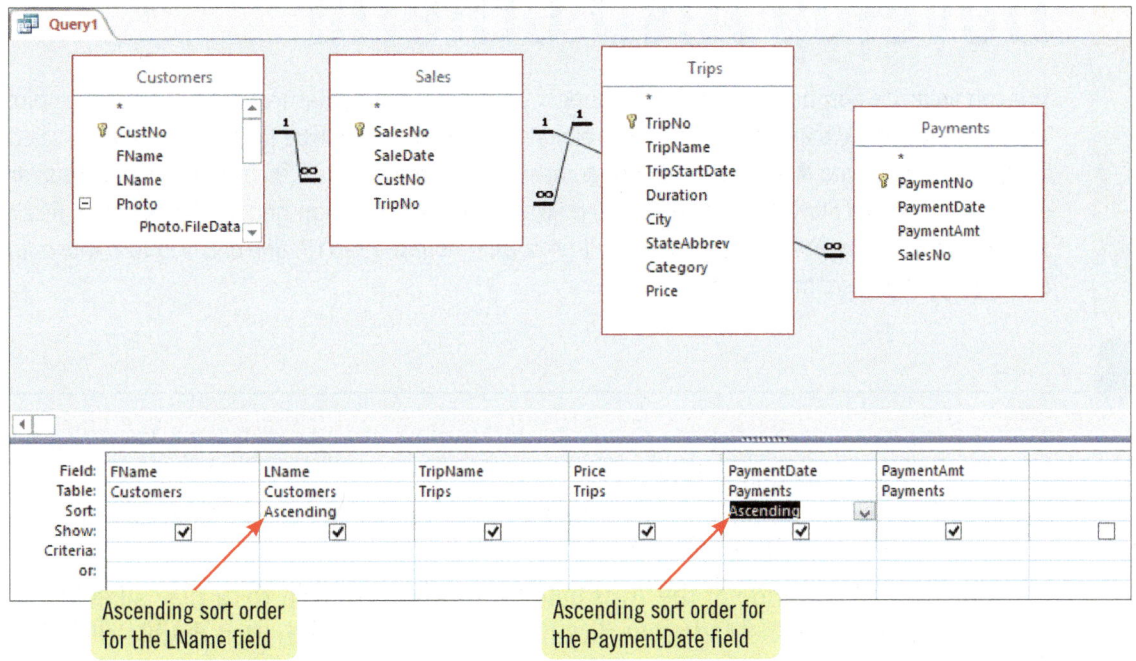

FIGURE 6-4: Records sorted by LName, then by PaymentDate

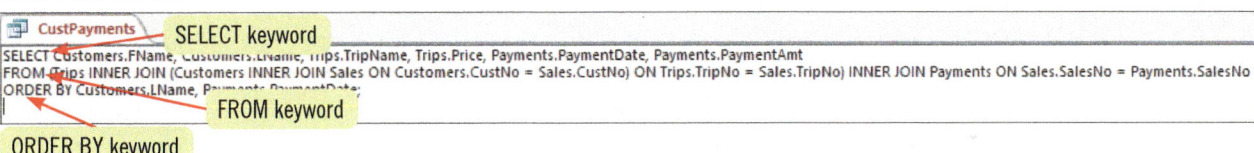

FIGURE 6-5: SQL View

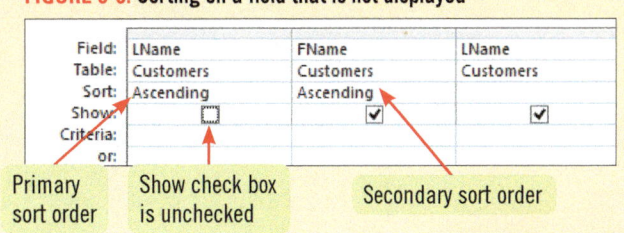

ORDER BY keyword
FROM keyword
SELECT keyword

Specifying a sort order different from the field order in the datasheet

If your database has several customers with the same last name, you can include a secondary sort on the first name field to distinguish the customers. If you want to display the fields in a different order from which they are sorted, you can use the solution shown in **FIGURE 6-6**. Add a field to the query design grid twice, once to select for the datasheet, and once to use as a sort order. Use the Show check box to deselect the field used as a sort order.

FIGURE 6-6: Sorting on a field that is not displayed

Field:	LName	FName	LName
Table:	Customers	Customers	Customers
Sort:	Ascending	Ascending	
Show:	☐	☑	☑
Criteria:			
or:			

Primary sort order — Show check box is unchecked — Secondary sort order

Develop AND Criteria

**Learning
Outcomes**
• Use the Like
 operator in query
 criteria
• Define advanced
 comparison
 operators

You can limit the number of records that appear on the resulting datasheet by entering criteria in Query Design View. **Criteria** are tests, or limiting conditions, that must be true for the record to be selected for a datasheet. To create **AND criteria**, which means the query selects a record only if all criteria are true, enter two or more criteria on the same Criteria row of the query design grid. **CASE** *Julia Rice predicts strong sales for ecological (Eco) trips that start on or after August 1, 2018. She asks you to create a list of the existing trips that meet those criteria.*

STEPS

1. **Click the Create tab, click the Query Design button, double-click Trips, then click Close in the Show Table dialog box**

   To query for ecological trips, you need to add the Category field to the query grid. In addition, you want to know the trip name and start date.

2. **Drag the bottom edge of the Trips field list down to resize it to display all fields, double-click the TripName field, double-click the TripStartDate field, then double-click the Category field**

   To find trips in the Eco category, you need to add a criterion for the Category field in the query grid.

3. **Click the first Criteria cell for the Category field, then type Eco**

   To find all trips that start on or after August 1st, use the >= (greater than or equal to) operator.

4. **Click the first Criteria cell for the TripStartDate field, type >=8/1/2018, then press [↓]**

   As shown in **FIGURE 6-7**, Access assists you with criteria syntax, rules by which criteria need to be entered. Access automatically adds quotation marks around text criteria in Short Text fields, such as "Eco" in the Category field, and pound signs around date criteria in Date/Time fields, such as #8/1/2018# in the TripStartDate field. The criteria in Number, Currency, and Yes/No fields are not surrounded by any characters. See **TABLE 6-1** for more information on common Access comparison operators and criteria syntax.

5. **Click the Save button 🖫 on the Quick Access Toolbar, type EcoAugust2018 in the Save As dialog box, click OK, then click the View button ▦ to view the query results**

   The query results are shown in **FIGURE 6-8**.

6. **Close the EcoAugust2018 datasheet**

FIGURE 6-7: Entering AND criteria on the same row

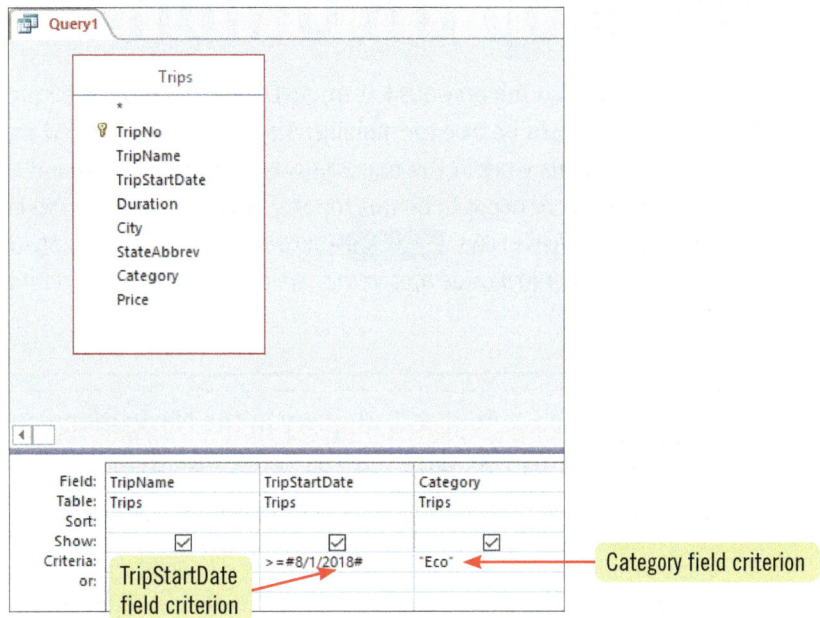

FIGURE 6-8: Datasheet for EcoAugust2018 records

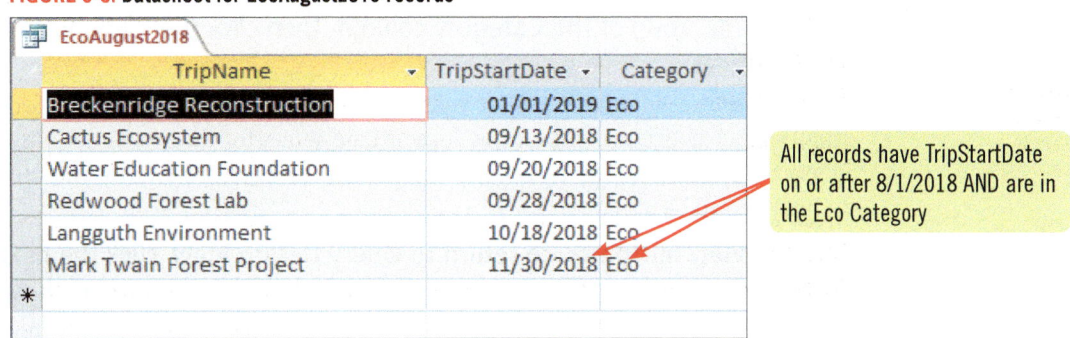

TABLE 6-1: Common comparison operators

operator	description	example	result
>	Greater than	>500	Value exceeds 500
>=	Greater than or equal to	>=500	Value is 500 or greater
<	Less than	<500	Value is less than 500
<=	Less than or equal to	<=500	Value is 500 or less
<>	Not equal to	<>500	Value is any number other than 500
Between...And	Finds values between two numbers or dates	Between #2/2/2017# And #2/2/2020#	Dates between 2/2/2017 and 2/2/2020, inclusive
In	Finds a value that is one of a list	In ("NC","SC","TN")	Value equals NC or SC or TN
Null	Finds records that have no entry in a particular field	Null	No value has been entered in a field
Is Not Null	Finds records that have any entry in a particular field	Is Not Null	Any value has been entered in a field
Like	Finds records that match the criterion, used with the * (asterisk) wildcard character	Like "C*"	Value starts with C
Not	Finds records that do not match the criterion	Not 100	Numbers other than 100

Develop OR Criteria

Learning Outcomes
- Use AND and OR criteria in the same query
- Define advanced wildcard characters

As you experienced in the previous lesson, AND criteria narrow the number of records in the datasheet by requiring that a record be true for multiple criteria. You also learned that AND criteria are entered on the same row. OR criteria work in the opposite way. **OR criteria** expand the number of records in the datasheet because a record needs to be true for only one of the criteria. You enter OR criteria in the query design grid on different criteria rows. **CASE** *Julia Rice asks you to modify the EcoAugust2018 query to expand the number of records to include trips in the Service category that start on or after 8/1/2018 as well.*

STEPS

1. **Right-click the EcoAugust2018 query in the Navigation Pane, click Copy, right-click a blank spot in the Navigation Pane, click Paste, type EcoServiceAugust2018 in the Paste As dialog box, then click OK**

   By making a copy of the EcoAugust2018 query before modifying it, you won't change the EcoAugust2018 query by mistake. To add OR criteria, you enter criteria in the next available "or" row of the query design grid. By default, the query grid displays eight rows for additional OR criteria, but you can add even more rows using the Insert Rows button on the Design tab.

2. **Right-click the EcoServiceAugust2018 query, click Design View, type Service in the next row (the "or" row) of the Category column, then click the View button 🔲 to display the datasheet**

   The datasheet expands from 6 to 10 records because four trips with a Category of Service were added to the datasheet. But notice that two of the TripStartDate values for the Service records are prior to 8/1/2018. To select only those Service trips with a TripStartDate on or after 8/1/2018, you need to add more criteria to Query Design View.

3. **Click the View button 📐 to return to Query Design View, click the next TripStartDate Criteria cell, type >=8/1/2018, then click elsewhere in the grid, as shown in FIGURE 6-9**

   Criteria in one row do not affect criteria in another row. Therefore, to select only those trips that start on or after 8/1/2018, you must put the same TripStartDate criterion in both rows of the query design grid.

4. **Click 🔲 to return to Datasheet View**

   The resulting datasheet selects 8 records, as shown in **FIGURE 6-10**. When no sort order is applied, the records are sorted by the primary key field of the first table in the query (in this case, TripNo, which is not selected for this query). All of the records have a Category of Eco or Service and a TripStartDate value greater than or equal to 8/1/2018.

5. **Save and close the EcoServiceAugust2018 query**

   The R2G-6.accdb Navigation Pane displays the three queries you created plus the RevByState query that was already in the database.

FIGURE 6-9: Entering OR criteria on different rows

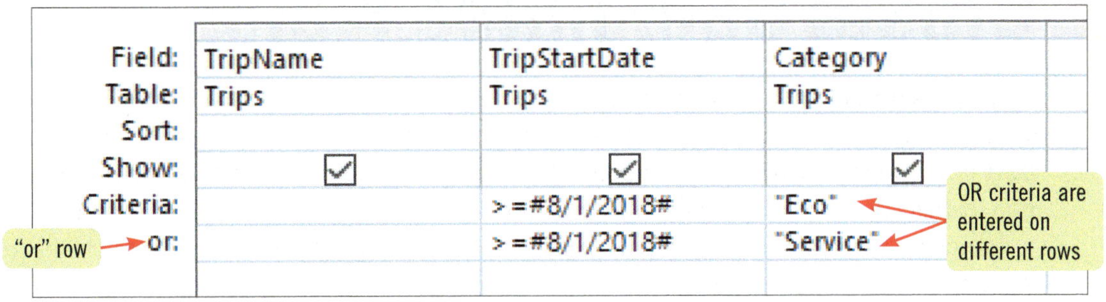

Field:	TripName	TripStartDate	Category
Table:	Trips	Trips	Trips
Sort:			
Show:	☑	☑	☑
Criteria:		>=#8/1/2018#	"Eco"
or:		>=#8/1/2018#	"Service"

"or" row → or:

OR criteria are entered on different rows

FIGURE 6-10: Datasheet for EcoServiceAugust2018 query

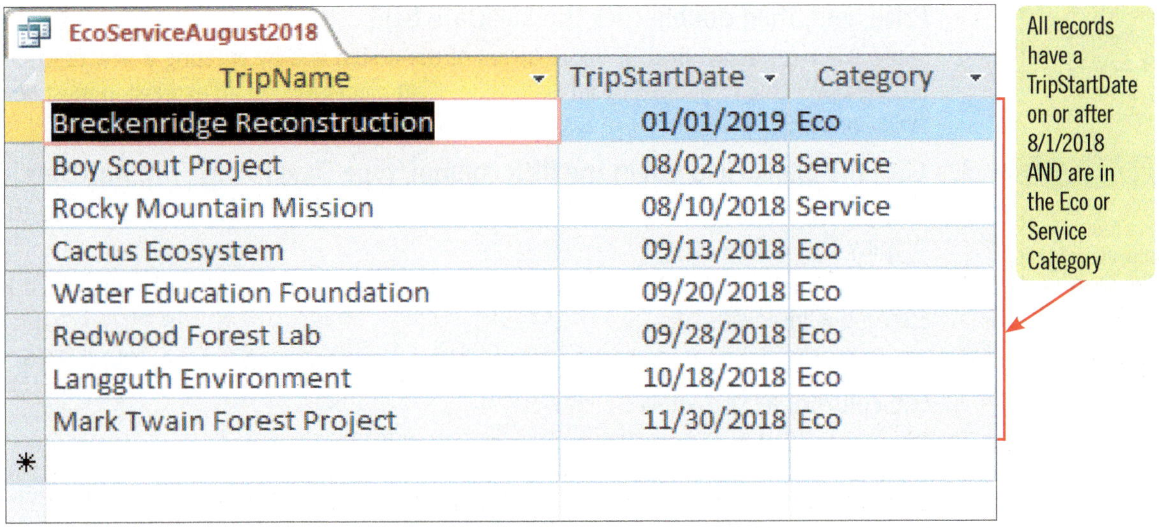

EcoServiceAugust2018

TripName	TripStartDate	Category
Breckenridge Reconstruction	01/01/2019	Eco
Boy Scout Project	08/02/2018	Service
Rocky Mountain Mission	08/10/2018	Service
Cactus Ecosystem	09/13/2018	Eco
Water Education Foundation	09/20/2018	Eco
Redwood Forest Lab	09/28/2018	Eco
Langguth Environment	10/18/2018	Eco
Mark Twain Forest Project	11/30/2018	Eco

All records have a TripStartDate on or after 8/1/2018 AND are in the Eco or Service Category

Using wildcard characters in query criteria

To search for a pattern, use a **wildcard character** to represent any character in the criteria entry. Use a **question mark (?)** to search for any single character, and an **asterisk (*)** to search for any number of characters. Wildcard characters are often used with the Like operator. For example, the criterion Like "10/*/2017" finds all dates in October of 2017, and the criterion Like "F*" finds all entries that start with the letter F.

Create Calculated Fields

Learning Outcomes
• Create calculated fields in queries
• Define functions and expressions

A **calculated field** is a field of data that can be created based on the values of other fields. For example, you can calculate the value for a discount, commission, or tax amount by multiplying the value of the Sales field by a percentage. To create a calculated field, define it in Query Design View using an expression that describes the calculation. An **expression** is a combination of field names, operators (such as +, –, /, and *), and functions that result in a single value. A **function** is a predefined formula that returns a value such as a subtotal, count, average, or the current date. See **TABLE 6-2** for more information on arithmetic operators and **TABLE 6-3** for more information on functions. **CASE** *Julia Rice asks you to find the number of days between the sale date and the trip start date. To determine this information, you create a calculated field called DaysToTrip that subtracts the SaleDate from the TripStartDate. You create another calculated field to determine the down payment amount for each trip sale.*

STEPS

1. **Click the Create tab on the Ribbon, click the Query Design button, double-click Trips, double-click Sales, then click Close in the Show Table dialog box**
   First, you add the fields to the grid that you want to display in the query.

QUICK TIP
Drag the bottom edge of the Trips field list down to display all fields.

2. **Double-click the TripName field, double-click the TripStartDate field, double-click the Price field, then double-click the SaleDate field**
   You create a calculated field in the Field cell of the design grid by entering a new descriptive field name followed by a colon, followed by an expression. Field names used in an expression must be surrounded by square brackets.

QUICK TIP
To display a long entry in a field cell, right-click the cell, then click Zoom.

3. **Click the blank Field cell in the fifth column, type DaysToTrip:[TripStartDate]-[SaleDate], then drag the ↔ pointer on the right edge of the fifth column selector to the right to display the entire entry**
   You create another calculated field to determine the down payment for each sale, which is calculated as 10% of the Price field.

TROUBLE
Field names in expressions are surrounded by [square brackets] not {curly braces} and not (parentheses).

4. **Click the blank Field cell in the sixth column, type DownPayment:[Price]*0.1, then widen the column, as shown in FIGURE 6-11**
   You view the datasheet to see the resulting calculated fields.

5. **Click the View button, press [Tab], type 7/20/18 in the TripStartDate field for the first record, press [Tab], type 1000 in the Price field for the first record, then press [↓]**
   A portion of the resulting datasheet, with two calculated fields, is shown in **FIGURE 6-12**. The DaysToTrip field is automatically recalculated, showing the number of days between the SaleDate and the TripStartDate. The DownPayment field is also automatically recalculated, multiplying the Price value by 10%.

6. **Click the Save button on the Quick Access Toolbar, type TripCalculations in the Save As dialog box, click OK, then close the datasheet**

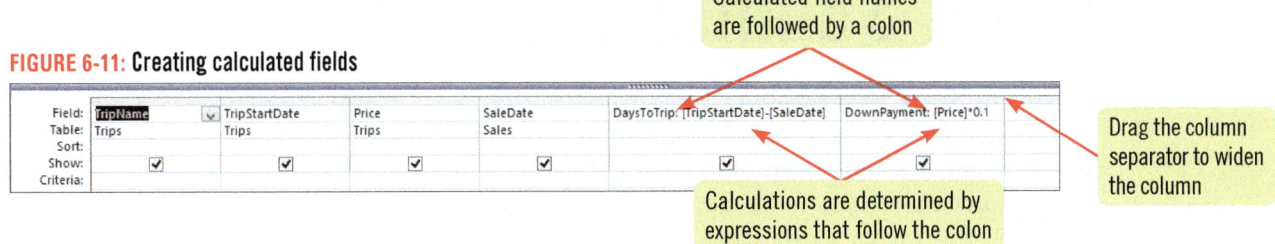

FIGURE 6-11: Creating calculated fields

FIGURE 6-12: Viewing and testing calculated fields

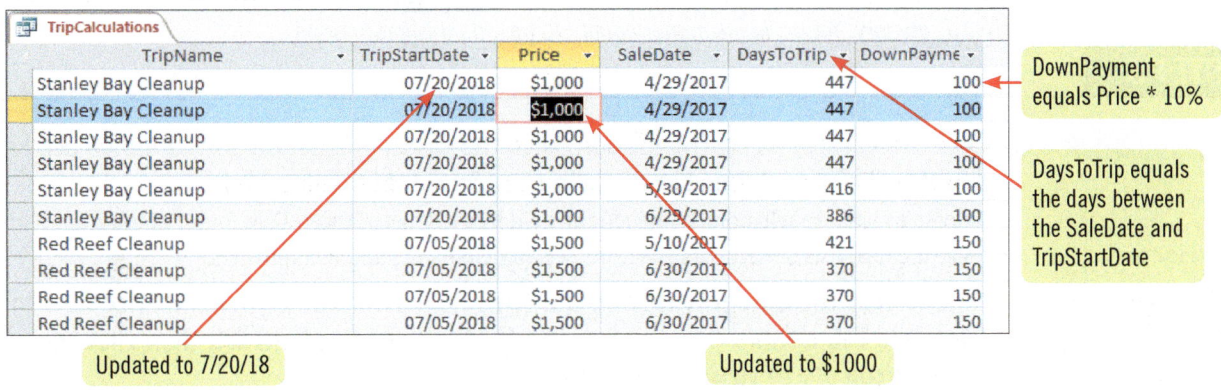

TABLE 6-2: Arithmetic operators

operator	description
+	Addition
−	Subtraction
*	Multiplication
/	Division
^	Exponentiation

TABLE 6-3: Common functions

function	sample expression and description
DATE	DATE()-[BirthDate] Calculates the number of days between today and the date in the BirthDate field; Access expressions are not case sensitive, so DATE()-[BirthDate] is equivalent to date()-[birthdate] and DATE()-[BIRTHDATE]; therefore, use capitalization in expressions in any way that makes the expression easier to read
PMT	PMT([Rate],[Term],[Loan]) Calculates the monthly payment on a loan where the Rate field contains the monthly interest rate, the Term field contains the number of monthly payments, and the Loan field contains the total amount financed
LEFT	LEFT([LastName],2) Returns the first two characters of the entry in the LastName field
RIGHT	RIGHT([PartNo],3) Returns the last three characters of the entry in the PartNo field
LEN	LEN([Description]) Returns the number of characters in the Description field

Build Summary Queries

A **summary query** calculates statistics for groups of records. To create a summary query, you add the **Total row** to the query design grid to specify how you want to group and calculate the records using aggregate functions. **Aggregate functions** calculate a statistic such as a subtotal, count, or average on a field in a group of records. Some aggregate functions, such as Sum or Avg (Average), work only on fields with Number or Currency data types. Other functions, such as Min (Minimum), Max (Maximum), or Count, also work on Short Text fields. **TABLE 6-4** provides more information on aggregate functions. A key difference between the statistics displayed by a summary query and those displayed by calculated fields is that summary queries provide calculations that describe a group of records, whereas calculated fields provide a new field of information for each record. **CASE** ▶ *Julia Rice asks you to calculate total sales for each trip category. You build a summary query to provide this information.*

STEPS

1. **Click the Create tab on the Ribbon, click the Query Design button, double-click Sales, double-click Trips, then click Close in the Show Table dialog box**

   It doesn't matter in what order you add the field lists to Query Design View, but it's important to move and resize the field lists as necessary to clearly see all field names and relationships.

2. **Double-click the Category field in the Trips field list, double-click the Price field in the Trips field list, double-click the SalesNo field in the Sales field list, then click the View button 🔲 to view the datasheet**

   One hundred and one records are displayed, representing all 101 records in the Sales table. You can add a Total row to any datasheet to calculate grand total statistics for that datasheet.

3. **Click the Totals button in the Records group, click the Total cell below the Price field, click the Total list arrow, click Sum, then use ✛ to widen the Price column to display the entire total**

   The Total row is added to the bottom of the datasheet and displays the sum total of the Price field, $129,550. Other Total row statistics you can select include Average, Count, Maximum, Minimum, Standard Deviation, and Variance. To create subtotals per Category, you need to modify the query in Query Design View.

4. **Click the View button 🔽 to return to Query Design View, click the Totals button in the Show/Hide group, click Group By in the Price column, click the list arrow, click Sum, click Group By in the SalesNo column, click the list arrow, then click Count**

   The Total row is added to the query grid below the Table row. To calculate summary statistics for each category, the Category field is the Group By field, as shown in **FIGURE 6-13**. With the records grouped together by Category, you subtotal the Price field using the Sum operator to calculate a subtotal of revenue for each Category of trip sales and count the SalesNo field using the Count operator to calculate the number of sales in each category.

5. **Click 🔲 to display the datasheet, widen each column as necessary to view all field names, click in the Total row for the SumOfPrice field, click the list arrow, click Sum, then click another row in the datasheet to remove the selection**

   The Eco category leads all others with a count of 42 sales totaling $47,450. The total revenue for all sales is still $129,550, as shown in **FIGURE 6-14**, but now each record represents a subtotal for each Category instead of an individual sale.

6. **Click the Save button 💾 on the Quick Access Toolbar, type CategorySales, click OK, then close the datasheet**

FIGURE 6-13: Summary query in Design View

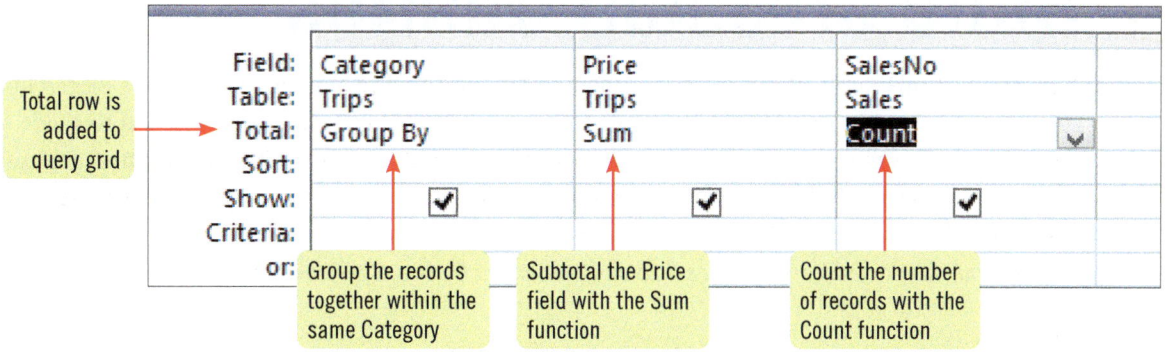

Total row is added to query grid →

Field:	Category	Price	SalesNo
Table:	Trips	Trips	Sales
Total:	Group By	Sum	Count
Sort:			
Show:	☑	☑	☑
Criteria:			
or:			

Group the records together within the same Category

Subtotal the Price field with the Sum function

Count the number of records with the Count function

FIGURE 6-14: Summary query datasheet

Query1

Group By the Category field →

Category	SumOfPrice	CountOfSalesNo
Adventure	$12,500.00	10
Cultural	$12,600.00	7
Eco	$47,450.00	42
Educational	$36,800.00	27
Family	$1,000.00	1
Service	$19,200.00	14
Total	$129,550.00	

Count the SalesNo field

Sum the Price field

Grand total for the Price field

TABLE 6-4: Aggregate functions

aggregate function	used to find the
Sum	Total of values in a field
Avg	Average of values in a field
Min	Minimum value in a field
Max	Maximum value in a field
Count	Number of values in a field (not counting null values)
StDev	Standard deviation of values in a field
Var	Variance of values in a field
First	Field value from the first record in a table or query
Last	Field value from the last record in a table or query

Build Crosstab Queries

A **crosstab query** subtotals one field by grouping records using two other fields that are placed in the column heading and row heading positions. You can use the **Crosstab Query Wizard** to guide you through the steps of creating a crosstab query, or you can build the crosstab query from scratch using Query Design View. **CASE** *Julia Rice asks you to continue your analysis of prices per category by summarizing the price values for each trip within each category. A crosstab query works well for this request because you want to subtotal the Price field as summarized by two other fields, TripName and Category.*

STEPS

1. **Click the Create tab on the Ribbon, click the Query Design button, double-click Trips, double-click Sales, then click Close in the Show Table dialog box**

   The fields you need for your crosstab query come from the Trips table, but you also need to include the Sales table in this query to select trip information for each record (sale) in the Sales table.

2. **Double-click the TripName field, double-click the Category field, then double-click the Price field**

   The first step in creating a crosstab query is to create a select query with the three fields you want to use in the crosstabular report.

3. **Click the View button [icon] to review the unsummarized datasheet of 101 records, then click the View button [icon] to return to Query Design View**

   To summarize these 101 records in a crosstabular report, you need to change the current select query into a crosstab query.

4. **Click the Crosstab button in the Query Type group**

   Note that two new rows are added to the query grid—the Total row and the Crosstab row. The **Total row** helps you determine which fields group or summarize the records, and the **Crosstab row** identifies which of the three positions each field takes in the crosstab report: Row Heading, Column Heading, or Value. The **Value field** is typically a numeric field, such as Price, that can be summed or averaged.

5. **Click the Crosstab cell for the TripName field, click the list arrow, click Row Heading, click the Crosstab cell for the Category field, click the list arrow, click Column Heading, click the Crosstab cell for the Price field, click the list arrow, click Value, click Group By in the Total cell of the Price field, click the list arrow, then click Sum**

   The completed Query Design View should look like **FIGURE 6-15**. Note the choices made in both the Total and Crosstab rows of the query grid.

6. **Click [icon] to review the crosstab datasheet**

   The final crosstab datasheet is shown in **FIGURE 6-16**. The datasheet summarizes all 101 sales records by the Category field used as the column headings and by the TripName field used in the row heading position. Although you can switch the row and column heading fields without changing the numeric information on the crosstab datasheet, you should generally place the field with the most entries (in this case, TripName has more values than Category) in the row heading position so that the printout is taller than it is wide.

7. **Click the Save button [icon] on the Quick Access Toolbar, type TripCrosstab as the query name, click OK, then close the datasheet**

   Crosstab queries appear with a crosstab icon to the left of the query name in the Navigation Pane.

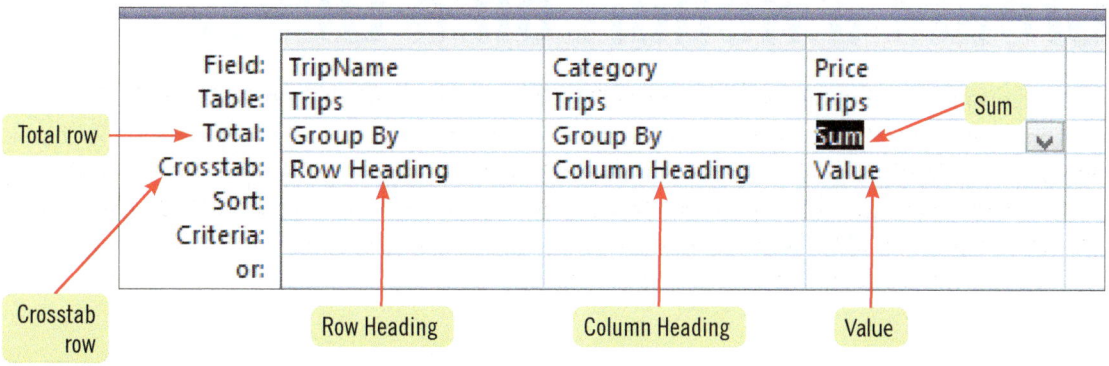

FIGURE 6-15: Query Design View of crosstab query

Total row → Crosstab row

Field:	TripName	Category	Price
Table:	Trips	Trips	Trips
Total:	Group By	Group By	**Sum**
Crosstab:	Row Heading	Column Heading	Value
Sort:			
Criteria:			
or:			

Sum

Row Heading   Column Heading   Value

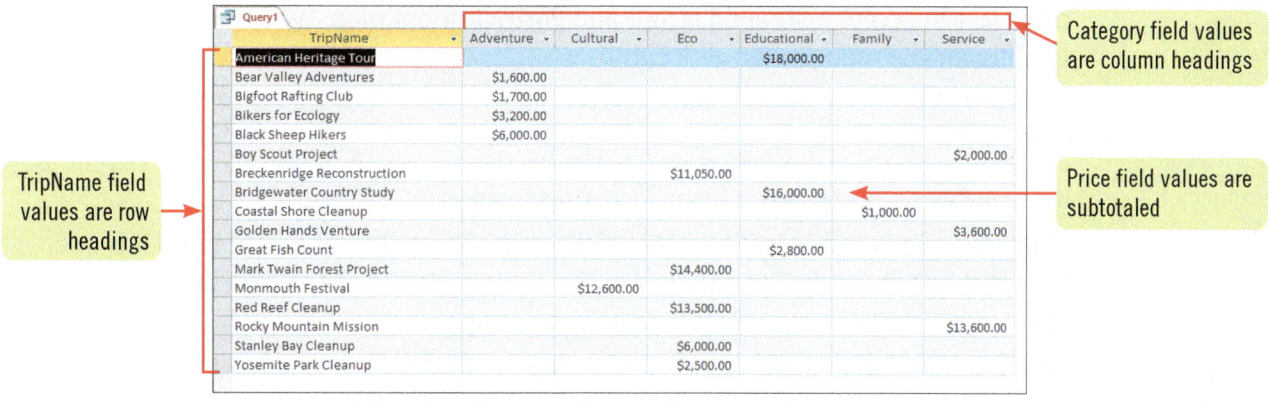

FIGURE 6-16: Crosstab query datasheet

Category field values are column headings

TripName field values are row headings

Price field values are subtotaled

TripName	Adventure	Cultural	Eco	Educational	Family	Service
American Heritage Tour				$18,000.00		
Bear Valley Adventures	$1,600.00					
Bigfoot Rafting Club	$1,700.00					
Bikers for Ecology	$3,200.00					
Black Sheep Hikers	$6,000.00					
Boy Scout Project						$2,000.00
Breckenridge Reconstruction			$11,050.00			
Bridgewater Country Study				$16,000.00		
Coastal Shore Cleanup					$1,000.00	
Golden Hands Venture						$3,600.00
Great Fish Count				$2,800.00		
Mark Twain Forest Project			$14,400.00			
Monmouth Festival		$12,600.00				
Red Reef Cleanup			$13,500.00			
Rocky Mountain Mission						$13,600.00
Stanley Bay Cleanup			$6,000.00			
Yosemite Park Cleanup			$2,500.00			

Using query wizards

Four query wizards are available to help you build queries including the Simple (which creates a select query), Crosstab, Find Duplicates, and Find Unmatched Query Wizards. Use the **Find Duplicates Query Wizard** to determine whether a table contains duplicate values in one or more fields. Use the **Find Unmatched Query Wizard** to find records in one table that do not have related records in another table. To use the query wizards, click the Query Wizard button on the Create tab.

Create a Report on a Query

When you want a more professional printout of the information than can be provided by a query datasheet, you use a report object. By first selecting the fields and records you want in a query and then basing the report on that query, you can easily add new fields and calculations to the report by adding them to the underlying query. When you base a report on a query, the query name is identified in the **Record Source** property of the report. **CASE** ▶ *Julia Rice asks you to create a report to subtotal the revenue for each trip.*

STEPS

1. **Double-click the RevByState query in the Navigation Pane to open its datasheet**

   The RevByState query contains the customer state, trip name, and price of each trip sold. Analyzing which trips are the most popular in various states will help focus marketing expenses. Creating a query to select the fields and records needed on a report is the first step in creating a report that can be easily modified later.

2. **Close the RevByState query, click the Create tab on the Ribbon, click the Report Wizard button, click the Select All button >> to select all fields in the RevByState query, then click Next**

   The Report Wizard wants to group the records by the State field. This is also how you want to analyze the data.

3. **Click Next, click TripName, then click the Select Field button > to add the TripName field as a second grouping level, click Next, click Next to not choose any sort orders, click Next to accept a Stepped layout and Portrait orientation, type Revenue by State as the title for the report, then click Finish**

   The report lists each trip sold within each state as many times as it has been sold. You decide to add the name of the customers who have purchased these trips to the report. First, you will need to add them to the RevByState query. Given that the Revenue by State report is based on the RevByState query, you can access the RevByState query from Report Design View of the Revenue by State report.

4. **Right-click the Revenue by State tab, click Design View, close the Field List if it is open, then click the Property Sheet button in the Tools group on the Design tab**

   The Property Sheet for the Revenue by State report opens.

5. **Click the Data tab in the Property Sheet, click RevByState in the Record Source property, then click the Build button ⋯ , as shown in FIGURE 6-17**

   The RevByState query opens in Query Design View.

6. **Double-click the FName field, double-click the LName field, click the Close button on the Design tab, then click Yes when prompted to save the changes**

   Now that the FName and LName fields have been added to the RevByState query, they are available to the report.

7. **Click the Design tab on the Ribbon, click the Text Box button ab|, click to the left of the Price text box in the Detail section, click the Text13 label, press [Delete], click Unbound in the text box, type =[FName] &" "&[LName], then press [Enter]**

   You could have added the FName and LName fields directly to the report but the information looks more professional as the result of one expression that calculates the entire name.

8. **Switch to Layout View, resize the new text box as shown in FIGURE 6-18 to see the entire name, save and close the Revenue by State report, close the R2G-6.accdb database, then exit Access**

FIGURE 6-17: Modifying a query from the Record Source property

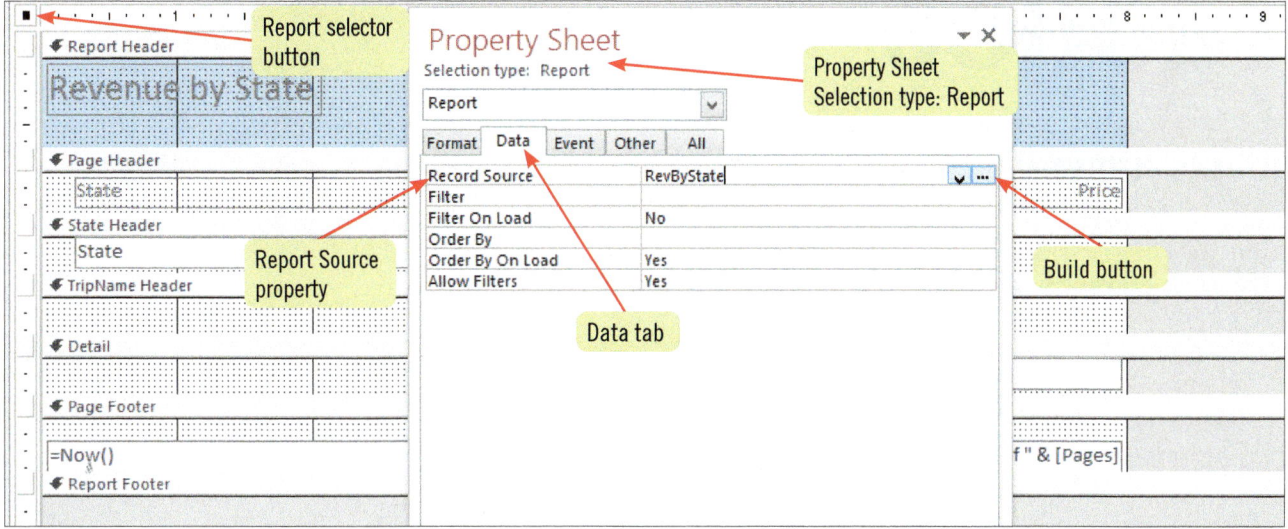

FIGURE 6-18: Final State Revenue Report

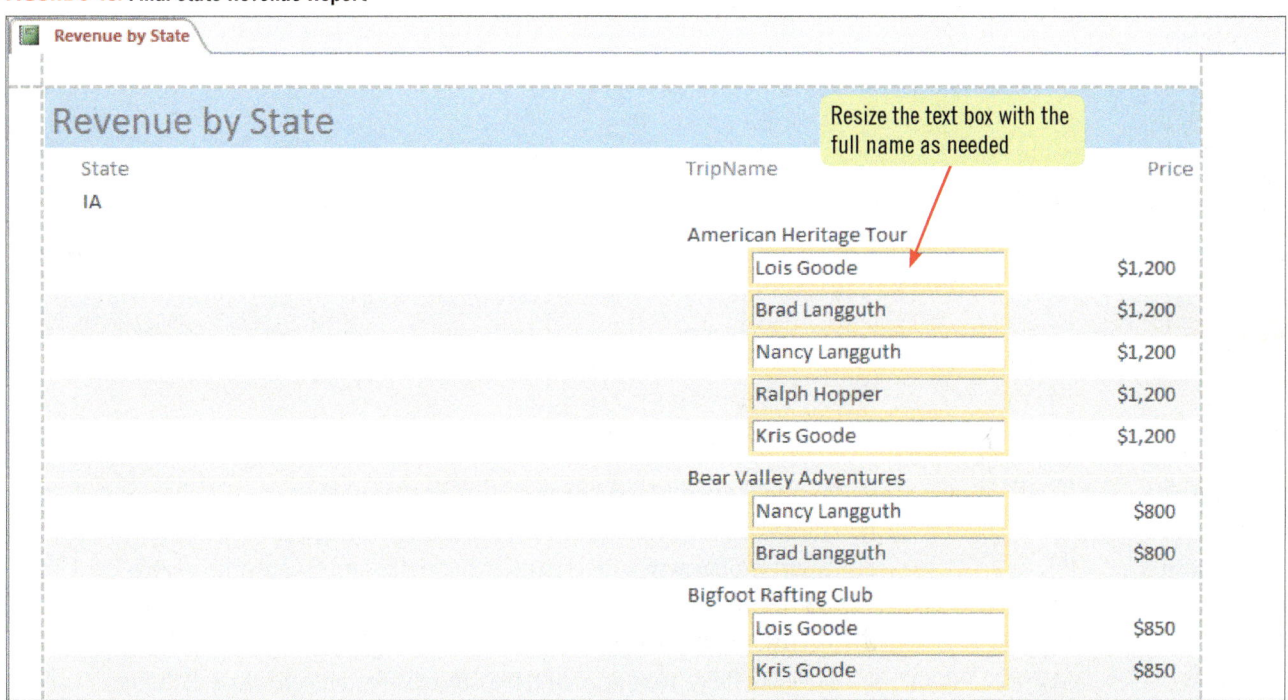

Practice

Concepts Review

Identify each element of Query Design View shown in FIGURE 6-19**.**

FIGURE 6-19

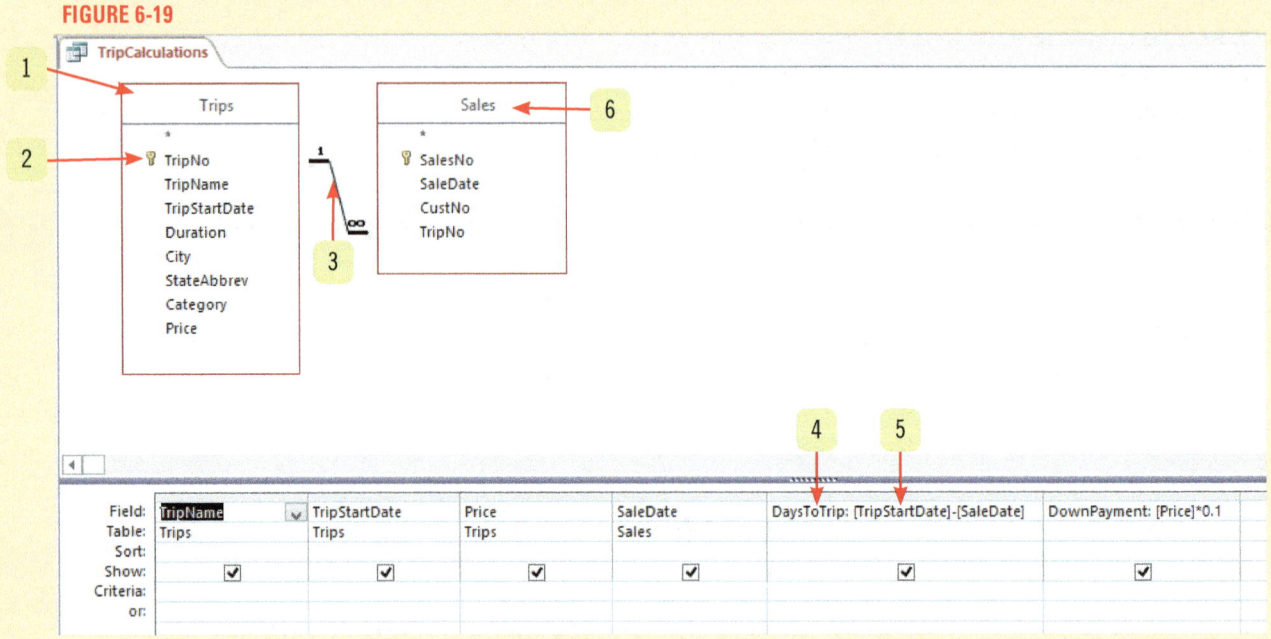

Match each term with the statement that best describes it.

7. **AND criteria**

8. **OR criteria**

9. **Record Source**

10. **Select query**

11. **Wildcard character**

12. **Sorting**

a. Placing the records of a datasheet in a certain order

b. Entered on more than one row of the query design grid

c. Report property that determines what fields and records the report will display

d. Asterisk (*) or question mark (?) used in query criteria

e. Retrieves fields from related tables and displays records in a datasheet

f. Entered on one row of the query design grid

Select the best answer from the list of choices.

13. **The query datasheet can best be described as a:**
    a. Logical view of the selected data from underlying tables.
    b. Duplication of the data in the underlying table's datasheet.
    c. Separate file of data.
    d. Second copy of the data in the underlying tables.

14. **Queries may not be used to:**
    a. Calculate new fields of data.
    b. Enter or update data.
    c. Set the primary key field for a table.
    d. Sort records.

15. **When you update data in a table that is also selected in a query:**
    a. You must relink the query to the table to refresh the data.
    b. The updated data is automatically displayed in the query.
    c. You must also update the data in the query datasheet.
    d. You can choose whether to update the data in the query.

16. **Which of the following is *not* an aggregate function available to a summary query?**
    a. Avg
    b. Count
    c. Subtotal
    d. Max

17. **The order in which records in a query are sorted is determined by:**
    a. The order in which the fields are defined in the underlying table.
    b. The importance of the information in the field.
    c. The alphabetic order of the field names.
    d. The left-to-right position of the fields in the query design grid that contain a sort order choice.

18. **A crosstab query is generally constructed with how many fields?**
    a. 1
    b. 2
    c. 3
    d. More than 5

19. **In a crosstab query, which field is the most likely candidate for the Value position?**
    a. FName
    b. Cost
    c. Department
    d. Country

20. **Which property determines the fields and records available to a report?**
    a. Field List
    b. Underlying Query
    c. Data
    d. Record Source

Skills Review

1. Create multitable queries.

  a. Start Access and open the Service-6.accdb database from the location where you store your Data Files, then enable content if prompted.

  b. Create a new select query in Query Design View using the Names and Zips tables.

  c. Add the following fields to the query design grid in this order:
  - FirstName and LastName from the Names table
  - City, State, and Zip from the Zips table

  d. In Datasheet View, replace the LastName value in the Martha Robison record with your last name.

  e. Save the query as **MemberList**, print the datasheet if requested by your instructor, then close the query.

2. Apply sorts and view SQL.

  a. Open the MemberList query in Query Design View.

  b. Drag the FirstName field from the Names field list to the third column in the query design grid to make the first three fields in the query design grid FirstName, LastName, and FirstName.

  c. Add an ascending sort to the *second* and *third* fields in the query design grid, and uncheck the Show check box in the *third* column. The query is now sorted in ascending order by LastName, then by FirstName, though the order of the fields in the resulting datasheet still appears as FirstName, LastName.

  d. Click the File tab, click Save As, then use Save Object As to save the query as **SortedMemberList**. View the datasheet, print the datasheet if requested by your instructor, then close the SortedMemberList query.

3. Develop AND criteria.

  a. Right-click the SortedMemberList query in the Navigation Pane, click Copy, right-click a blank spot in the Navigation Pane, click Paste, then type **KansasB** as the name for the new query.

  b. Open the KansasB query in Design View, then type **B*** (the asterisk is a wildcard) in the LastName field Criteria cell to choose all people whose last name starts with B. Access assists you with the syntax for this type of criterion and enters Like "B*" in the cell when you click elsewhere in the query design grid.

  c. Enter **KS** as the AND criterion for the State field. Be sure to enter the criterion on the same line in the query design grid as the Like "B*" criterion.

  d. View the datasheet. It should select only those people from Kansas with a last name that starts with the letter B.

  e. Enter your hometown in the City field of the first record to uniquely identify the printout.

  f. Save the KansasB query, print the datasheet if requested by your instructor, then close the KansasB query.

4. Develop OR criteria.

  a. Right-click the KansasB query in the Navigation Pane, click Copy, right-click a blank spot in the Navigation Pane, click Paste, then type **KansasBC** as the name for the new query.

  b. Open the KansasBC query in Design View, then enter **C*** in the second Criteria row (the or row) of the LastName field.

  c. Enter **KS** as the criterion in the second Criteria row (the or row) of the State field so that those people from KS with a last name that starts with the letter C are added to this query.

  d. View the datasheet. It should select only those people from Kansas with a last name that starts with the letter B or C. Print the datasheet if requested by your instructor, then save and close the query.

5. Create calculated fields.

  a. Create a new select query in Query Design View using only the Names table.

  b. Add the following fields to the query design grid in this order: FirstName, LastName, Birthday.

  c. Create a calculated field called Age in the fourth column of the query design grid by entering the expression: **Age: Int((Now()-[Birthday])/365)** to determine the age of each person in years based on the information in the Birthday field. The Now() function returns today's date. Now()-[Birthday] determines the number of days a person has lived. Dividing that value by 365 determines the number of years a person has lived. The Int() function is used to return the integer portion of the answer. So if a person has lived 23.5 years, Int(23.5) = 23.

Skills Review (continued)

   d. Sort the query in descending order on the calculated Age field.

   e. Save the query with the name **AgeCalc**, view the datasheet, print the datasheet if requested by your instructor, then close the query.

6. Build summary queries.

   a. Create a new select query in Query Design View using the Names and Activities tables.

   b. Add the following fields: FirstName and LastName from the Names table, and Hours from the Activities table.

   c. Add the Total row to the query design grid, then change the aggregate function for the Hours field from Group By to Sum.

   d. Sort in descending order by Hours.

   e. Save the query as **HoursSum**, view the datasheet, widen all columns so that all data is clearly visible, print the datasheet if requested by your instructor, then save and close the query.

7. Build crosstab queries.

   a. Use Query Design View to create a select query with the City and State fields from the Zips table and the Dues field from the Names table. Save the query as **DuesCrosstab**, then view the datasheet.

   b. Return to Query Design View, then click the Crosstab button to add the Total and Crosstab rows to the query design grid.

   c. Specify City as the crosstab row heading, State as the crosstab column heading, and Dues as the summed value field within the crosstab datasheet.

   d. View the datasheet as shown in **FIGURE 6-20**, print the datasheet if requested by your instructor, then save and close the DuesCrosstab query.

FIGURE 6-20

City	IA	KS	MO
Blue Springs			$50.00
Bridgewater	$50.00		
Buehler		$50.00	
Clear Water		$100.00	
Des Moines	$25.00		
Dripping Springs		$25.00	
Flat Hills		$50.00	
Fontanelle	$50.00		
Greenfield	$50.00		
Kansas City		$50.00	$100.00
Langguth		$25.00	
Leawood			$50.00
Lee's Summit			$75.00
Lenexa		$25.00	
Manawatta		$25.00	
Manhattan		$25.00	
Overland Park		$100.00	
Red Bridge		$425.00	
Running Deer			$25.00
Student Hometown		$200.00	

Skills Review (continued)

8. **Create a report on a query.**

   a. Use the Report Wizard to create a report on all of the fields of the SortedMemberList query. View the data by Names, add State as a grouping level, add LastName then FirstName as the ascending sort orders, use a Stepped layout and Landscape orientation, then title the report **Members by State**.

   b. In Design View, open the Property Sheet for the report, then open the SortedMemberList query in Design View using the Build button on the Record Source property.

   c. Add the Birthday field to the SortedMemberList query then close the query.

   d. To the left of the LastName field in the Detail section, add a text box bound to the Birthday field. (*Hint*: Type **Birthday** in place of Unbound or modify the text box's Control Source property to be Birthday.) Delete the label that is automatically created to the left of the text box.

   e. In Layout View, resize the City and Zip columns so that all data is clearly visible, as shown in **FIGURE 6-21**. Be sure to preview the report to make sure it fits on the paper.

   f. If requested by your instructor, print the first page of the Members by State report, save and close it, close the Service-6.accdb database, then exit Access.

FIGURE 6-21

Independent Challenge 1

As the manager of a music store's instrument rental program, you have created a database to track rentals to elementary through high school students. Now that several rentals have been made, you want to query the database and produce different datasheet printouts to analyze school information.

   a. Start Access and open the Music-6.accdb database from the location where you store your Data Files, then enable content if prompted.

   b. In Query Design View, create a query with the following fields in the following order:
   • SchoolName field from the Schools table
   • RentalDate field from the Rentals table
   • Description field from the Instruments table
   (*Hint*: Although you don't use any fields from the Students table, you need to add the Students table to this query to make the connection between the Schools table and the Rentals table.)

   c. Sort in ascending order by SchoolName, then in ascending order by RentalDate.

   d. Save the query as **SchoolActivity**, view the datasheet, replace Lincoln Elementary with your elementary school name, print the datasheet if requested by your instructor, then close the datasheet.

   e. Copy and paste the SchoolActivity query as **SchoolSummary**, then open the SchoolSummary query in Query Design View.

Independent Challenge 1 (continued)

f. Modify the SchoolSummary query by deleting the Description field. Use the Totals button to group the records by SchoolName and to count the RentalDate field. Print the datasheet if requested by your instructor, then save and close the SchoolSummary query.

g. Create a crosstab query named **SchoolCrosstab** based on the SchoolActivity query. (*Hint*: Select the SchoolActivity query in the Show Table dialog box.) Use Description as the column heading position and SchoolName in the row heading position. Count the RentalDate field.

h. View the SchoolCrosstab query in Datasheet View. Resize each column to best fit the data in that column, then print the datasheet if requested by your instructor. Save and close the SchoolCrosstab query.

i. Copy and paste the SchoolActivity query as **HSRentals**. Modify the HSRentals query in Query Design View so that only those schools with the words **"High School"** in the SchoolName field are displayed. (*Hint*: You have to use wildcard characters in the criteria.)

j. View the HSRentals query in Datasheet View, print it if requested by your instructor, then save and close the datasheet.

k. Close the Music-6.accdb database, then exit Access.

Independent Challenge 2

As the manager of a music store's instrument rental program, you have created a database to track rentals to elementary through high school students. You can use queries to analyze customer and rental information.

a. Start Access and open the Music-6.accdb database from the location where you store your Data Files, then enable content if prompted.

b. In Query Design View, create a query with the following fields in the following order:
- Description and MonthlyFee fields from the Instruments table
- LastName, Zip, and City fields from the Students table

(*Hint*: Although you don't need any fields from the Rentals table in this query's datasheet, you need to add the Rentals table to this query to make the connection between the Customers table and the Instruments table.)

c. Add the Zip field to the first column of the query grid, and specify an ascending sort order for this field. Uncheck the Show check box for the first Zip field so that it does not appear in the datasheet.

d. Add an ascending sort order to the Description field.

e. Save the query as **RentalsByZipCode**.

f. View the datasheet, replace Johnson with your last name in the LastName field, print the datasheet if requested by your instructor, then save and close the datasheet. (*Note*: If you later view this query in Design View, note that Access changes the way the sort orders are specified but in a way that gives you the same results in the datasheet.)

g. In Query Design View, create a query with the following fields in the following order:
- Description and MonthlyFee fields from the Instruments table
- LastName, Zip, and City fields from the Students table

(*Hint*: You'll need to add the Rentals table.)

h. Add criteria to find the records where the Description is equal to **cello**. Sort in ascending order based on the Zip then City fields. Save the query as **Cellos**, view the datasheet, print it if requested by your instructor, then close the datasheet.

i. Copy and paste the Cellos query as **CellosAndAnkeny**, then modify the CellosAndAnkeny query with AND criteria to further specify that the City must be **Ankeny**. View the datasheet, print it if requested by your instructor, then save and close the datasheet.

Independent Challenge 2 (continued)

j. Copy and paste the CellosAndAnkeny query as **CellosOrAnkeny**, then modify the CellosOrAnkeny query so that all records with a Description equal to Cello *or* a City value of **Ankeny** are selected. View the datasheet, print it if requested by your instructor, then save and close the datasheet.

k. Close the MusicStore-6.accdb database, then exit Access.

Independent Challenge 3

As a real estate agent, you use an Access database to track residential real estate listings in your area. You can use queries to answer questions about the real estate properties and to analyze home values.

a. Start Access and open the LakeHomes-6.accdb database from the location where you store your Data Files, then enable content if prompted.

b. In Query Design View, create a query with the following fields in the following order:
- AgencyName from the Agencies table
- RFirst and RLast from the Realtors table
- SqFt and Asking from the Listings table

c. Sort the records in descending order by the SqFt field.

d. Save the query as **BySqFt**, view the datasheet, enter your last name instead of Schwartz for the listing with the largest SqFt value, then print the datasheet if requested by your instructor.

e. In Query Design View, modify the BySqFt query by creating a calculated field that determines price per square foot. The new calculated field's name should be **PerSqFt**, and the expression should be the asking price divided by the square foot field, or **[Asking]/[SqFt]**.

f. Remove any former sort orders, sort the records in descending order based on the PerSqFt calculated field, and view the datasheet. Save and close the BySqFt query. ###### means the data is too wide to display in the column. You can make the data narrower and also align it by applying a Currency format.

g. Reopen the BySqFt query in Query Design View, right-click the calculated PerSqFt field, click Properties, then change the Format property to Currency. View the datasheet, print it if requested by your instructor, then save and close the BySqFt query.

h. Copy and paste the BySqFt query as **CostSummary**.

i. In Design View of the CostSummary query, delete the RFirst, RLast, and SqFt fields.

j. View the datasheet, then change the Big Cedar Realtors agency name to *your last name* followed by **Realtors**.

k. In Design View, add the Total row, then sum the Asking field and use the Avg (Average) aggregate function for the PerSqFt calculated field.

l. In Datasheet View, add the Total row and display the sum of the SumOfAsking field. Widen all columns as needed, as shown in **FIGURE 6-22**.

m. If requested by your instructor, print the CostSummary query, then save and close it.

n. Close the LakeHomes-6.accdb database, then exit Access.

FIGURE 6-22

CostSummary		
AgencyName	SumOfAsking	PerSqFt
Sunset Cove Realtors	$2,628,840.00	$113.87
Student Last Name Realtors	$3,835,214.40	$113.51
Green Mountain Realty	$1,493,940.00	$83.12
Total	$7,957,994.40	

Independent Challenge 4: Explore

You're working with the local high school guidance counselor to help her with an Access database used to manage college scholarship opportunities. You help her with the database by creating several queries. (*Note*: To complete this Independent Challenge, make sure you are connected to the Internet.)

a. Start Access, open the Scholarships-6.accdb database from the location where you store your Data Files, then enable content if prompted.

b. Conduct research on the Internet or at your school to find at least five new scholarships relevant to your major, and enter them into the Scholarships table.

c. Conduct research on the Internet or at your school to find at least one new scholarship relevant to a Computer Science major, and enter the two records into the Scholarships table. Enter **Computer Science** in the Major field.

d. Create a query called **ComputerScience** that displays all fields from the Scholarships table and selects all records with a **Computer Science** major. If requested by your instructor, print the ComputerScience query then save and close it.

e. Copy and paste the ComputerScience query as **BusinessOrCS**. Add OR criteria to the BusinessOrCS query to add all scholarships in the **Business** major to the existing scholarships in the Computer Science major. If requested by your instructor, print the BusinessOrCS query then save and close it.

f. Create a new query that selects the ScholarshipName, DueDate, and Amount from the Scholarships table, and sorts the records in ascending order by DueDate, then descending order by Amount. Name the query **AllScholarshipsByDueDate**. If requested by your instructor, print the AllScholarshipsByDueDate query then save and close it.

g. Use the Report Wizard to create a report on the AllScholarshipsByDueDate query, do not add any grouping levels or additional sort orders, use a Tabular layout and a Portrait orientation, and title the report **All Scholarships by Due Date**.

h. In Design View of the All Scholarships by Due Date report, open the Property Sheet, and use the Record Source Build button to open the AllScholarshipsByDueDate query in Design View. Add the Major field to the query, save and close it.

i. In Report Design View, open the Group, Sort, and Total pane, add the Major field as a grouping field. Add DueDate as a sort order from newest to oldest, then add Amount as a sort field from largest to smallest.

j. Add a text box to the Major Header section, and bind it to the Major field. (*Hint*: Type **Major** in place of Unbound or modify the text box's Control Source property to be Major.) Delete the label that is automatically created to the left of the text box. Preview the report, modify the ScholarshipName and DueDate labels in the Page Header section to show spaces between the words, and move and resize any controls as needed to match FIGURE 6-23. Print the report if requested by your instructor.

k. Save and close the All Scholarships by Due Date report, close the Scholarships-6.accdb database, then exit Access.

FIGURE 6-23

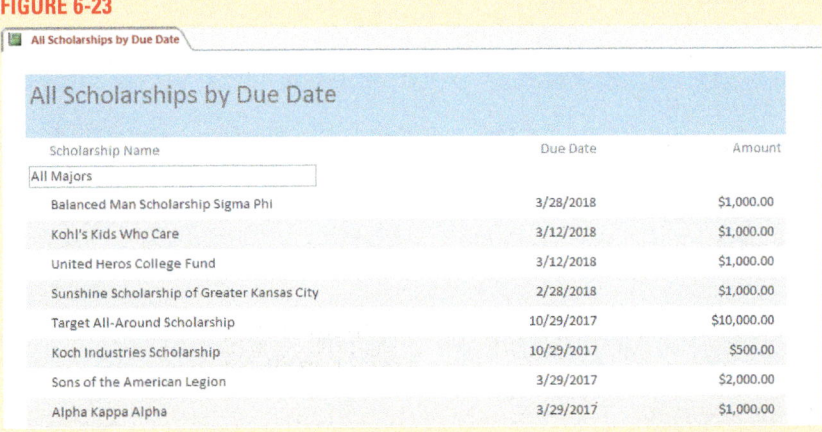

Scholarship Name	Due Date	Amount
All Majors		
Balanced Man Scholarship Sigma Phi	3/28/2018	$1,000.00
Kohl's Kids Who Care	3/12/2018	$1,000.00
United Heros College Fund	3/12/2018	$1,000.00
Sunshine Scholarship of Greater Kansas City	2/28/2018	$1,000.00
Target All-Around Scholarship	10/29/2017	$10,000.00
Koch Industries Scholarship	10/29/2017	$500.00
Sons of the American Legion	3/29/2017	$2,000.00
Alpha Kappa Alpha	3/29/2017	$1,000.00

Visual Workshop

Open the Training-6.accdb database from the location where you store your Data Files, then enable content if prompted. In Query Design View, create a new select query with the DeptName field from the Departments table, the CourseCost field from the Courses table, and the Description field from the Courses table. (*Hint*: You will also have to add the Employees and Enrollments tables to Query Design View to build relationships from the Departments table to the Courses table.) Save the query with the name **DeptCrosstab**, then display it as a crosstab query, as shown in FIGURE 6-24. Print the DeptCrosstab query if requested by your instructor, save and close it, then close the Training-6.accdb database.

FIGURE 6-24

Description	Accounting	Book	Human Resc	Information	Marketing	Operations	Shipping	Training	Warehouse
Access Case Problems	$400.00	$600.00			$200.00	$200.00		$200.00	$400.00
Computer Fundamentals	$200.00	$800.00	$400.00	$200.00	$600.00		$400.00	$400.00	$800.00
Dynamite Customer Service Skills		$100.00	$100.00	$100.00	$200.00				$200.00
Employee Benefits Made Clear		$150.00	$100.00	$50.00	$150.00	$50.00	$100.00	$50.00	$200.00
Excel Case Problems	$200.00		$200.00			$400.00	$400.00	$200.00	$400.00
Intermediate Access	$800.00	$1,200.00			$400.00	$400.00		$400.00	$800.00
Intermediate Excel	$400.00	$200.00	$200.00			$400.00	$400.00	$200.00	$400.00
Intermediate Internet Explorer	$400.00	$800.00	$400.00	$200.00	$400.00	$200.00	$200.00	$400.00	$600.00
Intermediate Phone Skils	$300.00	$300.00				$300.00		$150.00	$300.00
Intermediate PowerPoint	$400.00	$600.00	$200.00		$200.00	$200.00	$200.00	$400.00	$600.00
Intermediate Tax Planning	$100.00	$50.00	$50.00	$50.00		$50.00	$100.00	$50.00	$200.00
Intermediate Windows		$200.00	$400.00	$200.00	$400.00		$400.00	$200.00	$600.00
Intermediate Word		$200.00	$200.00	$200.00	$400.00				$400.00
Internet Fundamentals		$600.00	$400.00	$200.00	$600.00		$400.00	$400.00	$800.00
Introduction to Access	$400.00	$600.00	$200.00		$400.00	$200.00		$200.00	$400.00
Introduction to Excel	$400.00	$200.00	$200.00			$400.00	$400.00	$200.00	$800.00
Introduction to Insurance Planning	$150.00	$225.00	$75.00		$75.00	$75.00	$150.00	$150.00	$225.00
Introduction to Internet Explorer	$400.00	$800.00	$400.00	$200.00	$600.00	$200.00	$200.00	$400.00	$1,000.00
Introduction to Networking		$400.00	$400.00	$200.00	$600.00		$400.00	$200.00	$800.00
Introduction to Outlook	$400.00	$600.00	$400.00		$400.00	$400.00	$400.00	$400.00	$400.00
Introduction to Phone Skills	$300.00	$450.00			$150.00	$300.00	$150.00	$150.00	$450.00
Introduction to PowerPoint	$400.00	$800.00	$400.00	$200.00	$600.00	$200.00	$200.00	$400.00	$600.00
Introduction to Project	$1,200.00	$2,000.00	$400.00		$1,600.00	$1,600.00	$1,600.00	$1,200.00	$3,200.00
Introduction to Tax Planning	$100.00	$100.00	$50.00	$50.00	$50.00	$50.00	$100.00	$50.00	$200.00
Introduction to Windows		$600.00	$400.00	$200.00	$600.00	$200.00	$400.00	$400.00	$800.00

Record: 1 of 31 — No Filter — Search

Enhancing Forms

CASE ▶ Julia Rice wants to improve the usability of the forms in the Reason 2 Go database. You will build and improve forms by working with subforms, combo boxes, option groups, and command buttons to enter, find, and filter data.

Module Objectives

After completing this module, you will be able to:

- Use Form Design View
- Add subforms
- Align control edges
- Add a combo box for data entry
- Add a combo box to find records
- Add command buttons
- Add option groups
- Add tab controls

Files You Will Need

R2G-7.accdb	LakeHomes-7.accdb
Service-7.accdb	Scholarships-7.accdb
Music-7.accdb	Baseball-7.accdb

Use Form Design View

A **form** is a database object designed to make data easy to find, enter, and edit. You create forms by using **controls**, such as labels, text boxes, combo boxes, and command buttons, which help you manipulate data more quickly and reliably than working in a datasheet. A form that contains a **subform** allows you to work with related records in an easy-to-use screen arrangement. For example, using a form/subform combination, you can display customer data and all of the orders placed by that customer at the same time. **Design View** of a form is devoted to working with the detailed structure of a form. The purpose of Design View is to provide full access to all of the modifications you can make to the form. **CASE** ▶ *Julia Rice asks you to create a customer entry form. You create this form from scratch in Form Design View.*

STEPS

1. **Start Access, then open the R2G-7.accdb database from the location where you store your Data Files, enable content if prompted, click the Create tab on the Ribbon, then click the Form Design button in the Forms group**

   A blank form is displayed in Design View. Your first step is to connect the blank form to an underlying **record source**, a table or query that contains the data you want to display on the form. The fields in the record source populate the **Field List**, a small window that lists the fields in the record source. The Customers table should be the record source for the CustomerEntry form.

2. **Double-click the form selector button ▪ to open the form's Property Sheet, click the Data tab in the Property Sheet, click the Record Source list arrow, then click Customers**

   The Record Source property lists all existing tables and queries, or you could use the Build button ⋯ to create a query for the form. With the record source selected, you're ready to add controls to the form. Recall that bound controls, such as text boxes and combo boxes, display data from the record source, and unbound controls, such as labels and lines, clarify information.

3. **Click the Add Existing Fields button in the Tools group to open the Field List, click CustNo in the Field List, press and hold [Shift], click FirstContact in the Field List, then drag the selection to the form at about the 1" mark on the horizontal ruler**

   The fields of the Customers table are added to the form, as shown in **FIGURE 7-1**. The FirstContact field is added as a combo box because it has Lookup properties. The other fields are text boxes except for the Photo field, which is inserted as an **Attachment** control given the Photo field has an Attachment data type. Labels are created for each bound control and are captioned with the field name. You can rearrange the controls by moving them.

4. **Click the form to deselect all controls, click the Street text box, press and hold [Ctrl], click the City, State, Zip, and Phone text boxes as well as the FirstContact combo box to add them to the selection, then release [Ctrl]**

   Selected controls will move as a group.

5. **Use the ⬚ pointer to drag the selected controls up and to the right of the name controls, then click the View button 🖼 to switch to Form View**

   The new form in Form View is shown in **FIGURE 7-2**. You will improve and enhance it in later lessons.

6. **Click the Save button 💾 on the Quick Access Toolbar, type CustomerEntry as the form name, click OK, then close the CustomerEntry form**

FIGURE 7-1: Adding fields in Form Design View

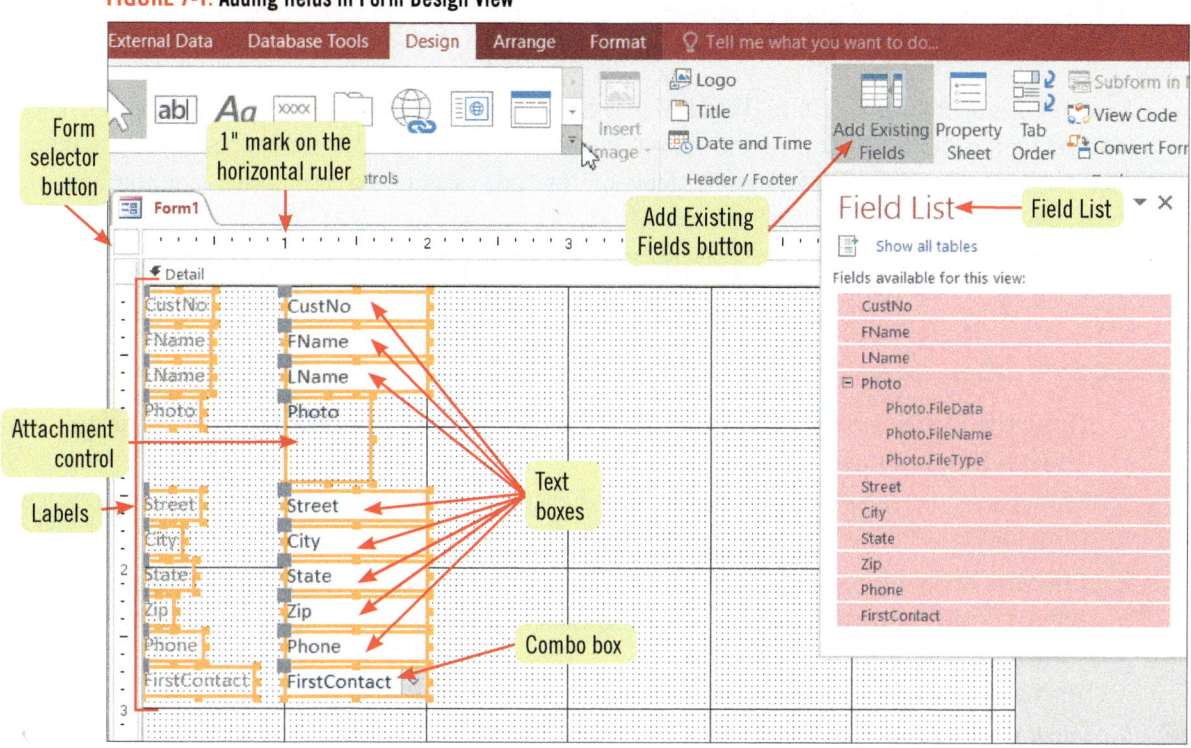

FIGURE 7-2: New form in Form View

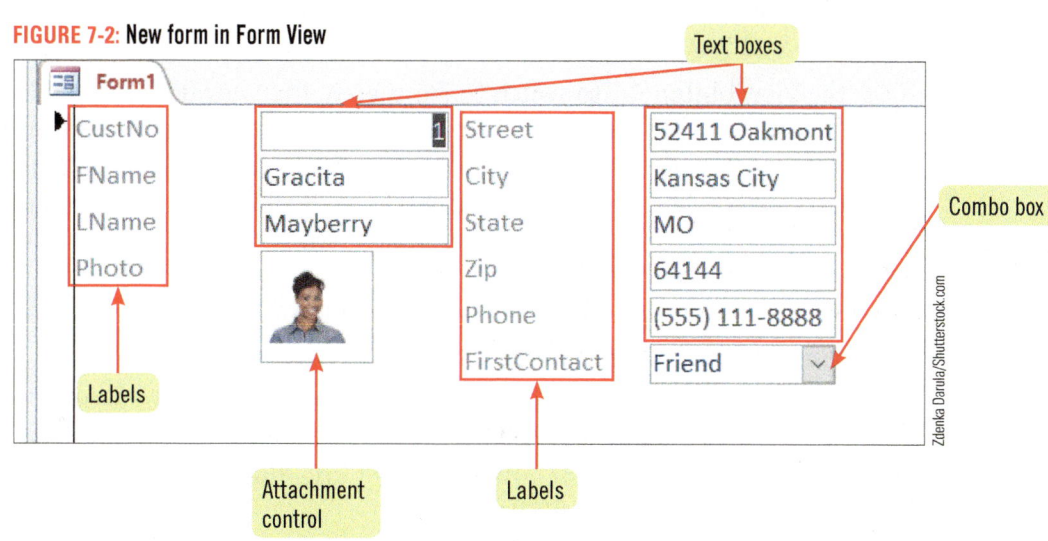

Zdenka Darula/Shutterstock.com

Add Subforms

A **subform** is a form within a form. The form that contains the subform is called the **main form**. A main form/subform combination displays the records of two tables that are related in a one-to-many relationship. The main form shows data from the table on the "one" side of the relationship, and the subform shows the records from the table on the "many" side of the relationship. **CASE** ▶ *Julia asks you to add a subform to the CustomerEntry form to show related sales for each customer.*

STEPS

1. **Open the CustomerEntry form in Design View, then close the Field List and Property Sheet if they are open**

   You add new controls to a form by dragging fields from the Field List or selecting the control on the Design tab of the Ribbon.

2. **Click the More button ⏷ in the Controls group to view all of the form controls, click the Subform/Subreport button 🖼, then click below the Photo label in the form, as shown in FIGURE 7-3**

   The Subform Wizard opens to help you add a subform control to the form.

3. **Click Next to use existing Tables and Queries as the data for the subform, click the Tables/Queries list arrow, click Query: SalesData, click the Select All Fields button ⟩⟩, click Next, click Next to accept the option Show SalesData for each record in Customers using CustNo, then click Finish to accept SalesData subform as the name for the new subform control**

   A form **layout** is the general way that the data and controls are arranged on the form. By default, subforms display their controls in a columnar arrangement in Design View, but their **Default View property** is set to Datasheet. See **TABLE 7-1** for a description of form layouts. The subform layout is apparent when you view the form in Form View.

4. **Click the View button 🖳 to switch to Form View, then navigate to CustNo 6, Kristen Lang, who has purchased four different trips, as shown in the subform**

   Sales information appears in the subform in a datasheet layout. As you move through the customer records of the main form, the information changes in the subform to reflect sales for each customer. The main form and subform are linked by the common CustNo field. Resize the columns of the subform to make the information easier to read.

5. **Point to the line between field names in the subform and use the ↔ pointer to resize the column widths of the subform, as shown in FIGURE 7-4**

   The CustomerEntry form now displays two navigation bars. The inside bar is for the subform records, and the outside bar is for the main form records.

6. **Right-click the CustomerEntry form tab, click Close, then click Yes when prompted to save changes to both form objects**

Linking the form and subform

If the form and subform do not appear to be correctly linked, examine the subform's Property Sheet, paying special attention to the **Link Child Fields** and **Link Master Fields** properties on the Data tab. These properties tell you which field serves as the link between the main form and subform.

FIGURE 7-3: Adding a subform control

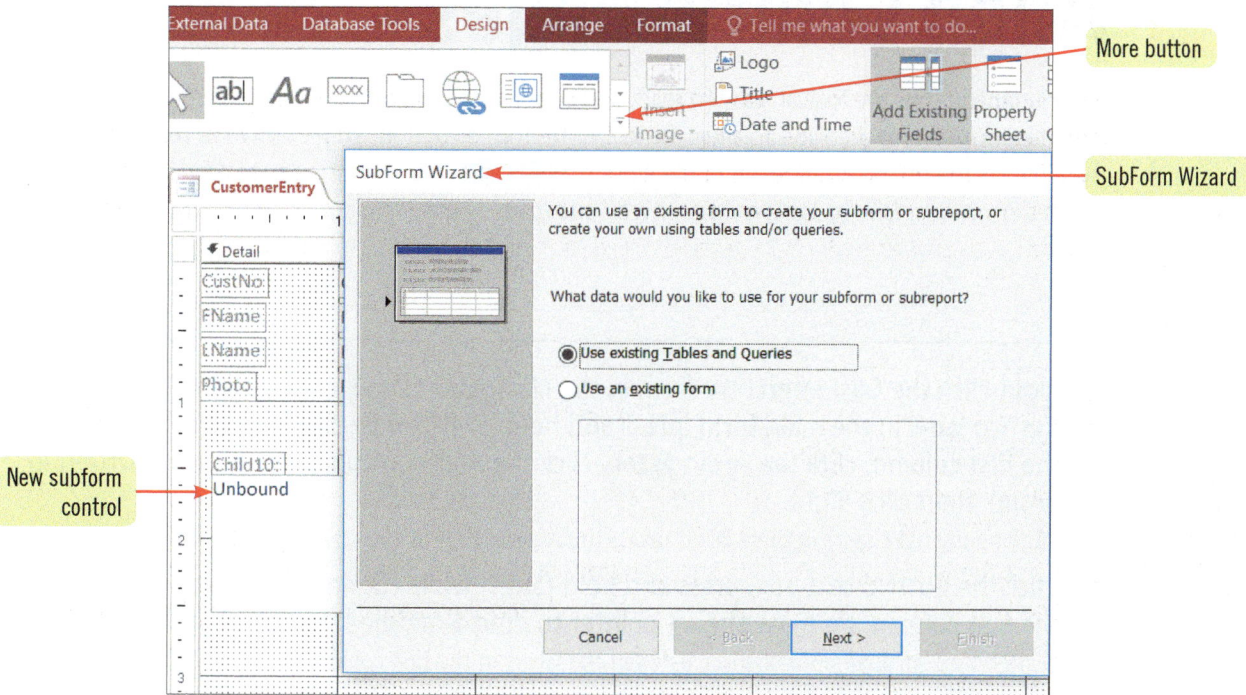

FIGURE 7-4: CustomerEntry form and SalesData subform

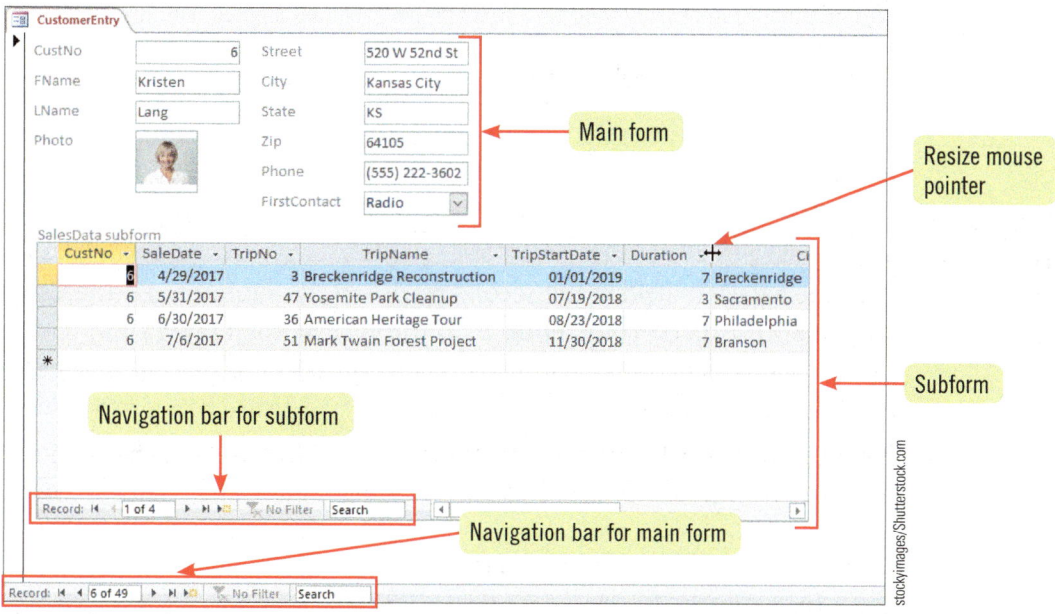

TABLE 7-1: Form layouts

layout	description
Columnar	Default view for main forms; each field appears on a separate row with a label to its left
Tabular	Each field appears as an individual column, and each record is presented as a row
Datasheet	Default view for subforms; fields and records are displayed as they appear in a table or query datasheet

Align Control Edges

Learning Outcomes
• Select multiple controls together
• Align the edges of controls

Well-designed forms are logical, easy to read, and easy to use. Aligning the edges of controls can make a big difference in form usability. To align the left, right, top, or bottom edges of two or more controls, use the Align button on the Arrange tab of the Ribbon. **CASE** ▶ *Julia Rice asks you to align and rearrange the controls in the main form to make it easier to read and to resize the Photo box so it is much larger.*

STEPS

1. **Right-click the CustomerEntry form in the Navigation Pane, click Design View, click the CustNo label in the main form, press and hold [Shift] while clicking the other labels in the first column, click the Arrange tab, click the Align button in the Sizing & Ordering group, then click Right**

   Aligning the right edges of these labels makes them easier to read and closer to the data they describe.

2. **Click the CustNo text box, press and hold [Shift] while clicking the other text boxes in the first column, then use the ↔ pointer to drag a middle-left sizing handle to the left**

   Leave only a small amount of space between the labels in the first column and the bound controls in the second column, as shown in **FIGURE 7-5**.

3. **Click the form to deselect the selected controls, press and hold [Shift] and click to select the six labels in the third column of the main form, click the Align button in the Sizing & Ordering group, then click Right**

   With the main form's labels and text boxes better sized and aligned, you decide to delete the Photo label and move and resize the Photo box to make it much larger.

4. **Click the form to deselect any selected controls, click the Photo label, press [Delete], click the Photo box to select it, use the ⬚ to move it to the upper-right corner of the form, use the ⤢ pointer to drag the lower-left sizing handle to fill the space, right-click the CustomerEntry form tab, then click Form View to review the changes**

   Use the subform to enter a new sale to Gracita Mayberry.

5. **Click the SaleDate field in the second record of the subform, use the Calendar Picker to choose 8/1/18, press [Tab], enter 3 for the TripNo, then press [Tab]**

   Once you identify the correct TripNo, the rest of the fields describing that trip are automatically added to the record. Continue to make additional enhancements in Form Design View as needed to match **FIGURE 7-6**.

6. **Save and close the CustomerEntry form**

Anchoring, margins, and padding

Anchoring means to position and tie a control to other controls so they move or are resized together. The control margin is the space between the content inside the control and the outside border of the control. Control **padding** is the space between the outside borders of adjacent controls. To apply anchoring, margins, or padding, work in Form Design View. Click the Arrange tab, select the control(s) you want to modify, and choose the Control Margins, Control Padding, or Anchoring buttons in the Position group.

FIGURE 7-5: Aligning and resizing controls

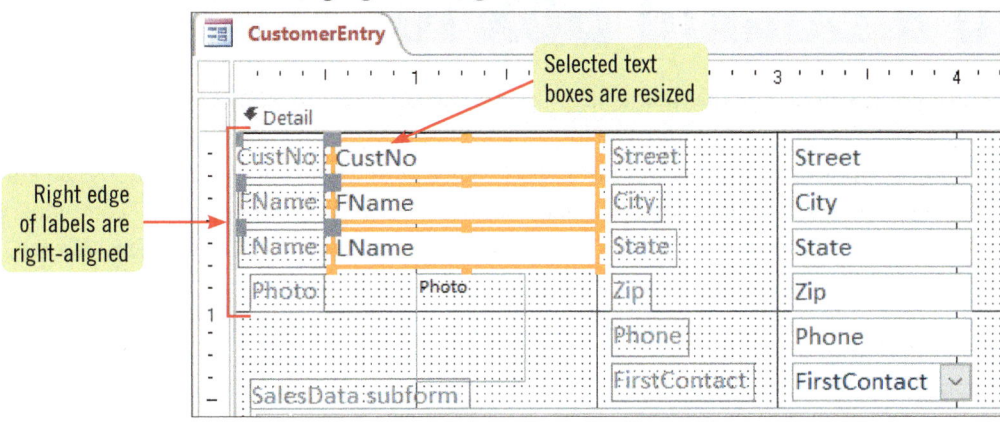

FIGURE 7-6: Updated CustomerEntry form

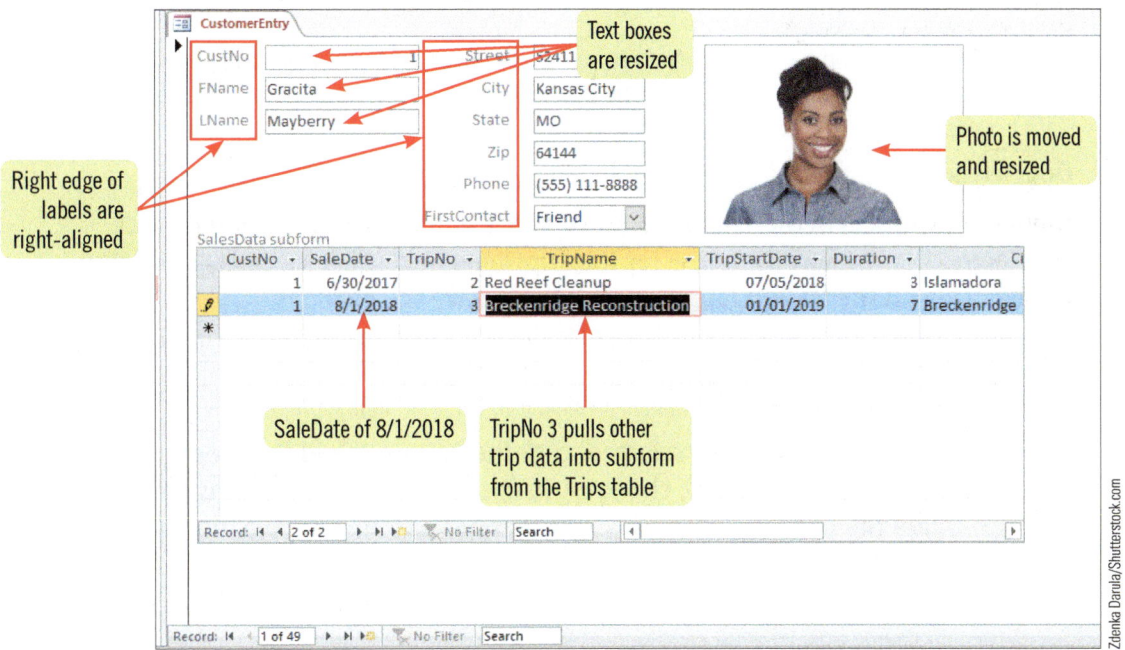

Add a Combo Box for Data Entry

If a finite set of values can be identified for a field, using a combo box instead of a text box control on a form allows the user to select a value from the list, which increases data entry accuracy and speed. Both the **list box** and **combo box** controls provide a list of values from which the user can choose an entry. A combo box also allows the user to type an entry from the keyboard; therefore, it is a "combination" of the list box and text box controls. You can create a combo box by using the **Combo Box Wizard**, or you can change an existing text box or list box into a combo box. Fields with Lookup properties are automatically created as combo boxes on new forms. Foreign key fields are also good candidates for combo boxes. **CASE** *Julia Rice asks you to change the TripNo field in the subform of the CustomerEntry form into a combo box so that when a customer purchases a new trip, users can choose the trip from a list instead of entering the TripNo value from the keyboard.*

STEPS

1. **Open the CustomerEntry form in Design View, click the TripNo text box in the subform to select it, right-click the TripNo text box, point to Change To on the shortcut menu, then click Combo Box**

   Now that the control has been changed from a text box to a combo box, you need to populate the list with the appropriate values.

2. **With the combo box still selected, click the Property Sheet button in the Tools group, click the Data tab in the Property Sheet, click the Row Source property box, then click the Build button** ⌄

   Clicking the Build button for the **Row Source property** opens the Show Table dialog box and the Query Builder window, which allows you to select the field values you want to display in the combo box list. You want to select the TripNo and TripName fields for the list, which are both stored in the Trips table.

3. **Double-click Trips, then click Close in the Show Table dialog box**

4. **Double-click TripNo in the Trips field list to add it to the query grid, double-click TripName, click the Sort list arrow for the TripName field, click Ascending, click the Close button on the Design tab, then click Yes to save the changes**

   The beginning of a SELECT statement is displayed in the Row Source property, as shown in **FIGURE 7-7**. This is an SQL (Structured Query Language) statement and can be modified by clicking the Build button. If you save the query with a name, the query name will appear in the Row Source property.

5. **With the TripNo combo box still selected, click the Format tab in the Property Sheet, click the Column Count property, change 1 to 2, click the Column Widths property, type 0.5;2, click the List Width property and change Auto to 2.5, save the form, then display it in Form View**

   Entering 0.5;2 sets the width of the first column to 0.5 inch and the width of the second column to 2 inches. To test the new combo box, you add another new sales record in the subform.

6. **Move to the second record for CustNo 2, click the TripNo list arrow in the second record in the subform, scroll as needed and click TripID 9 Bikers for Ecology on the list, press [Tab], enter 9/1/18 as the SaleDate value, then press [Enter]**

   The new record is entered as shown in **FIGURE 7-8**. Selecting a specific TripNo automatically fills in the correct Trip fields for that TripNo number.

FIGURE 7-7: Changing the TripNo field to a combo box

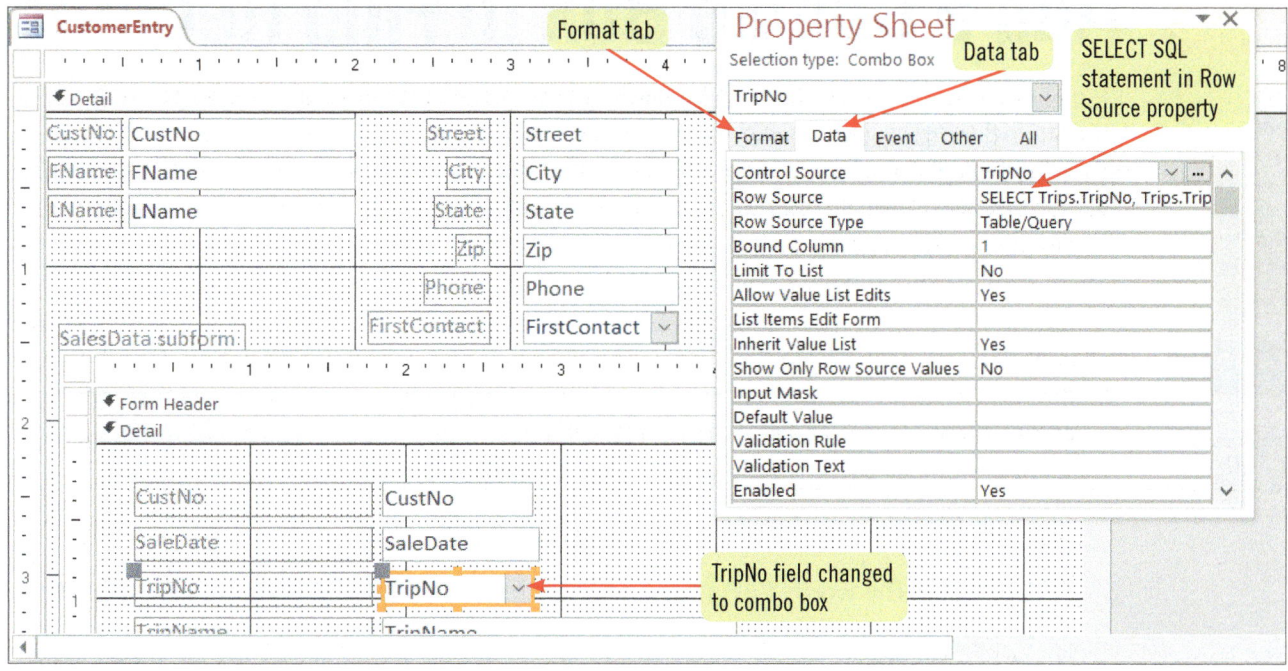

FIGURE 7-8: Using the TripNo combo box to enter a new record

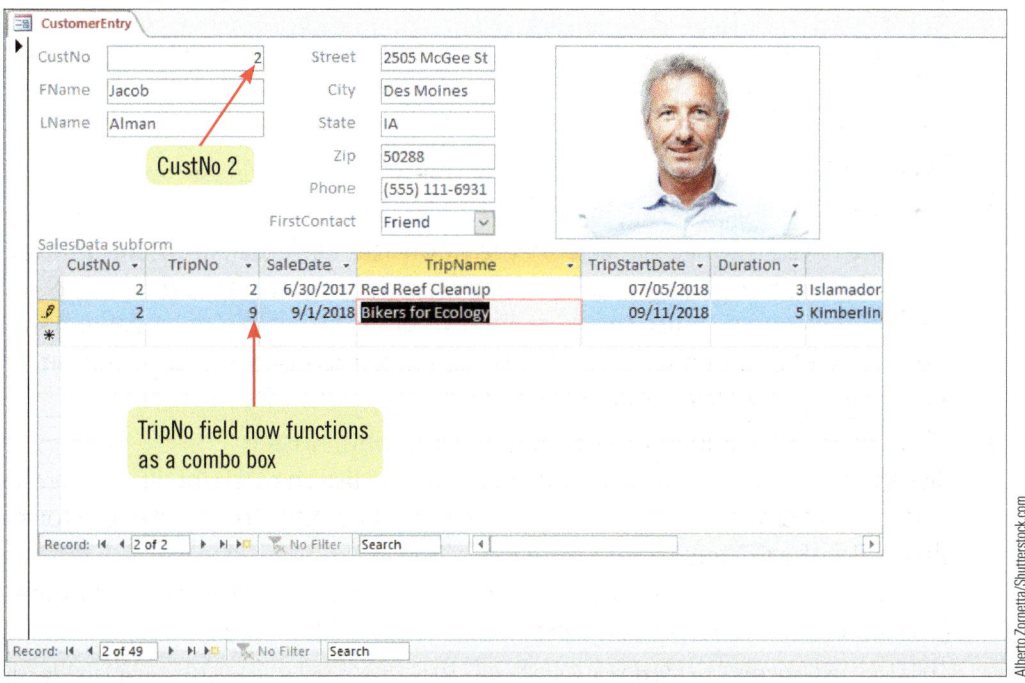

Choosing between a combo box and a list box

The list box and combo box controls are very similar, but the combo box is more popular for two reasons. While both provide a list of values from which the user can choose to make an entry in a field, the combo box also allows the user to make a unique entry from the keyboard (unless the **Limit To List property** is set to Yes). More important, however, is that most users like the drop-down list action of the combo box.

Add a Combo Box to Find Records

Learning Outcomes
- Add a combo box to find records
- Modify the Row Source property
- Search for data with a combo box

Most combo boxes are used to enter data; however, you can also use a combo box to find records. Often, controls used for navigation are placed in the Form Header section to make them easy to find. **Sections** determine where controls appear on the screen and print on paper. See **TABLE 7-2** for more information on form sections. **CASE** ▶ *Julia suggests that you add a combo box to the Form Header section to quickly locate customers in the CustomerEntry form.*

STEPS

1. **Right-click the CustomerEntry form tab, click Design View, close the Property Sheet if it is open, then click the Title button in the Header/Footer group on the Design tab**

   The **Form Header** section opens and displays a label captioned with the name of the form. You modify and resize the label.

2. **Click between the words Customer and Entry in the label in the Form Header, press the [Spacebar], then use the ↔ pointer to drag the middle-right sizing handle to the left to about the 3" mark on the horizontal ruler**

   Now you have space on the right side of the Form Header section to add a combo box to find records.

3. **Click the Combo Box button 🔲 in the Controls group, click in the Form Header at about the 5" mark on the horizontal ruler, click the Find a record option button in the Combo Box Wizard, click Next, double-click LName, double-click FName, click Next, click Next to accept the column widths and hide the key column, type Find Customer: as the label for the combo box, then click Finish**

   The new combo box is placed in the Form Header section, as shown in **FIGURE 7-9**. Because a combo box can be used for data entry or to find a record, a clear label to identify its purpose is very important. You modify the label to make it easier to read and widen the combo box.

4. **Click the Find Customer: label, click the Home tab, click the Font Color button arrow 🅰️ ▾, click the Dark Blue, Text 2 color box (top row, fourth from the left), click the Unbound combo box, use the ↔ pointer to drag the middle-right sizing handle to the right edge of the form to widen the combo box, then click the View button 🔲**

   You test the combo box in Form View.

5. **Click the Find Customer: list arrow, then click Lang, Kristen**

   The combo box finds the customer named Kristen Lang, but the combo box list entries are not in alphabetical order. You fix this in Form Design View by working with the Property Sheet of the combo box.

6. **Right-click the CustomerEntry form tab, click Design View, double-click the edge of the Unbound combo box in the Form Header to open its Property Sheet, click the Data tab, click SELECT in the Row Source property, then click the Build button ⋯**

   The Query Builder opens, allowing you to modify the fields or sort order of the values in the combo box list.

7. **Click Ascending in the Sort cell for LName, click Ascending in the Sort cell for FName, click the Close button on the Design tab, click Yes when prompted to save changes, click the View button 🔲, then click the Find Customer: list arrow**

   This time, the combo box list is sorted in ascending order by last name, then by first name, as shown in **FIGURE 7-10**.

8. **Scroll, click Alman, Jacob to test the combo box again, then save and close the CustomerEntry form**

   To modify the number of items displayed in the list, use the **List Rows property** on the Format tab.

FIGURE 7-9: Adding a combo box to find records

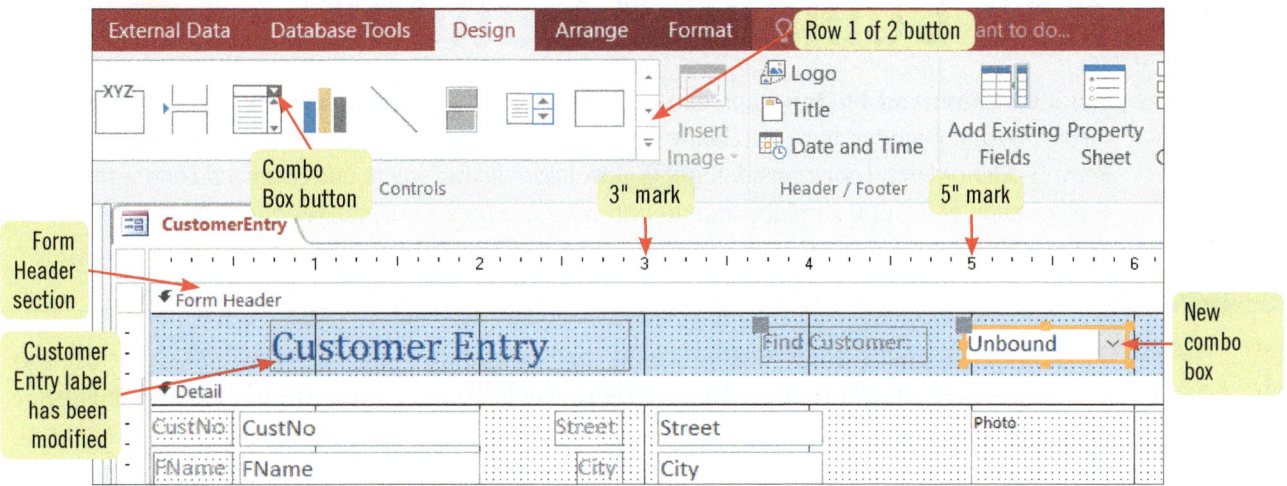

FIGURE 7-10: Using a combo box to find customers

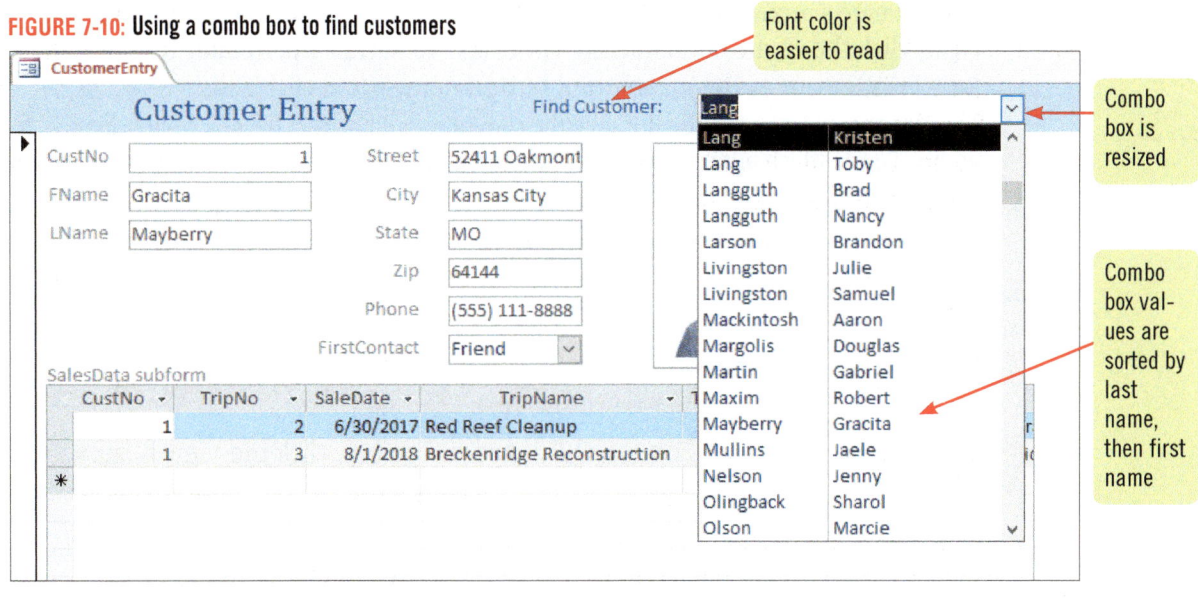

TABLE 7-2: Form sections

section	description
Detail	Appears once for every record
Form Header	Appears at the top of the form and often contains command buttons or a label with the title of the form
Form Footer	Appears at the bottom of the form and often contains command buttons or a label with instructions on how to use the form
Page Header	Appears at the top of a printed form with information such as page numbers or dates
Page Footer	Appears at the bottom of a printed form with information such as page numbers or dates

Add Command Buttons

Learning
Outcomes
• Add a command
button to a form

You use a **command button** to perform a common action in Form View such as printing the current record, opening another form, or closing the current form. Command buttons are often added to the Form Header or Form Footer sections. **CASE** ▶ *Julia Rice asks you to add command buttons to the Form Footer section of the CustomerEntry form to help other Reason 2 Go employees print the current record and close the form.*

STEPS

1. **Right-click the CustomerEntry form in the Navigation Pane, click Design View, close the Property Sheet if it is open, then scroll to the bottom of the form to display the Form Footer section**

   Good form design gives users everything they need in a logical location. You decide to use the Form Footer section for all of your form's command buttons.

2. **Click the Button button 🔲 in the Controls group, then click in the Form Footer at the 1" mark**

   The Command Button Wizard opens, listing 28 of the most popular actions for the command button, organized within six categories, as shown in **FIGURE 7-11**.

3. **Click Record Operations in the Categories list, click Print Record in the Actions list, click Next, click the Text option button, click Next to accept the default text of Print Record, type PrintRecord as the meaningful button name, then click Finish**

   Adding a command button to print only the current record prevents the user from using the Print option on the File tab, which prints *all* records. You also want to add a command button to close the form.

4. **Click the Button button 🔲 in the Controls group, then click to the right of the Print Record button in the Form Footer section**

5. **Click Form Operations in the Categories list, click Close Form in the Actions list, click Next, click the Text option button, click Next to accept the default text of Close Form, type CloseForm as the meaningful button name, then click Finish**

   To test your command buttons, you switch to Form View.

6. **Click the Save button 🔲 on the Quick Access Toolbar, click the View button 🔲 to review the form as shown in FIGURE 7-12, click the Print Record button you added in the Form Footer section, then click OK to confirm that only one record prints**

7. **Click the Close Form button in the Form Footer section to close the form**

   Using a command button to close a form prevents the user from unintentionally closing the entire Access application.

Shape effects

Shape effects provide a special visual impact (such as shadow, glow, soft edges, and bevel) to command buttons. To apply a shape effect, work in Form Design View. Click the Format tab, select the command button you want to modify, then click the Shape Effects button in the Control Formatting group to display the options.

Enhancing Forms

FIGURE 7-11: Command Button Wizard

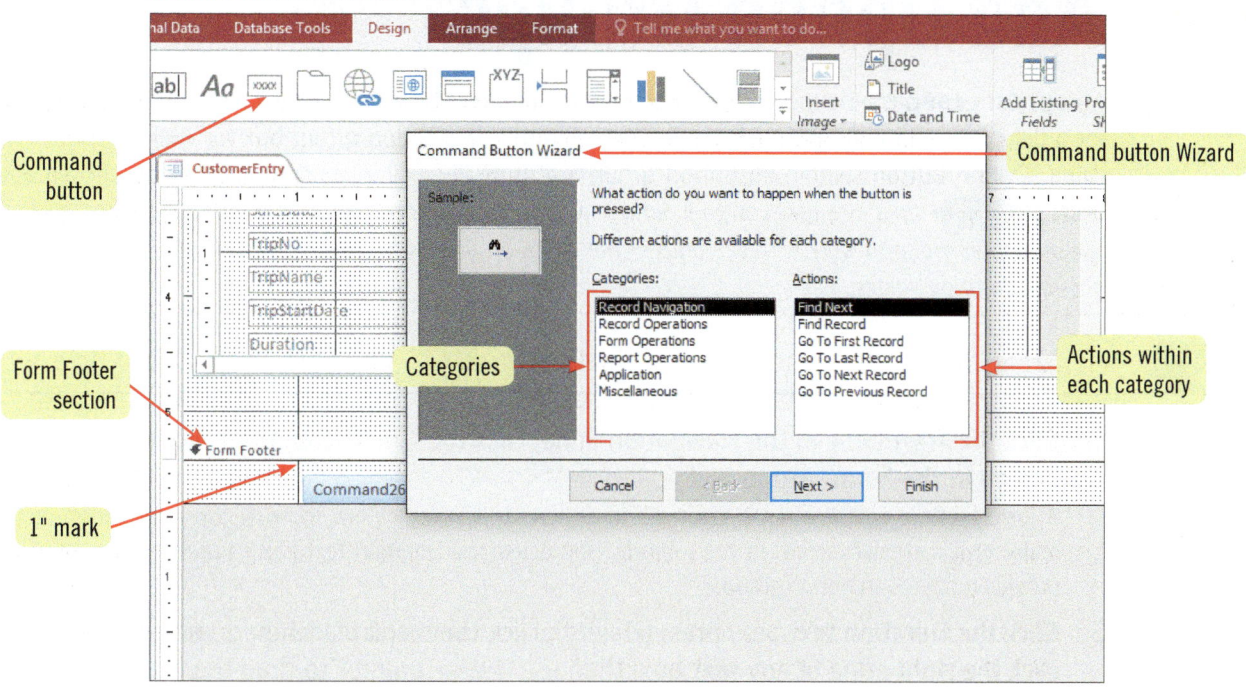

FIGURE 7-12: Final Customer Entry form with two command buttons

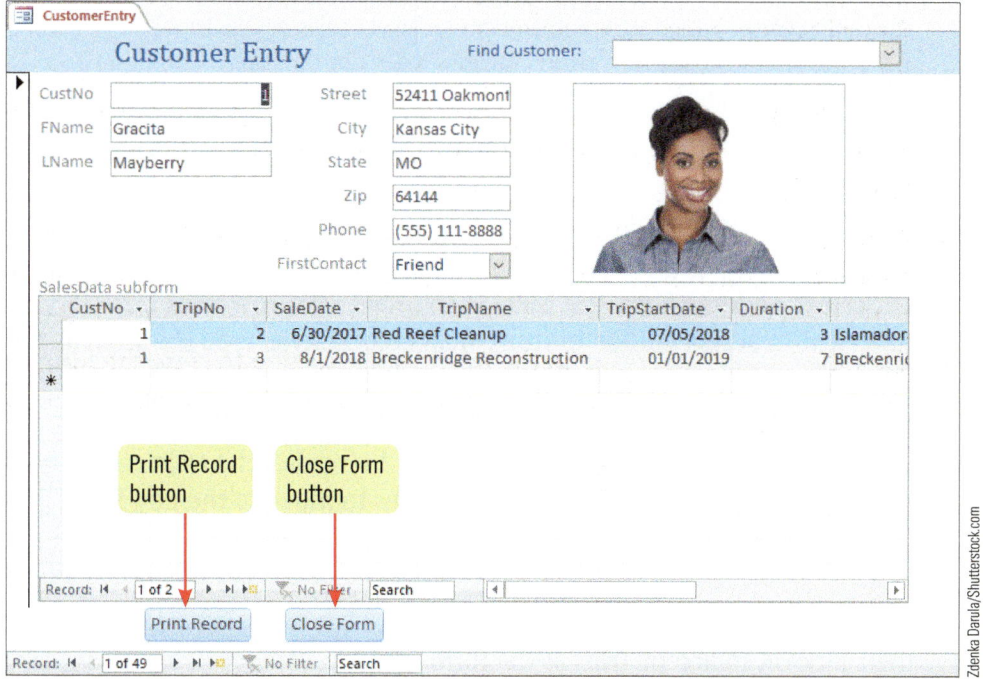

Access 2016

Zdenka Darula/Shutterstock.com

Add Option Groups

Learning Outcomes
- Add an option group to a form
- Add option buttons to an option group
- Use option buttons to edit data

An **option group** is a bound control used in place of a text box when only a few values are available for a field. You add one **option button** control within the option group box for each possible field value. Option buttons within an option group are mutually exclusive; only one can be chosen at a time. **CASE** *Julia Rice asks you to build a new form to view trips and sales information. You decide to use an option group to work with the data in the Duration field because R2G trips have only a handful of possible duration values.*

STEPS

1. **Click the Trips table in the Navigation Pane, click the Create tab, then click the Form button in the Forms group**

   A form/subform combination is created and displayed in Layout View, showing trip information in the main form and sales records in the subform. You delete the Duration text box and resize the controls to provide room for an option group.

   > **TROUBLE**
   > The blank placeholder is where the Duration text box formerly appeared.

2. **Click the Duration text box, press [Delete], click the blank placeholder, press [Delete], click the right edge of any text box, then use the ↔ pointer to drag the right edge of the controls to the left so they are about half as wide**

   You add the Duration field back to the form as an option group control using the blank space on the right that you created.

3. **Right-click the Trips form tab, click Design View, click the Design tab on the Ribbon, click the Option Group button [XYZ] in the Controls group, then click to the right of the TripNo text box**

   The Option Group Wizard starts and prompts for label names. All the trips sold by R2G have a duration of 3, 5, 7, 10, or 14 days, so the labels and values will describe this data.

   > **TROUBLE**
   > **FIGURE 7-13** shows the Option Group Wizard at the end of Step 4.

4. **Enter the Label Names shown in FIGURE 7-13, click Next, click the No, I don't want a default option button, click Next, then enter the Values to correspond with their labels, as shown in FIGURE 7-13**

   The Values are entered into the field and correspond with the **Option Value property** of each option button. The Label Names are clarifying text.

   > **QUICK TIP**
   > Option buttons commonly present mutually exclusive choices for an option group. Check boxes commonly present individual Yes/No fields.

5. **Click Next, click the Store the value in this field list arrow, click Duration, click Next, click Next to accept Option buttons in an Etched style, type Duration as the caption for the option group, then click Finish**

   View and work with the new option group in Form View.

6. **Click the View button [icon] to switch to Form View, click the Next record button [▶] in the navigation bar for the main form three times to move to the Boy Scout Project record, then click the 10 days option button**

   Your screen should look like **FIGURE 7-14**. You changed the duration of this trip from 7 to 10 days.

7. **Right-click the Trips form tab, click Close, click Yes when prompted to save changes, then click OK to accept Trips as the form name**

FIGURE 7-13: Option Group Label Names and Values

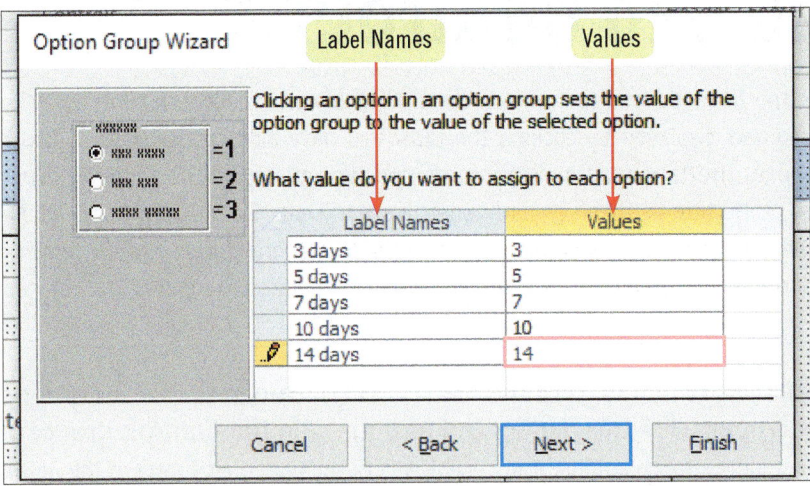

FIGURE 7-14: Trips form with option group for Duration field

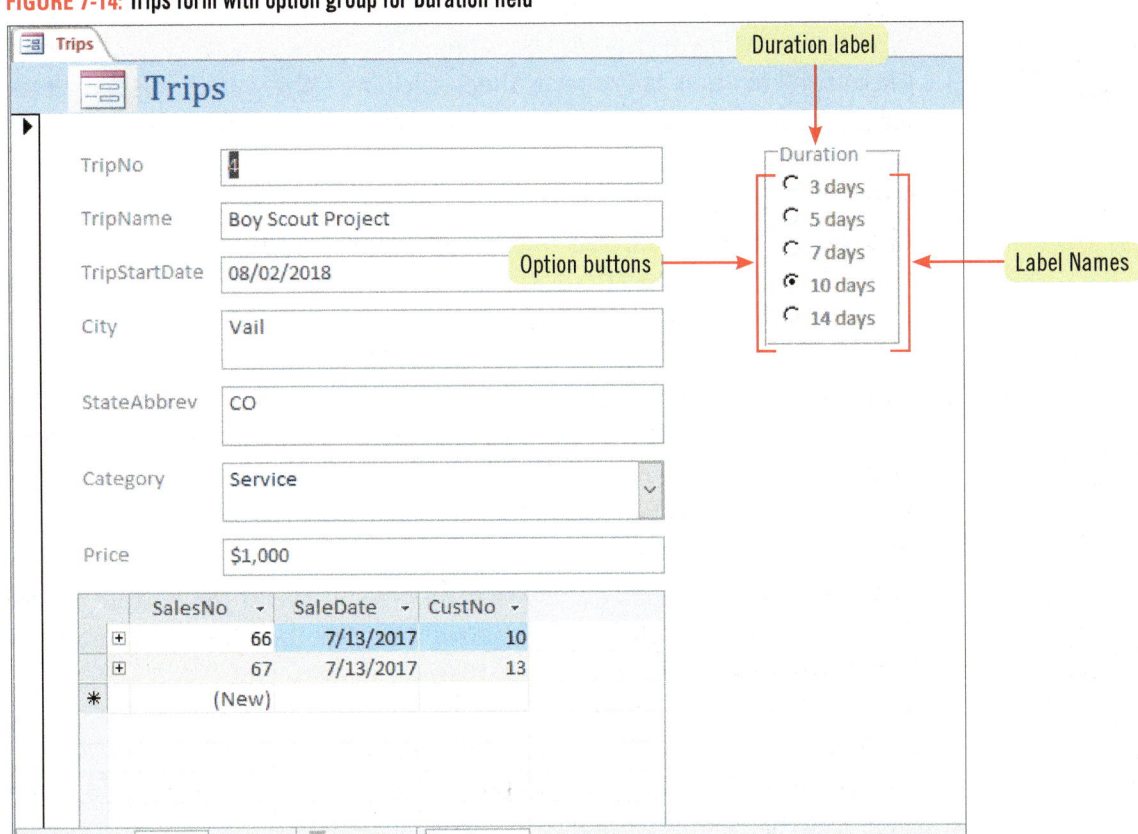

Protecting data

You may not want to allow all users who view a form to change all the data that appears on that form. You can design forms to limit access to certain fields by changing the Enabled and Locked properties of a control. The **Enabled property** specifies whether a control can have the focus in Form View. The **Locked property** specifies whether you can edit data in a control in Form View.

Add Tab Controls

Learning Outcomes
- Add a tab control to a form
- Modify tab control properties

You use the **tab control** to create a three-dimensional aspect to a form so that many controls can be organized and displayed by clicking the tabs. You have already used tab controls because many Access dialog boxes use tabs to organize information. For example, the Property Sheet uses tab controls to organize properties identified by categories: Format, Data, Event, Other, and All. **CASE** ▶ *Julia Rice asks you to organize database information based on two categories: Trips and Customers. You create a new form with tab controls to organize command buttons for easy access to trip and customer information.*

STEPS

1. **Click the Create tab, click the Blank Form button in the Forms group, close the Field List if it is open, click the Tab Control button ☐ in the Controls group, then click the form**

   A new tab control is automatically positioned in the upper-left corner of the new form with two tabs. You rename the tabs to clarify their purpose.

2. **Click the Page1 tab to select it, click the Property Sheet button in the Tools group, click the Other tab in the Property Sheet, double-click Page1 in the Name property, type Customers, then press [Enter]**

   You also give Page2 a meaningful name.

3. **Click Page2 to open its Property Sheet, click the Other tab (if it is not already selected), double-click Page2 in the Name property text box, type Trips, then press [Enter]**

   Now that the tab names are meaningful, you're ready to add controls to each page. In this case, you add command buttons to each page.

4. **Click the Customers tab, click the Button button ▦ in the Controls group, click in the middle of the Customers page, click the Form Operations category, click the Open Form action, click Next, click CustomerEntry, click Next, then click Finish**

   You add a command button to the Trips tab to open the Trips form.

5. **Click the Trips tab, click the Button button ▦, click in the middle of the Trips page, click the Form Operations category, click the Open Form action, click Next, click Trips, click Next, then click Finish**

   Your new form should look like **FIGURE 7-15**. To test your command buttons, you must switch to Form View.

6. **Click the View button ▦ to switch to Form View, click the command button on the Customers tab, click the Close Form command button at the bottom of the CustomerEntry form, click the Trips page tab, click the command button on the Trips page, right-click the Trips form tab, then click Close**

   Your screen should look like **FIGURE 7-16**. The two command buttons opened the CustomerEntry and Trips forms and are placed on different pages of a tab control in the form. In a fully developed database, you would add many more command buttons to make other database objects (tables, queries, forms, and reports) easy to find and open.

7. **Right-click the Form1 form tab, click Close, click Yes to save changes, type R2G Navigation as the form name, click OK, then close the R2G-7.accdb database**

FIGURE 7-15: Adding command buttons to a tab control

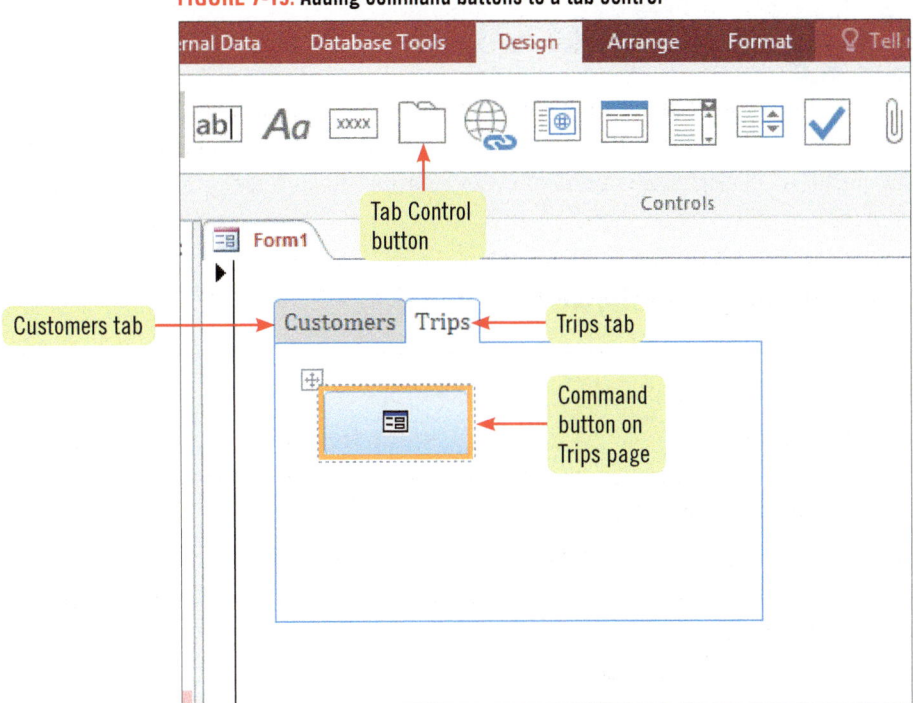

FIGURE 7-16: Form Navigation form

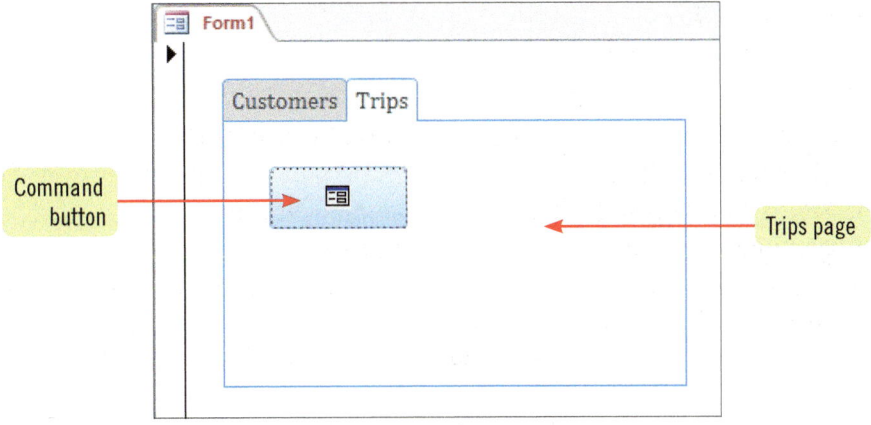

Practice

Concepts Review

Identify each element of Form Design View shown in FIGURE 7-17.

FIGURE 7-17

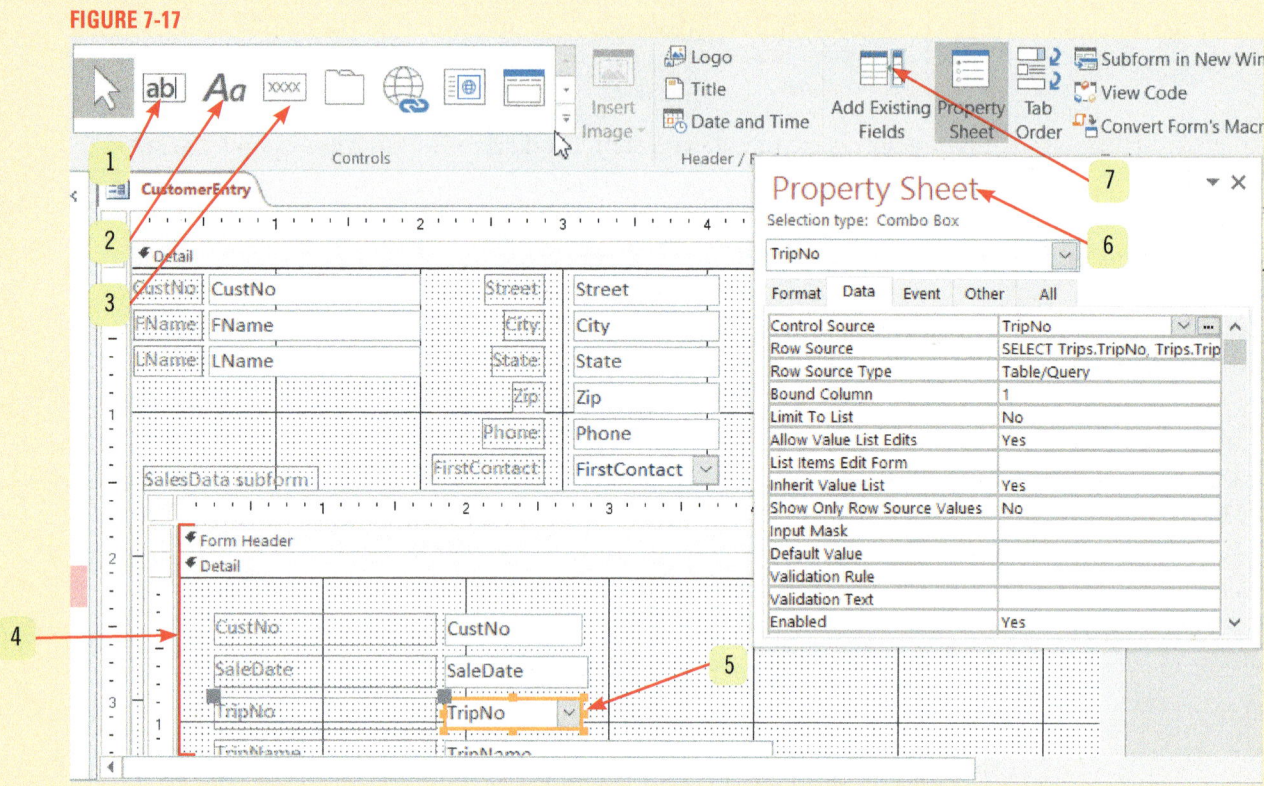

Match each term with the statement that best describes it.

8. **Combo box**

9. **Command button**

10. **Option group**

11. **Subform**

12. **Tab control**

a. A bound control that displays a few mutually exclusive entries for a field

b. A control that is used to organize other controls to give a form a three-dimensional quality

c. A bound control that is really both a list box and a text box

d. A control that shows records that are related to one record shown in the main form

e. An unbound control that executes an action when it is clicked

Select the best answer from the list of choices.

13. **Which control works best to display three choices—1, 2, or 3—for a Rating field?**
    - **a.** Text box
    - **b.** Label
    - **c.** Command button
    - **d.** Option group

14. **Which control would you use to initiate a print action?**
    - **a.** Text box
    - **b.** Option group
    - **c.** Command button
    - **d.** List box

15. **Which control would you use to display a drop-down list of 50 states?**
    - **a.** List box
    - **b.** Check box
    - **c.** Combo box
    - **d.** Field label

16. **To view many related records within a form, use a:**
    - **a.** Design template.
    - **b.** Subform.
    - **c.** Link control.
    - **d.** List box.

17. **Which of the following form properties defines the fields and records that appear on a form?**
    - **a.** Record Source
    - **b.** Row Source
    - **c.** Default View
    - **d.** List Items Edit Form

18. **Which is a popular layout for a main form?**
    - **a.** Datasheet
    - **b.** Global
    - **c.** Justified
    - **d.** Columnar

19. **Which is a popular layout for a subform?**
    - **a.** Justified
    - **b.** Columnar
    - **c.** Global
    - **d.** Datasheet

20. **To align controls on their left edges, first:**
    - **a.** Click the Layout tab on the Ribbon.
    - **b.** Click the Design tab on the Ribbon.
    - **c.** Select the controls whose edges you want to align.
    - **d.** Align the data within the controls.

21. **Which control is most commonly used within an option group?**
    - **a.** Check box
    - **b.** Command button
    - **c.** Option button
    - **d.** Toggle button

Skills Review

1. **Use Form Design View.**
   - **a.** Start Access and open the Service-7.accdb database from the location where you store your Data Files. Enable content if prompted.
   - **b.** Create a new form in Form Design View, open the Property Sheet for the new form, then choose the Members table as the Record Source.
   - **c.** Open the Field List, then add all fields from the Members table to Form Design View to the upper-left corner of the form.
   - **d.** Move the Birthday, Dues, MemberNo, and CharterMember controls to the right of the FirstName, LastName, Street, and Zip fields.
   - **e.** Save the form with the name **MemberHours**.

2. **Add subforms.**
   - **a.** In Form Design View of the MemberHours form, use the SubForm Wizard to create a subform below the Zip label.
   - **b.** Use all three fields in the Activities table for the subform. Show Activities for each record in Members using MemberNo, and name the subform **ActivityHours**.
   - **c.** Drag the bottom edge of the form up to just below the subform control.
   - **d.** View the MemberHours form in Form View, and move through several records. Note that the form could be improved with better alignment and that the Street text box is too narrow to display the entire value in the field.

Skills Review (continued)

3. Align control edges.

a. Switch to Form Design View, then edit the FirstName, LastName, MemberNo, and CharterMember labels in the main form to read **First Name**, **Last Name**, **Member No**, and **Charter Member**.

b. Select the four labels in the first column (First Name, Last Name, Street, and Zip) together, and align their right edges.

c. Move the Charter Member label to the left of the check box, below the Member No label. (*Hint*: Point to the upper-left corner of the Charter Member label to move the label without moving its associated check box.)

d. Select the four labels in the third column (Birthday, Dues, Member No, and Charter Member) together, and align their right edges.

e. Select the First Name label, the FirstName text box, the Birthday label, and the Birthday text box together. Align their top edges.

f. Select the Last Name label, the LastName text box, the Dues label, and the Dues text box together. Align their top edges.

g. Select the Street label, the Street text box, the Member No label, and the MemberNo text box together. Align their top edges.

h. Select the Zip label, the Zip text box, the Charter Member label, and the CharterMember check box together. Align their top edges.

i. Select the FirstName text box, the LastName text box, the Street text box, and the Zip text box together. Align their left edges and resize them to be wider and closer to the corresponding labels in the first column.

j. Align the left edges of the Birthday, Dues, and MemberNo text box controls.

k. Resize the Street text box to be about twice as wide as its current width.

l. Save the MemberHours form.

4. Add a combo box for data entry.

a. In Form Design View, right-click the Zip text box, then change it to a combo box control.

b. In the Property Sheet of the new combo box, click the Row Source property, then click the Build button.

c. Select only the Zips table for the query, then double-click the Zip, City, and State fields to add them to the query grid.

d. Close the Query Builder window, and save the changes.

e. On the Format tab of the Property Sheet for the Zip combo box, change the Column Count property to **3**, the Column Widths property to **0.5**;**2**;**0.5**, the List Width property to **3**, and the List Rows property from 16 to **50**.

f. Close the Property Sheet, then save and view the MemberHours form in Form View.

g. In the first record for Rhea Alman, change the Zip to **66205** using the new combo box.

5. Add a combo box to find records.

a. Display the MemberHours form in Design View.

b. Open the Form Header section by clicking the Title button in the Header/Footer section on the Design tab.

c. Modify the label to read **Member Activity Hours**, then narrow the width of the label to be only as wide as needed.

d. Add a combo box to the right side of the Form Header, and choose the "Find a record on my form…" option in the Combo Box Wizard.

e. Choose the MemberNo, LastName, and FirstName fields in that order.

f. Hide the key column.

g. Label the combo box **FIND MEMBER:**.

h. Move and widen the new combo box to be at least 2" wide, change the FIND MEMBER: label text color to black so it is easier to read, save the MemberHours form, then view it in Form View.

i. Use the FIND MEMBER combo box to find the Aaron Love record. Notice that the entries in the combo box are not alphabetized by last name.

j. Return to Form Design View, and use the Row Source property and Build button for the FIND MEMBER combo box to open the Query Builder. Add an ascending sort order to the LastName and FirstName fields.

Skills Review (continued)

k. Close the Query Builder, saving changes. View the MemberHours form in Form View, and find the record for Holly Cabriella. Note that the entries in the combo box list are now sorted in ascending order first by the LastName field, then by the FirstName field.

6. Add command buttons.

a. Display the MemberHours form in Design View.

b. Use the Command Button Wizard to add a command button to the middle of the Form Footer section.

c. Choose the Print Record action from the Record Operations category.

d. Choose the Text option button, type **Print Current Record**, then use **PrintButton** for the meaningful name for the button.

e. Use the Command Button Wizard to add a command button to the right of the other command button in the Form Footer section.

f. Choose the Close Form action from the Form Operations category.

g. Choose the Text option button, type **Close**, then use **CloseButton** for the meaningful name for the button.

h. Select both command buttons then align their top edges.

i. Save the form, display it in Form View, navigate through the first few records, then close the MemberHours form using the new Close command button.

7. Add option groups.

a. Open the MemberHours form in Form Design View.

b. Because the dues are always $25 or $50, the Dues field is a good candidate for an option group control. Delete the existing Dues text box and label.

c. Click the Option Group button in the Controls group on the Design tab, then click the form just to the right of the Birthday text box.

d. Type **$25** and **$50** for Label Names, do not choose a default value, and enter **25** and **50** for corresponding Values.

e. Store the value in the Dues field, use option buttons, use the Flat style, and caption the option group **Dues:**.

FIGURE 7-18

f. Save the MemberHours form, and view it in Form View. Move and align the other form controls as needed to match **FIGURE 7-18**.

g. Use the FIND MEMBER: combo box to find the record for Derek Camel, change his first and last names to your name, then change the Dues to $25 using the new option group. Print this record if requested by your instructor.

h. Use the Close command button to close and save the MemberHours form.

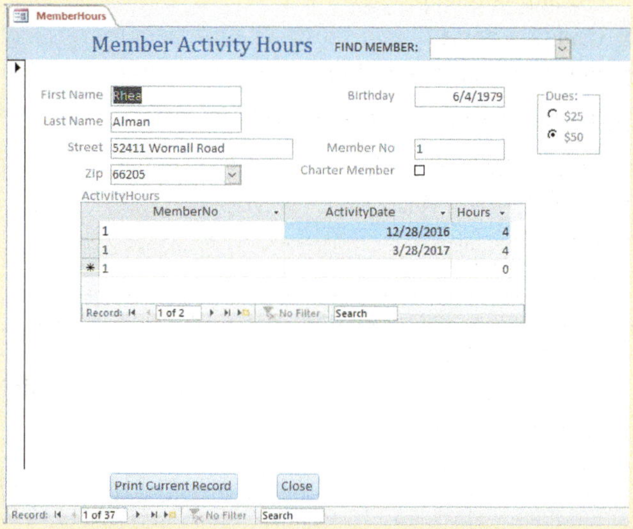

8. Add tab controls.

a. Create a new blank form, and add a tab control to it.

b. Open the Property Sheet, then use the Name property to rename Page1 to **Members** and Page2 to **Activities**. (*Hint*: Be sure to select the tab for the page and not the entire tab control.)

c. Right-click the Activities tab, click Insert Page, and use the Name property to rename the third page to **Dues**.

d. Save the form with the name **Navigation**.

Skills Review (continued)

e. On the Members page, add a command button with the Preview Report action from the Report Operations category. Choose the MemberRoster report, choose Text on the button, type **Preview Member Roster Report** as the text, and name the button **MemberRosterReportButton**.

f. On the Activities page, add a command button with the Open Form action from the Form Operations category. Choose the MemberHours form, choose to open the form and show all the records, choose Text on the button, type **Open Member Hours Form** as the text, and name the button **MemberHoursFormButton**.

g. On the Activities page, add a second command button below the first with the Preview Report action from the Report Operations category. Choose the ActivityListing report, choose Text on the button, type **Preview Activity Listing Report** as the text, and name the button **ActivityListingReportButton**.

h. Widen the command buttons on the Activities page as needed so that all of the text on the command buttons is clearly visible and the buttons are the same size. Also align the buttons as shown in **FIGURE 7-19**.

i. On the Dues page, add a command button with the Preview Report action from the Report Operations category. Choose the DuesByState report, choose Text on the button, type **Preview Dues by State Report** as the text, and name the button **DuesByStateReportButton**.

FIGURE 7-19

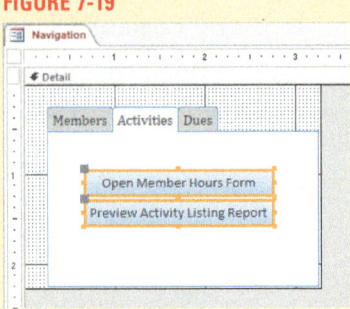

j. Save the Navigation form, then view it in Form View.

k. Test each button on each tab of the Navigation form to make sure it works as intended.

l. Close all open objects, then close the Service-7.accdb database.

Independent Challenge 1

As the manager of a music store's instrument rental program, you have created a database to track instrument rentals to students. You want to build a form for fast, easy data entry.

a. Start Access, then open the database Music-7.accdb from the location where you store your Data Files. Enable content if prompted.

b. Using the Form Wizard, create a new form based on all of the fields in the Students and Rentals tables.

c. View the data by Students, choose a Datasheet layout for the subform, then accept the default form titles of **Students** for the main form and **Rentals Subform** for the subform.

d. Add another record to the rental subform for Amanda Smith by typing **7711** as the SerialNo entry and **8/2/17** as the RentalDate entry. Note that no entry is necessary in the RentalNo field because it is an AutoNumber field. No entry is necessary in the CustNo field as it is the foreign key field that connects the main form to the subform and is automatically populated when the forms are in this arrangement.

e. Change Amanda Smith's name to your name.

f. Open the Students form in Design View. Right-align the text within each label control in the first column of the main form. (*Hint*: Use the Align Right button on the Home tab.)

g. Resize the Zip, CustNo, and SchoolNo text boxes to as wide as the State text box.

h. Move the CustNo and SchoolNo text boxes and their accompanying labels to the upper-right portion of the form, directly to the right of the FirstName and LastName text boxes.

i. Modify the FirstName, LastName, CustNo, and SchoolNo labels to read First Name, Last Name, Cust No, and School No.

j. Delete the RentalNo and CustNo fields from the subform.

k. Open the Field List, and drag the Description field from the Instruments table to the subform above the existing text boxes. (*Hint*: Show all tables, then look in the Fields available in related tables section of the Field List.)

Independent Challenge 1 (continued)

l. Shorten and move the subform up, and continue moving and resizing fields as needed so that your form in Form View looks similar to **FIGURE 7-20**.

m. Save and close the Students form, close the Music-7.accdb database, then exit Access.

FIGURE 7-20

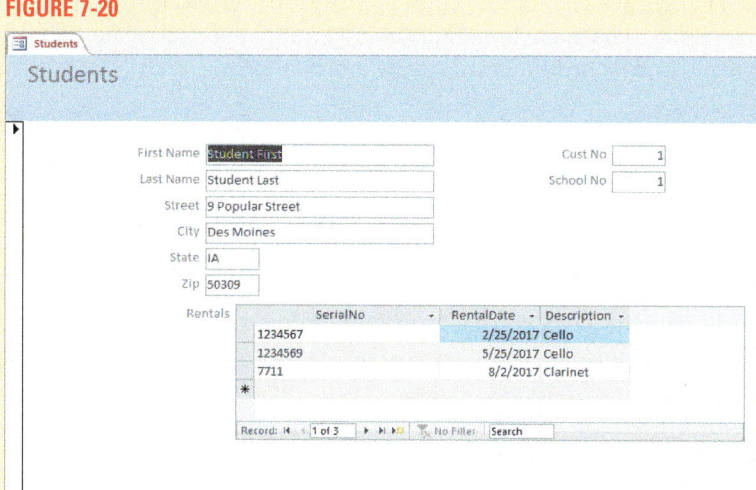

Independent Challenge 2

As the manager of a community effort to provide better access to residential real estate listings for a lake community, you have developed a database to track listings by realtor and real estate agency. You want to develop a form/subform system to see all listings within each realtor as well as within each real estate agency.

a. Start Access, then open the database LakeHomes-7.accdb from the location where you store your Data Files. Enable content if prompted.

b. Using the Form Wizard, create a new form based on all of the fields in the Agencies, Realtors, and Listings tables.

c. View the data by Agencies, choose a Datasheet layout for each of the subforms, and accept the default titles of **Agencies**, **Realtors Subform**, and **Listings Subform**.

d. In Form Design View, use the Combo Box Wizard to add a combo box to the Form Header to find a record. Choose the AgencyName field, hide the key column, widen the AgencyName column to see the entries clearly, and enter the label **FIND AGENCY:**.

e. Change the text color of the FIND AGENCY: label to black, and widen the combo box to about twice its current size.

f. Add a command button to a blank spot on the main form to print the current record. Use the Print Record action from the Record Operations category. Use a picture on the button, and give the button the meaningful name of **PrintButton**.

g. Use your skills to modify, move, resize, align text, and align control edges, as shown in **FIGURE 7-21**. Note that several labels have been modified, and many controls have been moved, resized, and aligned. Note that the subforms have also been resized and moved and that the ListingNo and RealtorNo fields in the Listings subform have been hidden. (*Hint*: To hide a field, right-click the fieldname in Form View and then click Hide Fields.)

h. Save the form, view it in Form View, then use the combo box to find Sunset Cove Realtors.

i. Resize the columns of the subforms to view as much data as possible, as shown in **FIGURE 7-21**, change Trixie Angelina's name in the Realtors subform to your name, then if requested by your instructor, print only the current record using the new command button.

j. Save and close the Agencies form, close the LakeHomes-7.accdb database, and exit Access.

FIGURE 7-21

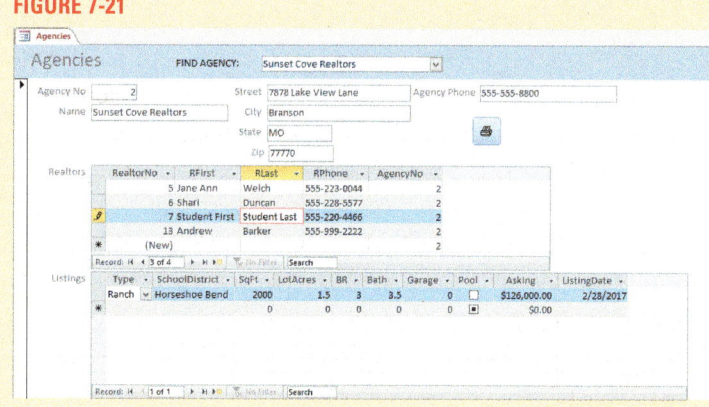

Independent Challenge 3

As the manager of a community effort to provide better access to residential real estate listings for a lake community, you have developed a database to track listings by realtor and real estate agency. You want to develop a navigation form to help find queries and reports in your database much faster.

a. Start Access, then open the database LakeHomes-7.accdb from the location where you store your Data Files. Enable content if prompted.

b. Create a new blank form, and add a tab control to it.

c. Open the Property Sheet and use the Name property to rename Page1 to **Realtors** and Page2 to **Listings**.

d. On the Realtors page, add a command button with the Preview Report action from the Report Operations category. Choose the RealtorsByAgency report, choose Text on the button, type **Preview Realtors by Agency** as the text, and name the button **cmdRealtors**. (Note that cmd is the three-character prefix sometimes used to name command buttons.)

e. On the Listings page, add a command button with the Run Query action from the Miscellaneous category. Choose the SchoolDistricts query, choose Text on the button, type **Open School Districts Query** as the text, and name the button **cmdSchools**.

f. On the Listings page, add a second command button with the Preview Report action from the Report Operations category. Choose the ListingsByType report, choose Text on the button, type **Preview Listing Report** as the text, and name the button **cmdListingReport**.

g. Save the form with the name **Lake Homes Navigation System**, then view it in Form View. The new form with the Listings tab selected should look like **FIGURE 7-22**.

h. Test each command button on both the Realtors and Listings pages.

i. Close all open objects, then close the LakeHomes-7.accdb database and exit Access.

FIGURE 7-22

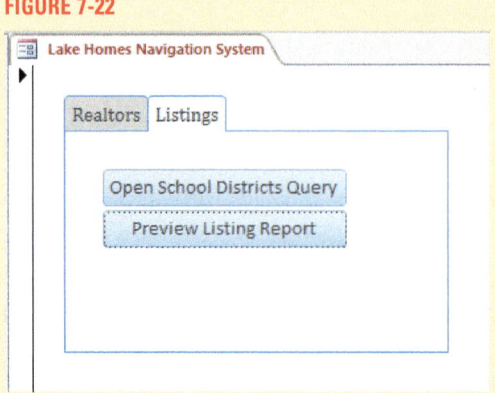

Independent Challenge 4: Explore

You have created an Access database to help manage college scholarship opportunities. You can keep the database updated more efficiently by creating some easy-to-use forms.

a. Start Access and open the Scholarships-7.accdb database from the location where you store your Data Files. Enable content if prompted.

b. Create a split form for the Scholarships table. Save and name the form **ScholarshipEntry**.

c. In Form Design View, narrow the label in the Form Header section to about half of its current size, then use the Combo Box Wizard to add a combo box to the Form Header section to find a scholarship based on the ScholarshipName field. Hide the key column, and use the label **FIND SCHOLARSHIP:**.

d. In Form Design View, widen the combo box as necessary so that all of the scholarship names in the list are clearly visible in Form View. Change the color of the FIND SCHOLARSHIP: text to black, and move and resize the label and combo box as necessary to clearly view them. Switch between Form View and Form Design View to test the new combo box control.

e. In Form Design View, change the combo box's List Rows property (on the Format tab) to **50** and use the Build button to modify the Row Source property to add an ascending sort order based on the ScholarshipName field. (*Hint*: The ID field needs to remain in the query, but it is hidden in the combo box as evidenced by the value in the Column Widths property of the combo box.)

f. Save the form, and in Form View, use the combo box to find the Papa Johns Scholarship. Change Papa Johns to your name as shown in FIGURE 7-23, then, if requested by your instructor, print only that record by using the Selected Record(s) option on the Print dialog box.

g. Save and close the ScholarshipEntry form, close the Scholarships-7.accdb database, then exit Access.

FIGURE 7-23

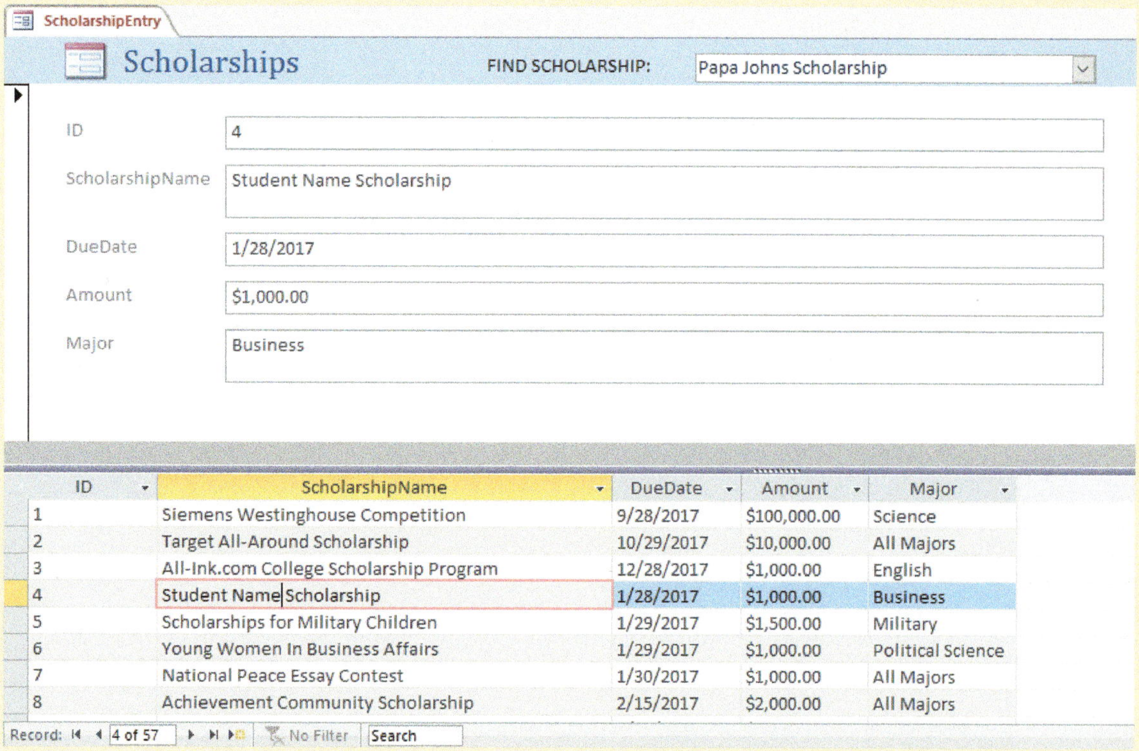

Visual Workshop

Open the Baseball-7.accdb database from the location where you store your Data Files. Enable content if prompted. Use Form Design View to create a form based on the Players table named **PlayersEntry**. Use your skills to modify, move, resize, align text, and align control edges as shown in FIGURE 7-24. Note that both the PlayerPosition as well as the TeamNo fields are presented as option groups. The values that correspond with each Position label can be found in the Field Description of the PlayerPosition field in Table Design View of the Players table. The Position option group is tied to the PlayerPosition field. The values that correspond with each Team label can be found by reviewing the TeamNo and TeamName fields of the Teams table. The Team option group is tied to the TeamNo field. Do not choose default values for either option group. Change Hank Aaron's name to your name, change the Position value to Pitcher, and change the Team to Dexter Cardinals. If requested by your instructor, print only that record.

FIGURE 7-24

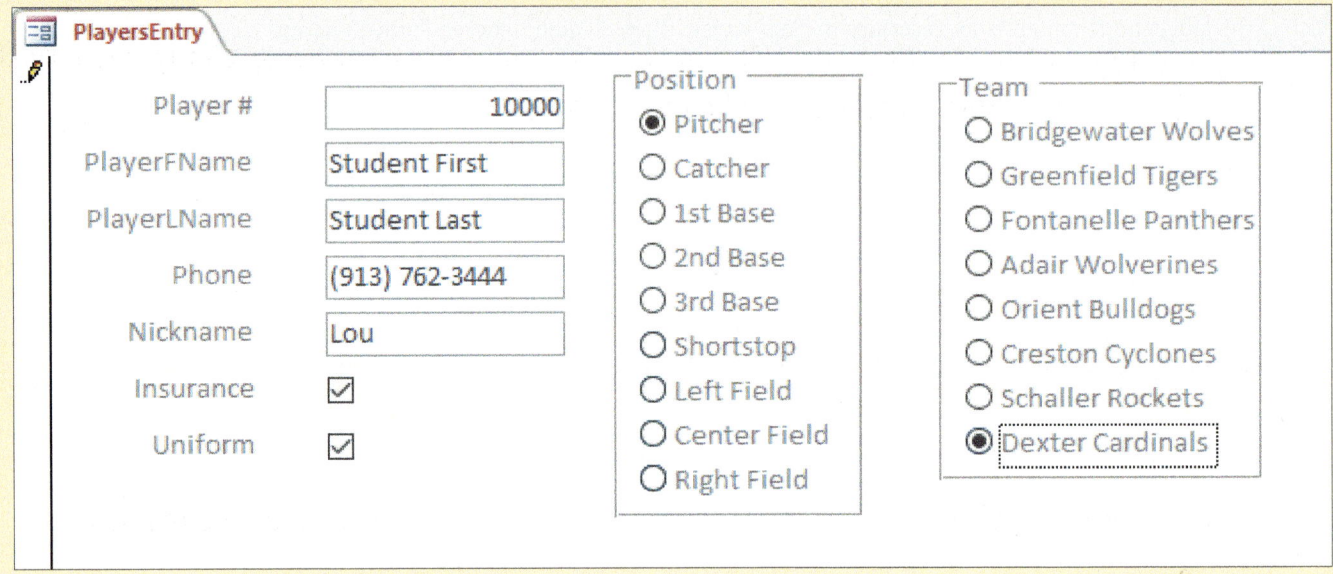

Analyzing Data with Reports

CASE ▶ Julia Rice asks you to create and enhance reports to analyze, clarify, and format important information at Reason 2 Go.

Module Objectives

After completing this module, you will be able to:

- Use Report Design View
- Create parameter reports
- Apply conditional formatting
- Add lines
- Use the Format Painter and themes
- Add subreports
- Modify section properties
- Create summary reports

Files You Will Need

R2G-8.accdb
LakeHomes-8.accdb
Music-8.accdb
Scholarships-8.accdb
Baseball-8.accdb

Use Report Design View

Although you can print data in forms and datasheets, **reports** give you more control over how data is printed and greater flexibility in presenting summary information. To create a report, you include text boxes to display data and use calculations and labels, lines, and graphics to clarify the data. **Report Design View** allows you to work with a complete range of report, section, and control properties. Because Report Design View gives you full control of all aspects of a report, it is well worth your time to master. **CASE** ▸ *Julia Rice asks you to build a report that shows all trips grouped by category and sorted in descending order by price. You use Report Design View to build this report.*

STEPS

1. **Start Access, open the R2G-8.accdb database from the location where you store your Data Files, enable content if prompted, click the Create tab, then click the Report Design button in the Reports group**

   The first step to building a report in Report Design View is identifying the record source.

2. **If the Property Sheet is not open, click the Property Sheet button in the Tools group, click the Data tab in the Property Sheet, click the Record Source list arrow, then click Trips**

   The Record Source can be an existing table, query, or SQL SELECT statement. The **Record Source** identifies the fields and records that the report can display. To build a report that shows trips grouped by category, you'll need to add a Category Header section. See **TABLE 8-1** for a review of report sections.

3. **Use the ✛ pointer to drag the top edge of the Page Footer section up to about the 1" mark on the vertical ruler, then click the Group & Sort button in the Grouping & Totals group to open the Group, Sort, and Total pane if it is not already open**

   Use the Group, Sort, and Total pane to specify grouping and sorting fields and open group headers and footers.

4. **Click the Add a group button in the Group, Sort, and Total pane; click Category; click the Add a sort button in the Group, Sort, and Total pane; click Price; click the from smallest to largest button arrow; then click from largest to smallest, as shown in FIGURE 8-1**

   With the grouping and sorting fields specified, you're ready to add controls to the report.

5. **Click the Add Existing Fields button in the Tools group, click TripNo in the Field List, press and hold [Shift] as you click Price in the Field List to select all fields in the Trips table, drag the selected fields to the Detail section of the report, then close the Field List window**

   Next, you move the Category controls to the Category Header section.

6. **Click the report to remove the current selection, right-click the Category combo box, click Cut on the shortcut menu, right-click the Category Header section, then click Paste on the shortcut menu**

   If the data on a report is self-explanatory, it doesn't need descriptive labels. Delete the labels, and position the text boxes across the page to finalize the report.

7. **Click each label and press [Delete] to delete the Category label as well as each label in the first column of the Detail section, then move and resize the remaining text boxes and shorten the Detail section, as shown in FIGURE 8-2**

8. **Click the Save button 🖫 on the Quick Access Toolbar, type TripsByCategory as the new report name, click OK, preview the first page of the report, as shown in FIGURE 8-3, then close the report**

Analyzing Data with Reports

FIGURE 8-1: Creating a report in Report Design View

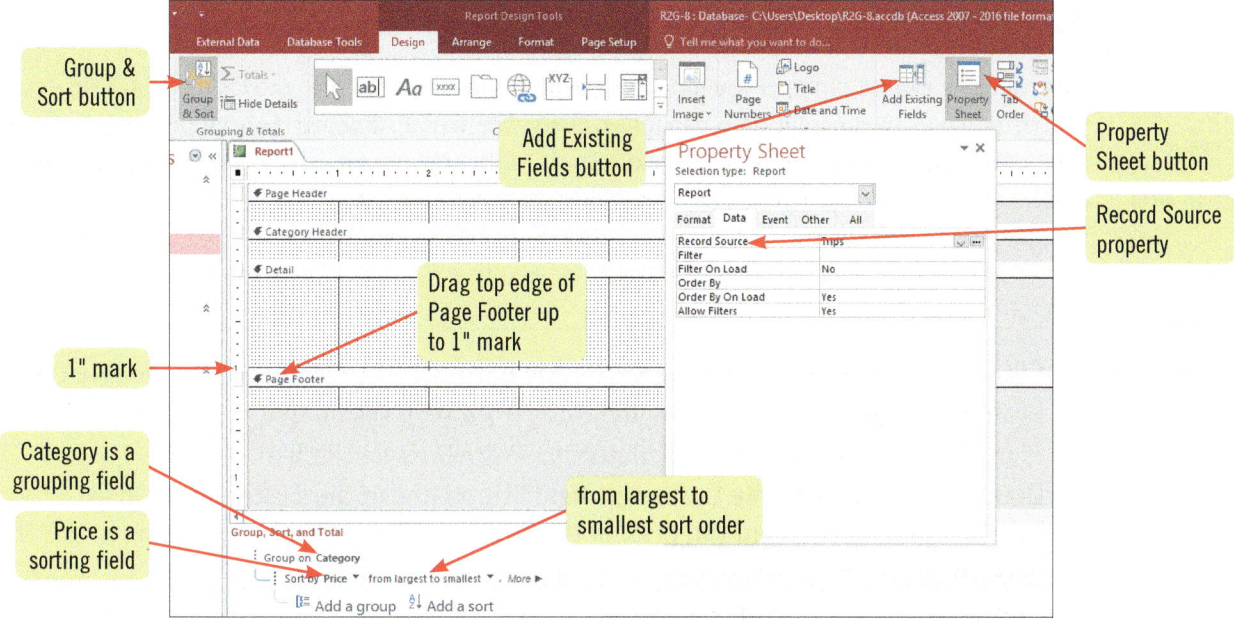

FIGURE 8-2: Moving and resizing the text box controls in the Detail section

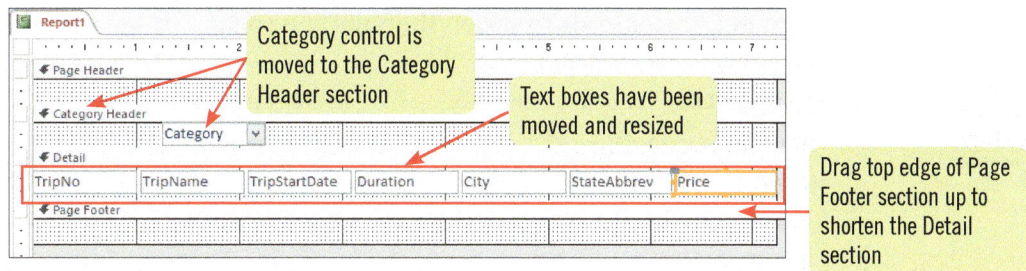

FIGURE 8-3: Previewing the TripsByCategory report

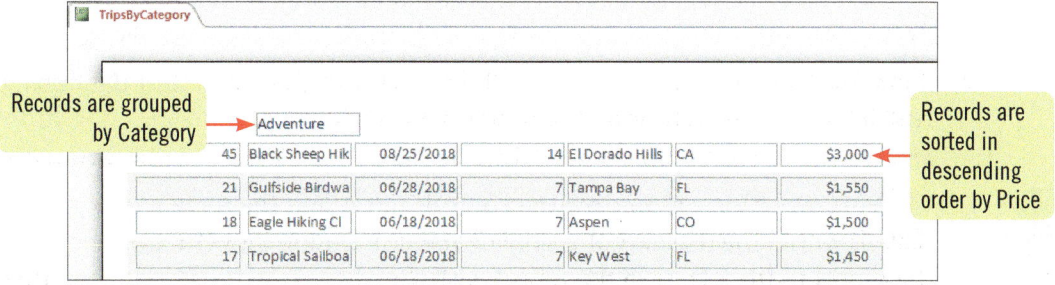

TABLE 8-1: Review of report sections

section	where does this section print?	what is this section most commonly used for?
Report Header	At the top of the first page of the report	To print a title or logo
Page Header	At the top of every page (but below the Report Header on page 1)	To print titles, dates, or page numbers
Group Header	Before every group of records	To display the grouping field value
Detail	Once for every record	To display data for every record
Group Footer	After every group of records	To calculate summary statistics on groups of records
Page Footer	At the bottom of every page	To print dates or page numbers

Create Parameter Reports

Learning Outcomes
- Enter parameter criteria
- Create a parameter report

A **parameter report** prompts you for criteria to determine the records to use for the report. To create a parameter report, you base it on a parameter query. The report's **Record Source** property determines what table or query provides the fields and records for the report. **CASE** *Julia Rice requests a report that shows all trip sales for a given period. You use a parameter query to prompt the user for the dates, then build the report on that query.*

STEPS

1. **Click the Create tab, click the Query Design button in the Queries group, double-click Customers, double-click Sales, double-click Trips, then click Close**

   You want fields from all three tables in the report, so you add them to the query.

TROUBLE
Resize the Trips field list to see all fields, or scroll down to find the Price field.

2. **Double-click FName in the Customers field list, LName in the Customers field list, SaleDate in the Sales field list, Price in the Trips field list, and then TripName in the Trips field list**

   To select only those trips sold in a given period, you add **parameter criteria**, text entered in [square brackets] that prompts the user for an entry each time the query is run, to the SaleDate field.

3. **Click the Criteria cell for the SaleDate field, type Between [Enter start date] and [Enter end date], then use ↔ to widen the SaleDate column to see the entire entry, as shown in FIGURE 8-4**

   To test the query, run it and enter dates in the parameter prompts.

QUICK TIP
You can also click the Run button to run a Select query, which displays it in Datasheet View.

4. **Click the View button 🔲 on the Design tab to run the query, type 6/1/17 in the Enter start date box, click OK, type 6/30/17 in the Enter end date box, then click OK**

   Fifteen records are displayed in the datasheet, each with a SaleDate value in June 2017.

5. **Click the Save button 🖫 on the Quick Access Toolbar, type SalesDateParam as the new query name, click OK, then close the SalesDateParam query**

   You use the Report button on the Create tab to quickly build a report on the SalesDateParam query.

6. **Click the SalesDateParam query in the Navigation Pane, click the Create tab, click the Report button in the Reports group, type 6/1/17 in the Enter start date box, click OK, type 6/30/17 in the Enter end date box, then click OK**

   The report is displayed in Layout View with records in June 2017. You decide to preview and save the report.

QUICK TIP
The Page buttons in the navigation bar are dim if the report contains only one page.

7. **Work in Layout View to narrow the controls (including the page number control) so that they fit within the margins of a single page, use Design View to drag the right edge of the report to the left, save the report with the name SalesDateParameter, then preview it as shown in FIGURE 8-5, entering 6/1/17 as the start date and 6/30/17 as the end date**

FIGURE 8-4: Entering parameter criteria in a query

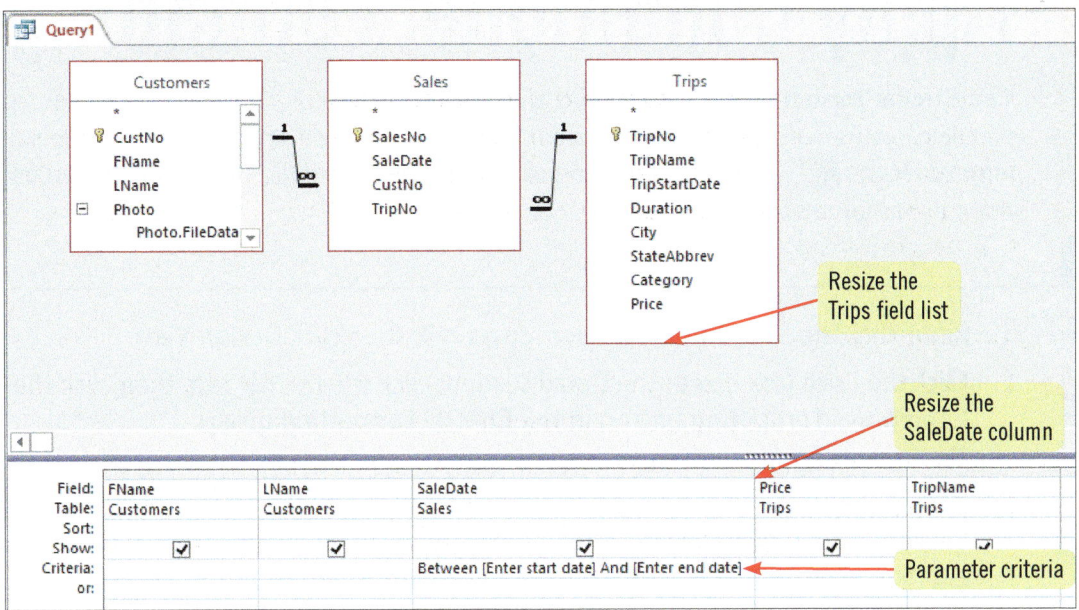

FIGURE 8-5: Previewing the SalesDateParameter report

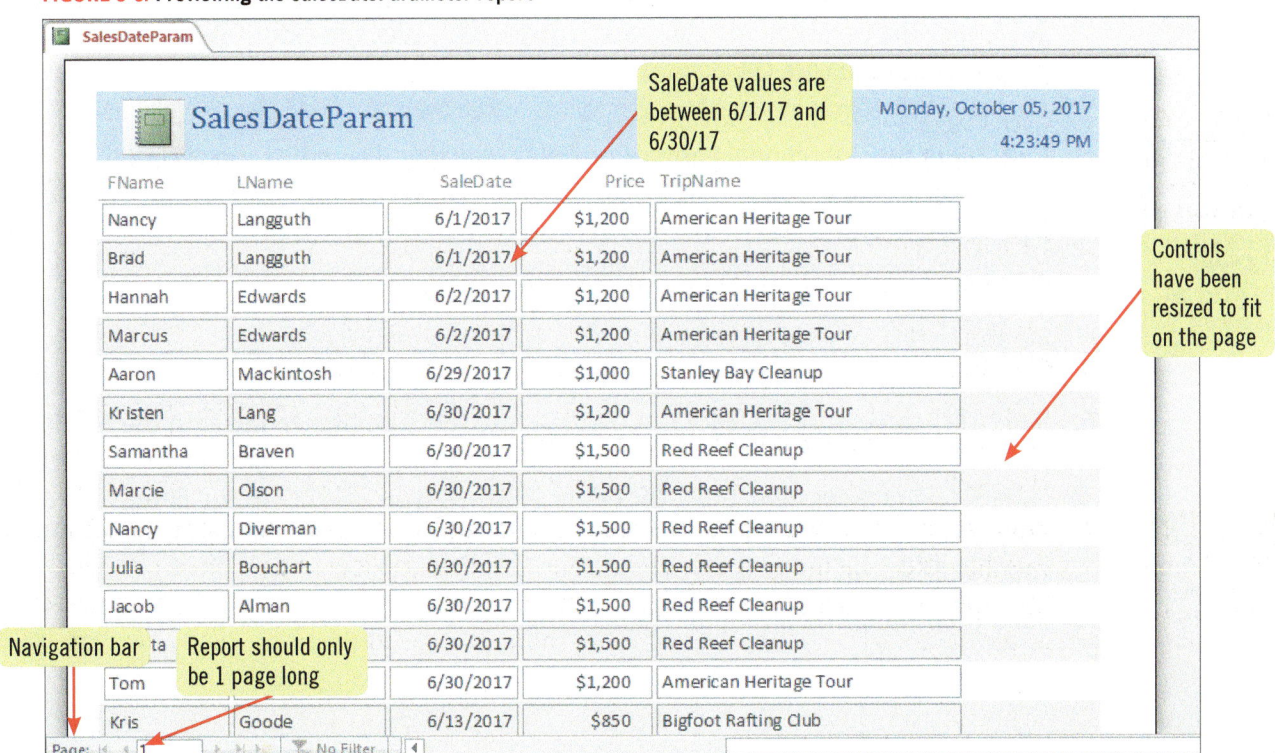

Parameter criteria

In Query Design View, you must enter parameter criteria within [square brackets]. Each parameter criterion you enter appears as a prompt in an Enter Parameter Value dialog box. The entry you make in the Enter Parameter Value box is used as the criterion for the field that contains the parameter criteria.

Apply Conditional Formatting

Conditional formatting allows you to change the appearance of a control on a form or report based on criteria you specify. Conditional formatting helps you highlight important or exceptional data on a form or report. **CASE** *Julia Rice asks you to apply conditional formatting to the SalesDateParameter report to emphasize different trip Price levels.*

STEPS

1. **Right-click the SalesDateParameter report tab, then click Design View**

TROUBLE
Be sure the Price text box (not Price label) is selected.

2. **Click the Price text box in the Detail section, click the Format tab, then click the Conditional Formatting button in the Control Formatting group**

   The Conditional Formatting Rules Manager dialog box opens, asking you to define the conditional formatting rules. You want to format Price values between 500 and 1000 with a yellow background color.

QUICK TIP
Between…and criteria include both values in the range.

3. **Click New Rule, click the text box to the right of the between arrow, type 500, click the and box, type 1000, click the Background color button arrow ⬛▾, click the Yellow box on the bottom row, then click OK**

   You add the second conditional formatting rule to format Price values greater than 1000 with a light green background color.

4. **Click New Rule, click the between list arrow, click greater than, click the value box, type 1000, click the Background color button arrow ⬛▾, click the Light Green box on the bottom row, then click OK**

   The Conditional Formatting Rules Manager dialog box with two rules should look like **FIGURE 8-6**.

QUICK TIP
The text box in the Report Footer section was automatically added when you used the Report button to create the report.

5. **Click OK in the Conditional Formatting Rules Manager dialog box, right-click the SalesDateParameter report tab, click Print Preview, type 7/12/17 in the Enter start date box, click OK, type 7/13/17 in the Enter end date box, then click OK**

   Conditional formatting rules applied a light green background color to the Price text box for two sales because the Price value is greater than 1000. Conditional formatting applied a yellow background color to the Price text box for seven sales because the Price value is between 500 and 1000.

   The text box in the Report Footer needs to be taller to display the information clearly.

6. **Right-click the report tab, click Design View, use the ↕ pointer to increase the height of the text box in the Report Footer section to clearly display the expression, right-click the SalesDateParameter report tab, click Print Preview, type 7/12/17 in the Enter start date box, click OK, type 7/13/17 in the Enter end date box, click OK, then click the report to zoom in as shown in FIGURE 8-7**

7. **Save, then close the SalesDateParameter report**

FIGURE 8-6: Conditional Formatting Rules Manager dialog box

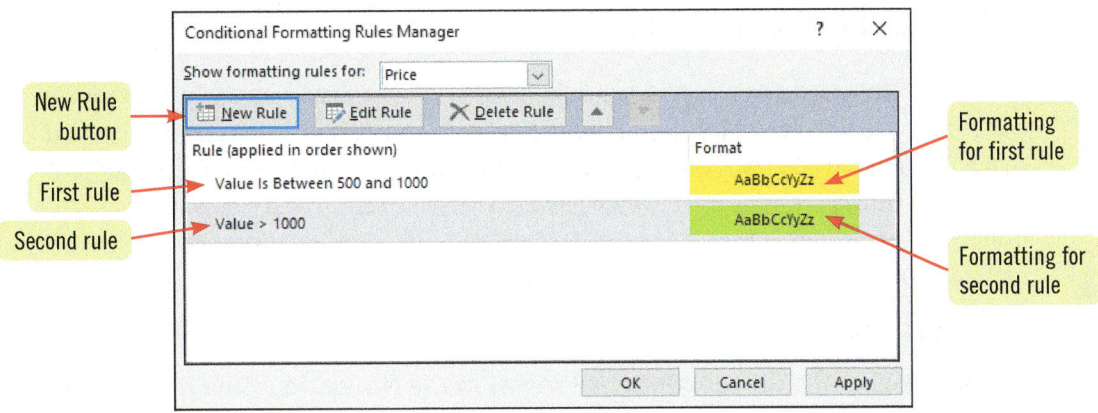

FIGURE 8-7: Conditional formatting applied to SalesDateParameter report

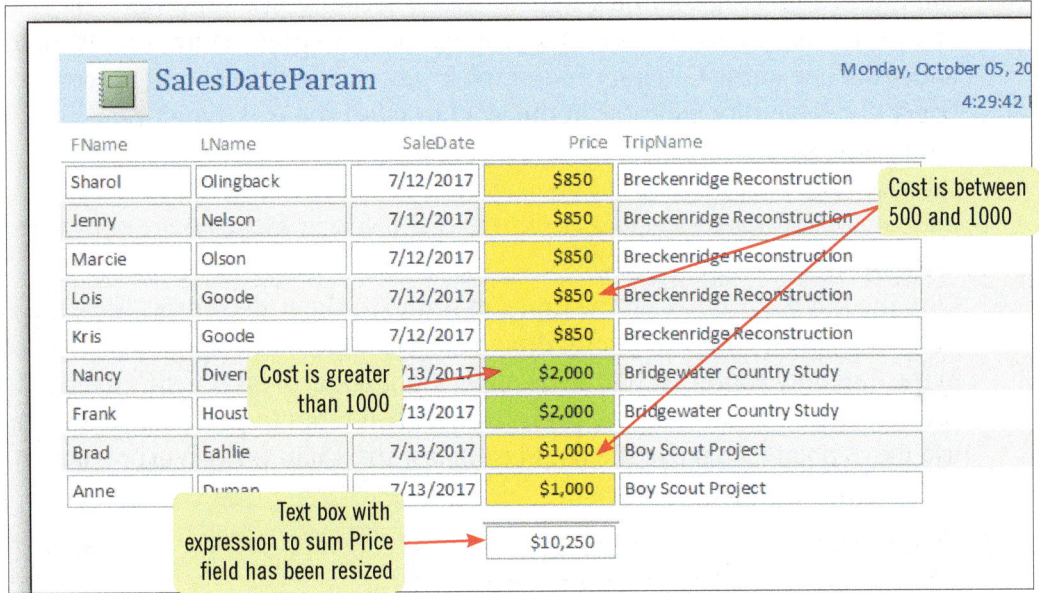

Conditional formatting using data bars

A feature of Access allows you to compare the values of one column to another with small data bars. To use this feature, use the "Compare to other records" rule type option in the New Formatting Rule dialog box, as shown in **FIGURE 8-8**.

FIGURE 8-8: Conditional formatting with data bars

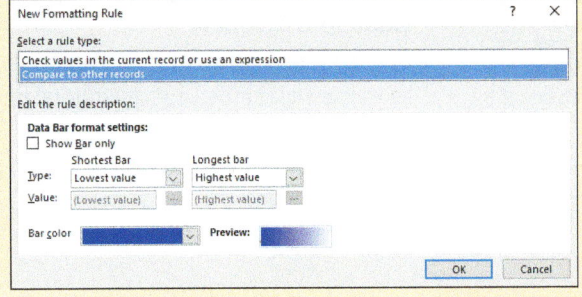

Add Lines

Learning Outcomes
• Add grand totals to a report
• Add lines to a report

Lines are often added to a report to highlight information or enhance its clarity. For example, you might want to separate the Report Header and Page Header information from the rest of the report with a horizontal line. You can also use short lines to indicate subtotals and grand totals. **CASE** ▶ *Julia Rice likes the data on the CategoryRevenue report, which has already been created in the R2G-8 database, but she asks you to enhance the report by adding a grand total calculation and separating the categories more clearly. Lines will help clarify the information.*

STEPS

QUICK TIP
Recall that Report View does not show page margins or individual pages of the report.

1. **Double-click the CategoryRevenue report in the Navigation Pane to open it in Report View, then scroll to the end of the report**

   The report could be improved if lines were added to separate the trip categories and to indicate subtotals. You also want to add a grand total calculation on the last page of the report. You use Report Design View to make these improvements and start by adding the grand total calculation to the Report Footer section.

2. **Right-click the CategoryRevenue report tab, click Design View, right-click the =Sum([Price]) text box in the Category Footer section, click Copy, right-click the Report Footer section, click Paste, press [→] enough times to position the expression directly under the one in the Category Footer, click Subtotal: in the Report Footer section to select it, double-click Subtotal: in the label to select the text, type Grand Total, then press [Enter]**

   The =Sum([Price]) expression in the Report Footer section sums the Price values for the entire report, whereas the same expression in the Category Footer section sums Price values for each category. With the calculations in place, you add clarifying lines.

TROUBLE
Lines can be difficult to find in Report Design View. See the "Line troubles" box in this lesson for tips on working with lines.

3. **Click the More button ⊽ in the Controls group to show all controls, click the Line button ◻, press and hold [Shift], drag from the upper-left edge of =Sum([Price]) in the Category Footer section to its upper-right edge, press [Ctrl][C] to copy the line, click the Report Footer section, press [Ctrl][V] two times to paste the line twice, then use the ⊹ pointer to move the lines just below the =Sum([Price]) expression in the Report Footer section**

   Pressing [Shift] while drawing a line makes sure that the line remains perfectly horizontal or vertical. The single line above the calculation in the Category Footer section indicates that the calculation is a subtotal. Double lines below the calculation in the Report Footer section indicate that it is a grand total. You also want to add a line to visually separate the categories.

QUICK TIP
Use the Rectangle button ▢ to insert a rectangle control on a form or report.

4. **Click the More button ⊽ in the Controls group to show all controls, click the Line button ◻, press and hold [Shift], then drag along the bottom of the Category Footer section**

   The final CategoryRevenue report in Report Design View is shown in **FIGURE 8-9**.

QUICK TIP
As a final report creation step, print preview a report to make sure it fits on the paper.

5. **Right-click the CategoryRevenue report tab, click Print Preview, then navigate to the last page of the report**

   The last page of the CategoryRevenue report shown in **FIGURE 8-10** displays the Category Footer section line as well as the subtotal and grand total lines.

FIGURE 8-9: Adding lines to a report

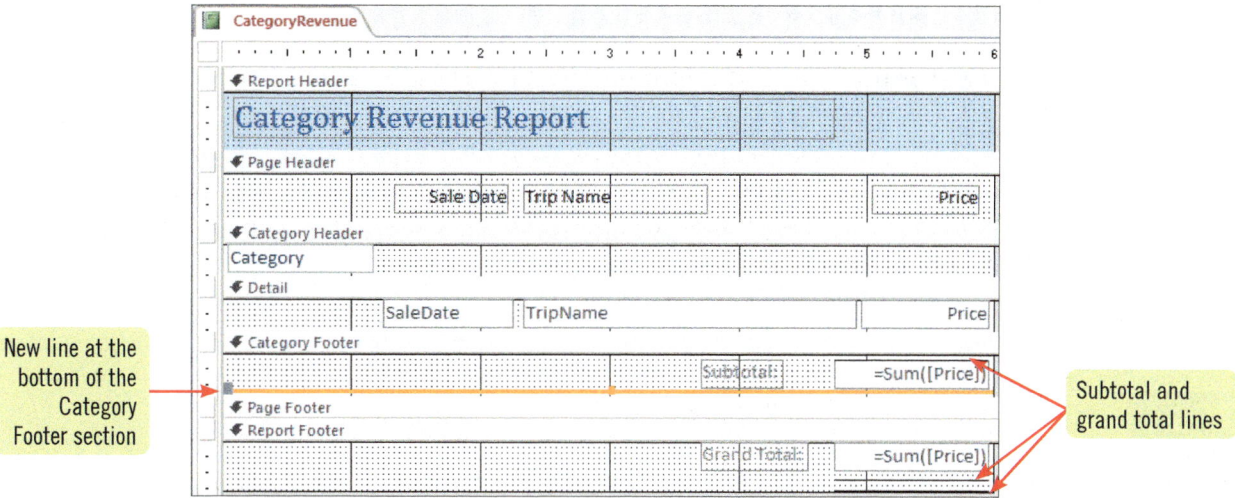

New line at the bottom of the Category Footer section

Subtotal and grand total lines

FIGURE 8-10: Previewing the last page of the CategoryRevenue report

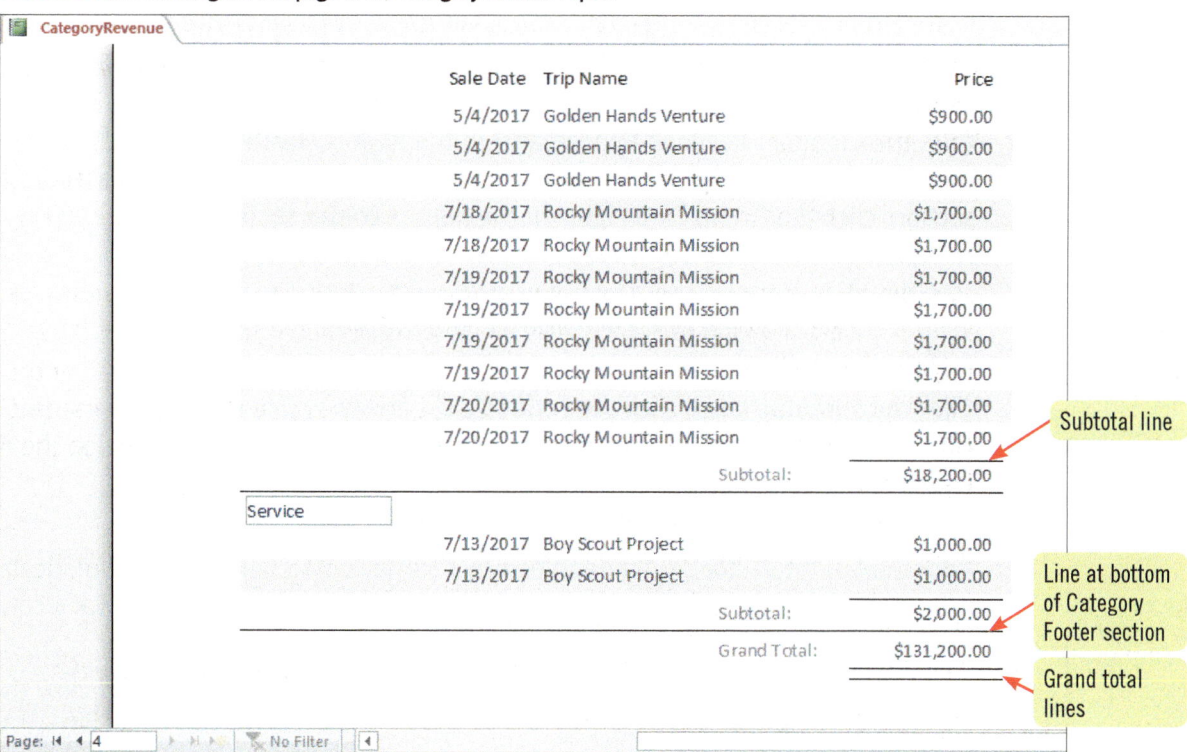

Subtotal line

Line at bottom of Category Footer section

Grand total lines

Line troubles

Sometimes lines are difficult to find in Report Design View because they are placed against the edge of a section or the edge of other controls. To find lines that are positioned next to the edge of a section, drag the section bar to expand the section and expose the line. Recall that to draw a perfectly horizontal line, you hold [Shift] while creating or resizing the line. It is easy to accidentally widen a line beyond the report margins, thus creating extra unwanted pages in your printout. To fix this problem, narrow any controls that extend beyond the margins of the printout, and drag the right edge of the report to the left. Note that the default left and right margins for an 8.5 x 11-inch sheet of paper are often 0.25 inches each, so a report in portrait orientation must be no wider than 8 inches, and a report in landscape orientation must be no wider than 10.5 inches.

Use the Format Painter and Themes

The **Format Painter** is a tool you use to copy multiple formatting properties from one control to another in Design or Layout View for forms and reports. **Themes** are predefined formats that you apply to the database to set all of the formatting enhancements, such as font, color, and alignment, on all forms and reports. **CASE** ▶ *Julia Rice wants to improve the CategoryRevenue report with a few formatting embellishments. You apply a built-in theme to the entire report and then use the Format Painter to quickly copy and paste formatting characteristics from one label to another.*

STEPS

QUICK TIP
The selected theme is applied to all forms and reports in the database.

1. **Right-click the CategoryRevenue report tab, click Design View, click the Themes button, point to several themes to observe the changes in the report, then click Ion, as shown in FIGURE 8-11**

   The Ion theme gives the Report Header section a light turquoise background. All text now has a consistent font face, controls in the same section are the same font size, and all controls have complementary font colors. You want the Subtotal: and Grand Total: labels to have the same formatting characteristics as the Category Revenue Report label in the Report Header section. To copy formats quickly, you will use the Format Painter.

QUICK TIP
Double-click the Format Painter to copy formatting to more than one control.

2. **Click the Category Revenue Report label in the Report Header, click the Home tab, double-click the Format Painter button, click the Subtotal: label in the Category Footer section, click the Grand Total: label in the Report Footer section, then press [Esc] to release the Format Painter**

   The Format Painter applied several formatting characteristics, including font face, font color, and font size from the label in the Report Header section to the other two labels. You like the new font face and color, but the font size is too large.

3. **Click the Subtotal: label, click the Font Size list arrow [18 ▾] in the Text Formatting group, click 12, click the Format Painter button, then click the Grand Total: label in the Report Footer section**

   The labels are still too small to display the entire caption.

TROUBLE
Double-click any corner sizing handle except for the move handle in the upper-left corner.

4. **Click the Subtotal: label, then double-click a corner sizing handle to automatically resize it to show the entire caption, click the Grand Total: label, then double-click a corner sizing handle**

5. **Right-click the CategoryRevenue report tab, then click Print Preview to review the changes as shown in FIGURE 8-12**

6. **Save and close the CategoryRevenue report**

FIGURE 8-11: Applying a theme to a report

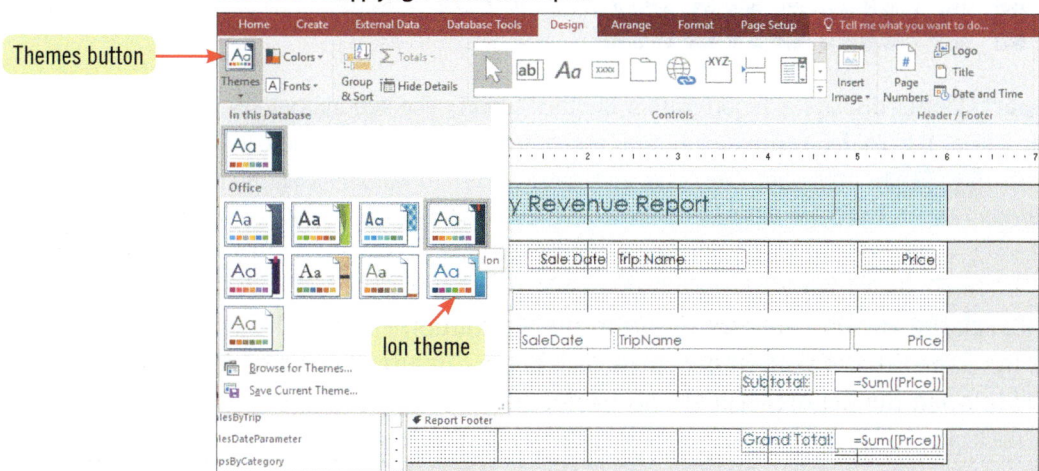

FIGURE 8-12: Ion theme applied to the CategoryRevenue report

Add Subreports

A **subreport** control displays a report within another report. The report that contains the subreport control is called the **main report**. You can use a subreport control when you want to connect two reports. **CASE** *You want the CategoryRevenue report to automatically print at the end of the TripsByCategory report. You use a subreport in the Report Footer section to accomplish this.*

STEPS

1. **Right-click the TripsByCategory report in the Navigation Pane, click Design View, right-click the Page Header section bar, then click Report Header/Footer on the shortcut menu to open the Report Header and Footer sections**

   With the Report Footer section open, you're ready to add the CategoryRevenue subreport.

> **TROUBLE**
> Be sure to put the subreport in the Report Footer section versus the Page Footer section.

2. **Click the More button ⏷ in the Controls group, click the Subform/Subreport button, then click the left edge of the Report Footer to start the SubReport Wizard, as shown in FIGURE 8-13**

   The SubReport Wizard asks what data you want to use for the subreport.

> **TROUBLE**
> You may need to scroll to find the None option in the list.

3. **Click the Use an existing report or form option button in the SubReport Wizard, click CategoryRevenue if it is not already selected, click Next, scroll and click None when asked how you want the reports to be linked, click Next, then click Finish to accept the default name**

   The Report Footer section contains the CategoryRevenue report as a subreport. Therefore, the CategoryRevenue report will print after the TripsByCategory report prints. You don't need the label that accompanies the subreport, so you delete it.

> **TROUBLE**
> You may need to move the subreport control to see the CategoryRevenue label.

4. **Click the new CategoryRevenue label associated with the subreport, press [Delete], then drag the top part of the Report Footer bar up to close the Page Footer section**

   Report Design View should look similar to FIGURE 8-14. If the subreport pushes the right edge of the main report beyond the 8" mark on the ruler, you may see a green error indicator in the report selector button because the report width is greater than the page width. To narrow a report, drag the right edge of a report to the left. Preview your changes.

5. **Right-click the TripsByCategory report tab, click Print Preview, then navigate through the pages of the report**

   The TripsByCategory report fills the first two pages. The CategoryRevenue subreport starts at the top of page three. There should be no blank pages between the printed pages of the report.

6. **Save and close the TripsByCategory report**

FIGURE 8-13: SubReport Wizard dialog box

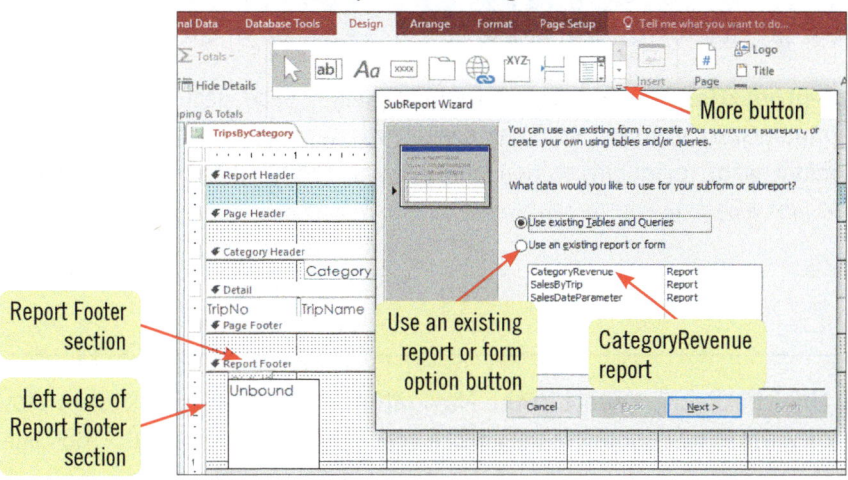

FIGURE 8-14: Subreport in Report Design View

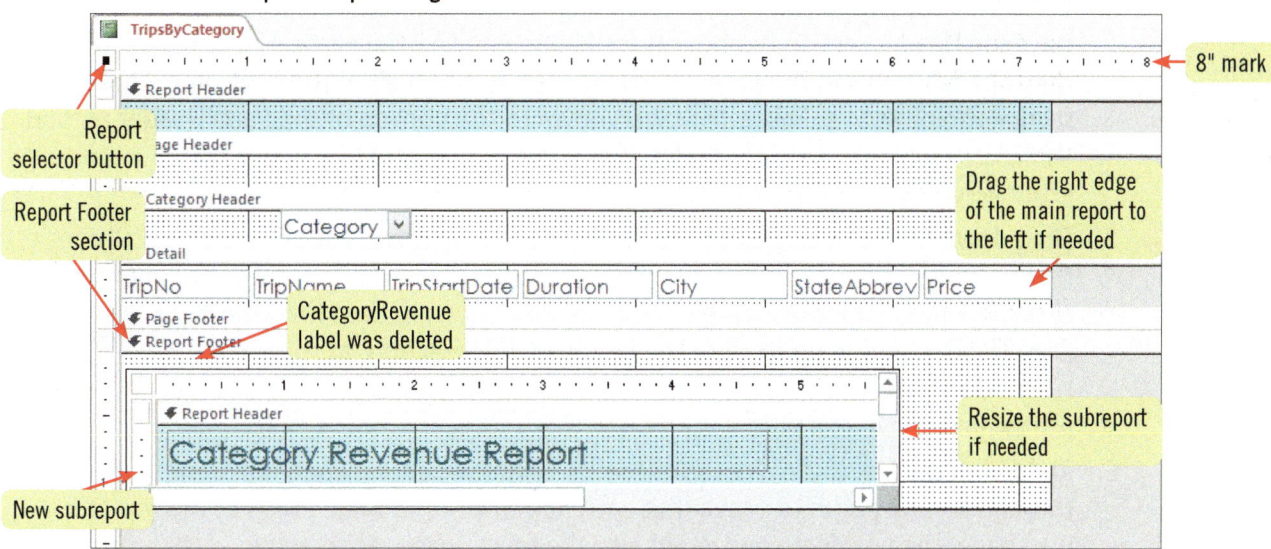

Modify Section Properties

Learning Outcomes
• Modify section properties
• Use rulers to select controls in Report Design View

Report **section properties**, the characteristics that define each section, can be modified to improve report printouts. For example, you might want each new Group Header to print at the top of a page. Or, you might want to modify section properties to format that section with a background color. **CASE** ▶ *Julia Rice asks you to modify the SalesByTrip report so that each trip prints at the top of a page.*

STEPS

1. **Right-click the SalesByTrip report in the Navigation Pane, then click Design View**
   To force each new trip to start printing at the top of a page, you open and modify the TripName Footer.

2. **Click the Group & Sort button to open the Group, Sort, and Total pane if it is not open; click the TripName More Options button in the Group, Sort, and Total pane; click the without a footer section list arrow; click with a footer section; then double-click the TripName Footer section bar to open its Property Sheet**
   You modify the **Force New Page** property of the TripName Footer section to force each trip name to start printing at the top of a new page.

3. **Click the Format tab in the Property Sheet, click the Force New Page property list arrow, then click After Section, as shown in FIGURE 8-15**
   You also move the Report Header controls into the Page Header so they print at the top of every page. First, you need to create space in the upper half of the Page Header section to hold the controls.

4. **Close the Property Sheet, drag the top edge of the TripName Header down to expand the Page Header section to about twice its height, click the vertical ruler to the left of the TripName label in the Page Header section to select all of the controls in that section, then use ⬚ to move the labels down to the bottom of the Page Header section**
   With space available in the top half of the Page Header section, you cut and paste the controls from the Report Header section to that new space.

5. **Drag down the vertical ruler to the left of the Report Header section to select all controls in that section, click the Home tab, click the Cut button in the Clipboard group, click the Page Header section bar, click the Paste button, then drag the top edge of the Page Header section up to close the Report Header section, as shown in FIGURE 8-16**
   Preview the report to make sure that each page contains the new header information and that each trip prints at the top of its own page.

6. **Right-click the SalesByTrip report tab, click Print Preview, navigate back and forth through several pages to prove that each new TripName value prints at the top of a new page, then navigate and zoom into the fourth page, as shown in FIGURE 8-17**
   Each trip now starts printing at the top of a new page, and the former Report Header section controls now print at the top of each page too, because they were moved to the Page Header section.

7. **Save and close the SalesByTrip report**

FIGURE 8-15: Changing section properties

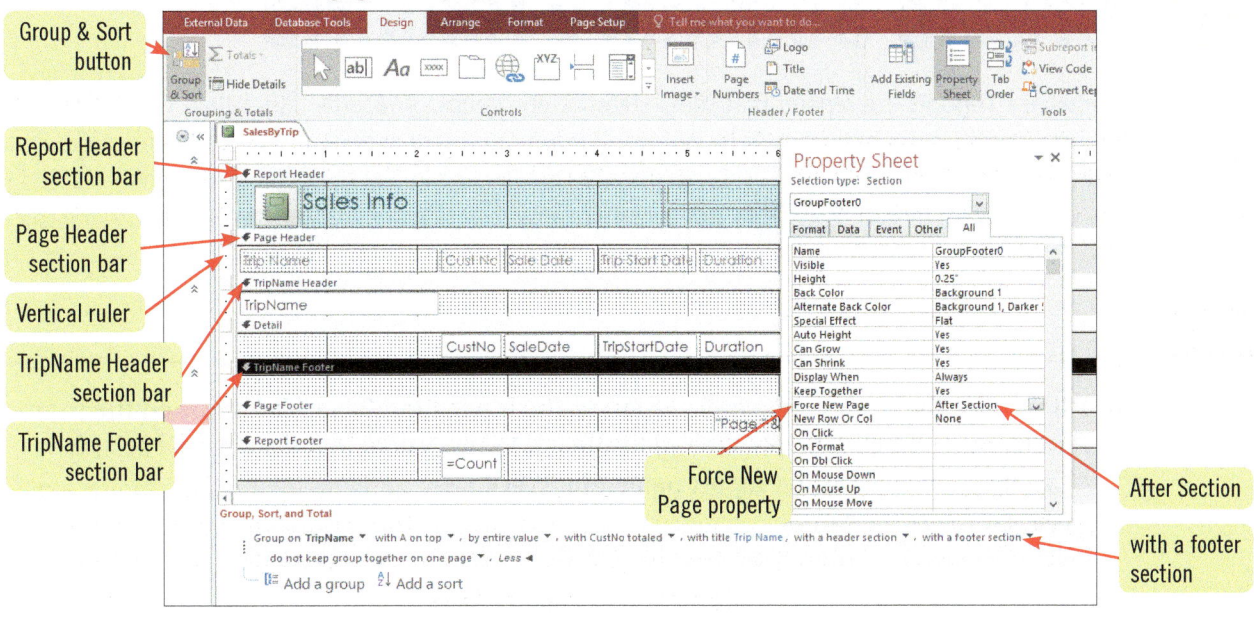

FIGURE 8-16: Moving controls from the Report Header to the Page Header

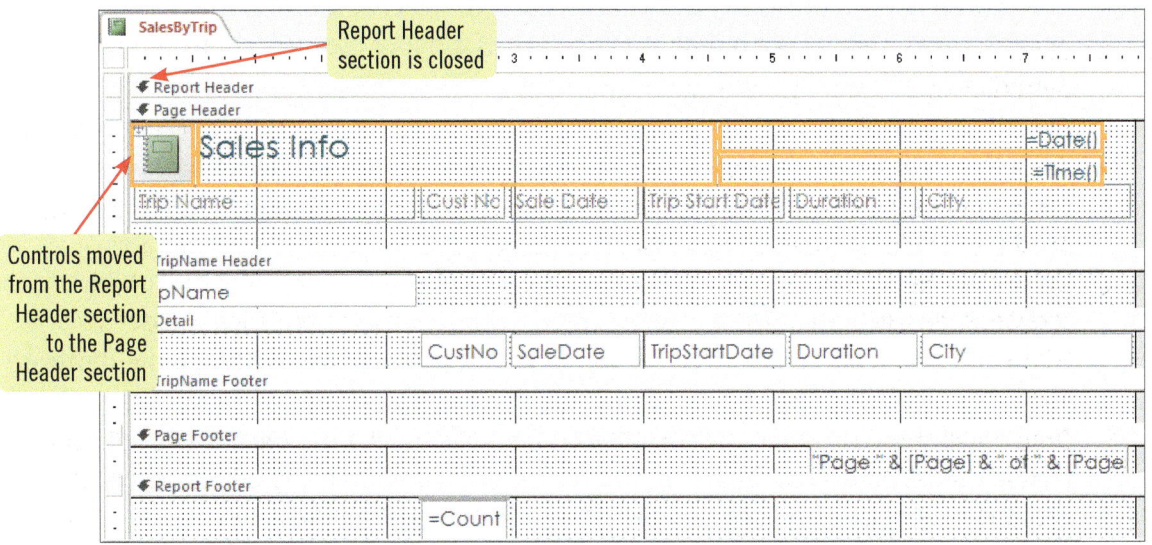

FIGURE 8-17: Fourth page of SalesByTrip report

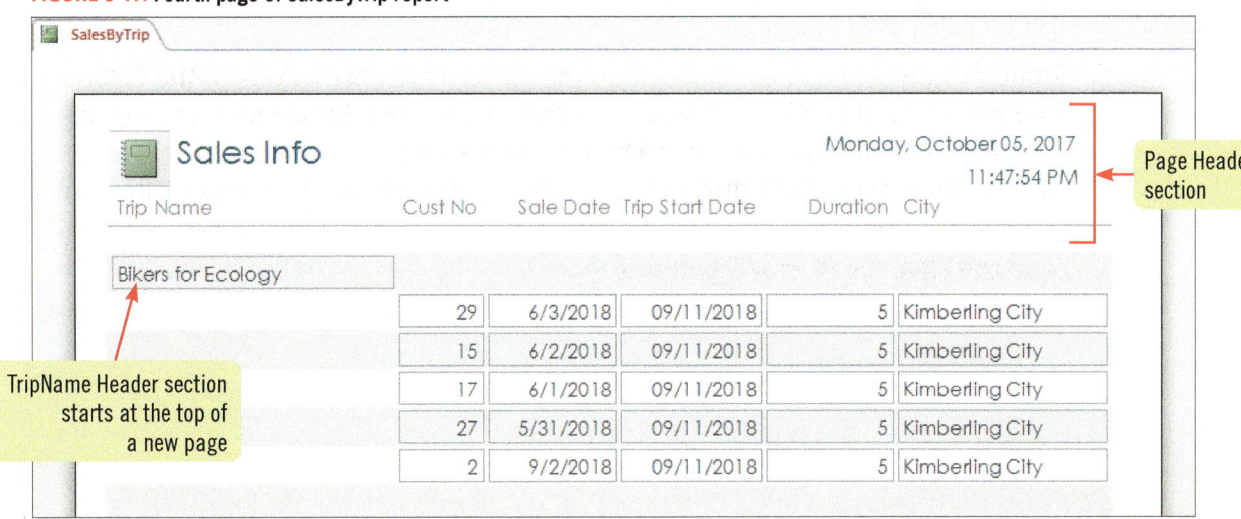

Create Summary Reports

Learning Outcomes
- Resize report sections
- Add calculations to Group Footer sections

Summary reports are reports that show statistics on groups of records rather than details for each record. You create summary reports by using Access functions such as Sum, Count, or Avg in expressions that calculate the desired statistic. These expressions are entered in text boxes most commonly placed in the Group Footer section. **CASE** ▶ *Julia Rice asks for a report to summarize the revenue for each trip category. You create a copy of the CategoryRevenue report and modify it to satisfy this request.*

STEPS

1. **Right-click the CategoryRevenue report in the Navigation Pane, click Copy on the shortcut menu, right-click below the report objects in the Navigation Pane, click Paste, type CategorySummary as the report name, then click OK**

   Summary reports may contain controls in the Group Header and Group Footer sections, but because they provide summary statistics instead of details, they do not contain controls in the Detail section. You delete the controls in the Detail section and close it.

2. **Right-click the CategorySummary report in the Navigation Pane, click Design View, click the vertical ruler to the left of the Detail section to select all controls in the Detail section, press [Delete], then drag the top of the Category Footer section bar up to close the Detail section**

   You can also delete the labels in the Page Header section.

3. **Click the vertical ruler to the left of the Page Header section to select all controls in the Page Header section, press [Delete], then drag the top of the Category Header section bar up to close the Page Header section**

   Because the Page Header and Page Footer sections do not contain any controls, those section bars can be toggled off to simplify Report Design View.

4. **Right-click the Report Header section bar, then click Page Header/Footer on the shortcut menu to remove the Page Header and Page Footer section bars from Report Design View**

   With the unneeded controls and sections removed, as shown in **FIGURE 8-18**, you preview the final summary report.

5. **Right-click the CategorySummary report tab, then click Print Preview**

   You could make this report look even better by moving the Category text box into the Category Footer section and deleting the Subtotal label and line.

6. **Right-click the CategorySummary report tab, click Design View, use the ⌖ pointer to drag the Category text box down from the Category Header section to the Category Footer section, click the Subtotal label in the Category Footer section, press [Delete], click the subtotal line just above the =Sum([Price]) text box in the Category Footer section, press [Delete], right-click the CategorySummary report tab, then click Print Preview**

   The summarized revenue for each category is shown in the one-page summary report in **FIGURE 8-19**.

7. **Save and close the CategorySummary report, then close R2G-8.accdb and exit Access**

FIGURE 8-18: Design View of the CategorySummary report

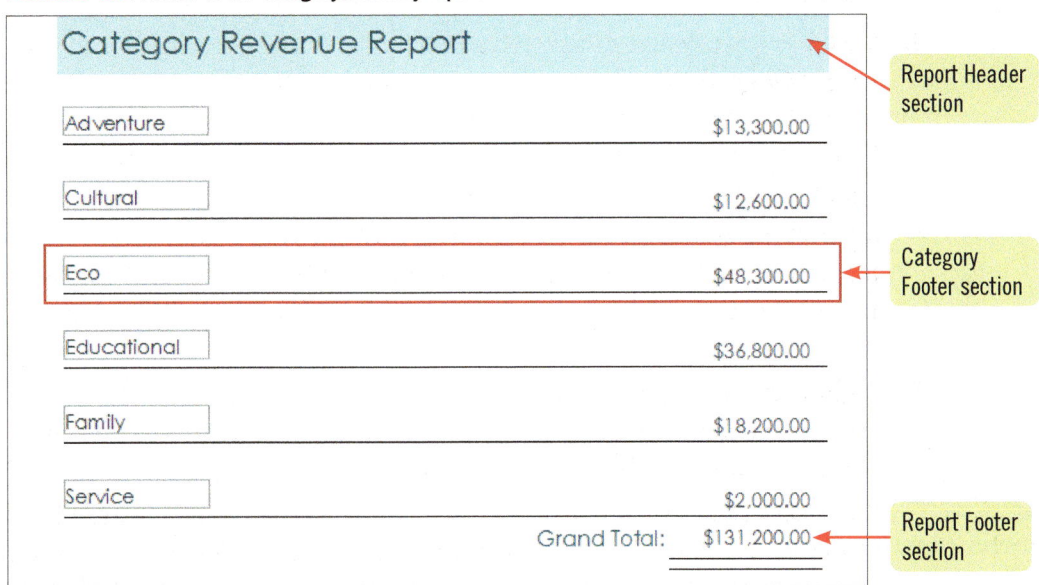

Page Header and Page Footer sections are removed

All controls in the Detail section are deleted and the Detail section is closed

CategorySummary

Report Header

Category Revenue Report

Category Header

Category

Detail

Category Footer

Subtotal: =Sum([Price])

Report Footer

Grand Total: =Sum([Price])

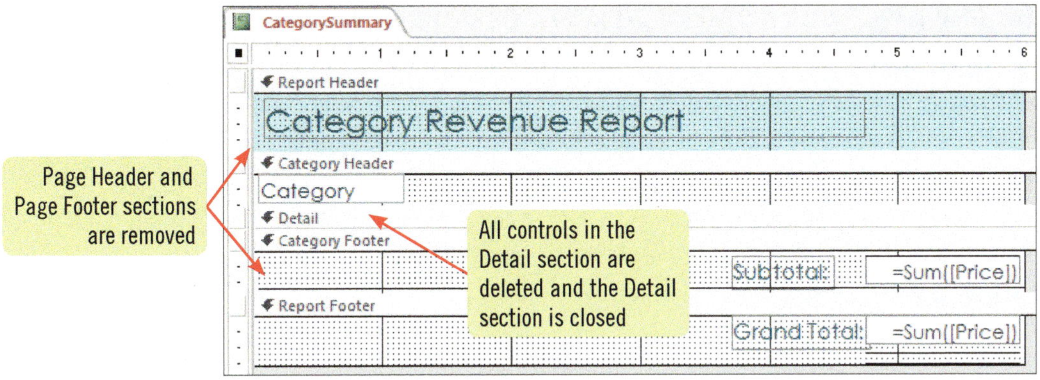

FIGURE 8-19: Preview of the CategorySummary report

Category Revenue Report

Report Header section

Adventure $13,300.00

Cultural $12,600.00

Eco $48,300.00

Category Footer section

Educational $36,800.00

Family $18,200.00

Service $2,000.00

Grand Total: $131,200.00

Report Footer section

Practice

Concepts Review

Identify each element of Report Design View shown in FIGURE 8-20.

FIGURE 8-20

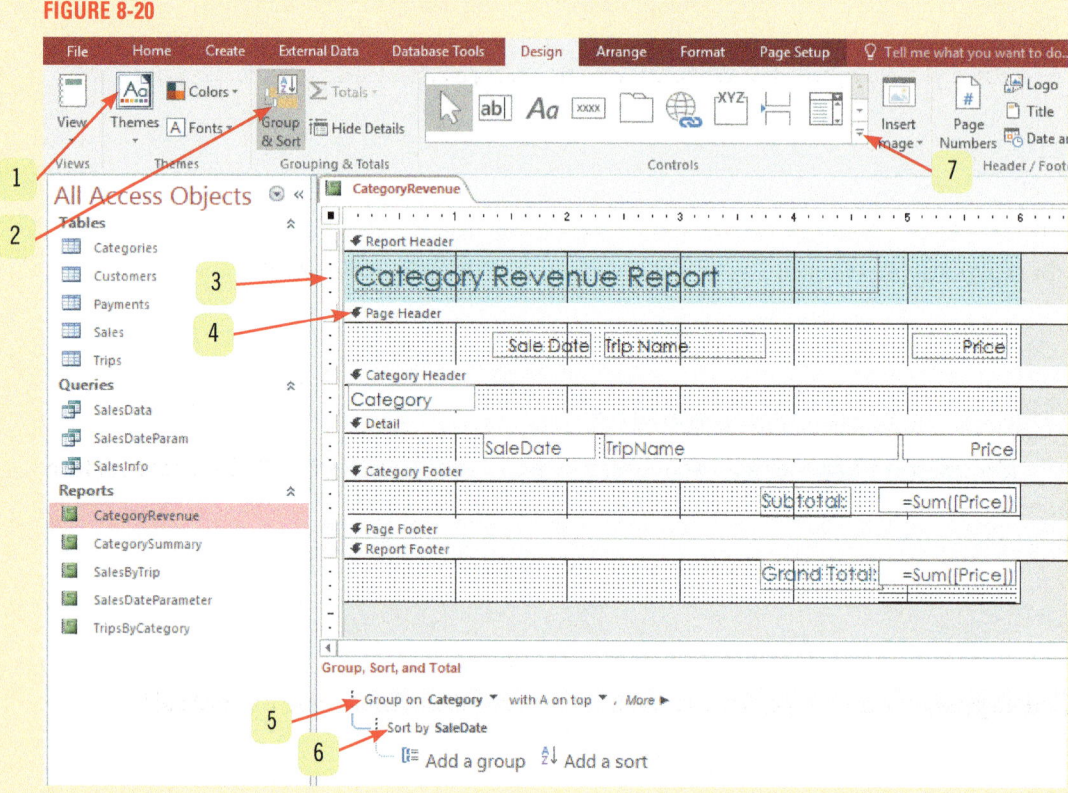

Match each term with the statement that best describes it.

8. **Theme**
9. **Parameter report**
10. **Summary report**
11. **Conditional formatting**
12. **Format Painter**

a. Used to copy multiple formatting properties from one control to another in Report Design View
b. Provides predefined formats that you apply to an entire form or report
c. Prompts the user for the criteria for selecting the records for the report
d. A way to change the appearance of a control on a form or report based on criteria you specify
e. Used to show statistics on groups of records

Select the best answer from the list of choices.

13. **Which control would you use to visually separate groups of records on a report?**
    a. Image
    b. Line
    c. Bound Object Frame
    d. Option group

14. **Which property would you use to force each group of records to print at the top of the next page?**
    a. Paginate
    b. Force New Page
    c. Calculate
    d. Display When

15. **What feature allows you to apply the formatting characteristics of one control to another?**
    a. Theme
    b. AutoContent Wizard
    c. Format Painter
    d. Report Layout Wizard

16. **Which key do you press when creating a line to make it perfectly horizontal?**
    a. [Alt]
    b. [Shift]
    c. [Home]
    d. [Ctrl]

17. **Which feature allows you to apply the same formatting characteristics to all the controls in a report at once?**
    a. AutoPainting
    b. Themes
    c. Format Wizard
    d. Palletizing

18. **In a report, an expression used to calculate values is entered in which type of control?**
    a. Label
    b. Text Box
    c. Combo Box
    d. Command Button

19. **Which section most often contains calculations for groups of records?**
    a. Page Header
    b. Page Footer
    c. Group Footer
    d. Detail

20. **Which control would you use to combine two reports?**
    a. List Box
    b. Subreport
    c. Combo Box
    d. Group & Sort Control

Skills Review

1. Use Report Design View.

 a. Open the LakeHomes-8.accdb database from where you store your Data Files and enable content if prompted.

 b. Open the RealtorList query, and then change Phil Kirkpatrick to your name. Close the query.

 c. Create a new report in Report Design View based on the RealtorList query.

 d. In the Group, Sort, and Total pane, select AgencyName as a grouping field and RLast as a sort field.

 e. Add the AgencyName field to the AgencyName Header. Delete the accompanying AgencyName label, position the AgencyName text box on the left side of the AgencyName Header, then resize it to be about 3" wide.

 f. Add the RealtorNo, RFirst, RLast, and RPhone fields to the Detail section. Delete all labels and position the text boxes horizontally across the top of the Detail section.

 g. Drag the top edge of the Page Footer section up to remove the blank space in the Detail section.

 h. Save the report with the name **RealtorList**, then preview it, as shown in **FIGURE 8-21**. The width and spacing of the controls in your report may differ. Use Layout View to resize each control so it is wide enough to view all data.

 i. Save and close the RealtorList report.

FIGURE 8-21

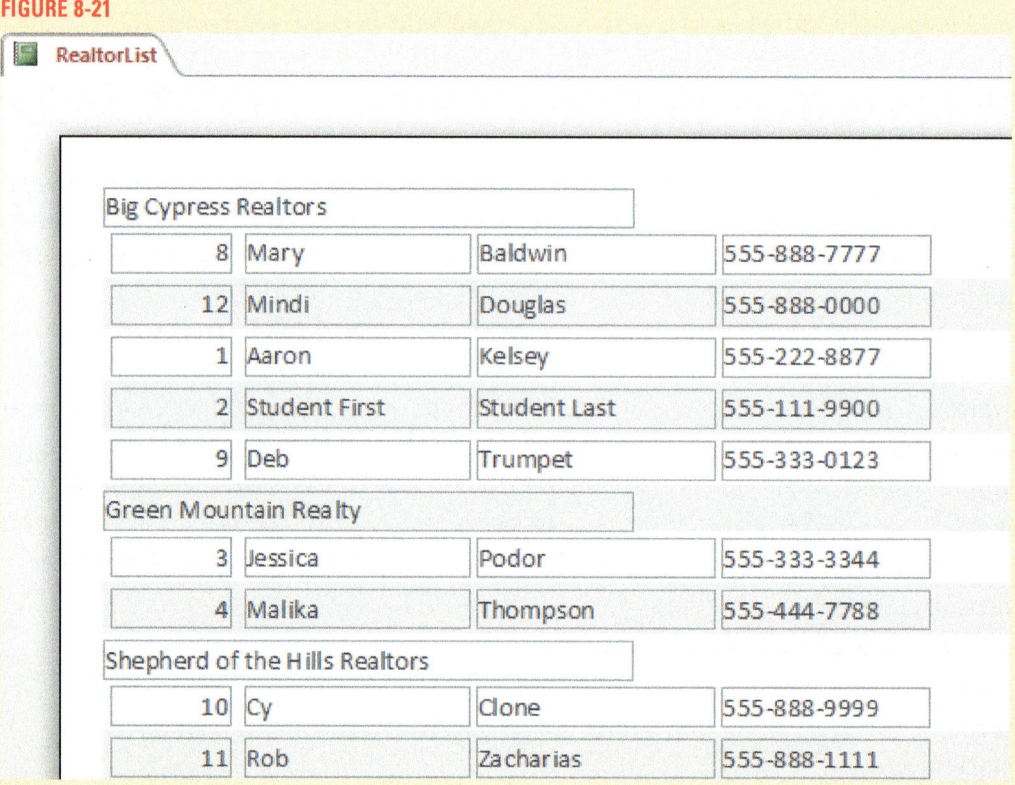

2. Create parameter reports.

 a. Create a query in Query Design View, including the RFirst, RLast, and RPhone fields from the Realtors table. Include the Type, SchoolDistrict, SqFt, and Asking fields from the Listings table.

 b. In the Asking field, include the following parameter criteria: **<=[Enter maximum asking price]**.

 c. Test the query by switching to Datasheet View, enter **300,000** in the Enter maximum asking price box, then click OK. The query should display 25 records, all with an asking price of less than or equal to $300,000. Save the query as **PriceParameter**, then close it.

Skills Review (continued)

d. Click the PriceParameter query in the Navigation Pane, then click Report on the Create tab. Enter **300,000** in the Enter maximum asking price box, then click OK.

e. Work in Layout View to narrow each column to be only as wide as necessary and to fit all columns across a single sheet of paper in portrait orientation.

f. In Report Design View, narrow the PriceParameter label to be about half as wide, then add a label with your name to the right side of the Report Header section.

g. In Report Design View, drag the right edge of the report to the left to make sure the report is no wider than 8 inches. This may include moving controls in the Page Footer or Report Footer to the left as well.

h. Preview the report again to make sure it is not too wide to fit on the paper, enter **300,000** in the prompt, then print the report if requested by your instructor.

i. Save the report with the name **PriceParameter**, then close it.

3. Apply conditional formatting.

a. Open the PriceParameter report in Report Design View, click the Asking text box, then open the Conditional Formatting Rules Manager dialog box.

b. Add a rule to format all Asking field values between **0** and **199999** with a light green background color.

c. Add a rule to format all Asking field values between **200000** and **300000** with a yellow background color.

d. Add a rule to format all Asking field values greater than **300000** with a red background color.

e. Test the report in Print Preview, entering a value of **500,000** when prompted. Make sure the conditional formatting colors are working as intended.

4. Add lines.

a. Open the PriceParameter report in Design View, then use the Group, Sort, and Total pane to add a sort order. Sort the fields in descending (largest to smallest) order on the Asking field.

b. Add a label to the Report Footer section directly to the left of the =Sum([Asking]) text box. Enter **Grand Total:** as the label text.

c. Expand the vertical size of the Report Footer section to about twice its current height and resize the =Sum([Asking]) text box in the Report Footer to better read the contents.

d. Draw two short horizontal lines just below the =Sum([Asking]) calculation in the Report Footer section to indicate a grand total.

e. Widen the Asking column if needed to display the values clearly, but be careful to stay within the margins of the report. Save the report, then switch to Print Preview to review the changes using a value of **300,000** when prompted. You should only see green and yellow background colors on the Asking field values.

5. Use the Format Painter and themes.

a. Open the PriceParameter report in Design View.

b. Change the PriceParameter label in the Report Header section to **Asking Price Analysis**.

c. Apply the Facet theme.

d. Change the font color of the RFirst label in the Page Header section to Automatic (black).

e. Use the Format Painter to copy the format from the RFirst label to the RLast, RPhone, Type, and SchoolDistrict labels in the Page Header section.

f. Change the font color of the SqFt label in the Page Header section to red.

g. Use the Format Painter to copy the format from the SqFt label to the Asking label.

h. Save and close the PriceParameter report.

Skills Review (continued)

6. Add subreports.

   a. Open the ListingReport and RealtorList reports in Print Preview. If needed, resize and align any text boxes that are not wide enough to show all data. Be careful to not extend the right edge of the report beyond one sheet of paper.

   b. Close the RealtorList report and display the ListingReport in Design View. Expand the Report Footer section, and add the RealtorList report as a subreport using the SubReport Wizard. Choose None when asked to link the main form to the subform (you may have to scroll), and accept the default name of RealtorList.

   c. Delete the extra RealtorList label in the Report Footer. (*Hint*: It will be positioned near the upper-left corner of the subreport, but it may be mostly hidden by the subreport.)

   d. Preview each page of the report to make sure all data is clearly visible. Widen any controls that do not clearly display information, again being careful not to extend the report beyond the right margin.

   e. Narrow the width of the report if necessary in Report Design View, then save and close it.

7. Modify section properties.

   a. In Report Design View of the ListingReport, modify the Realtors.RealtorNo Footer section's Force New Page property to After Section. (Note: The RealtorNo field is included in two tables, Realtors and Listings. Access uses the table-name.fieldname convention to specify that this RealtorNo field is from the Realtors table.)

   b. Open the Page Footer section, and add a label, **Created by Your Name**.

   c. Save and preview the ListingReport to make sure that the new section property forces each new realtor group of records to print on its own page, as shown in **FIGURE 8-22**. Also check that a label identifying you as the report creator appears at the bottom of each page. Remember that you must print preview the report (rather than display it in Report View) to see how the report prints on each page.

   d. Print the report if requested by your instructor, then save and close the report.

FIGURE 8-22

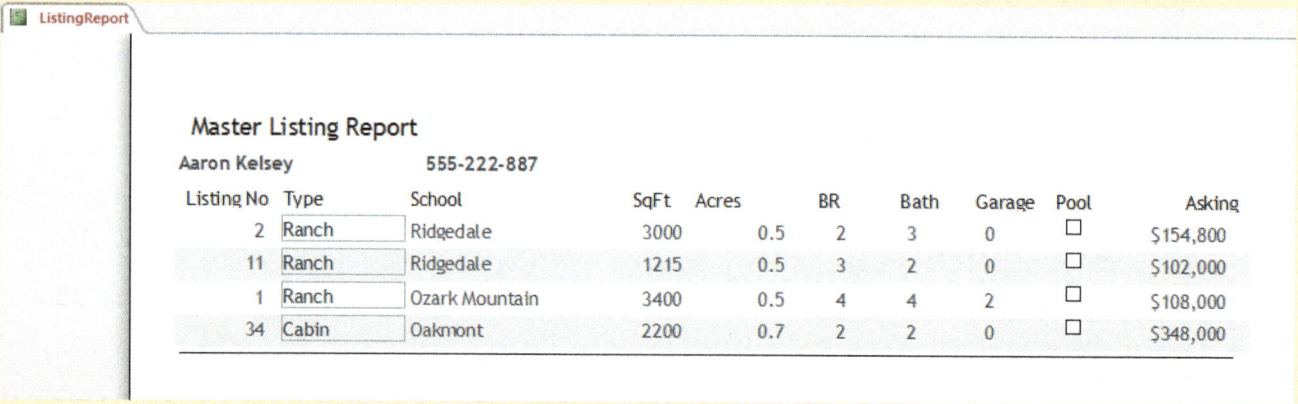

Skills Review (continued)

8. Create summary reports.

a. Right-click the ListingReport, click Copy, right-click the Navigation Pane, click Paste, then type **ListingSummary**.

b. Open the ListingSummary report in Design View, then delete the subreport from the Report Footer, all the controls in the Detail section, and all the labels in the Realtors.RealtorNo Header section. (*Hint*: Be careful not to delete the two text boxes in the Realtors.RealtorNo Header section.)

c. Close the extra space in the Report Footer, Detail, and Realtors.RealtorNo Header sections.

d. Expand the size of the Realtors.RealtorNo Footer section about 0.5", move the line to the bottom of that section, then add a text box to the right side of the section with the following expression: **=Sum([Asking])**.

e. Modify the new label to read **Subtotal of Asking Price:**, then move and resize the controls as needed so that both the label and text box can be clearly read in Report Design View.

f. Open the Property Sheet for the =Sum([Asking]) text box, click the Format tab, then choose **Currency** for the Format property and **0** for the Decimal Places property.

g. Expand the Report Footer section about 0.5 inches, copy the =Sum([Asking]) text box to the Report Footer section, move it directly under the =Sum([Asking]) text box in the Realtors.RealtorNo Footer section, then change the label to be **Grand Total:**.

h. Draw two short lines under the =Sum([Asking]) text box in the Report Footer section to indicate a grand total.

i. Change the Force New Page property of the Realtors.RealtorNo Footer section to None.

j. Move the two text boxes in the Realtors.RealtorNo Header section directly down to the Realtors.RealtorNo Footer section and then close the Realtors.RealtorNo Header section.

k. Position all controls within the 10.5" mark on the ruler so that the width of the paper is no wider than 10.5". Drag the right edge of the report as far to the left as possible so that it does not extend beyond 10.5".

l. Preview the report. Resize sections and move controls in Design View so the report matches FIGURE 8-23. Print the report if requested by your instructor, then save and close the report.

m. Close the LakeHomes-8.accdb database, and exit Access.

FIGURE 8-23

Master Listing Report			
Aaron Kelsey	555-222-8877	Subtotal of Asking Price:	$712,800
Student First Student Last	555-111-9900	Subtotal of Asking Price:	$985,936
Jessica Podor	555-333-3344	Subtotal of Asking Price:	$467,820
Malika Thompson	555-444-7788	Subtotal of Asking Price:	$1,026,120
Jane Ann Welch	555-223-0044	Subtotal of Asking Price:	$603,360
Shari Duncan	555-228-5577	Subtotal of Asking Price:	$144,000
Trixie Angelina	555-220-4466	Subtotal of Asking Price:	$126,000
Mary Baldwin	555-888-7777	Subtotal of Asking Price:	$914,279
Mindi Douglas	555-888-0000	Subtotal of Asking Price:	$1,222,200
Andrew Barker	555-999-2222	Subtotal of Asking Price:	$1,785,480
		Grand Total:	$7,987,994

Page: ◄ ◄ 1 ► ►► ► No Filter ◄

Independent Challenge 1

As the manager of a music store's instrument rental program, you created a database to track instrument rentals. Now that several instruments have been rented, you need to create a report listing the rental transactions for each instrument.

a. Start Access, open the Music-8.accdb database from where you store your Data Files, and enable content if prompted.

b. Use the Report Wizard to create a report based on the FirstName and LastName fields in the Students table, the RentalDate field from the Rentals table, and the Description and MonthlyFee fields from the Instruments table.

c. View the data by Instruments, do not add any more grouping levels, sort the data in ascending order by RentalDate, use a Stepped layout and Portrait orientation, and title the report **Instrument Rentals**.

d. Open the report in Design View, change the first grouping level from SerialNo to Description so that all instruments with the same description are grouped together, and open the Description Footer section.

e. Add a new text box to the Description Footer section with the expression **=Count([LastName])**. Change the label to **Number of Rentals:**, and position the controls close to the right side of the report.

f. Change the Force New Page property of the Description Footer section to After Section.

g. Add your name as a label to the Report Header section, and use the Format Painter to copy the formatting from the Instrument Rentals label to your name. Double-click a corner sizing handle of the label with your name to resize it to show your entire name, and align the top edges of both labels in the Report Header.

h. Save and preview the report, as shown in FIGURE 8-24. Move, resize, and align controls as needed to match the figure, make sure all controls fit within the margins of one sheet of paper, then print the report if requested by your instructor.

i. Save and close the Instrument Rentals report, close the Music-8.accdb database, then exit Access.

FIGURE 8-24

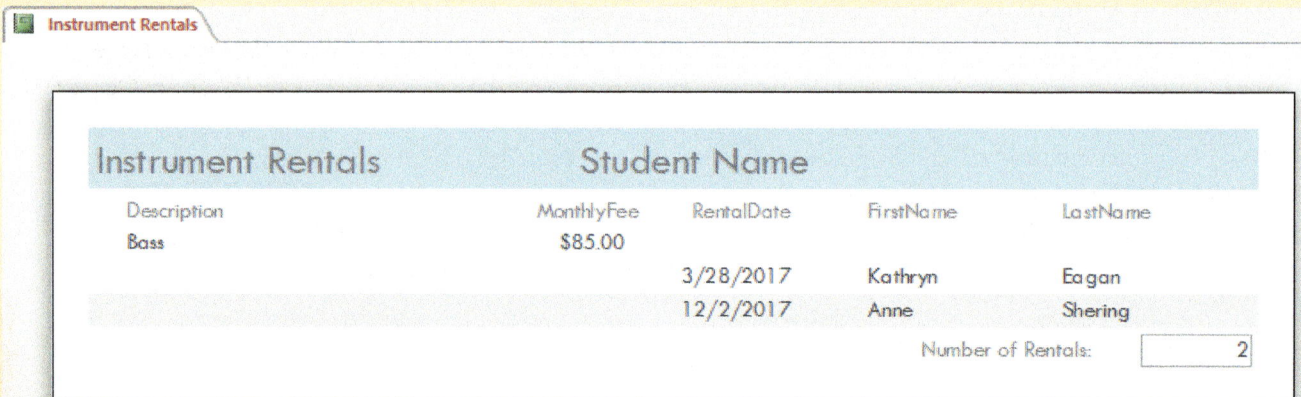

Independent Challenge 2

As the manager of a music store's instrument rental program, you have created a database to track instrument rentals. Now that the rental program is under way, you need to create a summary report that shows how many instruments have been rented by each school.

a. Start Access, open the Music-8.accdb database from the location where you store your Data Files, and enable content if prompted.

b. Build a query in Query Design View with the following fields: SchoolName from the Schools table and RentalDate from the Rentals table. (*Hint*: Include the Students table to build the proper relationships between the Schools and the Rentals table.) Save the query with the name **SchoolSummary**, then close it.

c. Create a new report in Report Design View. Use the SchoolSummary query as the Record Source property.

d. Add SchoolName as a grouping field, and add the SchoolName field to the left side of the SchoolName Header section. Delete the SchoolName label, and widen the SchoolName text box to about 4".

e. Drag the top edge of the Page Footer section up to completely close the Detail section.

f. Add a label to the Page Header section with your name. Format the label with an Arial Black font and a 14-point font size. Resize the label to display all the text.

g. Open the Report Header section, and add a label to the Report Header section that reads **New student musicians per school**. Format the label with Automatic (black) font color.

h. Add a text box to the right side of the SchoolName Header section with the expression **=Count([RentalDate])**. Delete the accompanying label.

i. Align the top edges of the two text boxes in the SchoolName Header.

j. Use the Format Painter to copy the formatting from the label with your name to the new label in the Report Header section, the SchoolName text box, and the =Count([RentalDate]) expression in the SchoolName Header section. Switch back and forth between Print Preview and Design View to resize the text boxes in the SchoolName Header section as needed to show all information in each box.

k. Open the Report Footer section, then copy and paste the =Count([RentalDate]) text box to the Report Footer section. Right-align the right edges of the =Count([RentalDate]) controls in the SchoolName Header and Report Footer sections.

l. Add one short line above and two short lines below the =Count([RentalDate]) text box in the Report Footer section to indicate a subtotal and grand total.

m. Save the report with the name **SchoolSummary**, then preview it, as shown in FIGURE 8-25.

n. Close the SchoolSummary report, close the Music-8.accdb database, then exit Access.

FIGURE 8-25

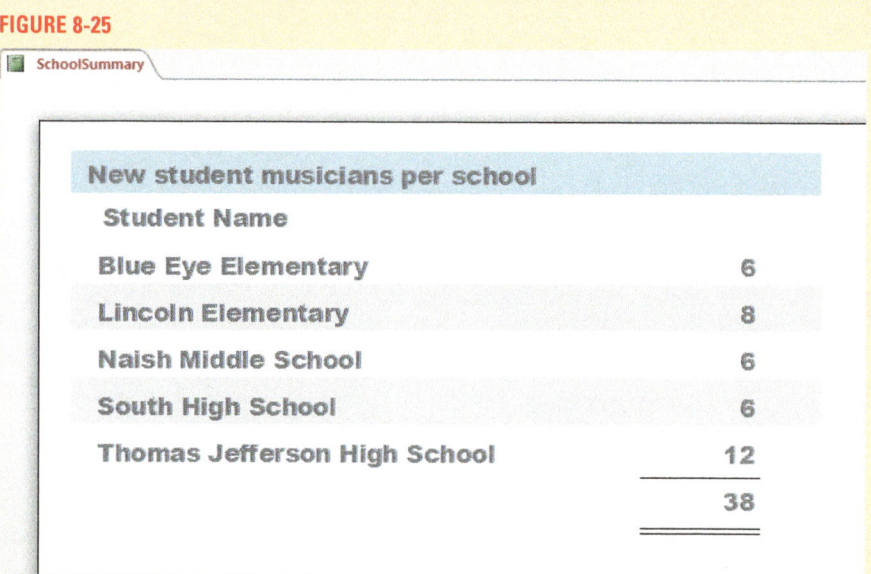

Access 2016

Independent Challenge 3

As the manager of a music store's instrument rental program, you have created a database to track instrument rentals. Now that the rental program is under way, you need to create a parameter report for each instrument type.

a. Start Access, open the Music-8.accdb database from where you store your Data Files, and enable content if prompted.

b. Create a query with the RentalDate field from the Rentals table, the Description and MonthlyFee fields from the Instruments table, and the FirstName and LastName fields from the Students table.

c. Enter the parameter criteria **Between [Enter start date] And [Enter end date]** for the RentalDate field and **[Enter instrument type such as cello]** for the Description field.

d. Save the query with the name **RentalParameter**, then test it with the dates **3/1/17** and **3/31/17** and the type **bass**. These criteria should select one record. Close the RentalParameter query.

e. Use the Report Wizard to create a report on all fields in the RentalParameter query. View the data by Instruments, do not add any more grouping levels, sort the records in ascending order by RentalDate, and use an Outline layout and a Portrait orientation. Title the report **Instrument Lookup**.

f. To respond to the prompts, enter **1/1/17** for the start date and **6/30/17** for the end date. Enter **viola** for the instrument type prompt.

g. In Report Design View, apply the Integral theme.

h. Add your name as a label to the Report Header section. Change the font color to black so that it is clearly visible.

i. Add spaces between all words in the labels in the Description Header section: MonthlyFee, RentalDate, FirstName, and LastName to change them to **Monthly Fee**, **Rental Date**, **First Name**, and **Last Name**. Be sure to change the label controls and not the text box controls.

j. Open the Description Footer section.

k. Add a text box to the Description Footer section that contains the expression **=Count([LastName])*[MonthlyFee]**. Change the accompanying label to read **Monthly Revenue:**, then move the text box with the expression below the LastName text box and resize both so that their contents are clearly visible.

l. Open the Property Sheet for the new expression. On the Format tab, change the Format property to **Currency** and the Decimal Places property to **0**.

m. Display the report for RentalDates **1/1/17** through **4/30/17**, instrument type **viola**. Your report should look like FIGURE 8-26.

n. Save the Instrument Lookup report, print it if requested by your instructor, close the Music-8.accdb database, then exit Access.

FIGURE 8-26

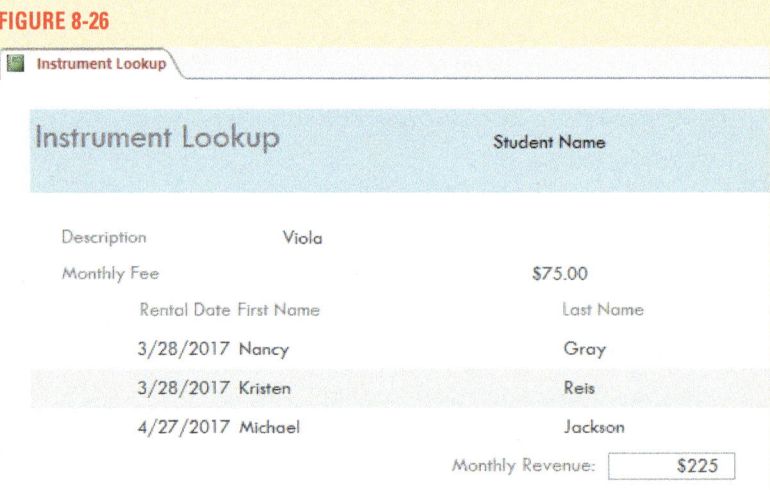

Independent Challenge 4: Explore

You have created an Access database to help manage college scholarship opportunities. You analyze scholarships by building a report with conditional formatting.

a. Start Access and open the Scholarships-8.accdb database from the location where you store your Data Files. Enable content if prompted.

b. Use the Report Wizard to create a report based on the Scholarships table. Include all of the fields. Add Major then Amount as the grouping levels, then click the Grouping Options button in the Report Wizard. Choose 5000s as the Grouping interval for the Amount field. Sort the records by DueDate in descending order. Use a Stepped layout and a Landscape orientation. Title the report **Scholarships by Major**.

c. Preview the report, then add your name as a label next to the report title.

d. In Layout View, add spaces to the DueDate and ScholarshipName labels to read **Due Date** and **Scholarship Name**.

e. Resize and narrow the columns to fit on a single sheet of landscape paper, then drag the right edge of the report to the left in Report Design View to make sure it is within the 10.5" mark on the horizontal ruler.

f. Expand the Page Header section to about twice its height, move the labels in the Page Header section to the bottom of the Page Header section, move the labels from the Report Header section to the top of the Page Header section, then close up the Report Header section.

g. Open the Major Footer section, then change the Force New Page property of the Major Footer section to After Section.

h. Click the Amount text box in the Detail section, then apply a new rule of conditional formatting. Use the Compare to other records rule type, and change the Bar color to light green.

i. Preview page 4 of the report for the Computer Science majors, as shown in **FIGURE 8-27**.

j. Save and close the Scholarships by Major report and the Scholarships-8.accdb database.

FIGURE 8-27

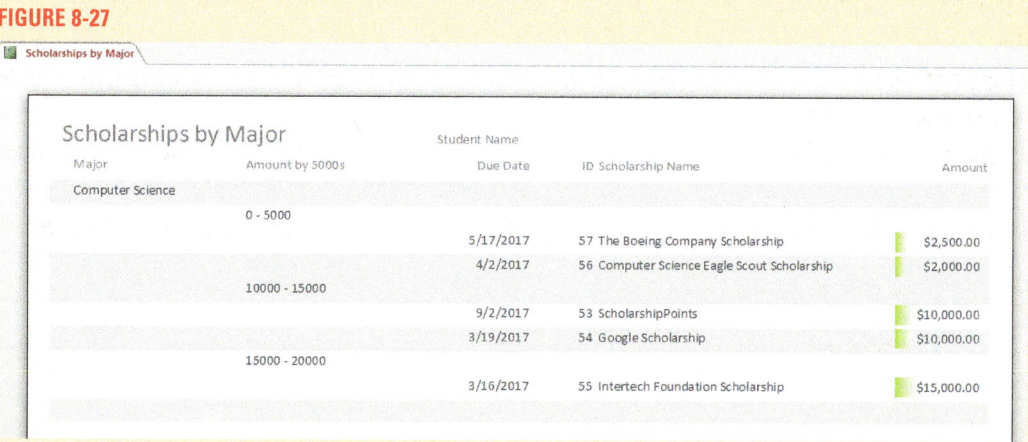

Access 2016

Visual Workshop

Open the Baseball-8.accdb database from the location where you store your Data Files and enable content if prompted. Using the Report Wizard, build a report on the PlayerLName field from the Players table and the AtBats and Hits fields from the PlayerStats table. View the data by Players, do not add any more grouping or sorting fields, and use a Stepped layout and Portrait orientation. Enter **Batting Average** as the name of the report. In Report Design View, open the PlayerNo Footer section and move the PlayerLName text box down to the same position in the PlayerNo Footer section. Add new text boxes to the PlayerNo Footer section to sum the AtBats, sum the Hits, and calculate the overall batting average per player. The expression to find the batting average is **=Sum([Hits])/Sum([AtBats])**. Delete any extra labels that are created when you add the text boxes, and delete all of the controls in the Detail section. Close the PlayerNo Header and Detail sections, and resize the PlayerNo Footer section to remove blank space. Modify the Decimal Places property of the batting average calculation to show **3** digits to the right of the decimal point, and modify the Format property to be Standard. Apply a conditional format to the batting average expression so that if it is greater than or equal to **0.5**, the text is bold and red. Add a label to the Page Header section to identify the batting average, add a label to the Report Header section with your name, and then edit the labels and align the controls, as shown in FIGURE 8-28. As a final step, change the Group on field from PlayerNo to PlayerLName so the records are sorted by player last name, change the Alternate Back Color of the PlayerLName Footer section to Background 1, and add a line at the bottom of the PlayerLName Footer section as shown in FIGURE 8-28. Save the Batting Average report, print the report if requested by your instructor, and then close it.

FIGURE 8-28

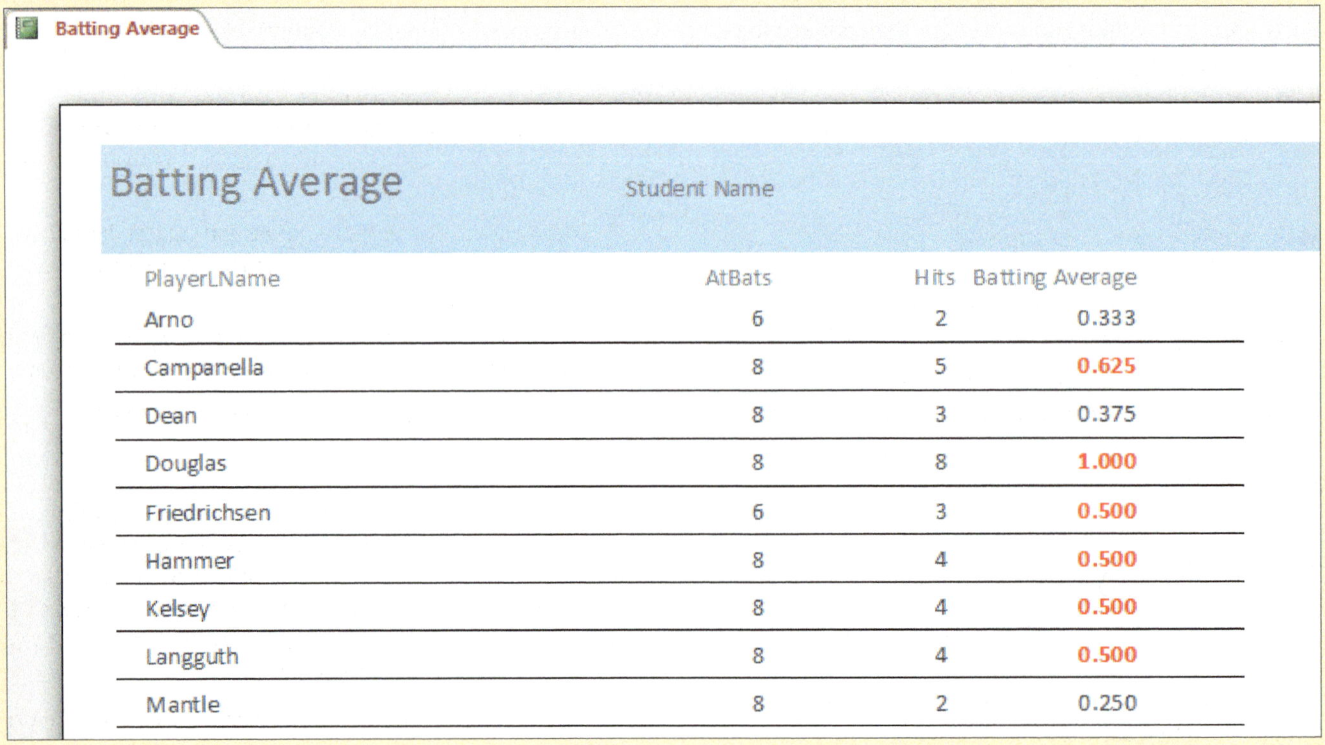

PlayerLName	AtBats	Hits	Batting Average
Arno	6	2	0.333
Campanella	8	5	0.625
Dean	8	3	0.375
Douglas	8	8	1.000
Friedrichsen	6	3	0.500
Hammer	8	4	0.500
Kelsey	8	4	0.500
Langguth	8	4	0.500
Mantle	8	2	0.250

Glossary

.accdb The file extension that means the database is an Access database, created with Access 2007, 2010, 2013, or 2016.

.jpg The filename extension for JPEG files.

.mdb The file extension for Access 2000 and 2002–2003 databases.

Active The currently available document, program, or object; on the taskbar, when more than one program is open, the button for the active program appears slightly lighter.

Add-in Software that works with an installed app to extend its features.

Aggregate function function such as Sum, Avg, and Count used in a summary query to calculate information about a group of records.

Alignment command A command used in Layout or Design View for a form or report to left-, center-, or right-align a value within its control using the Align Left, Center, or Align Right buttons on the Home tab. In Design View, you can also align the top, bottom, right, or left edge of selected controls using the Align button.

Allow Multiple Values A lookup property that lets you create a multivalued field.

Allow Value List Edits The Lookup field property that determines whether users can add to or edit the list of items in a lookup field.

Alternate Back Color property A property that determines the alternating background color of the selected section in a form or report.

Anchoring A layout positioning option that allows you to tie controls together so you can work with them as a group.

AND criteria Criteria placed in the same row of the query design grid. All criteria on the same row must be true for a record to appear on the resulting datasheet.

Animation emphasis effect In Sway, a special effect you can apply to an object to animate it.

Application developer The person responsible for building and maintaining tables, queries, forms, and reports for all of the database users.

Argument Information that a function uses to create the final answer. Multiple arguments are separated by commas. All of the arguments for a function are surrounded by a single set of parentheses.

Asterisk (*) A wildcard character used to search for any number of characters in query criteria.

Attachment A field data type for adding one or more files, such as images, to database records.

Attachment field A field that allows you to attach an external file such as a Word document, PowerPoint presentation, Excel workbook, or image file to a record.

Autofilter A feature that lets users quickly sort or filter a datasheet by a particular field.

AutoNumber A field data type in which Access enters a sequential integer for each record added into the datasheet. Numbers cannot be reused even if the record is deleted.

Avg function A built-in Access function used to calculate the average of the values in a given field.

Background image An image that fills an entire form or report, appearing "behind" the other controls; also sometimes called a watermark.

Backstage view Appears when the File tab is clicked. The navigation bar on the left side contains commands to perform actions common to most Office programs, such as opening a file, saving a file, and closing the file.

Backward-compatible Software feature that enables documents saved in an older version of a program to be opened in a newer version of the program.

Bound control A control used in either a form or report to display data from the underlying field; used to edit and enter new data in a form.

Byte A field size for Number fields that allows entries only from 0 to 255.

Calculated field A field created in Query Design View that results from an expression of existing fields, Access functions, and arithmetic operators. For example, the entry Profit:[RetailPrice]-[WholesalePrice] in the field cell of the query design grid creates a calculated field called Profit that is the difference between the values in the RetailPrice and WholesalePrice fields.

Calculation A new value that is created by an expression in a text box on a form or report.

Calendar Picker A pop-up calendar from which you can choose dates for a date field.

Card A section for a particular type of content in a Sway presentation.

Child table The "many" table in a one-to-many relationship.

Clip A short segment of audio, such as music, or video.

Clipboard A temporary Windows storage area that holds the selections you copy or cut.

Cloud computing Using an Internet resource to complete your work such as saving a database to Microsoft OneDrive or maintaining Microsoft Office 365.

Column separator The thin line that separates field names to the left or right in a datasheet or the query design grid.

Combo box A bound control used to display a drop-down list of possible entries for a field in which you can also type an entry from the keyboard. It is a "combination" of the list box and text box controls.

Combo Box Wizard A wizard that helps you create a combo box control on a form.

Command button An unbound control commonly called a button, used to provide an easy way to initiate an action on a form.

Compatibility The ability of different programs to work together and exchange data.

Conditional formatting Formatting that is based on specified criteria. For example, a text box may be conditionally formatted do display its value in red if the value is a negative number.

Contextual tab A tab that appears only when a specific task can be performed; contextual tabs appear in an accent color and close when no longer needed.

Control Any element on a form or report such as a label, text box, line, or combo box. Controls can be bound, unbound, or calculated.

Control Source property A property of a bound control in a form or report that determines the field to which the control is connected.

Cortana The Microsoft Windows virtual assistant that integrates with Microsoft Edge to find and provide information.

Creative Commons license A public copyright license that allows the free distribution of an otherwise copyrighted work.

Criteria Entries (rules and limiting conditions) that determine which records are displayed when finding or filtering records in a datasheet or form, or when building a query.

Criteria syntax Rules by which criteria need to be entered. For example, text criteria syntax requires that the criteria are surrounded by quotation marks (" "). Date criteria are surrounded by pound signs (#).

Crosstab query A query that represents data in a cross-tabular layout (fields are used for both column and row headings), similar to PivotTables in other database and spreadsheet products.

Crosstab Query Wizard A wizard used to create crosstab queries and which helps identify fields that will be used for row and column headings, and fields that will be summarized within the datasheet.

Crosstab row A row in the query design grid used to specify the column and row headings and values for the crosstab query.

Current record The record that has the focus or is being edited.

Data cleansing The process of removing and fixing orphan records in a database.

Data type A required property for each field that defines the type of data that can be entered in each field. Valid data types include AutoNumber, Short Text, Long Text, Number, Currency, Yes/No, Date/Time, and Hyperlink.

Database designer The person responsible for building and maintaining tables, queries, forms, and reports.

Database user The person primarily interested in entering, editing, and analyzing the data in the database.

Datasheet A spreadsheet-like grid that displays fields as columns and records as rows.

Datasheet View A view that lists the records of an object in a datasheet. Tables, queries, and most form objects have a Datasheet View.

Date function A built-in Access function used to display the current date on a form or report; enter the Date function as Date().

Default View property A form property that determines whether a subform automatically opens in Datasheet or Continuous Forms view.

Design View A view in which the structure of an object can be manipulated. Every Access object (table, query, form, report, macro, and module) has a Design View.

Dialog box launcher An icon you can click to open a dialog box or task pane from which to choose related commands.

Docs.com A Microsoft website designed for sharing Sway sites.

Document window Most of the screen in Word, PowerPoint, and Excel, where you create a document, slide, or worksheet.

Drawing canvas In OneNote, a container for shapes and lines.

Edit List Items button A button you click to add items to a combo box list in Form View.

Edit mode The mode in which Access assumes you are trying to edit a particular field, so keystrokes such as [Ctrl][End], [Ctrl][Home], [↓], and [↑] move the insertion point within the field.

Edit record symbol A pencil-like symbol that appears in the record selector box to the left of the record that is currently being edited in either a datasheet or a form.

Enabled property A control property that determines whether the control can have the focus in Form View.

Error indicator An icon that automatically appears in Design View to indicate some type of error. For example, a green error indicator appears in the upper-left corner of a text box in Form Design View if the text box Control Source property is set to a field name that doesn't exist.

Expression A combination of values, functions, and operators that calculates to a single value. Access expressions start with an equal sign and are placed in a text box in either Form Design View or Report Design View.

Field In a table, a field corresponds to a column of data, a specific piece or category of data such as a first name, last name, city, state, or phone number.

Field list A small window that lists the fields in a table for a query or the fields in the record source for a form or report.

Field name The name given to each field in a table.

Field properties Characteristics that further define the field. Field properties are displayed in Table Design view.

Field Properties pane The lower half of Table Design View, which displays field properties.

Field selector The button to the left of a field in Table Design View that indicates the currently selected field. Also the thin gray bar above each field in the query grid.

Field Size property A field property that determines the number of characters that can be entered in a field.

File A stored collection of data; in Access, the entire database and all of its objects are in one file.

Filter A way to temporarily display only those records that match given criteria.

Filter By Form A way to filter data that allows two or more criteria to be specified at the same time.

Filter By Selection A way to filter records for an exact match.

Find Duplicates Query Wizard A wizard used to create a query that determines whether a table contains duplicate values in one or more fields.

Find Unmatched Query Wizard A wizard used to create a query that finds records in one table that doesn't have related records in another table.

Focus The property that indicates which field would be edited if you were to start typing.

Force New Page A property that forces a report section to start printing at the top of a new page.

Foreign key field In a one-to-many relationship between two tables, the foreign key field is the field in the "many" table that links the table to the primary key field in the "one" table.

Form An Access object that provides an easy-to-use data entry screen that generally shows only one record at a time.

Form Header The section of a form that appears at the beginning of a form and typically displays the form title.

Form section A location in a form that contains controls. The section in which a control is placed determines where and how often the control prints.

Form View View of a form object that displays data from the underlying recordset and allows you to enter and update data.

Form Wizard An Access wizard that helps you create a form.

Format Painter A tool you can use when designing and laying out forms and reports to copy formatting characteristics from one control to another.

Format property A field property that controls how information is displayed and printed.

Formatting Enhancing the appearance of information through font, size, and color changes.

Free response quiz A type of Office Mix quiz containing questions that require short answers.

FROM A SQL keyword that determines how tables are joined.

Function A special, predefined formula that provides a shortcut for a commonly used calculation, for example, SUM or COUNT.

Gallery A visual collection of choices you can browse through to make a selection. Often available with Live Preview.

Graphic image *See* Image.

Grouping A way to sort records in a particular order, as well as provide a section before and after each group of records.

Groups Each tab on the Ribbon is arranged into groups to make features easy to find.

Hub A pane in Microsoft Edge that provides access to favorite websites, a reading list, browsing history, and downloaded files.

Image A nontextual piece of information such as a picture, piece of clip art, drawn object, or graph. Because images are graphical (and not numbers or letters), they are sometimes referred to as graphical images.

Infinity symbol The symbol that indicates the "many" side of a one-to-many relationship.

Ink to Math tool The OneNote tool that converts handwritten mathematical formulas to formatted equations or expressions.

Ink to Text tool The OneNote tool that converts inked handwriting to typed text.

Inked handwriting In OneNote, writing produced when using a pen tool to enter text.

Inking toolbar In Microsoft Edge, a collection of tools for annotating a webpage.

Input Mask A field property that provides a visual guide for users as they enter data.

Insertion point A blinking vertical line that appears when you click in a text box; indicates where new text will be inserted.

Integrate To incorporate a document and parts of a document created in one program into another program; for example, to incorporate an Excel chart into a PowerPoint slide, or an Access report into a Word document.

Interface The look and feel of a program; for example, the appearance of commands and the way they are organized in the program window.

Is Not Null A criterion that finds all records in which any entry has been made in the field.

Is Null A criterion that finds all records in which no entry has been made in the field.

Join line The line identifying which fields establish the relationship between two related tables. Also called a link line.

JPEG (Joint Photographic Experts Group) Acronym for Joint Photographic Experts Group, which defines the standards for the compression algorithms that allow image files to be stored in an efficient compressed format. JPEG files use the .jpg filename extension.

Junction table A table created to establish separate one-to-many relationships to two tables that have a many-to-many relationship.

Key symbol The symbol that identifies the primary key field in each table.

Label control An unbound control that displays text to describe and clarify other information on a form or report.

Label Wizard A report wizard that precisely positions and sizes information to print on a vast number of standard business label specifications.

Landscape orientation A printout that is 11 inches wide by 8.5 inches tall.

Launch To open or start a program on your computer.

Layout A way to group several controls together on a form or report to more quickly add, delete, rearrange, resize, or align controls.

Layout View An Access view that lets you make some design changes to a form or report while you are browsing the data.

Left function An Access function that returns a specified number of characters, starting with the left side of a value in a Text field.

Len function Built-in Access function used to return the number of characters in a field.

Like operator An operator used in a query to find values in a field that match the pattern you specify.

Limit to List A combo box control property that allows you to limit the entries made by that control to those provided by the combo box drop-down list.

Line A graphical element that can be added to a report to highlight information or enhance its clarity.

Link Child Fields A subform property that determines which field serves as the "many" link between the subform and main form.

Link line The line identifying which fields establish the relationship between two related tables.

Link Master Fields A subform property that determines which field serves as the "one" link between the main form and the subform.

List box A bound control that displays a list of possible choices for the user. Used mainly on forms.

List Rows A control property that determines how many items can be displayed in a list, such as in a combo box.

Live Preview A feature that lets you point to a choice in a gallery or palette and see the results in the document or object without actually clicking the choice.

Locked property A control property specifies whether you can edit data in a control on Form View.

Logical view The view of a query that shows the selected fields and records as a datasheet.

Long Integer The default field size for a Number field.

Lookup field A field that has lookup properties. Lookup properties are used to create a drop-down list of values to populate the field.

Lookup properties Field properties that allow you to supply a drop-down list of values for a field.

Lookup Wizard A wizard used in Table Design View that allows one field to "look up" values from another table or entered list. For example, you might use the Lookup Wizard to specify that the Customer Number field in the Sales table display the Customer Name field values from the Customers table.

Macro An Access object that stores a collection of keystrokes or commands such as those for printing several reports in a row or providing a toolbar when a form opens.

Main form A form that contains a subform control.

Main report A report that contains a subreport control.

Many-to-many relationship The relationship between two tables in an Access database in which one record of one table relates to many records in the other table and vice versa. You cannot directly create a many-to-many relationship between two tables in Access. To relate two tables with such a relationship, you must establish a third table called junction table that creates separate one-to-many relationships with the two original tables.

Margin The space between the outer edge of the control and the data displayed inside the control.

Microsoft OneNote Mobile app The lightweight version of Microsoft OneNote designed for phones, tablets, and other mobile devices.

Module An Access object that stores Visual Basic programming code that extends the functions of automated Access processes.

Multiuser A characteristic that means more than one person can enter and edit data in the same Access database at the same time.

Multivalued field A field that allows you to make more than one choice from a drop-down list.

Name property A property that uniquely identifies each object and control on a form or report.

Navigation buttons Buttons in the lower-left corner of a datasheet or form that allow you to quickly navigate between the records in the underlying object as well as add a new record.

Navigation mode A mode in which Access assumes that you are trying to move between the fields and records of the datasheet (rather than edit a specific field's contents), so keystrokes such as [Ctrl][Home] and [Ctrl][End] move you to the first and last field of the datasheet.

Navigation Pane A pane in the Access program window that provides a way to move between objects (tables, queries, forms, reports, macros, and modules) in the database.

Note In OneNote, a small window that contains text or other types of information.

Notebook In OneNote, the container for notes, drawings, and other content.

Null entry The state of "nothingness" in a field. Any entry such as 0 in a numeric field or a space in a text field is not null. It is common to search for empty fields by using the Null criterion in a filter or query. The Is Not Null criterion finds all records where there is an entry of any kind.

Object A table, query, form, report, macro, or module in an Access database.

OLE A field data type that stores pointers that tie files, such as pictures, sound clips, or spreadsheets, created in other programs to a record.

OneDrive Microsoft storage system that lets you easily save, share, and access your files from any device with Internet access.

One-to-many line The line that appears in the Relationships or query design window and shows which field is used between two tables to serve as the linking field. The one-to-many line displays a "1" next to the field that serves as the "one" side of the relationship and displays an infinity symbol next to the field that serves as the "many" side of the relationship when referential integrity is specified for the relationship. Also called the one-to-many join line.

One-to-many relationship The relationship between two tables in an Access database in which a common field links the tables together. The linking field is called the primary key field in the "one" table of the relationship and the foreign key field in the "many" table of the relationship.

Online collaboration The ability to incorporate feedback or share information across the Internet or a company network or intranet.

Option button A bound control used to display a limited list of mutually exclusive choices for a field, such as "female" or "male" for a gender field in form or report.

Option group A bound control placed on a form that is used to group together several option buttons that provide a limited number of values for a field.

Option Value An option button property that determines the values entered into a field when the option button is selected.

OR criteria Criteria placed on different rows of the query design grid. A record will appear in the resulting datasheet if it is true for any single row.

ORDER BY A SQL keyword that determines how records in the query result are sorted.

Orphan record A record in the "many" table of a one-to-many relationship that doesn't have a matching entry in the linking field of the "one" table. Orphan records cannot be created if referential integrity is enforced on a relationship.

Padding The space between the outside borders of adjacent controls.

Page In OneNote, a workspace for inserting notes and other content, similar to a page in a physical notebook.

Parameter criteria Text entered in [square brackets] that prompts the user for an entry each time the query is run.

Parameter report A report that prompts you for criteria to determine the records to use for the report.

Parent table The "one" table in a one-to-many relationship.

Pixel (picture element) One pixel is the measurement of one picture element on the screen.

Pmt function Built-in Access function used to calculate the monthly payment on a loan; enter the Pmt function as Pmt([Rate],[Term],[Loan]).

Portrait orientation A printout that is 8.5 inches wide by 11 inches tall.

Previewing Prior to printing, seeing onscreen exactly how the printout will look.

Primary key field A field that contains unique information for each record. A primary key field cannot contain a null entry.

Print Preview An Access view that shows you how a report or other object will print on a sheet of paper.

Property A characteristic that further defines a field (if field properties), control (if control properties), section (if section properties), or object (if object properties).

Property Sheet A window that displays an exhaustive list of properties for the chosen control, section, or object on a form or report.

Property Update Options A Smart Tag that applies property changes in one field to other objects of the database that use the field.

Query An Access object that provides a spreadsheet-like view of the data, similar to that in tables. It may provide the user with a subset of fields and/or records from one or more tables. Queries are created when the user has a "question" about the data in the database.

Query Datasheet View The view of a query that shows the selected fields and records as a datasheet. Query Datasheet View is displayed when you run a query.

Query design grid The bottom pane of the Query Design View window in which you specify the fields, sort order, and limiting criteria for the query.

Query Design View The window in which you develop queries by specifying the fields, sort order, and limiting criteria that determine which fields and records are displayed in the resulting datasheet.

Question mark (?) A wildcard character used to search for any single character in query criteria.

Quick Access Toolbar A small toolbar on the left side of a Microsoft application window's title bar, containing icons that you click to quickly perform common actions, such as saving a file.

Read-only An object property that indicates whether the object can read and display data, but cannot be used to change (write to) data.

Reading view In Microsoft Edge, the display of a webpage that removes ads and most graphics and uses a simple format for the text.

Record A row of data in a table.

Record Source A property of a form or report that identifies the table or query containing the data to display.

Referential integrity A set of Access rules that govern data entry and help ensure data accuracy. Setting referential integrity on a relationship prevents the creation of orphan records.

Relational database software Software such as Access that is used to manage data organized in a relational database.

Relationship report A printout of the Relationships window that shows how a relational database is designed and includes table names, field names, primary key fields, and one-to-many relationship lines.

Report An Access object that creates a professional printout of data that may contain such enhancements as headers, footers, and calculations on groups of records.

Report Design View An Access view that allows you to work with a complete range of report, section, and control properties.

Report Wizard An Access wizard that helps you create a report.

Resize bar A thin gray bar that separates the field lists in the query design grid.

Responsive design A way to provide content so that it adapts appropriately to the size of the display on any device.

Ribbon Appears below the title bar in every Office program window, and displays commands you're likely to need for the current task.

Right function Built-in Access function used to return the specified number of characters from the end of a field value.

Row Source A property that defines the values to display in a list, such as in a Lookup field or combo box.

Ruler A vertical or horizontal guide that appears in Form and Report Design View to help you position controls.

Run a query To open a query and view the fields and records that you have selected for the query presented as a datasheet.

Sandbox A computer security mechanism that helps to prevent attackers from gaining control of a computer.

Save As command A command on the File tab that saves the entire database (and all objects it contains) or only the current object with a new name.

Screen capture An electronic snapshot of your screen, as if you took a picture of it with a camera, which you can paste into a document.

Screen clipping In OneNote, an image copied from any part of a computer screen.

Screen recording In Office Mix, a video you create by capturing your desktop and any actions performed on it.

Scrub the database To remove and fix orphan records and otherwise improve the quality and consistency of data in the database.

Section A location in a form or report that contains controls. The section in which a control is placed determines where and how often the control prints.

Section properties Characteristics that define each section in a report.

Section tab In OneNote, a divider for organizing a notebook.

SELECT A SQL keyword that determines what fields a query selects.

Select query The most common type of query that retrieves data from one or more linked tables and displays the results in a datasheet.

Shape effect A special visual impact (such as shadow, glow, soft edges, and bevel) applied to command buttons.

Simple Query Wizard An Access wizard that prompts you for information it needs to create a new query.

Sizing handles Small squares at each corner of a selected control in Access. Dragging a handle resizes the control. Also known as handles.

Slide Notes In Office Mix, the written and displayed version of notes typically used to recite narration while creating a slide recording.

Slide recording In Office Mix, a video you create by recording action with a webcam, a camera attached or built into a computer.

Smart Tag A button that provides a small menu of options and automatically appears under certain conditions to help you work with a task, such as correcting errors. For example, the AutoCorrect Options button, which helps you correct typos and update properties, and the Error Indicator button, which helps identify potential design errors in Form and Report Design View, are smart tags.

Sort To reorder records in either ascending or descending order based on the values of a particular field.

Split form A form split into two panes; the upper pane allows you to display the fields of one record in any arrangement, and the lower pane maintains a datasheet view of the first few records.

SQL (Structured Query Language) A language that provides a standardized way to request information from a relational database system.

SQL View A query view that displays the SQL code for the query.

Storyline In Sway, the workspace for assembling a presentation.

Subdatasheet A datasheet that is nested within another datasheet to show related records. The subdatasheet shows the records on the "many" side of a one-to-many relationship.

Subform A form placed within a form that shows related records from another table or query. A subform generally displays many records at a time in a datasheet arrangement.

Subreport A control that displays a report within another report.

Suite A group of programs that are bundled together and share a similar interface, making it easy to transfer skills and program content among them.

Sum function A mathematical function that totals values in a field.

Summary query A query used to calculate and display information about records grouped together.

Summary report A report that calculates and displays information about records grouped together.

Sway site A website Sway creates to share and display a Sway presentation.

Sync In OneNote, to save a new or updated notebook so that all versions of the notebook, such as a notebook on OneDrive and a copy on a hard drive, have the same contents.

Syntax Rules for entering information such as query criteria or property values.

Tab control An unbound control used to create a three-dimensional aspect to a form so that other controls can be organized and shown in Form View by clicking the "tabs."

Tab Index property A form property that indicates the numeric tab order for all controls on the form that have the Tab Stop property set to Yes.

Tab order property A form property that determines the sequence in which the controls on the form receive the focus when the user presses [Tab] or [Enter] in Form view.

Tab Stop property A form property that determines whether a field accepts focus.

Table A collection of records for a single subject, such as all of the customer records; the fundamental building block of a relational database because it stores all of the data.

Table Design View The view in which you can add, delete, or modify fields and their associated properties.

Tabs Organizational unit used for commands on the Ribbon. The tab names appear at the top of the Ribbon and the active tab appears in front.

Template A sample file, such as a database provided within the Microsoft Access program. In OneNote, a page design you can apply to new pages to provide an appealing background, a consistent layout, or elements suitable for certain types of notes, such as meeting notes or to-do lists.

Text Align property A control property that determines the alignment of text within the control.

Text box The most common type of control used to display field values.

Theme A predefined set of colors, fonts, line and fill effects, and other formats that can be applied to an Access database and give it a consistent, professional look.

Title bar Appears at the top of every Office program window; it displays the document or database name and program name.

To Do tag In OneNote, an icon that helps you keep track of your assignments and other tasks.

Total row Row in the query design grid used to specify how records should be grouped and summarized with aggregate functions. Total row also refers to the last row of a datasheet where the values in a field may be summarized in a number of ways such as summed or counted.

Unbound control A control that does not change from record to record and exists only to clarify or enhance the appearance of the form, using elements such as labels, lines, and clip art.

User interface A collective term for all the ways you interact with a software program.

Validation Rule A field property that helps eliminate unreasonable entries by establishing criteria for an entry before it is accepted into the database.

Validation Text A field property that determines what message appears if a user attempts to make a field entry that does not pass the validation rule for that field.

View Each Access object has different views for different purposes. For example, you work with data in Datasheet View. You modify the design of the object in Layout and Design Views. You preview a printout in Print Preview. Common views include Datasheet View for a table or query, or Design View for any Access object.

Web Note In Microsoft Edge, an annotation on a webpage.

Wildcard A special character used in criteria to find, filter, and query data. The asterisk (*) stands for any group of characters. For example, the criteria M* in a State field criterion cell would find all records where the state entry was Massachusetts, Missouri, Montana, MA, MO, MT, and any other entry that starts with M. The question mark (?) wildcard stands for only one character. In this example, M? would only find MA, MO, or MT.

Zooming in A feature that makes a printout appear larger but shows less of it on screen at once; does not affect the actual size of the printout.

Zooming out A feature that shows more of a printout on screen at once but at a reduced size; does not affect the actual size of the printout.

...dex

Microsoft Sway, PA 6–9
 adding content, PA 7
 creating presentations, PA 6–7
 designing presentations, PA 8
 publishing presentations, PA 8
 sharing presentations, PA 8
Microsoft Word 2016
 filenames and default file extension, OFF 8
 start screen, OFF 4, OFF 5
Min function, AC 149
minus sign (-), subtraction operator, AC 147
More Forms tool, AC 56
mouse pointer shapes, AC 58
moving. *See also* navigating
 controls, AC 90
 datasheet columns, AC 17
multiplication operator (*), AC 147
multiuser capabilities, Excel and Access compared, AC 3
multiuser databases, AC 14
Multivalued fields, AC 112

N

Name property, AC 66
navigating between Office programs, OFF 4
navigation buttons, AC 14
Navigation mode, AC 14
 keyboard shortcuts, AC 15
Navigation Pane, AC 4
Navigation tool, AC 56
not equal to operator (<>), AC 36, AC 143
Not operator, AC 143
note(s), PA 2. *See also* Microsoft OneNote 2016
 taking, PA 3
notebooks, PA 2. *See also* Microsoft OneNote 2016
Null operator, AC 143
Number data type, AC 7
Number fields
 modifying, AC 116–117
 properties, AC 116, AC 117

O

object linking and embedding (OLE) data type, AC 122
objects, AC 4, AC 5, AC 9
 deleting or removing, AC 148
 read-only, AC 80

 renaming, AC 8
 views, AC 10
Office 365. *See* Microsoft Office 365
Office 2016 suite, OFF 2–3. *See also* Microsoft Office 2016
Office Clipboard, OFF 5, OFF 13
OLE (object linking and embedding) data type, AC 122
OLE Object data type, AC 7
OneDrive. *See* Microsoft OneDrive
OneNote. *See* Microsoft OneNote 2016
one-to-many join lines, AC 12, AC 110, AC 138
one-to-many relationships, AC 10, AC 12–13, AC 106, AC 109, AC 110–111
online collaboration, OFF 2, OFF 9
Open dialog box, OFF 10, OFF 11
opening
 files. *See* opening files
 Property Sheets, AC 152
opening files, OFF 10, OFF 11
 as copies, OFF 10
 documents created in older Office versions, OFF 11
 read-only files, OFF 10
option buttons, forms, AC 63, AC 176
option groups, forms, AC 63, AC 176–177
Option Value property, AC 176
OR criteria, AC 40–41, AC 144–145
ORDER BY keyword, AC 140
orphan records, AC 56, AC 107

P

padding, forms, AC 67, AC 168
Page Footer section, AC 84
 forms, AC 173
 reports, AC 191
Page Header section, AC 84
 forms, AC 173
 reports, AC 191
page orientation, AC 80, AC 81
parameter criteria, AC 192, AC 193
parameter reports, AC 192–193
parent table, AC 111
plus sign (+), addition operator, AC 147
PMT function, AC 147
portrait orientation, AC 80, AC 81
pound sign (#), criteria, AC 38

T

tab(s), OFF 6, OFF 7
tab controls, forms, AC 63, AC 178–179
Tab Index property, AC 66
tab order, AC 66–67
Tab Order dialog box, AC 67
tab stop(s), AC 66
Tab Stop property, AC 66
table(s), AC 4, AC 5, AC 9
  adding to queries, AC 148
  child, AC 111
  creating, AC 8–9
  filtering data, AC 36–37
  finding data, AC 34, AC 35
  layouts, AC 59
  one-to-many relationships, AC 12–13
  parent, AC 111
  queries, adding or deleting, AC 32
  sorting data, AC 34, AC 35
Table Datasheet View, modifying fields, AC 117
Table Design View, AC 6, AC 7, AC 108, AC 109
Tabular layout, AC 167
templates, AC 6, OFF 4, PA 2
text, converting handwriting to, PA 3–4
Text Align property, AC 62
text boxes, forms, AC 54, AC 63
text fields, short, modifying, AC 114–115
themes, forms, AC 198, AC 199
title bar, OFF 6
To Do Tags, PA 2
toggle buttons, forms, AC 63
Toggle Filter button, AC 35
Total row, AC 148, AC 150
touch screen, Office 2016 apps, OFF 4

U

unbound controls, AC 61
Undo button, AC 168

unfreezing fields in datasheets, AC 30
unhiding fields in datasheets, AC 30
user(s), databases, AC 54
user interfaces, OFF 6

V

Validation Rule property, AC 120–121
Validation Text property, AC 120–121
Value field, AC 150
Var function, AC 149
video clips, capturing, PA 11
views, OFF 12, OFF 13
  logical, AC 138
  objects, AC 10
  reports, AC 83
  switching between, AC 66
virtual assistant, Edge, PA 14–15

W

web browser. *See* Microsoft Edge
Web Note tools, PA 15
webpages
  annotating, PA 15
  live, inserting in slides, PA 12
wildcard characters, AC 36, AC 145
Word. *See* Microsoft Word 2016

Y

Yes/No data type, AC 7

Z

Zoom In button, Microsoft Office 2016, OFF 6, OFF 7
Zoom Out button, Microsoft Office 2016, OFF 6, OFF 7